Churchill's Colonel

For
Granny and Grandpa,
Cara and Posie

Churchill's Colonel

The War Diaries of Lieutenant Colonel Anthony Barne

Edited by Charles Barne

Pen & Sword
MILITARY

First published in Great Britain in 2019 by
Pen & Sword Military
An imprint of
Pen & Sword Books Ltd
Yorkshire – Philadelphia

ISBN 978 1 52675 970 2

Printed and bound in England
By TJ International Ltd.

Pen & Sword Books Ltd incorporates the Imprints of Pen & Sword
Books Archaeology, Atlas, Aviation, Battleground, Discovery, Family
History, History, Maritime, Military, Naval, Politics, Railways, Select,
Transport, True Crime, Fiction, Frontline Books, Leo Cooper,
Praetorian Press, Seaforth Publishing, Wharncliffe and White Owl.

For a complete list of Pen & Sword titles please contact

PEN & SWORD BOOKS LIMITED
47 Church Street, Barnsley, South Yorkshire, S70 2AS, England
E-mail: enquiries@pen-and-sword.co.uk
Website: www.pen-and-sword.co.uk

or

PEN AND SWORD BOOKS
1950 Lawrence Rd, Havertown, PA 19083, USA
E-mail: uspen-and-sword@casematepublishers.com
Website: www.penandswordbooks.com

Contents

Abbreviations   vi
Foreword   ix
Prologue   x
Maps   xiii

Chapter 1   Early Life   1

Chapter 2   Gathering Clouds   7

Chapter 3   War in the Western Desert   52

Chapter 4   Rejoining the Royals   91

Chapter 5   El Alamein   144

Chapter 6   The Wilderness   194

Chapter 7   The 4th Hussars   209

Chapter 8   Mainland Europe   227

Chapter 9   Barne's Taxi Service   260

Epilogue   314
Appendix: A: Speeches Mentioned in the Diaries   317
Appendix B   322
Acknowledgements   323

Abbreviations

AA	Anti-Aircraft
AAG	Assistant Adjutant General
ACV	Armoured Command Vehicle
AFHQ	Allied Forces Headquarters
AMS	Assistant Military Secretary
B3	Supply echelons, located about 20 miles behind the line
BEF	British Expeditionary Force
BTE	British Troops in Egypt
BGS	Brigadier General Staff
CGS	Chief General Staff
CIH	Central India Horse (21st King George V's Own Horse) Regiment
CLY	County of London Yeomanry
CRA	Commander Royal Artillery
CRE	Commander Royal Engineers
DAQMG(M)	Deputy Assistant Quarter Master General (Major)
DCM	District Court Martial
DLI	Durham Light Infantry
DY	Derbyshire Yeomanry
EME	Electrical & Mechanical Engineer
FGCM	Field General Court Martial
G2	Staff branch responsible for intelligence and security
GOC	General Officer Commanding
GHQ	General Headquarters
KDG	1st King's Dragoon Guards
LAD	Light Aid Detachment, unit attached to REME
L/Cpl	Lance Corporal
LG	Landing Ground

LRDG	Long Range Desert Group
MO	Medical Officer
MS	Military Secretary
MTC	Mechanised Transport Corps
NAAFI	Navy, Army and Air Force Institutes
OC	Officer Commanding
OE	Old Etonian
OR	Other Ranks
PT	Physical Training
RA	Royal Artillery
RAAF	Royal Australian Air Force
RAL	Rear Admiral Liaison
RAMC	Royal Army Medical Corps
RAOC	Royal Army Ordnance Corps
RASC	Royal Army Service Corps
RE	Royal Engineers
REME	Royal Electrical & Mechanical Engineers
RFC	Royal Flying Corps
RN	Royal Navy
RNAS	Royal Navy Air Service
RSM	Regimental Sergeant Major
RTR	Royal Tank Regiment
RYC	Royal Yacht Club
SAAF	South African Air Force
SMO	Senior Medical Officer
SQMS	Staff Quarter-Master Sergeant
SSM	Staff Sergeant Major
STO	Stores & Transport Officer
TAC HQ	Tactical Headquarters
TEWT	Tactical Exercise without Troops
TJFF	Trans-Jordanian Frontier Force
VAD	Voluntary Aid Detachment
WD	Western Desert
3H	3rd the King's Own Hussars
4th SA	4 Field Brigade, South African regiment
7H	7th Queen's Own Hussars

9L	9th Queen's Royal Lancers
11th H	11th Hussars (Prince Albert's Own)
12L	12th (Prince of Wales') Royal Lancers
13L	13th Lancers, armoured regiment of the Indian Army
15th/19th H	15th/19th The King's Royal Hussars
27L	27th Lancers
60th	The King's Royal Rifle Corps

Foreword

Lieutenant Colonel Anthony Barne's wonderful diaries give us an extraordinary insight into the day to day lives of the young men and women who were caught up in the maelstrom of the Second World War, who tried to continue their lives, start a family and play their part in the conflict. I thoroughly enjoyed them.

His extraordinary war service, which placed him in so many well-known theatres of the Second World War in Africa and mainland Europe, allows a fascinating insight into a soldier's experience of war, with its various difficulties, excitements and sorrows, as well as the view of how the war was unfolding from the perspective of those on the front lines.

More than anything it serves as a reminder that the reality of war is best seen not through troop movements, battle lines and large-scale campaigns, but through the eyes of the men and women whose lives are irrevocably shaped by it. At 'Walking With The Wounded', we support many people who have been impacted by conflict and their service in the Armed Forces. We recognise their significant contribution to society while serving, as well as after they leave the military, and provide a structure for them to reintegrate into their communities. These diaries serve as a vivid and colourful reminder of what we owe these men and women.

Edward Parker
Co-Founder, Walking With The Wounded

Prologue

On 2 September 1945 Winston Churchill arrived at Villa Rosa on the shore of Lake Como in Italy. Two months after the German surrender, and a month before the Japanese capitulation, there had been a general election resulting in an unexpected and emphatic swing from Churchill's Conservatives to Clement Attlee's Labour Party and his promises of social reform. Having served as prime minister for the final five years of the Second World War, Churchill found himself powerless to help rebuild Britain in the peacetime he had worked so hard to achieve. At seventy years old, Churchill's legendary stamina was flagging, and a holiday seemed long overdue.

Given the obvious dangers of such a well-known figure visiting a country he had so recently led a war against, he was given a guard from his old regiment, the 4th Hussars. Their commanding officer, Lieutenant Colonel Anthony Barne, was invited to visit Churchill as a guest and made the 450-mile drive from Austria, where the regiment had been stationed since the end of hostilities. During the drive there was a serious incident when his car was deliberately forced off a mountain pass at 50mph by a German lorry driver.

Lord Moran, Churchill's personal physician, recalled Barne's arrival at Villa Rosa in his book, *Winston Churchill: The Struggle for Survival 1940–1965*:

> I told him Winston was out. We talked in a desultory way for some time. He was a typical cavalry soldier of the old kind, very conscious of the fabric of English society and of the anatomy of the horse …
>
> When at last we had discovered his room, he retired, to emerge later in a very smart gabardine uniform. He was keyed up for the meeting with the PM. Winston, he said, had once invited him to dine at No 10. On four occasions the PM had inspected the Regiment during the war. No other Colonel had such a record.

About 8.15, as we stood gazing down over the terrace to the lake, the launch came into sight. The Colonel smoothed his hair. Far below we could see Winston landing; we watched him walk slowly up a path till he disappeared from view, down some steps which saved the climb to the house. Suddenly, while we were talking, Winston entered the room. He walked up to the Colonel, who instinctively stood to attention.

'Your name?' he asked, with a conciliatory smile.

I was sorry for the Colonel. He was disappointed, of course, that Winston had forgotten he was coming but, after all, he knew that he had many things on his mind. What he could not understand was that Winston had failed to recognise him ...

Then Winston strode upstairs as if the Colonel was done with. But during dinner the four-hundred-and-fifty mile drive and the somersault came out. Winston was interested and even touched by the odyssey.

'You mean you have come all that way to see me, and risked your life in this accident?'

The situation was entirely retrieved. The Colonel became one of the family. Winston told how his regiment set out to win the regimental polo; he said he had allowed no mere military considerations to interfere with that ambition. It seemed more important to him than anything in his life, more exciting than anything in the war. The Colonel followed every word of this confession with affectionate pride. If it had been possible, Winston would have risen in his estimation, that this great man should attach the same importance to horsemanship as he had always done gave him a comfortable feeling of reassurance.

Barne stayed for four nights, spending the days picnicking, boating and accompanying Churchill to various spots where he would spend hours painting watercolours of the lakes. Barne later reminisced:

We had a speed boat and a police launch so could evade the Italians. Once he wanted a swim and nearly swamped our light craft when getting overboard. I could then not get him back onboard though we both struggled hard so I towed him in to the shallows and signalled to Sarah [Churchill's daughter]. She waded out to help him. He looked like a great pink baby emerging from the water.

On 5 September Churchill wrote to his wife, Clementine, back in the UK:

I am guarded by the 4th Hussars. 24 men and two officers travelled 400 miles (I blush to say) from Austria to be my personal protectors here and the Colonel, Barne, arrived also yesterday, a most agreeable man, who, again, has come this enormous distance. On the road he had a motor accident of a most dangerous character which might easily have killed him and the two others on board. The car was gradually forced off the road by a lorry, struck the embankment, went over a 12-foot drop turning twice in the air, to be smashed out of all recognition. The Colonel, his servant and the driver were all unhurt. Fancy what I should have felt if they or any of them had been killed!

On 17 September Churchill was about to depart from Lake Como and sent a letter addressed to 'My dear Colonel':

We have had wonderful weather, and I have eight large paintings in an advanced state of decomposition. We have been a very happy party, and I have formed a great regard for John and Tim, whose kindness has been unfailing. We have had no visitors at all since the Field Marshall [Alexander] left except Monsieur Montag, the art critic, who has been very helpful and brought a most magnificent present of paint colours from Zurich. Sarah has deserted the arts since you departed, and Tim is too shy to plunge in with the brush.

It has been a great compliment to me to be guarded by my own Regiment, and I am touched by the sentiment which inspired the action of my great friend, which has led you to many victories.

Yours very sincerely,
W. S. C.

P.S. I shiver when I think of your escape. All's well that ends well.

Map 1: The Middle East.

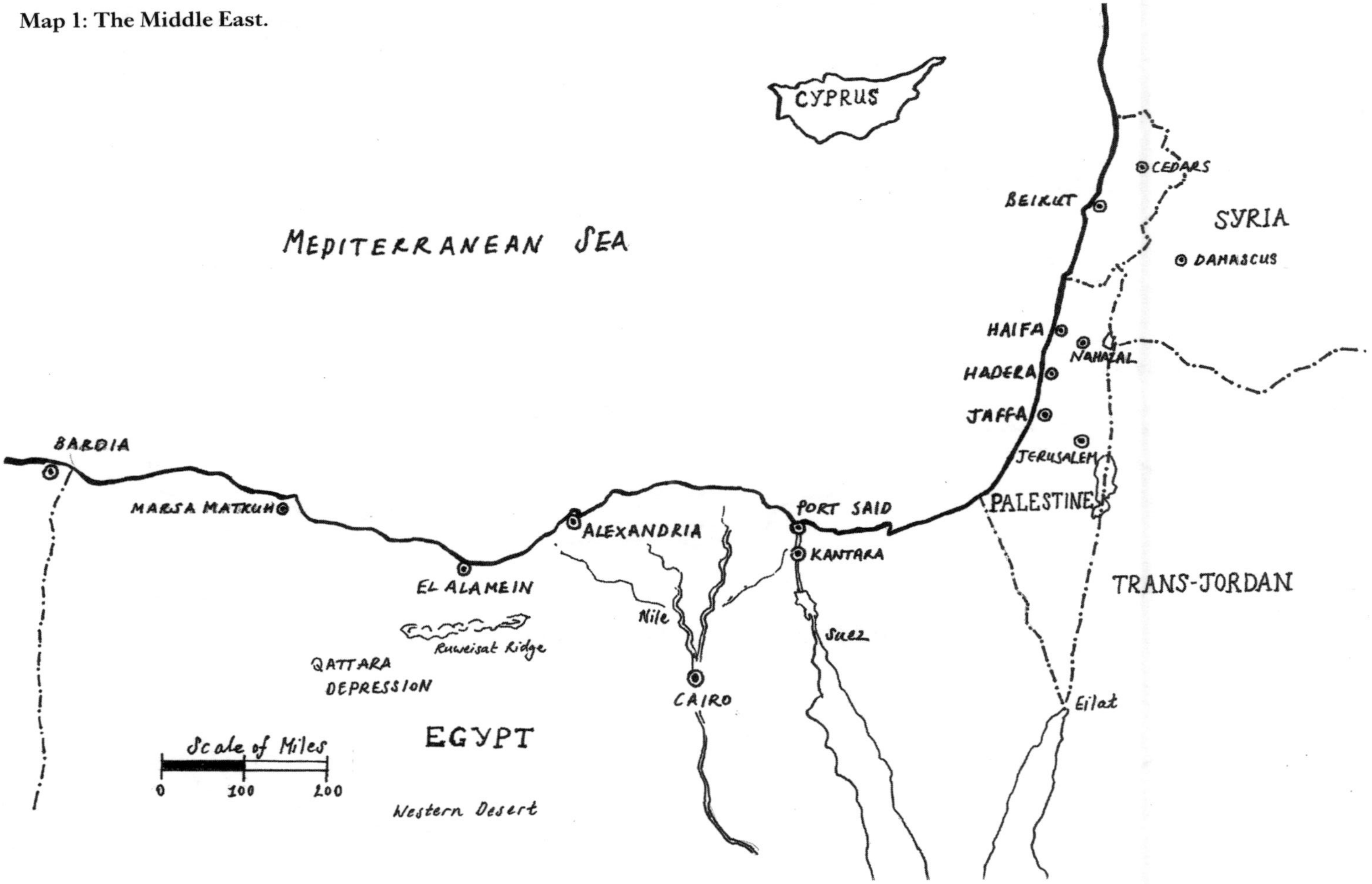

Map 1: The Middle East.

Map 2: The North African Campaign.

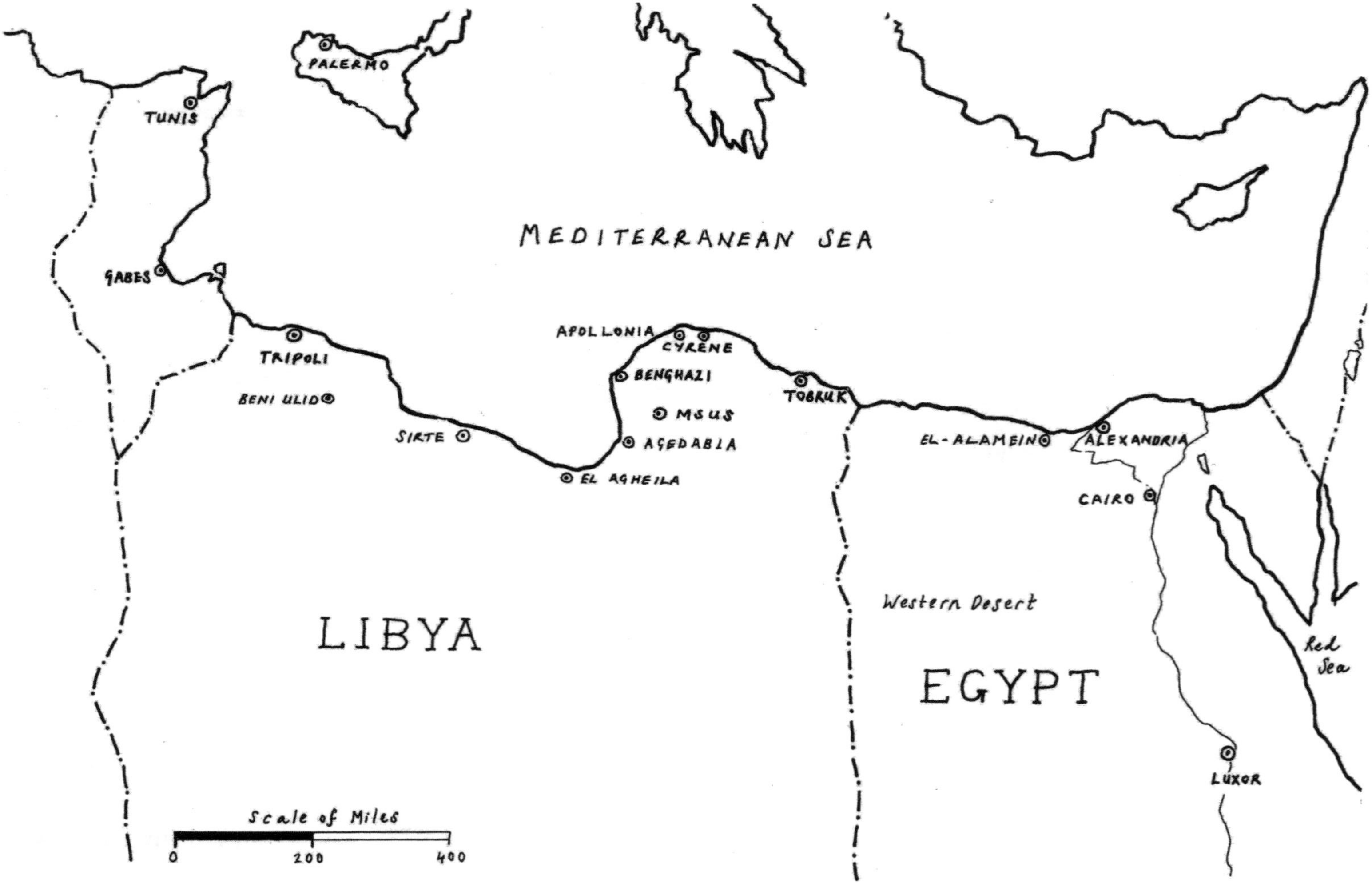

MEDITERRANEAN SEA

PALERMO

TUNIS

GABES

TRIPOLI

BENI ULID

SIRTE

EL AGHEILA

AGEDABIA

MSUS

BENGHAZI

APOLLONIA

CYRENE

TOBRUK

EL-ALAMEIN

ALEXANDRIA

CAIRO

LUXOR

Red Sea

LIBYA

EGYPT

Western Desert

Scale of Miles

0   200   400

Map 3: Mainland Europe.

Chapter 1

Early Life

Anthony Miles Barne, was born on 20 November 1906 at Sotterley Hall, the Barne family home since 1744. He had an older brother, Michael born in 1905, and two younger siblings, Nigel born in 1909 and Elizabeth born in 1911.

They grew up at Sotterley, a large Georgian country house set amongst wooded parkland in Suffolk. Religion played a considerable part in life at Sotterley, and the Sabbath was respected without question. This meant the children learning the collect of the day and reciting it to their mother before breakfast, followed by a long service at the estate church. The afternoons were spent quietly: they were forbidden to climb trees, a favourite and highly competitive pastime, and no toys were allowed.

The children spent the majority of their time out in the parkland, learning to appreciate nature, constructing traps, collecting eggs and ferreting. Natural history was an important part of their upbringing and a passion that was to last a lifetime. With extensive stabling and fields to ride in, they all became accomplished riders at an early age. Their father, Miles, had served in the Boer War, and the boys loved camping in the woods with him, boiling eggs in the tea billy as he had done in South Africa and taking turns on sentry duty.

Tony and Michael were sent to a private prep school where they were irritated by their dentist's son who was constantly tinkling on the piano. Benjamin Britten was to become one of the most celebrated composers of his generation.

As it did to many other families, the First World War brought devastating loss. Their father was recalled to his old regiment, the Scots Guards, in June 1915 and a month later was serving on the Western Front. Whilst temporarily commanding his battalion over Christmas 1915 he became embroiled in a brief informal truce with the Germans and was court-martialled – but later fully exonerated. Having survived the dreadful winter of 1916/17 on the Somme, he returned on leave to Sotterley in August 1917 and spent a week with his young family. Tragically, on his way back to rejoin his regiment he was fatally wounded near Ypres when a stricken British aeroplane accidentally dropped a bomb behind Allied lines. To add further sorrow, Miles' brother and brother-in-law were also killed in action. The losses left a huge hole in the family, but Violet, their mother, dealt with the tragedies with Victorian stoicism and looked after her family with calm dedication.

At the age of thirteen Tony passed the entrance exams to join the Royal Navy and went for his initial interview, but this coincided with a period of military cutbacks following the First World War, and his place was revoked. Instead, he went on to continue his education at Marlborough College, where he became friends with John Betjeman. It is clear that Tony was not a natural academic, and his report from 1922 seems to be representative of an undistinguished school career:

> His knowledge is very limited and his results are of a feeble description – particularly his grammar and spelling. He appears to be a woolly little person who has done his best though with not much success.

Tony's mother seemed to share the school's pessimism as to his prospects and, as a hedge, bought him 5,000 acres of uncleared bush in Kenya at one shilling an acre. Tony, however, was determined to join the Army and worked hard to prepare himself. He suffered a motorbike accident two weeks before the exams, leaving him badly concussed. Nevertheless he sat the entrance papers and then went on to watch Suzanne Lenglen, wearing a long skirt and serving underarm, win the Ladies' Singles at Wimbledon. To everybody's surprise, Tony passed the entry exams to the Royal Military College, Sandhurst, and the Kenyan land was sold at a small profit some time later.

Already a strong horseman, Tony thrived at Sandhurst and had the rare honour of being permitted to wear spurs in his first term at the riding school. In the prestigious competition for the Saddle he lost on the toss of a coin and had to accept the Hunting Crop, the second prize and one his father had also won. On leaving Sandhurst he had his pick of regiments and joined the Royal Dragoons, the most sought after of the cavalry regiments.

Lieutenant Barne joined the Royals in 1927 as the regiment was moving to the large heath of Hounslow, close to the open countryside surrounding the hamlet of Heathrow. A young officer was expected to work hard: cleaning the stables and riding before breakfast, followed by a rigorous programme of riding school and troop drill. Boots and breeches were worn from dawn to dusk.

Junior officers were not well paid, but belonging to a good regiment was an expensive privilege. A certain standard of living was expected in the Royals, and the outgoings must have been enormous: uniforms, London club subscriptions, mess bills, saddlery, a servant and grooms, as well polo ponies and horses at livery in good hunting country.

When not on duty, a young cavalry officer's life was an endless cycle of hunting, shooting, mess dinners, balls and country house weekends. London in the 1920s still had many horses on the road, the main streets were paved with wooden blocks and after midnight gangs of street sweepers with hoses, brushes and carts would emerge to clean up. Lieutenant Barne and friends, refreshed after a good night, would drive back to Hounslow in the small hours attempting to perform 360° skids on the wet paving. Occasionally a car would turn over, and the street cleaners and friendly bobbies would help put it back on its wheels.

The Royals sailed for Egypt in September 1927, not to return to the UK for any great stretch for nearly twenty years. On boarding the ship all swords, pistols and spurs were handed into the armoury and returned on landing. In Egypt the regiment conducted intense training, but the officers still found time for playing polo three times a week, plentiful duck shooting and regular horse racing. Being of a slight build, Lieutenant Barne was able to get his weight below eight stone and rode a number of notable winners.

In 1928 Barne used his leave to travel to Kenya and see the farmland that once was to be his. Staying with family friends, he settled in well to the colonial lifestyle of race meetings, polo and enormous dinner parties. The trip was also notable for this incident:

On our second morning trekking from Nairobi I walked out while breakfast was being cooked as I had seen vultures collected. I could find no kill, so put my rifle against a big tree and lowered my trousers. While contemplating the infinite, I noticed a long tail swinging about 10 feet over my head and a large face looking down on me. Holding my shorts with one hand and my rifle with the other, I ran into the open ground – the direction I thought the leopard would be unlikely to go if scared or wounded. I had a single-barrel Rigby, not recommended for dangerous game. I moved slowly to where I could see his heart with no twigs intervening and the leopard dropped to the ground, dead. He had killed a young zebra and such was his strength, he had jumped over 10 feet into the tree to eat at his leisure. I watched this wonderful beast for several minutes but there was no movement. I was trembling from excitement, pleased that I had taken the right action and at the same time a feeling of regret that such a noble animal should be my prey – useless for food, of no offence to mankind and dead because of my hunting lust and pride in having such a trophy.

In 1929 the Royals moved to Secunderabad in central India, where the British had pledged to the local ruler, His Exalted Highness the Nizam, to maintain the largest garrison in India. As a major supplier of diamonds, the Nizam was one of the world's wealthiest men and is reputed to have fathered 149 children. The British military were in the process of 'Indianisation': Indian officers were trained at Sandhurst and much of the army's time in India was spent doing joint exercises.

The regiment moved on to Meerut, near Delhi in northern India, where the tough programme aimed to make the trooper, already well versed in weaponry, into an expert scout. Lieutenant Barne had developed a reputation for mapping and map reading and each year in India he was sent off for a ten-day expedition to find a new area for brigade exercises. With a couple of servants he would set off into an uncharted area to mark up bivouac sites, watering points and river crossings, whilst avoiding the various wild animals that had killed several of his friends.

The military authorities encouraged officers to go pig-sticking as training because 'a startled or angry boar is ... a desperate fighter [and therefore] the pig-sticker must possess a good eye, a steady hand, a firm seat, a cool head and a courageous heart.'

Fox hunting I loved, steeplechasing was a thrill but for sheer exhilaration there was nothing to compare with pig-sticking and all that went with it. The scene is set in the early dawn among the vast flats alongside the River Ganges with the backdrop of the snow-covered Himalayas, although anything up to 200 miles away. As soon as the sun rose the mountains disappeared in the ever increasing heat and by the time we were mounted, there was no sign of anything beyond the brown flat grass land of the Khadir. Not of course that it was really flat; there were areas of open ground called 'midan' with menacing thorn scrub that would rip the thickest breeches and wells two to three feet deep, and equally wide, that were known only to the pig, the coolie who had dug it and eventually to the Spear who was led over it by the hunted quarry.

I took as many falls as anyone but on one occasion I speared a pig and the shaft of my spear broke, leaving the razor sharp head sticking out on the other side of the pig. He was a monster of great age, in a fury and not weakened by the wound. I threw myself off the horse, who galloped off, and tackled the pig with the heavy lead butt of the spear, careful to avoid his tusks and also getting impaled on my own spear. Eventually he got me down and I was gripping his tusks just above my head. I tried to knock him out with the lead butt which was still in my hand, but his skull was like old oak. After a while we were both so exhausted that we paused to regain our breath and strength as it looked to be a fight to the finish. I realised that the other two members of my heat [team] had got lost so it was unlikely that I should be found for some time, if ever. Incredibly, a coolie came across me and despatched the boar. It was some time before a rescue party arrived and could lift the dead pig off me. Our doctor decided I also had a broken back, but as it was 17 miles to a road, I had to ride. Two coolies held a leg each on the ride as at times I was passing out from the pain. We found the car and went to Meerut Hospital where they decided there was nothing really wrong with me. However, I remained in great pain and wrote to my Ma (a letter took eighteen days then) who arranged for me to fly home and see her specialist (she had been badly hurt when run over by a taxi in a blackout in the War). From his own x-ray the doctor saw at once that I had cracked a bone in my spine. By manipulation and rest I was relieved of the worst of the pain and was playing polo again next winter in India.

It was in India that Lieutenant Barne met Cara Holmes-Hunt at a polo tournament. Brought up in Melbourne, the daughter of a successful gas businessman and a regular in the Australian society pages, she spent a 'season' in India, where young ladies (disparagingly known as the 'fishing fleet') came to meet eligible bachelors amongst the British officers. Cara was an acknowledged beauty, petite, with a sharp mind and quick sense of humour. She was to become a devoted wife and support for the next six decades.

In 1935 the Royals were en route back to England on standard peacetime rotation when world affairs intervened. Mussolini had started flexing his muscles in Abyssinia, and relations between Britain and Italy were becoming increasingly strained. On arrival at Suez the regiment was ordered to stop in Egypt, where they were to remain for the next year as reserve troops.

During this spell in Egypt, Lieutenant Barne was seconded from the regiment for a strategic assignment. Following the suicide of seven-foot Captain 'Tiny' Hexham, he was to take over supervision of 8,000 Egyptians laying a railway into the Western Desert, choosing the site for the El Alamein station (an area he was to revisit regularly in the years to come) and helping to strengthen the frontier. Importantly, the limited access to life's indulgences allowed him to spend a year clearing his overdrafts before returning to the UK.

Cara was now living in England, and they spent much of their time together. They were soon engaged, and married on 10 June 1937. In keeping with their peripatetic lifestyle, they did not have long together, and in 1938 Cara sailed for Australia to see her parents while Lieutenant Barne and the Royals sailed to Palestine.

Chapter 2

Gathering Clouds

At the end of the First World War, the British secured a mandate to govern Palestine under the Sykes-Picot Agreement, and over the next twenty years the competing and entirely incompatible interests of the Jewish and Arab populations led to several uprisings, the most notable being the 'Great Revolt' by the Arabs starting in 1936.

With Germany's Jewish population excluded from society, bullied and persecuted when Hitler came to power, many decided to emigrate. This resulted in a large and determined stream of immigrants into Palestine, far exceeding the British quota. The Arabs, unsettled by the growing Jewish population and shifting balance of power, began a general strike. This soon descended into a violent revolt against the British and open hostilities against the Jews, laying mines and sniping at the Jewish agricultural colonies. The Jews were ill-prepared to deal with these attacks and relied on British forces to protect them.

The campaign of killing and sabotage continued throughout 1937, and in early 1938 the British sent out reinforcement troops from England. At this stage the Royals were one of only two British cavalry regiments that had retained their horses and were ideally suited to mounted patrols on the rocky, mountainous terrain. By the end of 1938 the organized rebellion had been quashed and order restored, but guerrilla activity continued in rural areas until the outbreak of the Second World War.

* * *

The diaries commence with these prescient words: 'This Diary was started shortly after leaving England to return to Palestine as it was thought that the period between departure from Palestine and an unknown date in the future might be of interest many years hence.'

Saturday 19th August 1939

My much longed for leave started today. At breakfast my attention is drawn to a paragraph of late news that looks ominously like Hitler is rolling up his sleeves for war.[1]

I catch the ration convoy into Haifa and spend the day fixing my ticket, money, bathing etc. I go down to the docks and see two small ships with 840 Jewish refugees aboard brought in. The poor devils have been at sea for weeks and originally were in four boats but one burnt and another ran aground.

Have a hell of a party in the evening. Drink too much and behave just no how at dinner and then afterwards at the casino. It's chiefly a celebration of Harry Webb's engagement to a most unattractive young woman.

Sunday 20th August 1939

Rise at 9am and feel pretty good. King packs up for me and I dither 'til the plane leaves. We get away at noon and rise to over 12,000 foot. It's sweaty hot and I start to feel queer with hands and feet tingling. I stand up and immediately pass out. A fellow passenger said I turned blue in the face and thought I'd suffocated.

We land in Rhodes to refuel and see a mass of Italian bombers in the sheds. Stay the night in Athens and beat it up. Dine at the hotel and then go to the cabaret. Don't get home 'til after 4am and have a very good laugh.

Monday 21st August 1939

Rise at 5.30am after an hour's disturbed doze but have time to sleep on the planes. We land at Brindisi and then Rome where we change planes. At Toulon we see the defence boom across the harbour and then, after a stop at Marseilles, fly directly to Paris to change planes again. Eventually we land at Croydon at 8.45pm and find Cara at the customs barrier.

She's looking awfully well, happy and pretty. She has the Packard with a chauffeur and we go back to the club for the night. London quite empty as one might expect in August but, my God, it's good to be back in England again. I never want to go abroad again.

Tuesday 22nd August 1939

After some sorting out and repacking we drive round to see Granny. She looks the same as ever and rises to see us in a spritely way.

---

1. On 17 August Hitler closed the German border with Poland and started the process of confiscation of German property owned by Polish Jews.

We do some shopping, pick up Cara's luggage and then drive home to Suffolk, arriving about 6pm. Mummy and Elizabeth there. It's very pleasant to be home and see Lizzie's beaming face. Linda [AMB's beloved springer spaniel] is not sure of me for a second but then it all comes back to her and her welcome is overwhelming. There cannot be a dog as faithful and affectionate as her and she never leaves my side, gazing up at my face continually.

Wednesday 23rd August 1939
Spend a thoroughly quiet day. It's very warm and we spend the day wandering round the garden and dozing under the cherry tree. At 4pm we go to a large tennis party, everyone seems to think war inevitable.

Go to bed early and Nigel arrives back at 11pm in a stinking condition. I shall ask Mummy to talk to him seriously as some of his friends are not pleasant and Nigel has a weak head. I daren't think what Mummy would say if she knew he was coming in drunk.

Thursday 24th August 1939
Cara and I have an early breakfast and go in to Norwich to see the dentist. As soon as I'm in the chair Nigel phones to say a wire has come: 'RETURN AT ONCE ROYALS'. Cara seems so cheerful I don't know how I'm going to break it to her but leave it 'til we return home. She takes it very well, certainly better than last year.

Then have a filthy day wiring and phoning about sailings. Mummy very upset and Michael and Peggy rush back from Scotland as the crisis looks so bad.

The news is not yet good but I cannot believe Hitler has reached such a serious state of madness as to be prepared to take on Poland, France and us and yet refuse the aid of Italy. She has lost Spain and Japan's friendship by the Russian pact.[2]

Friday 25th August 1939
After lengthy discussion, eventually decide to drive to London to get my wisdom tooth looked at by a specialist and make sure of my ticket to Egypt. We take food and wraps as hear on the wireless that refugees are streaming out of London. The roads are actually pretty empty, the most noticeable thing being the RAF lorries.

Hear that the War Office has cancelled my sailing with P&O so I get fixed up on a troop ship. No date fixed but they'll wire me.

---

2. The Molotov-Ribbentrop Pact, a neutrality pact between Nazi Germany and the Soviet Union, was signed in Moscow on 23 August 1939.

Saturday 26th August 1939

Leave London and arrive home in time for lunch. Mummy is out organising for refugees – she is a marvel the way she works. Go at tea time to see the children at Southwold and find a great searchlight battery installed behind Frostenden spring!

A Dutch girl refugee has arrived to stay and says plenty of people are crowding out of Europe. Ma has everything organised to take thirty-one Scots Guards wives and families to stay in the Nursery wing.

War seems a long way from Sotterley but the news seems bleak. I find a wire awaiting me to report to Southampton at 1pm Monday. Oh well, five days with Cara is better than no leave at all.

Sunday 27th August 1939

We all go to church and the new parson, Hawthorn, preaches quite a good but political sermon. I don't know why but I've never felt so depressed. I now have a feeling that war is inevitable but the general feeling is that Hitler would be mad to plunge us all into a war – or is he more prepared than we all realise?

Poor old Linda knows something awful is about to happen and cries when she loses sight of me. Cara is much braver and the only cheerful member of the household.

Monday 28th August 1939

Called at 6am and get away at 7am punctually. It's beastly leaving Cara after only five days having already been apart for ten months. Old Linda knew perfectly well that I was leaving her and I left her on Cara's bed exactly as I did last October.

Nigel drives down with me in the Packard and we get to London by 9.30am. The nearer one gets to London the more normal things seem although there are hardly any buses on the streets. The balloons are filled and floating everywhere and there are many odd uniforms about.

We reach Southampton by 12.30pm and find I am to sail on MV *Devonshire*. I send Cara a telegram and then we set sail at 4.45pm. At the Needles we meet HMS *Cape Town* who will escort us. We delay an hour to swing the compass[3] as this is a maiden voyage. Rumours are rife and it's all rather grim.

---

3. The process of compensating a compass on new ship to account for the influence of the ship's structure or close objects.

Tuesday 29th August 1939

Everyone seems determined to give me a job so am made baggage officer. This entails sorting all the bags in the holds for the various ports: Gibraltar, Malta, Alexandria, Port Said, Palestine, India and beyond. Very few pieces seem properly labelled with both name and destination on it which makes the task somewhat trying.

Have also been given the unpleasant little job of acting, assistant, unpaid quartermaster. There are several tons of supplies and stores completely unorganised. This really should be the Navy's pigeon but Colonel Whitworth has let it flutter over to him and he has let it flutter over to perch on my shoulder.

Friday 1st September 1939

Partridge season opens – who will be shooting them?

Wake up steaming into Gibraltar and see a mass of shipping waiting to be allowed into the Mediterranean. There are very few warships however as the plan is for France to guard the western end.

At 4pm we get shore leave 'til 11pm. The police are like London bobbies and they carry gas masks. The town must have been very much more attractive twenty-five years ago but does not lack charm.

In the evening Hopkinson and I visit *Cape Town* to thank them for their protection. They have a very nice crowd onboard who nearly drown us in draught beer! They are nearly all dugouts [retired officers] or reserves but I'm glad we went. We crawl home at 11.30pm and hope our absence or condition are not held against us in the morning.

Saturday 2nd September 1939

Wake up feeling extremely fresh having left the porthole open all night but after breakfast I am rocketed for being late which dampens the mood somewhat.

I watch two sloops sweep for mines outside the harbour. A big French destroyer calls in for oil and water followed by a great white vessel called *Atlantis*. Later on we see the three cruisers *Dauntless*, *Despatch* and *Durban* putting out to sea which makes us wonder if war has been declared. A man-of-war going out is a truly inspiring sight, especially just now when nobody knows what will happen next.

After dinner we walk along the quay and look at the defence boom which is put out at sunset. It stretches out in two long curved lines into the gloom. There is not a ripple in the water and with the lights everywhere it is hard to believe we are on the eve of war. The AA gunners are sitting around their guns and searchlights in tin hats and we spend some time chatting to them.

Sunday 3rd September 1939

Chamberlain makes a broadcast announcing Hitler has failed to answer the ultimatum and that a state of war exists [*see* Appendix A]. We listen to it in a crowded smoke room and at the far end the nurses continue to calmly try on gas masks. Italy seems to be backing out but even with her also against us I believe we will humble Hitler.

After days of tension we really are at war now. The wireless goes continuously with official announcements and at 6pm HM speaks. It fades out occasionally but it's a moving little talk and no doubt reassures many. I think of Cara and Mummy listening to it too, no doubt in the drawing room. Pray God we all meet again one day. It must be rotten for Cara not knowing where I am.

Monday 4th September 1939

It's a fine sight from my porthole to see the Spanish hills with their tops swathed in rolls of white mist and the French fleet lying opposite reflected in the smooth water.

Censorship of correspondence is now strictly in force. This makes letter writing very different as one can literally say nothing. The P&O from China comes in but we fail to get our mail on to her.

Still no news on when we'll sail – it looks like we'll be sitting off Gibraltar 'til the war is over! All very depressing.

Tuesday 5th September 1939

Italy's intentions seem peaceful and the news seems more positive. South Africa has also come in with us. We've carried out two big air raids dropping pamphlets, one with over six million copies.

After lunch we hold rowing races with the ship's lifeboats. In the evening I walk around the docks. *Alaunia* is next to us and being fitted out as an armed cruiser. I also watch destroyer *Keppel* in dry dock being renovated. They are wonderful long, lean boats and bristle with every imaginable engine of destruction.

Wednesday 6th September 1939

Garrett presents me at breakfast with a letter from Cara. Most lucky and the only one in our ship to get a letter, I believe. Very glad to get some news.

A rumour I'd heard last night is substantiated by a terrific bustle at 9am as a coat of grey paint is being plastered onto the ship's sides. It seems we'll sail tomorrow at dusk.

I lunch at Government House with the governor and his wife, both charming and natural. They show us the house and gardens, including a tree reputed to be 2,000 years old. It looks a little like a palm but had smaller branches. It's known as a 'Dragon Tree'.[4]

By dark almost the whole ship has been painted after ten hours' work. A few life boats and the upper deck stanchions are all that are left white.

We sail at 8.30pm but without an escort. The destroyers we had expected to come with us have had to deal with a fleet of enemy submarines based around the Canary Islands. The pocket battleship *Deutschland* is also supposed to be in this area.

Thursday 7th September 1939

Wake up rather late and feel beastly having had to sleep with porthole closed. I'm inclined to think a lilo on deck might be a better option. I would be wakened early by the deck scrubbing but at least I'd get air and it's a safer place if we get torpedoed.

We are going fast and zigzagging in case of a submarine. We have now been joined by an escort and keep sight of shore at all times.

Friday 8th September 1939

Normal routine by day. General Nosworthy[5] gives a lecture on the general European picture but is unable to tell us much as he is not much more in the know than anyone else.

We continue to zigzag and a notice is put up relaxing ship-darkening provisions. This is immediately cancelled, however, so we presume a submarine has been located.

Saturday 9th September 1939

We sight Malta at about 3pm and see several large flying boats and other airplanes flying around, all heavily laden with bombs. The harbour is completely empty other than one cruiser and one elderly sloop.

In the evening we are not allowed ashore so we have a party and drink a couple of bottles of Burgundy for dinner.

There is very little in the news. Canada is coming in with us, as expected, but what sounds ominous is that Russia seems to be calling up reserves and making a certain amount of troop movements. It may be that she takes this opportunity to settle some differences with Japan. I fear this will become a world war again and could last several years.

---

4. In 1975 it was reappraised as around 250–365 years old.
5. Lieutenant General Sir Francis Nosworthy KCB, DSO, MC (1887–1971) became commander-in-chief of West Africa Command.

Sunday 10th September 1939

The second Sunday onboard and it seems an age since I was in church in Garboldisham singing the same hymns we are now singing on the foredeck.

The zigzagging makes the ship turn half over with every change of direction which makes it very uncomfortable for us. We steam straight after dark as there is no moon and our grey hull must make us nearly invisible.

We are lectured in the morning on anti-submarine defences and then in the evening we have a very dull one on the RNAS.

At about 11pm I take my lilo to sleep on deck but a band of drunk Marines pour out of the bar singing. By midnight they've been through their bawdy repertoire and are reduced to hymns! 'I was a skivvy' becomes 'The day thou gavest Lord is ended'.

Tuesday 12th September 1939

Again see no shipping all day until we're almost into Alexandria. We anchor at noon and after a lot of complications berth around 4pm. Hardly any of the fleet in the harbour – Egypt seems to be taking the war pretty quietly.

Hop, Garrett and I go ashore and dine at the Union Bar and then go on to beat up the old haunts – they are completely unchanged!

Wednesday 13th September 1939

Sail at 5.30am. It's pretty tricky getting in and out with booms, nets, mines etc.

At Port Said I am ordered to catch the 9pm train to Kantara. We cross the canal by ferry and at midnight catch the Palestine train.

Thursday 14th September 1939

Wake up at Rafa at about 5.30am. Shave and wash before anyone else wakes up. It's beautifully cool but the flies are bad and there's a lot of dust about. It's odd to be back amongst the old familiar sights, sounds and smells when I thought I'd seen the last of it all.

Friday 15th September 1939

I go to Nahalal to meet the squadron. They are in a most cosy camp in our old wood. They have been out since 3am and many are already bedded down. Our strength is about 140 men and 110 horses. We are pretty well self-contained and the men look fit and happy. The officers sleep outside but meal in. The men are in orderly lines in a young pine wood with two men to a tree. The horse lines are in the same wood and I should defy any aeroplane to spot us.

Saturday 16th September 1939
The best night's sleep I've had for a long time. I hate a shut window and always sleep best outside. The sun is too hot to allow one to stay in bed past 6.30am but there are not many chances of lying late anyway.

I'm very glad to have my King back. He's scrupulously clean and pleasantly attentive. He'll make the ideal butler at Sotterley one day.

An Arab inspector comes in. It's extraordinary how the Jew hates the Arab and vice versa and yet here comes an Arab into a Jewish colony and probably commanding Jewish police. It's a bizarre mix-up.

Sunday 17th September 1939
Very hot morning and sticky. Hear that a truck has been blown up at Sarid by a landmine. They are the most devilish contraptions.

I take a troop out to escort a dog following the scent of the perpetrator. It's interesting to watch these dogs work as they never lose the line even if donkeys, camels, chickens etc cross it. Yet if once they lift their noses they are completely lost and struggle to pick it up again. Sadly a whole day's Bedouin activity across the line in a populous camp, combined with hot sun for 10 hours, defeated our dog, Molly. We did, however, capture the *Mukhtar* [village headman] who was trying to slip away.

We watered and fed and start back for camp at 5.30pm. At dusk, an hour later, I turn around and look at the troop. Every man was riding on a loose rein and every horse walking with not a single one out of position. A year ago yesterday we went into camp and very few of the men could ride; now a full night's marching or a forty-eight hour bivouac is considered normal.

Monday 18th September 1939
I have a long hot drive around Haifa and Acre. Bivouac at Sakhnin where there is awful water shortage. It's hard on the inhabitants but they are a bad lot and we would not be bothering them if they behaved.

The country looks very different from when I was last here, dry and burnt up. The olive orchards around here are enormous and the trees look like they must have been planted by the Romans.

Tuesday 19th September 1939
I take a recce party to Deir Hannah and Ailabun to find water for the horses. Both are crusader villages and the inhabitants are pale Christians.

At 6pm I take out two ambush parties and remain out 'til midnight but fail to contact a night walker. As there's a curfew anyone out after dark is usually armed and we are authorised to shoot first and ask after.

Saturday 23rd September 1939

Return to Nahalal. As soon as we leave camp a crowd of natives and small children rush in to unearth tins, bottles etc. Soon the tidy site becomes a rubbish dump in a few minutes.

We halt at the top of a pass to give the horses a breather. I should think we can see a third of Palestine. There seems to be a migration of birds of prey towards the south; eagles, kites, hawks and kestrels seem to be moving in their hundreds and at great height.

Tuesday 26th September 1939

Colonel Macleod when walking from the cookhouse yesterday with a piece of meat was attacked by a kite. It has remained with him ever since. It sits on his bed and one can stroke it like a parrot.

We get news of a big gang leader, Yusef Hamdar, having shot up an Arab family in the area. We are to look for him tomorrow.

Wednesday 27th September 1939

We divide into two parties, half with Ronnie[6] go down to Megiddo to work north and the remainder with self and Brian [Ralph 'Brian' Gore] go to Umm Az Zinat and work south. We don't find the gang leader and have no adventures other than when Brian misreads his map and enters a village I was already investigating.

Thursday 28th September 1939

Ronnie, Geoffrey and I start off at 5am with a Jewish Sergeant Pressman and the night watchman of the local colony to shoot hares in the vineyards. A very unusual sort of shoot and not easy as the hares never ran a line, giving only a very fleeting opportunity. We get twelve hare and find the two Jews are mad keen and most unorthodox!

For supper we have jugged hare. The troops also eat hare and our servants say it is the best meal they've had since Christmas!

Friday 29th September 1939

It turns out to be one of the hottest days of the year. The coolest place after lunch is 103°. We are to return to Kakur tomorrow but decide to march tonight in case tomorrow will be equally hot.

We dine with the Jewish Council and other members of the colony. They are charming to us and give us roast turkey. It is embarrassing when they

---

6. Lieutenant Colonel Ronnie Joy DSO (1898–1974), also a notable cricketer, playing for Essex 1922–8.

drink our health and wish us 'victory'. Ronnie answers for us and keeps his speech in a lighter vein.

There is a full moon and the temperature is pleasant when we move off at 11.30pm. A large crowd cheers us away. Many of the troops have had too much beer and will feel the full effect around dawn.

Saturday 30th September 1939
Except for periods of heavy dust we have a pleasant ride. It's extraordinary how one's mind can wander when riding in the dark. The old horse plods on and one can abandon all local thoughts. We get to Hadera at around 7.45am having enjoyed the cooling breeze for the few miles before arrival. We spend most of the day sleeping – we have a lot of sleep to make up.

The more I see of the men the more I admire them. They get through an incredible amount of work despite the intense heat and, with a few exceptions, are always cheerful and satisfied.

Sunday 1st October 1939
Spend morning working out tomorrow's move. Ronnie meanwhile attends a conference to discuss matters concerning the rumour of seven officers and 200 reservists being on the high seas bound for here. Tony Pepys and Bob will become squadron leaders and I the senior 2i/c.

Monday 2nd October 1939
Go over to Karkur. Our new mess here is very pleasant and airy and from the veranda one can look over the whole camp. My room faces south-west and King arranges my things with taste. After moving so much it is nice to settle and feel one may have two months in one spot.

The news is very cheerful today. Winston Churchill makes a very fine speech [*see* Appendix A] which anticipates and forestalls (I think) Hitler's next move which will be to appeal to the world when his peace treaty is rejected. There is no doubt that alcohol does not affect Winnie's brain!

Wednesday 4th October 1939
The draft is coming next week and there are a hundred problems to solve, the greatest being accommodation.

Settle into daily routine which is to have a doze in the afternoon, walk round the evening stables and then listen to the wireless news 'til dinner. We only wear a white shirt and blue trousers for dinner – very informal but comfortable.

It's now a year since that horrible dawn when I left Cara, one of the nastiest moments of our life. Pray God it won't be another year 'til we can set up house again.

Friday 6th October 1939

Robert Crockett tells me he is getting his girl out here to marry her and share a house with at Hermon's at Nathanya. I am sorely tempted to try and get Cara out here but feel strongly that the war is not going to last so long and Mummy can't be left alone for the winter. I'd only see Cara three days a fortnight if she came out, to say nothing of the chances of me being moved on to a staff job somewhere.

Finish Evelyn Waugh's *Black Mischief*. Must recommend to Cara – it is distinctly humorous.

Saturday 7th October 1939

We catch three Arab boys stealing from the NAAFI. SSM Lewis is very funny with them and puts them on fatigues. They scrub out the guard room and are sent off with a flea in their ear.

Arrange for the police to kill off the surplus dogs that roam around the camp, partly because their howling makes it impossible to sleep and partly because of a story that a mad jackal attacked another camp and killed thirteen dogs, injuring others. I hate the idea of a rabies scare here.

Hear Berlin's translation of Hitler's speech [*see* Appendix A]. It's laughably weak. I can't believe Germany will last out 'til after Christmas with Hitler already losing his grip. Russia is fast becoming a menace in the background and I don't see a peaceful solution to world problems as yet.

Thursday 10th October 1939

I spend the entire morning in the local court as a military representative at local land dispute settlements. The local tribe of Arab Turkmen claim the right as tenants to plough certain Jewish land. The managing director of the Jewish company disputes this but seems entirely ignorant of what has been going on on his land for the last two years.

It is quite obvious that the Arab is fighting for his livelihood while the Jew is out to push him off the land. Some of the Arabs are very fine looking men and have spent much of the winter both in the hills and in the cage.

Thursday 12th October 1939

In the afternoon we go down to the sea and shoot off anti-aircraft practices. We have small balloons as targets which come over us fast and rising on fresh wind. It is surprising what number are hit by rifle fire – over half. The Bren guns are not so good but one could see from the tracer that the shooting was accurate enough to upset any pilot.

Friday 13th October 1939

This should be an unlucky day for somebody. It turns out to be very unlucky for the local dogs as the police come round and destroy four but far from instantaneously.

In the evening I give an impassioned address to the squadron about saving money. I would very much like to start them all off on Post Office savings. Later in the evening I discuss the matter with King. I suspect life here is more expensive than in India but feel sure that the modern man is less adept at looking ahead. The general attitude appears to be 'it's my money and I can do what I like with it.'

Sunday 15th October 1939

In the evening I see the new moon and make the correct obeisance and make a wish. On entering the house I find a fat letter from Cara and one from Ma with several enclosures from Nigel and Lysbeth. Later a second one from Cara is brought in – they are dated 24th and 27th!

Nigel has enlisted and has been sent to France as Driver Barne of RASC, a very noble effort. Elizabeth is working in the Connaught Hospital. Cara seems very happy and settled.

I remain convinced that Hitler must crack up soon and I feel sure the next six months will see the end of the organised war.

Wednesday 18th October 1939

Elizabeth's birthday. I hope she's not on night duty and manages to have a bit of a party. I should have liked to raise a glass to her health but am feeling far from fit having been inoculated yesterday. My temperature is a shade over 104° and apparently a lot of the squadron are similarly suffering. One never used to feel the effects of it like this in India.

Friday 27th October 1939

We have a late *Reveille* and at about 11am the reservists arrive. There are a curious looking old collection and very much of a type. We take over billets at noon with two bungalows for officers and sergeants.

Reggie rings up to say we're to form a mechanised squadron, Gawd help us … it is quite incredible how we've changed in a year; we've become as malleable as putty.

European news remains positive and Ribbentrop [German foreign minister] made a blundering speech [*see* Appendix A]. Hitler seems to be at his wit's end.

Sunday 29th October 1939

Have to interview various Jews; one wants to plant potatoes on our football ground, one wants money for eggs. An Arab comes in to complain that the Jews have taken 200 sheep and then the Jews come in to say they only took one and that's because the Arabs stole their vegetables. One has to imitate Solomon to the best of one's ability.

Have a film in the evening. Good news reel but the main film is rather sordid. It's all about tarts in a nightclub.

Wednesday 1st November 1939

Another 'opening day' [of the fox-hunting season] arrives with me abroad. This is the eleventh, and every one I swear will be my last. Personally, despite the government's declaration of preparation for three years of war, I think we'll be home for next season.

Saturday 11th November 1939

Wood, the storeman, comes up with poppies for us. It seems incredible that with a war raging we should go on trying to remember the last one. As yet casualties are few, except for Ball who was at Catterick with me in '28, and I know no one amongst the roll of honour. After two months of fighting in 1914 the death roll of people one knew was enormous. I suppose now the cavalry are extinct and the Guards are not in the line. So far it's all been RAF, *Royal Oak*[7] and *Courageous*[8] casualties.

Spend the entire day on a DCM defending Lance Corporal Biggs. A silly case and he obviously deserves conviction. Eddie prosecutes and, as always, he's easy money. The court is Duncan and Seaton of the Welch Regiment and Brian G. Seaton comes back with us for a drink after the court. He is the son of a Russian Countess and is as wild as a hawk, especially when in drink.

Tuesday 14th November 1939

I'm bored stiff here – one year has been more than sufficient. I'm now financially back on my feet again but feel I ought to be doing something in this war. If not, I should at least have a definite job with my wife beside me.

---

7. HMS *Royal Oak* was torpedoed by a U-boat and sunk at Scapa Flow in Orkney on 14 October 1939. Of the crew of 1,234 men, 833 were killed. The sinking had considerable effect on wartime morale as the naval base at Scapa Flow had been considered impregnable to submarine attack.

8. HMS *Courageous* was torpedoed by a U-boat and sunk off the coast of Ireland on 17 September with the loss of 519 crew, including her captain.

Monday 20th November 1939
My birthday. Thirty-three years behind me and not much to show for them.

It's a foul day and there's a lot of work to be done clearing up after last night's storm. It raged all night long with the heavy hail breaking windows. The gale blew over a watchtower and lifted a whole sixty-foot veranda in the air and landed it on the roof!

Ronnie comes in after lunch with a message from Reggie to say I've been ordered to take over running the port in Haifa. The only good news is that General Barker gives permission for wives to land if they can get permission to leave England.

Wednesday 22nd November 1939
Finish handing over to Terry Gosling, who will replace me.

I go in to Haifa at 10.30 taking King. He unpacks for me as I set about learning the routine from Biddy, Roddy and the commander (General Langham), with whom I'll be living 'til Cara comes out.

Friday 24th November 1939
After lunch we go fishing and catch nothing but later return after dark and get into a *garkur*, 4lb and strong as a horse; they're a type of sea bass. It's lovely down by the breakwater with a nearly full moon rising over the hills.

Saturday 25th November 1939
Teddy rings up first thing to say that wives that are not already in Palestine or en route are being stopped so we must take urgent steps before the order comes into force. Have a hectic morning sending wires and cables – it is imperative I get Cara out here but now must sit and await an answer.

Wednesday 29th November 1939
Big day. *Devonshire* is arriving at dawn and so have to be down to meet her. We have to take off a small party and then put on 500. All this requires careful organisation and supervision.

Receive a cable from Cara saying she's finding it difficult to get an exit permit from England, as I'd feared. I must not give up hope.

We have a very drunken orgy in the evening with the Finlays and Brasseys and others. It's a real good party with masses of pop flowing free and everyone in good heart. Robert Crockett gets very drunk and wild – lets his pistol off and uses the most offensive language which I don't approve of in public.

Thursday 30th November 1939

Russsia invaded Finland this morning.[9] Very depressing news as it looks like encouraging our conflict into a real World War. As usual when depressed I fly to send a cable to Cara in the hopes of urging on her efforts to get out here.

Friday 1st December 1939

Start off at 6.30am with Captain Lyddeker, John Chetwode, Guy and Charles Herbert for Beirut. We are on a liaison mission with the French and it's deeply interesting to see what I take to be history in the making.

I can follow the French when they speak but cannot say much in return. The whole meeting is on the most cordial terms and the French put every card on the table except one; one that is not hard to miss when one looks at the map on the wall.

The French were charming and surprisingly efficient and Charles did very well at keeping to the points at hand. I was not asked much thankfully.

We all lunch at the St George, have a lot of good wine and a nice cigar to finish. Merton, the war correspondent follows us out of the restaurant – he'd give his eyes to know what we talked about!

Tuesday 5th December 1939

Spend a couple of hours in Charles' office reading up on the files as we are reorganising the movements: I'll have Ships, Trains and Transport under me.

Still no news from Cara. I write her an absolute stinker, poor lamb, but fear it might be the only way to rouse her. I fear friends back home are giving her ignorant and ill-timed advice about coming out here.

Saturday 16th December 1939

Take King on driving instruction, he may turn out to be quite a good driver. As the town is celebrating the Sabbath it's a good day to take him round.

The German colony is being evacuated and cleared by the police and as a consequence there are cordons everywhere. Poor Ma App and her maids will have a day of tears but I'm not sorry for them – if they will bow down to false Gods then they must suffer.

---

9. Known as the Winter War, the conflict between Russia and Finland was to last until the Moscow Peace Treaty of 13 March 1940. The Soviets gained 11 per cent of Finnish territory but suffered over 300,000 casualties.

Sunday 17th December 1939

Visit my proposed new office in the station (Haifa East). When installed I shall have an office next to Charles Herbert and a mass of clerks with typewriters so probably won't be able to hear a word on the telephone. I hate that instrument.

Wednesday 20th December 1939

Captain Lyddeker, Roddy, Lieutenant Commander Mandley and I all go down to Jaffa to look at the port with a view to landing or embarking troops. The port is really only a lighter basin [harbour with a shallow draught] with a very tricky entrance. It is very interesting watching the lightermen and they seem to be highly skilful.

Saturday 23rd December 1939

King and I go off to do a driving test for our licences. King does extremely well, very cool and gives a smooth exhibition.

After lunch I receive a cable from Cara saying she's starting in January from Marseilles. It is the most thrilling news I have ever heard as I really was getting desperate. I must now start some serious house hunting. There are plenty of German houses free as all the 'enemy' are now in camps.

Monday 25th December 1939

Roddy and I go to early church at St Luke's. A very nice service and the little church is nearly full.

The rest of the day, I'm afraid, is a riot. We start by drinking at most of the police messes and by lunch we're rather tight. I go up the hill to the Parkers and have an uproarious party and then take King out to the hospital to see some Royals and give them cigarettes and papers.

Stay for tea with the nurses and while there hear the King's speech [*see* Appendix A]. It is a good speech and well pronounced. Whilst at tea Roddy takes Jill Bishop out and proposes marriage so for the rest of the day he's unplayable.

In the evening we attend a rather strange dinner party with the Webbs. A good deal of liquor is consumed. Afterwards everyone decants to the Savoy Bar but I clear out and walk home. It seems I was lucky as Roddy succeeds in breaking up the car and breaking Guy's nose badly. He ends up in hospital.

Thursday 28th December 1939

A terrible day. *Neuralia*, scheduled for dawn, only arrives at 11.30am and we are to take off 80 nurses and 300 RAMC and then put on the West Yorks and their baggage. The winches break and even when repaired are terribly slow. The ship is old and decrepit and we have an awful time getting the West Yorks on, especially as there's no lighting in the holds.

Saturday 30th December 1939
Feel like death all day with a bloody cold.

Guy comes out of hospital today looking pretty ugly but thankfully he's got no serious or lasting injury.

Sunday 31st December 1939
Still feel like death but go down to the docks early to help disembark the *Inventor*. The master is the most extraordinary old boy, Mr Bostock by name and rather like Uncle Mike.[10]

Guy's nose bleeds all day long and we end up having to take him back to the hospital. Poor Guy – he needs some time off.

Drink and dine with John Chetwode but break up before midnight. I have no wish to see this bloody year out – failed for Staff College, seen Cara for five days and war has blackened the whole world.

Monday 1st January 1940
Wake up full of good intentions – I only hope they'll last.

Thompson and I go out early, first to see the AA guns off the ship and then take some photos against a magnificent rainbow.

By 10am it's raining hard and we go to see Guy in hospital. He's in a bad way, under morphia and with his vein plugged.

Saturday 6th January 1940
Christen the new office and telephones. Corporal Smart is going to be my chief clerk. He's not much to look at but he's supposed to be good to his name.

Visit the bank to prepare my finances for when Cara arrives. My allowance should be about £43 pm, add £29 pm pay and 5/- pd for staff captain. This

---

10. Captain Michael Barne DSO, RN (1877–1961). A Second Lieutenant on RRS *Discovery* during Scott's first Antarctic expedition (1901–4) with responsibility for magnetometry and depth sounding, he participated in several sledge journeys, the longest of which he led himself to what is now known as Barne Inlet. On his return from Antarctica he rejoined the Royal Navy. In the First World War he was awarded a DSO following service in the Dardanelles and the Dover Patrol. He also received the Royal Humane Society's Silver Medal for diving overboard and attempting to rescue a sailor during a storm in the Atlantic. He retired from the Royal Navy in 1919 as a Captain but returned during Second World War to take command of an anti-submarine patrol ship.

should be sufficient for our needs without touching Coutts, but money is bound to be tight after the war so we must save all we can.

Tuesday 9th January 1940

Rise at 5.30am to meet the convoy. The heavy swell and terrific rain make boarding difficult but eventually manage to start unloading. We try to get the Warwicks off according to the programme and eventually get one train off but the floors are so slippery the horses cannot stand.

It is one of the worst days I've known. We work 'til 9pm without a break except for breakfast with everything and everyone soaked. The only thing that has kept me going was a wire to say that Cara would arrive into Tel Aviv on Monday.

Thursday 11th January 1940

Lovely day. Down at the docks by 7am and work the Cheshire Yeomanry. The first horse comes off at 7.35am and by 9.10am the first train is ready to depart. The whole ship, *Tairea*, was clear by 12.30pm and the remains of the Cheshire on the *Rhona* were out by 10am. Their horses looked bigger and better than others but they were lucky with the weather – altogether nine died and thirty-three admitted to the veterinary hospital out of 1,975. Of nearly 4,000 men over ninety were admitted to hospital, mostly for throats.

Friday 12th January 1940

Can't get any news of Cara's ship. The Tel Aviv people know of no ship on 15th. She may be landing here or Beirut or I may get a wire from Alexandria.

Saturday 13th January 1940

Get a wire from Cara in the afternoon to say she's at Alexandria and coming to Beirut. I shall be able to meet her on the frontier.

To catch up with *Glenapp*'s fast unloading rate, we work 'til 1am. The labourers get very tired and we end up doing most of the work ourselves. Bitterly cold and back-breaking.

Monday 15th January 1940

Go to the frontier and Cara turns up looking radiant. She arrives in a taxi with three missionary women. It is a most joyful moment for both of us and from now Palestine will be a different country!

We have tea at Appinger's and a constant stream of people come in. All very bewildering for Cara who had a nasty 24 hours at sea; the ship was empty and was tossed around like a cork apparently.

Sunday 21st January 1940

See a lot of horses off to Hadera; Cheshire, Warwicks and Staffs send seventy each to the Royals. We have been warned to be ready for war in six weeks' time. Can't believe that it is possible but there's no doubt about something blowing in the wind. The TJFF are concentrating on the Saudi Arabia frontier and we are going as far as Beisan to relieve them from this side.

Wednesday 24th January 1940

Get a calm and collected letter from Mummy to say that poor old Granny is dying. She's a very great character and Mummy has been a very faithful daughter to her. It's sad that the family should be so scattered and that Mummy has to bear it all alone.

Saturday 27th January 1940

Before lunch we have a drink on an old tub *Sakara* that has sailed under three flags and three names. In the afternoon, the ship lands its ballast too quickly and quietly rolls 50 degrees. By dark after frantic unloading it turns over on the other side.

Sunday 28th – Wednesday 31st January 1940

This period has passed like a bad dream. Dawn of Sunday broke cold and wet and so it has continued, interrupted only by periods of gale.

Have six horse boats to discharge plus there's eleven ships sitting out in the bay who daren't lie in the harbour. *Talumba* kills a man when she slips her moorings. She then drifts broadside out of the harbour in a gale and narrowly misses an Australian destroyer.

Cara comes down frequently to see how things are getting on and she takes great interest in it all.

Saturday 3rd February 1940

Cara, Tommy Baylis and and I start off at 7.30am for Jerusalem in convoy with Charles Herbert. Glorious morning and the Plain of Esdraelon is covered in mist. We stop at Jacob's Well and then go straight through.

In the afternoon I conduct Cara and Tommy around the Old City. Poor Cara has a tummy bug but Tommy enjoys every minute of it. After tea we attend Philip and Douglas Kaye's party. The chief drink is Tiger's Milk [brandy, rum, milk, sugar syrup and cinnamon], a ghastly poison.

Monday 5th February 1940

Hang about HQ all morning discussing Australian moves and local queries.

Return by the coast road after lunch. Again Cara and Tommy enjoy it very much indeed and the countryside is looking at its very best. Hold office over a whisky in the evening and catch up on events of the last two days.

Wednesday 7th February 1940

Very big day as apply for ten days leave in Syria starting 25th. Also start fixing up my early departure for the canal. We're going down on Friday as Egypt seem to want us to fix things for them, blast them!

Syrian Prince is in with over 24,000 packages to be discharged. Busy times.

Friday 9th February 1940

Start off at 7am for Port Said, taking the sick horses on the back of the train to Lydda. Get into Kantara at 6pm and met by Mallins of Essex Regiment and Washer the Washout who is going to be the STO of the move, a terrible blow as he's useless. Both are blind drunk when they meet us, apparently their standard condition.

Saturday 10th February 1940

I hear some queer stories about Mallins who has a weak head but won't give up alcohol. He's been near to being court martialled several times.

Very hush hush news comes through that Anthony Eden [Secretary of State for Dominion Affairs] is coming down to meet the Dominion troops. It's annoying as the bigger the noise the more difficult and delaying it is for us.

Nothing has been fixed here and we have to work out the whole move ourselves despite the order that BTE would do the move and we'd help! Spend most of the day at Kantara seeing all the important people. Surprisingly, very few ships are using the canal. We see a small Indian liner playing our national anthem and a large, luxurious Dutch one, *Dempo*, go southbound carrying troops.

We dine on *Lucinda*. She's one of the most luxurious craft one can imagine; about 400 tons and 41 years old. A bad sea boat but as a houseboat nothing could be nicer. Her late owner was a smuggler who saw sense and chartered her to the Admiralty before she was confiscated!

Monday 12th – Wednesday 14th February 1940

After a conference with full staff it is decided that it is imperative that I go down to meet the ships to prepare them for disembarkation.

In the evening I drive down to the canal and go out to *Orford* and *Otranto*, both looking very fine in the evening light. Board each one and explain the plan – am treated like a royal guest! Dine on *Otranto* and then come up on her to Kantara. She has 102 officers and 1,350 troops onboard, all very cheerful and looking fit, tough but oldish. The officers on the whole appear to have no breeding and seem a little afraid of their men. Lieutenant Colonel Dougherty is their CO and is very pleasant. Anthony Eden received them this morning and I just missed him at Ishmailia. We disembark the whole ship – and their baggage – by one ladder in 2 hours, 10 minutes.

Between 12.30am Tuesday and 8.30am Wednesday we manage to disembark over 6,500 Australians with no hitches. We have a doze on Wednesday afternoon but feel surprisingly untired given we've been over 60 hours without sleep.

Thursday 15th February 1940

A dull train journey back and am met by Cara at the station. She appears to have had a gay time and I'm very glad.

After dinner we go to a recital by Huberman [Bronislaw Huberman, the Polish violinist]. We are in the second row, much the best seats for a violin solo. It's well worth attending but I'm not sure he's as good as he was a year ago. I may be getting critical – his technique is, of course, amazing and his fingers are a joy to watch.

Saturday 24th February 1940

Set off late morning for skiing in Lebanon, getting through both frontiers by lunchtime and reaching Beirut by 3.15pm. Whole drive in solid rain. After an early tea we get all the skiing necessities and get an early night.

Sunday 25th February 1940

Set off again at 9.30am having bought 40 litres of petrol. The hill up is terrific after Tripoli. The gorge we follow is enormously deep with vertical sides and following it round thirty-seven hairpin bends takes most of my attention. We lunch en route and arrive at the Cedars [ski resort] by 3pm. Have to kick a Frenchman and Syrian tart out of our room but have time to get changed and get an hour and a half on skis. For every slide one has to climb an equal distance.

Monday 26th February 1940

Ski all morning on the local slope and then in the afternoon taken to the *Prière de Déjeuner*, a 1,200 foot climb on skis. It's too much for most of us and we are too tired to have much control over our skis. We climb in nothing over a shirt but on the way down need windproof clothes.

Have a strong mustard bath in the evening and pray we won't be too stiff in the morning.

Wednesday 28th February 1940

In the morning Colonel and Mrs Large take us up Orange Peel twice and on the second run I suddenly find my legs.

One of the nicest things about this leave is the complete absence from sitting around making small talk. One doesn't get in from skiing 'til after 5pm and by the time one has tea-ed, bathed and rested it's dinner time.

Saturday 2nd March 1940
Rise at 7am and eat breakfast alone. With much trepidation I join the Jewish party taking part in the downhill race from *Pierre de Nord*. There's not a single English-speaking person present but they are all very nice to me (in French). The climb up at 9am is in good snow but by the time we race at 11am it has already got slushy. The course is a steep downhill with seven turns and then a schuss for a mile. I take three falls and would have given up but an excited Frenchman comes and urges me on.

Monday 4th March 1940
Michael and I organise a race for amateurs from Orange Peel. We have fourteen competitors but not all start – or finish. I'm put scratch but fall heavily and lose a ski. Cara has a 24-second start and goes jolly well. She's a neat little skier, certainly bold enough and comes third.

After lunch we climb up to a desperate place with not another soul about and the weather closing in. A great storm is coming but it's our last day and the snow is perfect.

Wednesday 6th March 1940
Find the new offices in the dock are nearly completed and very smart indeed. Sadly, though, Boulton and Griffiths have done damn all in my absence and I'm inundated with unanswered letters.

All ranks now have to wear uniform all the time, which is a nuisance but I felt sure it would come.

Sunday 10th March 1940
Guy calls me at 6am to say that *Rajula* and *Rohua* are in sight. They are alongside by 7.30am and start discharging their horses. By 3pm we have finished forming the second horse train in icy cold wind and rain. There is also 100 tons of hay to be taken off each ship and the *Rajula* goes on 'til about midnight.

Monday 11th March 1940
After lunch Cara and I go up Mount Carmel after flowers. We find thirty-seven varieties with tulips and a big orange ranunculus being the most attractive. Cara finds a tiny field mouse, probably just weaned. I bring it down in my pocket and she makes the most of her tiny pet. It absorbs her

entire interest. What will happen when she has a child of her own I daren't think – I'll be completely out of the picture.

Thursday 21st March 1940

Cara gets news of a nice flat becoming available in the near future. I'm all in favour of it. It's higher up the hill than Appinger's but I think it will keep her occupied and work out cheaper than the hotel. In any case I am sick of hotel life and Appinger's is deteriorating rapidly. We will, however, miss the flow of visitors that come and go.

All chance of a quiet Easter now vanished with the *Talamba* coming in on Saturday and two supply ships on Easter Day.

Cara and I go up to see the flat in the evening. It's really rather attractive with three bedrooms, dining and drawing rooms, large hall, kitchen etc as well as a servant who does everything and has a room downstairs.

Sunday 24th March 1940

Rise at 6am and go down to get *Talumba* finished. She goes on discharging hay and forage 'til 3pm.

Attention then turns to *Glen*. She has the new magnetic belt to protect her from magnetic mines. She discharges a large quantity of ordnance which seems a little queer. There is talk of this becoming a theatre of war with wives to be evacuated but this contradicts the official line. This rather changes my view on taking a flat if there's a chance Cara could be evacuated.

Thursday 28th March 1940

Have to go to pack Bayliss off to hospital. Poor little man – he looks pathetic and I'm not at all sure he hasn't been giving himself his own medicine. His cupboard is full of empty gin bottles and one glass smelt strongly. His speech is far from coherent and I only hope my suspicions are not correct as he's a nice sort.

Monday 1st April 1940

I hear that my fears about Bayliss were well founded. He is in hospital with alcohol poisoning and was blind drunk when I took him in. Silly little old man.

Have Ruth Wood for lunch who tells how she has just written to the Secretary of State for War (her uncle Oliver Stanley!) over the wife problem. Very naughty of her but one can't help laughing.

Tuesday 9th April 1940

At 11am great excitement is caused by the news that Germany has invaded Denmark and Norway.[11] Everyone v thrilled and at lunchtime we are all crowded into the lounge to hear the wireless.

Wednesday 10th April 1940

The whole place is full of rumours with the Navy caught napping and landings taking place. It's quite obvious whatever is happening now cannot be relayed for a bit so we must just wait and see. It does appear, however, that the Northern Front is now front page news and we can only hope we have not been bluffed. I would not be surprised to see Italy come in now against us as most of their navy is now in home waters.

After dinner we listen to the news which is extremely good. With the loss of only two of our destroyers we seem to have disposed of the majority of the German Navy and supply ships. I can't help feeling this is Hitler's first great blunder and will shorten the war considerably.

Thursday 11th April 1940

Bayliss ill again. I strongly suspected he was tight yesterday morning and possibly since Monday.

Peter Ryder, now a captain, turns up in the evening to stay the night. I'm inclined to think he's getting a bit of a bore and is definitely conceited. He tells us he was shown secret documents by the RAF stating our losses in the Sylt raid were 85%.[12] It's unbelievable and completely against our policy. It's also a dangerous statement to go whispering round and undermines confidence in our own government.

Friday 12th April 1940

Bayliss still in bed. Charles is furious and talking about arresting him. I think the little man is penitent and needs a chance to recover. I go and talk to him in the afternoon and he seems anxious to reform. I go to old Mrs Abbott whom I feel sure can keep him in hand. She is going to give him a room and keep him under observation.

---

11. Operation *Weserübung*, the German invasion of Denmark and Norway, was presented as a preventative move against the mooted Franco–British occupation of neutral Norway. Germany was heavily reliant on Swedish iron ore imported from northern Norway which would have been at risk if the Allies established naval bases in the Baltic.

12. The attack on the German seaplane base in Sylt took place during the night of 19/20 March 1940. At that time it was the biggest air attack undertaken by either side. Of the twenty British bombers that set out, only one was shot down.

When having a drink at the Windsor later, the barman informs me that Bayliss had a bottle of brandy on Thursday and a bottle of gin on Friday. I have ordered that he be given no more.

Very little news today. Exports to Scandinavia from GB have been banned. Also an enormous minefield has been laid which will hem in Germany and not threaten Sweden's neutrality. I hear the navy is being strengthened in the Med and the French are also massing in northern Syria. Are we going to jump? If so, how soon?

Saturday 13th April 1940

News extremely good. We are reported to have sunk seven German destroyers and made a landing at Narvik.[13] The German people must hear of these losses and will soon become depressed. Italy at the moment is very hostile but unless they (or we) have the wrong end of the stick, they'll soon climb down.

Monday 15th April 1940

A big Norwegian ship has come in empty and is immediately detained. *Lesbos* is hard at work discharging timber and some corrugated iron. *Hatsu* doesn't quite finish and in the morning drops eight cases of bacon overboard. The bacon is £5 per case and we think it's worthwhile to use a diver to recover them!

Friday 19th April 1940

The papers have several grave headlines: England's warning to Italy, unrest in the Balkans, USA's warning to Japan, German advances in Norway, but what about Russia? There seems little mention of her and she can play a very important part either by coming in or staying out.

At 9.30pm there is a practice blackout. On the whole it's pretty effective but not a practical exercise as it was a full moon!

Monday 22nd April 1940

Cara starts her new job at the Cypher Office[14] and she's a little nervy at the thought of it! She wakes up early and says it feels like she's going back to

---

13. The second naval battle of Narvik resulted in eight German destroyers and a U-boat sunk or scuttled, against three British destroyers damaged. Despite the naval defeat, the port of Narvik and the surrounding areas remained under German control as there were no Allied forces available to land there. On 10 June 1940 the Norwegian Army eventually capitulated, after the longest period any occupied country withstood a German invasion before succumbing.

14. The British used Typex cypher machines from 1937 onwards to exchange encrypted messages. Experienced operators could manage to decipher up to twenty words a minute that were then printed on paper tape.

school. She hasn't got a very nice boss – Mr Thomson and his wife run the office. Both are school teachers by profession and have no sense of humour. Cara will be earning £15 pm, £1 more than the trained stenographer in my office!

Thursday 25th April 1940
Pick Cara up at her office at 11.30am and after a quick change rush on to Tel Aviv for the local races.

We have an extremely amusing afternoon. I meet up with an owner, Mr Nathanson, and after a lot of talk manage to wangle a ride on his brother's bay horse. I get the very severe bit removed and put my own saddle on but I don't do any good- chiefly because I can't get round one very sharp corner, unknown both to the horse and me. I let two people through and then can't catch either.

The grandstand is Napoleon's Hill surmounted by flags and teaming with Jewish youth. The horses were mostly Arab owned and not much to look at.

Sunday 28th April 1940
A message comes in to say that shipping is being diverted round the Cape and the Mediterranean is partially closed – an ominous sign. From the signals it appears that we are collecting a fleet in the eastern Mediterranean.

Wednesday 1st May 1940
Come in to office to find Charles in a real flap – it seems the secret of the closing of the Mediterranean to our ships has been disclosed and Cara is getting the blame. Actually he inadvertently let the cat out but very nobly was only perturbed about Cara!

We can't get hold of Lyddeker as he's spent the morning arranging a tennis tournament (a good wartime job!) so we beard him later in the afternoon and get a full apology from him. John C, his secretary, seems a most competent liar but gets a real rocket from Lydekker, Charles and then myself.

Thursday 2nd May 1940
The papers give a far from happy set of headlines. The PM admits we've had a bit of a setback in Norway but the wireless is more cheerful. In my own mind I'm convinced that in our unprepared state for the Norwegian invasion we'll have to lose a lot before we start gaining.

Friday 3rd May 1940
We find Lydekker hard at work loading Lewis gun magazines. The war has been in progress for eight months and he's been boasting about commanding the port, responsible for security etc but hasn't done a damn thing until we're

on the brink. Italian bombers could have the port office in ruins before he would give his men even one practice shoot. No doubt he'll get a decoration after the war, unless he's caught out by Mussolini.

Owing to the closing of the Mediterranean, Haifa is almost empty.

Friday 10th May 1940
Everyone stirred by the wireless announcement that Hitler has invaded Holland, Belgium and Luxembourg. It must be the last throw of a madman. Like Samson he intends to die and cause as much havoc as he can in the collapse.

While this is happening, the Labour Party try to cause a split in the government and criticise poor old Chamberlain. If they knew the effect on the Arab, Jew and all other foreigners they'd be ashamed to be called English. I fear that Chamberlain will resign and I fear still that Churchill will become PM. I should like Halifax.

At 10pm old Chamberlain speaks to say he's resigned. He's a great man and has presided over three of the most troublesome years in history. No one could have done more and now our ungrateful people can only tear him to pieces.

Churchill is now PM. A gentleman has gone and a clever cad has replaced him.[15] No doubt he will be hailed with great joy in most quarters because he has not forgotten to advertise himself. I only hope I live to eat this page!

Tuesday 14th May 1940
Spend a miserable day in bed with a temperature of 101°. Charles comes in in the afternoon to say the Australian move is on on the 18th/20th and I must go down on Thursday.

Thursday 16th May 1940
Still feeling weak as a kitten but leave on the 8.30am from Haifa. We have two young officers attached: Robinson of the King's Own, a nice energetic lad, and Blackman of the Queen's who is less bright and keen.

Spend the night at Port Said. There seems to be very little shipping about and everyone fearful that Italy about to come in against us. The Western Front situation is also very grave with the Germans pushing right into East France.

---

15. AMB's father seemed to have an equally low opinion of Churchill. He wrote in his diary on 14 December 1915 from just behind the Western Front near Ypres, 'Met Winston Churchill in the street yesterday, a terrible looking person – never saw anything so unlike a soldier – such a low flabby face – more like an "unemployable" from the East End.'

Friday 17th – Sunday 19th May 1940

As seems usual for troop moves, the weather lets us down properly. A strong *khamseen* [hot, dry, sandy wind from the south] obliterates the sun and covers everything in a dry, powdery sand. At lunchtime the cutlery is too hot to touch, even inside the tents.

Ramilies, a French cruiser and two destroyers come through the Canal during the night. She has four searchlights on and looks magnificent. The destroyers slip through with no lights on like rats creeping along a fence.

The first ship in is *Strathaird*, followed by *Neuralia* (my first trooper in September 1927) and then later *Ettrick*. We work all night offloading the troops and supplies and finish at 10am. We're exhausted but no sleep is possible with the heat and howling gale.

We feed at 7pm and prepare for a second night's work. This does not go quite so smoothly as the officers who went down to explain our plans seem to have failed, with chaotic results. I am forced to flatly refuse the demands of a Colonel (Mitchell) with DSO and bar, but 'orders is orders'. He's very incensed and for a moment I thought he would put me under arrest.

The Captain of *Ettrick* is Legg, a most princely looking man with a white beard and moustache cut into fine points. He gave me breakfast and I've never met a man with more perfect manners. He's like a man out of a play with perfectly modulated speech and a delightfully old fashioned choice of wording.

We spend the second lousy, sleepless day on our beds and then at 10.30pm catch the night train back to Haifa.

Monday 20th May 1940

Arrive back to the news that I am to be posted to General Headquarters Middle East and must make for Cairo at once.

My first reaction is for Cara and the future. It will be very hot for her and with Italy on the fence there is no knowing how we will be affected or where I may be sent to.

Wednesday 22nd – Friday 24th May 1940

We are up to our eyes in packing up, handing over my job, winding up the Australian move and organising a farewell party.

I now realise how much we have dug ourselves in and how happy we've been. At our cocktail party, to which we invite thirty and thirty turn up, we say farewell to some wonderful people. Included in this is Gerald Bayliss who we have cured, I hope, of DTs and is a genuine little man.

And so on Friday we go to bed rather sadly and rather tight feeling we've closed a very happy chapter in our little lives.

Saturday 25th May 1940

Have a hot dusty journey down to Cairo.

Things do look very bad – Germans in the Channel ports and Italy on the verge of joining in. Cairo is in partial blackout with troops everywhere who 'stand to' morning and evening to guard against parachutes. Our general policy, as usual, seems to be to sit and wait for the enemy to move so that we can make the next move to counteract. Why the hell can't we dictate to Italy? We just need to say, 'What is your policy? Either you come in with us or we must take you to be an enemy and act accordingly.'

Sunday 26th May 1940

I visit my new HQ at 9am. Not a soul about and at 10am a few float in but I manage to get very little idea about my future.

I'm in a bad position financially because I've no account here, have run out of English cheques and have no allowance due to the end of the month – and that will be paid into Haifa! I want to change my hotel as the Continental is too expensive but I can't leave it 'til I pay the bill! In consequence I go to bed supperless. Not that it's any hardship – it's too hot to eat. Tonight there's a total blackout which is not much fun. I should hate to be driving my car in it or even to be walking.

Monday 27th May 1940

We start work at 8.15am and continue 'til 1.15am. This seems to be the regular programme with 2 hours off in the evening 6–8pm. Saturday and Sunday are no longer treated as holidays but everyone to get one day off a week.

I change hotels after lunch; moving to the Metropolitan. Much cheaper and no less clean.

Tuesday 28th May 1940

I take a trip around Abbassia [Royal Armoured Corps base on the outskirts of Cairo]. It is completely transformed. The whole desert right out to the ranges and beyond the old ordnance depot is a solid mass of depots, sidings, repair shops etc.

The lunchtime news is extremely bad. Belgium has capitulated which rather leaves the BEF in the air. No doubt all our friends and contemporaries are now going through hell. The casualty list will be frightful and I fear that many of the flower of the old cavalry will be in it. All this at the whim of one man.

Dine with Atkinson on the roof of my hotel. A pleasant evening but rather spoilt by some very noisy drunken RAF and attendant women. They don't leave 'til 3am and wake me up. I pour my entire pot of hot water on them as they are all screaming and standing about under my window 'til I can bear it no longer. The effect is excellent.

Wednesday 29th May 1940

Saunders, from whom I am taking over, takes me round to see BTE staff officers, Topham and Elrington. The latter with the reddest hair I've ever seen. They tell a tale of natives being shot on the canal bank; the former insisting they were saboteurs and that the fifth column [spies, saboteurs, etc.] is in our midst, the latter merely feeling sorry for what he considered to be two harmless fishermen.

Am accosted at breakfast by someone who turns out to be Kenneth Grant, an old flame of Elspeth's and not very popular with the family. He is of 'fiddling with the dashboard' fame.

Dine in hotel and bed early. The whole capital seems surrounded by searchlights, AA guns etc. It's as well to be prepared but I can't see the Italians bombing Cairo. There are too many ice-creamers [Italians] here and they hold too much of the property to make it popular.

Friday 31st May 1940

I hear from Naval Intelligence that Italy is coming in on 5th June. I don't believe it.

Cara leaves Haifa at 8.30am, the same time I start my tour of the Western Desert. Alexandria is sticky but cooler than Cairo. The fleet is in the harbour in force while one battleship is in the floating dock. It gives one an idea of the enormous size of a battleship. She can be seen from the streets towering over the warehouses.

The desert has quite a lot of green showing and it's amazing how much barley has been garnered. There seem to be far more camel about than I remember – no doubt being later in the year they have brought them up to the coastal wells.

Stop at Hillyers Hotel for the night. It is gloriously fresh and cool. The sunset on the lagoon is perfectly lovely. I wish vehemently that Cara would be with me and not at Kantara awaiting the Cairo Express.

Saturday 1st June 1940

Saunders is in a perpetual hurry to return to Cairo. Have a truck tour and then down to Sidi Haneish to meet the trolley. We arrive in at 5.50pm, have a drink in town and then get then catch the 7pm train to Cairo. Find Cara in bed and fast asleep. Very nice to be together.

Sunday 2nd June 1940

Go to office and find a lot of work already starting for me. Have long interviews regarding the Western Desert tour – Italy does look like coming in and we must get a move on to make sure everything is ready.

Wednesday 5th June 1940

In the evening we look at Jane's Cairo flat that Cara has found. It is most attractive, very roomy and with great airy windows and balconies. At £12 a month furnished with all Jane's glass and linen etc, it's a real bargain.

Saturday 8th June 1940

Spend the entire and heated morning at Abbassia testing loading tanks and lorries on and off the station platforms using portable ramps. We find General Neame[16] and many Red Hats [staff officers] present when we turn up and it takes a little time to get things together as it was meant to be a trial, not a demonstration.

That evening Cara tells me that Robert has been killed. Poor Norman and Laura. It's hard to realise the boy had grown up. He was one of the best lads that ever walked. It's ghastly to think one man can wield enough power to destroy so much. I've heard of many other friends of mine sacrificed in this struggle against evil. At times I wish I could get away from here to fight but there has to be an army here and it would be cruel on Cara.

The Germans are attacking the line at the Somme again in force. Apparently with two million men. How the devil they get them up and maintain them I don't know – we couldn't do it in peace conditions.

Sunday 9th June 1940

First night at the flat and we have a quiet first dinner lit by candles. Abdul is an excellent waiter and Morsi, the cook, has an excellent reputation. I'm thankful Cara has a home of sorts as hotel life is wretched. She's lost a lot of weight and now weighs 6st 3 lb – far too little.

Hear that Sotterley has been taken over by the government. Daren't think what that means but anything better than the Hun there.

Monday 10th June 1940

Our third anniversary. It's very hard to remember a time when we were not married and what a lot has happened in those three years. Bad years for the

---

16. Lieutenant General Sir Philip Neame VC, KBE, CB, DSO (1888–1978), the only person to win both the Victoria Cross and an Olympic gold medal (won at the 1924 Paris Games for rifle shooting).

world but we've enjoyed them in the periods we've been together: Lyburn Lodge, Switzerland, Palestine, Syria and here – Peace and War. What a strange life we live.

In the evening Musso announces that he has declared war on the Allies but not on Egypt.[17] This puts us in a very curious position – I suppose we ought to be interned! And I presume we can't lock up any Italians.

We get electric light that evening at about 5pm and so can turn on the wireless. Musso is taking no offensive action but warns Greece, Turkey, Jugoslavia, Switzerland and Egypt to keep out. What a rat that man is. In one week I'll bet he'll have drawn in at least two of those countries.

Tuesday 11th June 1940
We hear for once we've taken the initiative and instead of Italy drawing first blood we've bombed most of their colonial airbases and captured twenty-seven ships. America seems disgusted with Mussolini, and the Italians here are not too happy about it. The whole situation is far from clear. The Germans were shut up here in September but we are told we can't touch the Italians. Where is the difference?

Wednesday 12th June 1940
Duty officer. Rush home for lunch and dinner then back for a peaceful night on the boat. Once bitten twice shy so now bring my bed and sleep on the ship. It's beautifully cool and the sound of Father Nile lapping close by is soothing.

Thursday 13th June 1940
Hear the 11th H captured two Italian officers and sixty-one men yesterday. We've also taken the air initiative. The battle for Paris still raging. We've lost half a division on the coast. The Germans can't keep up this sustained effort. They will have to quieten down to consolidate and reorganise soon. Their letters of credit must be non-existent and I can't believe the French would leave them much in the way of supplies.

Friday 14th June 1940
Cara starts work in the Middle East Cypher Office. Lieutenant Baxter is her boss but she finds Miss Wavell, the commander-in-chief's daughter, is even more bossy. Her hours are the same as ours 8.15am–1.15pm and 6–8pm. Of course these are liable to be prolonged, 2pm and 9pm being more usual.

---

17. 'People of Italy, take up your weapons and show your tenacity, your courage and your valour.' After this declaration, anti-Italian riots broke out in Britain resulting in the ransacking of Italian-owned shops, with 100 arrests in Edinburgh alone.

I have a busy day with trollies, AA trucks also keeping me working as I seem to be picking up the baby of security in the Western Desert. No one else seems to want the responsibility.

We hear in the evening that the French have let the Boche into Paris and have taken up a line to the rear. It's all tragic.

Saturday 15th June 1940

The situation is looking as black as anything can be. I don't see how the French can go on. They seem to hold no reserves. Every man is in the line and every man exhausted. The Germans however seem to be holding reserves and throwing in fresh troops.

Every day one hears of more deaths, Tony H-R[18] has been killed on the beach in Dunkirk. Cowdray has lost an arm, Anthony Taylor dead – in fact, only four 15th/19th H have got home unscathed.

Our little local successes – Libya, Eritrea etc – make good headlines but God knows what the real issue will be. The USA talks a lot about Elysian Fields of Paris and other nonsense but don't help. I fear even if they came in this evening their aid would be too late.

We dine on the Turf Club roof with Denny and Davidson and don't get home 'til after 3am. Don't feel like a party when I think of all my friends and contemporaries at home. So many that one had had parties with in the old days are now lying cold and still in France – probably never even to receive a burial.

Tuesday 18th June 1940

Poor old Royals – sitting in Palestine peacetime training and out of everything with the chances of doing anything growing less.

Visit Alexandria and experience an air raid warning. The traffic is very well drilled, everything stops and silence reigns. Tin hats get very hot in the sun – thank heaven I got a special lining made. The Italian planes get turned back near Mastruh but we spend a long time in a trench and do our work there.

I get fresh veg to take out to the divisional mess at Bagush, the very spot where four years ago I used to bathe. Then there was never another soul in sight, now the whole desert is people with little tents, large mess tents, lorries, wireless cars etc. O'Connor is commanding. We have a short chat. He is a bit shaken as almost caught a bomb today.

---

18. Lieutenant Hon Gustavus Hamilton Russell (1907–1940), older brother of AMB's close friends in the Royals, Jack and Desmond.

Hear of a plot being hatched to catch some Iti aeroplanes with a Spitfire that has just come up the line. Our old Gladiators are far too slow and the Iti is growing bold.

Wednesday 19th June 1940

I hear our trap was successful and resulted in the Spitfire polishing off three Itis and possibly two more while we lost one, probably the bait.

We go for a cold beer and meet a typical little army padre. He has rather an evil face and starts off with a really dirty story to show what a good chap he is.

We bed down at 9pm. The moon comes through the sand cloud at about 10pm and I am enabled to see my beastly little companions. I catch 21 bed bugs before 3.30am and then bang, crash, the first bomb drops!

Thursday 20th June 1940

I had heard the aircraft before but as there was no warning or firing did not wake the others. Though I'm awake and the others in their beauty sleep I find I'm almost last out. Two appear stark naked but most have donned something.

There are three Itis visible in the full moon. They have no opposition and are down to under 2,000 feet but the tarmac road glistening with dew misleads them and they hit nothing. It's not frightening – merely irritating to have to squat there and not hit back. In those little trenches I feel that nothing but a direct hit would have killed us although the blast is very strong. I hear later the bombing could be heard at Daboa, over 100 miles away.

Nineteen bombs are dropped, none doing any damage. In fact, if one had selected nineteen harmless spots those would have been the sites. As it's getting daylight the flies are making life unbearable, so go round and inspect the damage. All very slight and no casualties. At 7am three more Iti fighters appear over the old aerodrome but don't worry us. At 8am one Blenheim [British light bomber] appears and is fired on by the Egyptian AA battery.

I catch the train to Daboa where I stay the night to hold discussions with SMO about casualties and chain of command. We drink a lot and talk more. Go to bed dinnerless – once again. Sleep very well despite the noise of our bombers going off to rattle Tobruk and units of the Iti Navy.

Friday 21st June 1940

Conclude business and catch train to Alexandria. Go on to the docks. There are two French battleships still there but most of fleet out. Rush to catch Cairo train but it doesn't run on Fridays so have to spend night at Cecil's. Soon after we get to bed an air raid starts. Lasts most of night and is very noisy. AA guns firing into the sky and air wardens driving rather rashly full of their own importance. Watch it from the verandah then get bored. One bomb drops in the old harbour quite close by. The searchlights pick up the plane but the shooting can't even frighten the pilot.

Saturday 22nd June 1940

Have an awful scramble for the 6.30am train. Just as I step onboard there is some gunfire and they foolishly keep the train in the station.

Have a full day's work and am also duty officer. See Cara for an hour in the evening and find she experienced Cairo's first alarm all by herself in the flat. Poor little mite – she must have been terrified.

Terrible night – I split the top sheet with my toe and a stream of insects come and go all night. It must look like a beehive. I ask the officer on guard to stop the men from pushing past my bed from 5–7am and wake to find a sentry with fixed bayonet at each end of my bed! Rather surprising but so typical of the Guards – super efficiency. Roderick gasped at hearing it and said, 'Iimagine that in a Highland Regiment!' Imagine it in any other bloody regiment!

Sunday 23rd June 1940

Supposed to have the day off but only get the afternoon off.

France has crashed – she's signed an armistice of complete submission.[19] Terms I don't think the people will accept, at least I hope not.

Now it's us against the world and we'll win.

Friday 28th June 1940

Tiny Edwards, who seems to be King's messenger these days, comes in to the office. He saw Michael a few days ago says he's very well and people at home have not got their tails down.

Saturday 29th June 1940

Adeane comes to dine, arriving very late and we get rather hilarious. We start the evening disliking the Wops but before we've finished we've decided even the French are dagoes. The whole lot, bar the gentilhomme at Djibouti, have ratted – and the navy shows no sign of being loyal to us.

---

19. The Armistice of 2 June 1940 was signed in Compiègne Forest, symbolically chosen by the Germans as the site of the 1918 Armistice. The surrender established a German occupation zone in north and west France, allowing Hitler strategically important access to the English Channel and Atlantic ports, with the rest of (Vichy) France a client state of Germany under Marshal Pétain.

Nigel's birthday, hence the celebrations. Hear he's back safe in England.[20]

Sunday 30th June 1940

Duty officer and head far from good.

Spread my bed at 1.30pm for a lie down and at 1.31pm the telephone goes, then continues to go solidly 'til 5pm. Sometimes three phones going together and have five people in to see me. Poor Mrs Calloty has to be hauled in to help me time a special train. At 5pm I'm hauled off to a conference with all the big boys – very frightening.

Little 'Basil' Hamilton,[21] O.C. Black Watch, also summoned and the plan discussed for sending his battalion off complete in a cruiser. Destination so secret I'll disclose it later in my diary. Baggage, rations, stores etc have to be organised for loading and it can't be discussed over the telephone. There will be a great deal to do.

Monday 1st July 1940

We start off at 6.30am next morning for the port passing the cruiser on the way. She is looking very weather-beaten and her guns all blistered. Discover she's *Liverpool* and was one of the five that chased the five Wop destroyers and sank one.

Hamilton arrives at 8.30am, his vehicles at 9am and the ship comes alongside at 10.30am after bunkering. The ship takes off her seaplanes and gives us the hangar accommodation. Here we stow eleven vehicles and a lot of stores. It's quite incredible how much can go onboard and what a lot of fighting material constitutes a battalion. Not one unnecessary article is taken.

Leave at 6pm just as the ship is sailing. Say goodbye to Hammie who send a message to Cara to say he hopes he won't be 'under the weeds'. I think they are in for a party all right, and I don't think they could be better led. Not a soul knows where they are going – a well-kept secret (unusual).[22]

Thursday 4th July 1940

I take the day off from 10.30am 'til 6pm. We do a lot of shopping – buy a case of whisky in case there's a shortage and two large camel leather suitcases. They say there should be no shortage of anything for some time to come but by then I hope we'll have the Red Sea open.

---

20. Nigel had been evacuated from Dunkirk, along with 338,000 Allied troops.
21. Lieutenant Colonel Adrian Hamilton DSO, MC (1897–1960).
22. The 2nd Battalion, the Black Watch, were being sent to strengthen the Commonwealth forces in British Somaliland.

The big news of the day is that at last we've taken the initiative and taken over the French fleet. Any ships resisting are to be sunk.[23] Admiral Somerville, meeting resistance at Oman, cracked in to a large battle squadron, sinking many and running others ashore. It's terrible in a way but I feel it will show the world that we are in earnest.

Friday 5th July 1940

Colonel Turner proposes he and I go out to Western Desert on tour. I love going but Cara hates it. Can cheer her today by saying we've brought down nine Wop planes in the last 24 hours so they won't be bothering us much.

Not much work on in the evening so go lobbying. See O'Brian who is a second echelon clerk. As I go in he was writing to the regiment to say there was a vacancy for Major. That puts Francis up. I wish I could get mine through.

Sunday 7th July 1940

Catch the 3.30pm to Alex [Alexandria]. Our late Doc (Rowland) on the train. He's heading off to the WD in disgrace as he fired his revolver in the Continental Cabaret. He was under close arrest for nine days, released of his gun and sent out to WD.

We get no further than Ikingi Maryet when an air raid begins. We have a first class view and hear one raider starting his power dive directly above us – it's like teal in an early morning flight. About twenty bombs are dropped and twenty times that number of shells are fired. I count twenty lights focused on each plane. We think one machine might be hit so on the off chance celebrate it with another whisky.

Monday 8th July 1940

Arrive at Mersa at 6.25am to a lovely clear morning. Dash off on a trolley to Alex. The Hampshire Regiment run the trolleys and also the AA trucks which are on every possible train.

Haselton and Anderson, who I met at Fuka in '36, meet us. Have a bath and whisky & soda then talk solidly from 6.30pm to 11pm, eating dinner meanwhile. Notebooks play a prominent part on the dinner table.

Poor old Teale comes in later. He's been sick – shock from the bombing at Mersa being the cause. He's trying hard to maintain his self-esteem but it's

---

23. Despite assurances from the Vichy government that the French navy would remain under their control and not fall into German hands, the British War Cabinet felt that it could not take the risk and insisted the fleet be moved to British ports. The French refused and on 3 July 1940 the Royal Navy controversially attacked the French fleet at Mers-el-Kebir, killing 1,297 French sailors and putting six French warships out of action.

rather pathetic. He's not a young man and went through the last war. He is full of enthusiasm and I hope can get a quieter job elsewhere.

Wednesday 10th July 1940
Air raid warnings at 2am, 8am and 9am but we talk on.

Visit the docks where the French Navy, now un-gunned, proudly continues to fly its flag and the *matelots* [sailors] continue to walk arm in arm with our sailors although just along this same coast we've killed many unfortunate men due to the pigheadedness of their admiral.

Tuesday 16th July 1940
Hear the Wops have bombed Haifa and set fire to the oil tanks. We really deserve to lose this war. After five weeks at war with Italy, and knowing every Wop pilot knows his way blindfolded to Haifa and where the distilleries are, we take no protective measures whatsoever.

We dine à deux. We eat roast pheasant, corn cobs and mango. A very curious meal but very good. The pheasant must have been dead for two years. It's wonderful to think Fortnum's canning is so secure – the tins have not been kept in a cool place for six months.

Wednesday 17th July 1940
Cara's birthday – she loves her birthdays and Christmas but not much to celebrate today though. I manage to get a cable from Australia on her plate for breakfast but office work goes on as usual.

Cara is working longer hours now and finds it very interesting. She takes a lively interest in all that is going on and I think is very good at keeping quiet about what she knows.

Saturday 20th July 1940
Leckie and I fly to Alexandria. We fly round Cairo and over the Pyramids but see very little owing to cloud. At Dekheila observe a large bomb hole in the mud flats – I think this is the one I heard from the train on the 7th.

After breakfast I go down to the docks and see *Havoc* landing over 500 Wops. Most are stark naked and they seem a lousy collection.

I board the South Staffs special train from Qabbari siding. It's supposed to be a secret move but all the locals know about it and the hawkers are waiting. Many have watermelon for sale at exorbitant prices, others lemonade bottles filled with local dirty water.

Sunday 21st July 1940

I get out at Sidi Haneish and spend the day and night with division HQ.

Peter de Salis comes to see me and we sit drinking 'til late. He's divisional intelligence officer and very interesting. Hear of one colonel who was caught with the entire scheme to be brought into action if we attacked heavily. He was carrying it quite happily in an area we would not carry local code cards even. He shot himself, poor man.

We also raided a police post and unknowingly amongst the bumf was the complete Wop battle order. This was confirmed with an air recce and is still unchanged even now ten days after! All most useful.

At dusk a flight of Blenheims goes off bombing. They come over me like duck at twilight. At 1am they return, just as I'm off to bed. I anxiously count them in and thank heaven they've all returned.

Monday 22nd July 1940

Spend two nights at Daboa in the Engineers' Rest House. Mess with Auxiliary Pioneer Corps commanded by Brian Goddard and Francis Lennox-Boyd 2i/c. All the rest bar RSM and four sergeants are foreigners. The MO is Russian and all the lieutenants are from Slav countries. The men are a mixture of the lowest up to lawyers, doctors etc. One, Corporal Nu-Nu, was 15 years in the Foreign Legion and always carries a rhino-hide whip. There's also a Jew thrown out of Germany who has Swastikas branded on the soles of his feet. He was going to France but just missed the bus.

Thursday 1st August 1940

I attend the usual conference. There is a lot to discuss. It seems that we are giving up harassing tactics in the WD and retiring to a certain extent. It sounds mad to me but they don't seem to mind a bit if we give up Sollum or Mersa – Mersa, where we have spent hundreds of thousands of pounds on water supply, aerodrome, harbour etc, to say nothing of the prestige value in Egyptian eyes.

Sunday 4th August 1940

Things seem to be moving out here. Wavell[24] is flying home to see Churchill which is bound to produce some sort of action somewhere.

We lunch with Judge Barne.[25] A most comic little man. Very pompous, talkative but kind and with a sense of humour. We never get a word in

---

24. Field Marshal Archibald Wavell, 1st Earl Wavell GCB, GCSI, CMG, MC, KStJ, PC (1883–1950), commander-in-chief Middle East.
25. Major Henry Hume Barne (d. 1960) served in the Royal Army Service Corps in the First World War. After the war he continued working as a solicitor in London and York before becoming a judge in Cairo. He was awarded the Order of the Nile, the highest state honour, in 1950.

edgeways but have one of the best lunches I've ever eaten in the Near East.

I don't think we are related – he can date his family back about as far as our branch but there doesn't seem to be any connecting link. They've been Yeomen in Devon since the sixteenth century and at that time we were prospering in London.

Monday 5th August 1940
Things are beginning to happen. The Wops have invaded Somaliland at least a week earlier than our bright staff allowed for. It may prove rather embarrassing, I fear.

Tuesday 6th August 1940
Spend a busy morning preparing for impending moves. It all seems in flux at the moment with the Wops in Somaliland a week early and also massing on the Libyan frontier. Once again we have failed to take the initiative and will have to change our plans to conform to the Italian moves. Our trouble seems to lie in the fact that we take so long preparing and when we are almost ready to strike, find the enemy has struck first and we have to adopt to a new posture to ward off the blow.

Haifa is raided while I'm talking on the telephone to them. One bomb falls very near my old office, splintering the woodwork and making Carlson furious. He had a lucky escape.

Saturday 10th August 1940
We're working hard to get reinforcements to Somaliland. The situation is critical and Bofors AA guns[26] are the best antidote.

I'm also busy preparing for emergency moves within Egypt and Palestine.

Sunday 11th August 1940
Woken up at 2am by Colonel Cavendish. Spend the rest of a hectic morning telephoning Suez about the two Bofors guns that are missing. The four gunners we flew down to Somaliland yesterday look like they have no weapons!

Monday 12th August 1940
I feel deadbeat despite a good night's rest. There seems to be an immense amount of work in hand. I'm taking over all rail moves in Egypt, Western Desert, Sudan and Palestine. A nice parish!

---

26. The Bofors 40mm gun, a multipurpose automatic cannon first used in the 1930s and still in active service into the twenty-first century.

Wednesday 14th August 1940

Woken at 5.30am by telephone. Flap on as the chief [Wavell] wants certain information for the cabinet by 10am. Rather a thrill to think my knowledge required!

Long, hectic day in the office. Sussex Regiment going off by cruiser to reinforce Somaliland and 4th Indian Division move advanced by two days. Many other moves on and projected.

Thursday 15th August 1940

Learn that Somaliland has packed up[27] and all hurriedly arranged moves are cancelled. The fall of Somaliland is bad – a very great loss of prestige in a part of the world where prestige is of great importance. Can't help but feeling our G-branch [department of MI5 concerned with wartime espionage operations] is not up to scratch. They are slow, dull and lack the power to look forward.

Friday 16th August 1940

The impression at home is that an attack on the Western Desert is a certainty. Three tank trains are being loaded today.

Very funny joke going round. On 11th May the King told Anthony Eden he didn't want to see him again 'til he had some good news. The next day in came Eden: 'Sire, I am glad to inform you we have no allies.' To which the King replied, 'Well at any rate we can at least say we got to the bloody final!'

Monday 19th August 1940

A large mail in from Mummy, Nigel and Elizabeth. The chief brought it back – the first mail we've had for months.

Attend the usual BTE conference at 8.30am. A concentration of troops is definitely starting. It's very tricky as I know a good deal that BTE does not yet know about and when arguing it is difficult to avoid letting out facts that should be retained as secrets.

The Nile is rising fast and the current is tremendous. An enormous amount of rubbish is being swept down and the river has turned a rich brown. At dusk the whole island seems to be filled with frogs as the water must have reached the level of their hibernation and woken them up.

---

27. The Italian, Eritrean and Somali forces vastly outnumbered the British and Commonwealth troops and had the advantage of better artillery. The British forces were gradually overcome until they were forced to stage an embarrassing withdrawal. Churchill criticised Wavell, the theatre commander, because of the low number of casualties and publicly suggested the colony had not been adequately defended.

Friday 23rd August 1940
Again try to rouse BTE to take an interest in WD water. Malcolm W-M refuses to even try to collect numbers for me. Eventually persuade Jack Lease to hold a meeting on Monday. It's all a constant source of worry to me – surely we've had enough lessons to realise we must look ahead.

Tuesday 27th August 1940
A black day. An amendment to the evacuation of families order has come out stating all illegals will be compulsorily expelled on the first boat. There seems to be no loophole, despite Cara being highly trained and irreplaceable at short notice. It's hell – the powers that be are behaving extraordinarily badly.

Wednesday 28th – Friday 30th August 1940
Continue working without respite. For once in my life I'm genuinely worked too hard and at the back of my mind is the haunting thought of Cara being forcibly evacuated at short notice. I can't bear the thought of it, we've been separated too much already.

The WD problem is coming to a head. After several conflabs I decide to go out with Jack on Saturday to see for ourselves what the situation is.

Saturday 31st August 1940
Jack and I leave at 6.50am in a super V8 driven by Bishop, an ex-Midlands bus driver. We eat up the new desert road to Alex as far as Awrya at about 120 kilometres an hour. Arrive at Maaten Bagush by 5pm and sleep with blanket for the first time.

Sunday 1st September 1940
Go off early to reconnoitre the harbour for maintenance of the seaplanes. There's a fine crane but not with much scope. I fear Jack is a little pessimistic about its capabilities. It strikes me as curious that the CRE not only didn't know it was there but that his practical knowledge of the place was nil. So many of these minor 'key men' lack drive. Probably good fellows but they won't move until they are pushed.

Monday 2nd September 1940
Get to Cairo by 7pm and feel we've done a good weekend's work. Spend an hour in the office then Cara takes me home. Poor dear, she's been feeling this wretched evacuation of families as much as I and after we go to bed she breaks down. She's been working far too hard and has had no support from her unpleasant boss.

Thursday 5th September 1940
Suez gets bombed slightly by a single aircraft. Probably on a recce so worse to come. However, our air situation here is improving daily and the fleet is very much top dog in the Mediterranean. I hear the Wop fleet was too quick back into harbour for even our aircraft to catch it on Monday!

Sunday 8th September 1940
We get Cara to the office at 8.15am to find we're the only car there. Poor Cara, she's being worked far too hard – all the other clerks get an extra hour off on Sundays.

At 10am we go off to a special war service at the cathedral. An enormous crowd present. A very gay throng with all the women in summer dresses and nurses and officers in light khaki. I'm not sure quite how much genuine prayer rose from the cathedral and how much it was just a fashionable gathering. I see the chief for the first time. He never visits the offices which is bad.

Monday 9th September 1940
Cara has been detailed for night shift, midnight 'til 8am all week. It's too much for her and I'm going to object.

We all dine with Leckie Ewing 'til 11.30pm then Cara goes to work and I to bed. What a life!

Tuesday 10th September 1940
Cara sleeps all day. At 4.30pm she gets up and we go to the club for tea. Thank heaven it's cooler and not so exhaustingly hot for her. The chief's daughter, Felicity, is on the same times. We can only hope this will exhaust her too! I have written a strong letter but don't know what effect it will have.

Thursday 12th September 1940
Joan Paton lunches with us. She brings cuttings about Wintle's court martial.[28] Ironside was a witness! Joan is going to be enormous by the time

---

28. Lieutenant Colonel Alfred Wintle MC (1897–1966), officer in the Royals and a notable eccentric. During the First World War he saw extensive action at Ypres and the Somme and earned an MC for an attack in which he personally accounted for thirty-five prisoners. During the Third Battle of Ypres he was wounded, leaving him without one kneecap, several fingers and his left eye – forcing him to wear a monocle on the other. He found the period between the wars 'intensely boring' and when the Second World War started he was desperate to get back in the action. Following the French surrender he demanded an aircraft to go to France to rally the French Air Force. When he was refused he pulled a gun on an RAF officer and threatened to shoot them both if he didn't get his plane. For this he was imprisoned in the Tower of London, awaiting his court martial. Remarkably, two of the three charges against him were dropped and he was let off with a formal reprimand for the assault on the RAF officer.

she's 35! A strange contrast to Guy, who is like a lamp post. She thinks she's bit of a local 'queen' which cuts no ice with me.

Saturday 14th September 1940

Margot and Gilly come to tea and take Cara to the club but I have a lot of work in hand – horrid on a Sat night when one knows all other offices are closed.

Get back v late and join the girls for dinner at Mena [camp just outside Cairo at the foot of the Great Pyramid of Cheops]. Afterwards by the light of a large moon we walk around the Pyramids and Sphinx which they've have never seen. It's vastly different to what I remember in 1927 – diggings everywhere. I'm not sure they haven't built a new one!

Chapter 3

War in the Western Desert

With the British declaration of war in September 1939, the British Expeditionary Force was sent to defend France. Until May 1940 there was very little military action, but this changed with the German invasion of France and the Low Countries, leading to the dramatic evacuation from the beaches of Dunkirk. By July the Battle of Britain had begun, as the Luftwaffe strove to achieve air supremacy and to break British morale with indiscriminate raids on the civilian population. Germany intended to blockade Britain, cutting off vital shipping routes and forcing her into a negotiated peace settlement. With the swift French capitulation and the Italian entry to the war in June 1940, Britain and its dominions and colonies stood alone in carrying the burden of fighting the Axis powers.

It was in this context that the Italians launched an invasion of Egypt from their neighbouring colony of Libya. Italian forces were planning to advance along the Egyptian coast, gaining access to several strategically important and well-equipped ports and finally capturing the Suez Canal. If they held the canal Axis forces would effectively control the Mediterranean, and the British would be forced to sail the longer and more dangerous route around Africa to link up with their colonies in the east. It was therefore vital for Britain to hold on to Egypt.

*   *   *

Monday 16th September 1940
Excitement in the Western Desert as the Wops are advancing over the border.

It's awful to think of London being subjected to the awful bombardment that we read of daily in the papers. Yesterday apparently a one-ton bomb was dropped outside St Paul's and was removed by a band of heroes before it could explode. On Hackney Marsh, where it was taken, it made a crater 100 foot wide.[1]

---

1. On 12 September 1940 a night-time raid left an unexploded bomb lodged 30ft deep in the road next to St Paul's. The bomb was also close to a gas main which had been damaged in

Tuesday 17th September 1940
Daddy was killed today 23 years ago — and the Germans are as ruthlessly as ever murdering our civil population and destroying our historic buildings. If decent people must die to conquer this savage people then let us be ruthless also and ensure they rise only once in 50 years and not every quarter century. They must be stamped out now for good and all.

Sunday 29th September 1940
Cara gets news in the afternoon that her mother is definitely dying – she is terribly distressed and it's hard to give any comfort.

Thursday 3rd October 1940
Am met at the office with a wire to say that Mrs H-H [Frances Holmes-Hunt, née Lugg] died peacefully yesterday. Cara will be terribly upset – she has enough worries at the moment without this extra grief. Her mother must have been a very brave woman as she never missed a mail or complained to Cara of the pain she must have been suffering.

It's like a novel – I can't tell Cara the news 'til after lunch when she finishes work and she, at the same time, has news for me that we have Great Expectations next June. She had a test last Tuesday which has had a positive result.

Poor little thing, the news about her mother has broken her heart and she has a terrible afternoon of grief.

Friday 4th October 1940
A black day. Hate leaving Cara even for a short time. Send her Pa a cable to ask if Cara is advised to fly home. Not anxious for it myself but I won't stand in her way.

She is in a grievous state and even a small thing is capable of her sending her off in tears, poor dear.

Saturday and Sunday 5th and 6th October 1940
After finishing at the office I take Cara out to Mena for the weekend. The heat, oppression and stickiness is awful – next time we must take a north-facing room instead of facing the old pyramids.

In the evening we sit watching a never-ending stream of sightseers. A few civilians but mostly servicemen. Some by car, some in lorries, some in charabancs, a few walking, brave ones on ponies, camels and donkeys,

---

the raid. A team of Royal Engineers spent three days digging the bomb out before putting it on a truck and driving it to Hackney Marshes. Two George Crosses were awarded to the team.

soldiers, sailors, airmen – British, Australian, New Zealanders, Indians and a few French. All brought together by war. What mighty forces Hitler has stirred up against his country.

Friday 11th October 1940
Get up early to see 3H off to the desert. They have light tanks – don't envy them. If I'd gone to them I'd now be about 2i/c. Am not anxious to remain forever at this job but am not optimistic of my chances of getting on.

We hear that approval has been given for the cavalry division to be mechanised and Royals recommended for armoured cars. A nice compliment. The Greys are to be left horses. The world has marched past the poor old horse. There seems no room for him now.

Wednesday 16th October 1940
Play polo in the pm on Jimmy Jones' ponies. Thoroughly enjoy it but I get very rubbed up as I haven't played in at least two years.

Saturday 26th October 1940
Ronald, Lin Showers [Colonel Lionel Showers DSO, 1904–77] and I go off to climb the Second Pyramid [the Pyramid of Khafre, the second tallest and second largest at Giza]. Lin and Ronald get to the top but I'm ashamed to say I funk the last 40 foot. I think I could have done it but feel responsibility to Cara these days! We see a pair of peregrines and am told they nest yearly here.

We go into the Cheops Pyramid [the Great Pyramid, oldest of the Seven Wonders of the Ancient World]. Not very exciting and rather like the London tube in rush hour.

Monday 28th October 1940
Catch the 0930 – just – to Alex with George M. On arrival find that Greece has been invaded by Italy.[2] This will mean a lot of work. Jack Haseldon is in an awful flap as there are some quick moves already required. He's a bad flapper.

---

2. Very early on 28 October, the Italian ambassador to Greece had presented the Greek prime minister with an ultimatum demanding that Axis forces be allowed to enter Greek territory and occupy unspecified strategic locations or face war. The apocryphal response was a single word, *Ohi* (no). Within three hours Italian troops stationed in Albania started attacking the Greek border. The date is still commemmorated throughout Greece and Cyprus as Ohi Day.

Tuesday 29th October 1940
By train to Sidi Haneish, very crowded. The Australian brigade move is about 4 hours late which proves the necessity of carrying full rations and refilling water bottles somewhere. Arrive after dark. Blackout intense and we have great difficulty finding our way.

Mess with Jerry and Bobby Kidd. Bobby very depressed about his lot and he has a right to be. He's down from lieutenant colonel to G2 chemical warfare!

Wednesday 30th October 1940
George and I head to Mersa. The town looks a good deal more beaten up but there's been very little loss of life or military stores. Visit the harbour where they are working on the pipeline.[3]

There's a big air raid up the line. I believe we brought down eighty-four bombers and four fighters. We did a big air raid this morning – the ten Blenheims coming back in are a fine sight.

Friday 1st November 1940
Return to Cairo. Get in very late and find Cara back. She has thoroughly enjoyed her Ishmailia visit and looks well and back on form.

Monday 4th November 1940
Cara gets a letter from her father about the will. All very disturbing for her again. Her mother seems to have left everything to her as she knew what a spendthrift Phie[4] is and expects Cara to look after her if, and when, Phie's marriage becomes unstuck.

Thursday 7th November 1940
We hear Roosevelt has been elected American President for the third time. A good thing as we know where we stand with him and the papers seem cheerful. Poor little Greece is holding her own and we now have a foothold on south European territory. I can't believe this is a cut and dried Hitler plan but time will show.

Monday 11th November 1940
We all wear poppies – curious that even in the midst of this war we should find time to remember the last. The only point for remembering the last war

---

3. A freshwater pipeline was constructed by the Allies along the coast road from the Roman aqueduct at Mersa Matruh.
4. Phyllis 'Phie' Holmes-Hunt, Cara's sister, married and later divorced Wilfred Tennant Hunter. She had a reputation as a beautiful, high-living socialite.

was to make sure there would never be another and the point of poppies now is to collect money for the poor devils maimed in the last war.

Friday 15th November 1940
Cara and I catch the 7.50pm train to Shellal. Dining car and sleeper onboard as far as Sohag where the bridge is broken. We have to walk by the light of the full moon to the other train.

Saturday 16th November 1940
Breakfast in a basket at Luxor and very good too. Reach Shellal at 12.30pm and board the steamer *Hyksos*. Fletcher, a queer card, late RA, late police, now a refugee from Constanza, also on board and in charge of the staging camp (as yet unformed). We are very comfortable onboard and I think he is glad of the company. This truly is the last outpost of the Empire.

As there is no lighting we turn in about 8.30pm. Lovely cool night and fish plop all night around the ship. War seems very far from here.

Sunday 17th November 1940
Do a recce of the transit camp site about 1km north of Shellal which seems like a suitable site in every respect. I am strongly in favour of getting something going without delay but doubt anything will happen this winter.

Monday 18th November 1940
Drive into Aswan and take coffee with a most charming Egyptian brigade major. George Birawiki. The Sudan agent then turns up and takes charge of everything. He's a nice, shrewd little Palestinian, very capable and honest and definitely pro-British. He knows which side his bread is buttered on.

Tuesday 19th November 1940
Spend all morning at Karnak Temple and we are suitably impressed. What strikes me as the most amazing thing is the ambition of these men. They seem to have had no thought for themselves on earth and all their energy was devoted to their temple to sing their praises to God.

We tea at the house of Hassan and meet the old father. They are a nice couple and very attentive hosts. They show us many things from the tombs, including a lot from Tutankhamen's tomb which they never never should have possessed. They obtained them from Lord Carnarvon's labourers who found them buried by other labourers.

Wednesday 20th November 1940
My birthday – 34 years old. This is the first birthday we've had together for two years.

We spend the day across the river at Thebes. Tombs of Kings, Queens, Nobles, Ramesseum, etc.

Row back across the river in a lovely sunset and the whole scene in Egypt feels as it ought to be. We catch the 7.30pm train back to Cairo and leave in a shower of bows, hand kissing and bouquets from the hall porter.

Friday 29th November 1940

No work at all in our branch. There seems to be an ominous lull in proceedings. The Royals are likely to be coming down here soon as they are to be mechanised as quickly as possible.

We've been dining out every night – and lunching too. Last night dined with the Delaneys and Jackson's at the Continental. Roger is very intoxicated and tight in the arms of Mrs Digby, one of the floor hostesses. He invents a new dance which we call the 'subway rub'. Cara very angry with him.

Freya Stark,[5] the explorer, is present at the party. She wears a fine head of hair, kept in place by a band right around her head. Her figure is not perfect, nor her features. She has tiny screwed up eyes and an enormous bottom. Truly she could go through the heart of Arabia unmolested. When she leaves she puts on an Arab Legion cloak of scarlet and white silk.

Thursday 5th December 1940

Rex Hewer,[6] now Brigadier, arrives to take up the job of director of movements. I meet him in the evening at the Continental and he's on very good form. He flew in from Lagos and it took him 5 days. He also says London has had a lot of damage by this filthy indiscriminate bombing. Thankfully there seems to be no food shortage and Trumpers [the gentleman's barber in Mayfair] is still in existence.

Saturday 7th December 1940

Greek flags are very prominent now in the streets. The Greek Victory is no doubt having a great effect in this part of the world.[7]

There is also something going on in the WD. It's a very well-kept secret but one can feel the undertone of excitement in the BTE.

---

5. Dame Freya Stark (1893–1993), British-Italian explorer and travel writer. She wrote more than two dozen books covering her travels through the Middle East and Afghanistan.
6. Major General Reginald 'Rex' Hewer CB, CBE, MC (1892–1970).
7. By mid-November the Greeks had blunted the Italian attack and pushed the invading force back into Albania. This was seen as the first Axis setback of the war.

Monday 8th December 1940

The news comes out that we are making a good strong attack in the WD and by evening we have over 400 prisoners, killed Maletti[8] and have trapped about two divisions. The news tomorrow may be terrific – rumours are rife.

Tuesday 9th December 1940

The excitement is intense over the WD show. The closing score is over 4,000 prisoners and one complete tank battalion. To my mind the best part of it is the wonderful secrecy maintained by the BTE. No one in GHQ, except the chief, seemed to know anything.

Thursday 11th December 1940

Roger flies to HQ WD and returns in the evening. The battle is over with few casualties to us and we are left with 37,000 prisoners to water, feed, clothe and keep. A prodigious job.

Saturday 14th December 1940

Lunch with Mrs Carver – she has a charming young RNAS officer who was pilot of a torpedo-dropping plane at Taranto. Apparently they had to drop in over a balloon barrage and then come down to 60–100 foot off the water. He humbly admitted he was terrified!

Monday 16th December 1940

A lovely sunset. A great cloud that looks like the breast feathers of a teal, suddenly turns deep red. Perhaps it is the reflection of the blood of those slaughtered out in the Western Desert?

Saturday 21st December 1940

I am afraid that Cara is beginning to worry about her departure and the sea voyage. She unfortunately heard that nineteen mines have been swept up between Melbourne and Tasmania.

Have a bright little dinner then go on to the Metropolitan Cellar, a very gay spot and crowded out. The cost of champagne is scandalous but if people are such fools as to pay, one can't blame the management.

Tuesday 24th December 1940

Philip Kaye comes down from Palestine. He brings a lot of luggage and a live turkey for us. We have to collect it from the Continental kitchen where it has

---

8. Major General Pietro Maletti (1880–1940) commanded a rapidly assembled collection of motorized infantry and tanks called the 'Maletti Group'.

spent the day feeding on chopped onions. Cara carries it out through the crowded foyer. The turkey gives tongue but not a soul even smiles!

Wednesday 25th December 1940

Cara wakes me at daylight to open her stocking and put mine at the end of the bed – she's like a small child over it all. It's only our second Christmas together since we got married 4 years ago.

We go to early church at the cathedral, picking up Judge Barne en route. He looks more Pickwickian than ever. He barely reaches 5 foot and scarcely looks like the dignified, important figure as he would like to see himself. Nevertheless, in his judicial chair and under a wig I'm sure he looks much the part.

Hear the King's speech [*see* Appendix A]. As usual it's simple, sincere and good. Poor man – his stuttering was more noticeable but no doubt the strain of life must be terrible for him.

Bump into Wintle at the Continental. It's the first time I've seen him since his court martial and detention in the Tower of London. I feel one can't be completely and openly rude to him. He is still a Royal and I still retain a great deal of admiration for him but I can never feel quite the same to him. He has not done the regimental name any good.

Saturday 28th December 1940

A large detachment of Royals arrive to start training in mechanics. Arrangements have been bad and I fear there will be a shemozzle.

Tuesday 31st December 1940

The last day of the year. A rotten one for most people but wonderful for Cara and I as we have been able to be together continuously.

We go up to Abbassia to see the regiment. They look very comfortable and pleased to see us.

We have a very hectic party at Robert Adeane's flat in the evening. The flat is ultra-modern and obviously designed for a lady of the oldest profession. To bed about 2.30am, full of champagne instead of good resolutions.

Wednesday 1st January 1941

Ride early and almost the only one out. Heartily repent of my rashness and feel an extra hour in bed would have been better for me.

Thursday 2nd January 1941

George Luck, a gunner, arrives from England. He's part of the gang who did movement control in France and are starting to impose themselves on us. We have twenty-seven staff captains in the Middle East and just over 200 officers in movement control. As such, my job becomes a first grade appointment but I'm considered too young to be a lieutenant colonel! A pity but I value these few years.

Hopkins comes to dine, his leg still in plaster. He shares a flat with George Malcolm, such a nice chap and was in the RFC in the last war. He has lived in America since but came back straight away when the war started. I wonder if I would have done so …?

Monday 6th January 1941

After the conference I buttonhole Charles Russell and complain that my job is insufficient and that when BTE closes down I shall be squeezed out. I feel if I'm not required any longer then it is better to get out now and back to the regiment while it is still in embryo mechanised form. Russell agrees and will talk to Rex Hewer.

At 4.30pm I'm called and given DAQMG(M) Tobruk – which will be captured from the Italians shortly! It's quite a big job and damn interesting but rotten for poor Cara. I am to go off tomorrow as the recce party must be in at the earliest moment.

Wednesday 8th January 1941

Tobruk does not seem to be ready for an attack for a few days so am put on 12 hours' notice. Every time the telephone rings Cara expects to hear the worst – I'm afraid she's going through hell. We must treasure every moment we have together.

I give Cara £40 to tide over extra expenses as I want her to have at least £200 to leave the country with, if she needs to.

Friday 10th January 1941

At 2.30pm they ring me saying I must decamp to Alexandria immediately. As the only train goes at 4.45pm, I have little time to make a plan, go to GHQ to fix things, up to Abbassia to dispose of car, pack, see Cara and depart. She takes it all v philosophically. Ahmed and Morsi seem the most upset.

Saturday 11th January 1941

Meet Baxendale, the late Haifa pilot, who will be with me at Tobruk and also Tommy Thompson looking the same as ever. Go out in the Alexandria harbour to try out a movement control speedboat and see what is in. Look over two of the ships that I'll be handling. They've been carrying PoWs and stink something awful. The men cleaning them out keep coming out for air and are as sick as cats.

A thousand Australians come in by special train from Amriya. The whole town is full and many are drunk by the time they are due to leave.

Dine with Tommy. Poor old boy has just learnt that his house and girl's school have been destroyed but the family are safe.

Sunday 12th January 1941

Terrible dust storm when we wake up and impossible even to see across the breakwater. Go down to the dock and spend all day being a cad, cornering people and telling them how bad their work is. Drastic remedy is necessary as they take it for granted that a small ship can take five days to load. I get forty-three trucks discharged in less than 3 hours by sheer bullying. Chapman admits the Mahmoudia Quay has never looked so clear.

Must watch the future as feel if Cara can't get away by sea then I should be muscling in on a full time job here so that she could summer here and have the baby in Cairo.

Tuesday 14th January 1941

Spend the day loading *Draco* and *Hanne* and continue 'til midnight. There's a lot of pilfering going on at night. Nothing has been done about it and the natives have been quite open about it. Some that I caught I handed over to the local police, others I got a sergeant to beat up. It makes one very angry to think of troops going hungry because no precautions are taken here.

Friday 17th January 1941

Prisoners from Bardia[9] continue to come in by sea. They are all white, well dressed and very young looking. They go off in 'highsiders' with 120 per wagon. They all looked very pleased to be back in civilisation again.

Another state today as *Chakla* should have sailed at 10.00am but at 9.20am a lot more ammo turns up. The RAL comes down to the office in person in a fury. Luckily after a poor explanation I'm summoned to the flagship, HMS *Barham*. See the commander-in-chief, Cunningham,[10] who was made admiral of the fleet yesterday. Wavell turns up having first flown back from Greece but I'm only there for the small talk.

Things start happening at Tobruk tomorrow so I should be off shortly. Two air raid warnings in the night.

---

9. The Battle of Bardia was fought in Western Desert 3–5 January 1941. It was the first battle in which the Australian Army took part and to be commanded by an Australian general. Despite the Allies being heavily outnumbered it was a great success, with 36,000 Italian prisoners captured.
10. Admiral of the Fleet Andrew Cunningham, 1st Viscount Cunningham of Hyndhope (1883–1963).

Tuesday 21st January 1941

The attack on Tobruk starts today so we haven't got much longer now. Every time I come home I see Cara scanning my face fearing I've brought back bad news that I'm off.

Wednesday 22nd January 1941

George M telephones to say I'm to start off tomorrow. Break news to Cara after lunch and immediately pack up and don't stop 'til train goes at 4.15pm. Poor pet, she's been so brave and controlled all emotion but I know when she goes to bed tonight all alone she'll be as miserable as a lost little girl. It's so much harder for her. I have my job and cheerful friends and strange and interesting surroundings to keep myself from brooding.

I don't think I'm a coward. I do hope that if I get into a tight corner that I behave like a man but I know I do fear for Cara if anything should happen to me. We're such companions that one is completely lost without the other. Our three-and-a-half years of marriage have merely increased our love. Perhaps this is a disadvantage in wartime but I think we have a great deal more than most people to look forward to afterwards.

Thursday 23rd January 1941

Start at 9am but car breaks down after 40 miles and we run on to Dabba on three cylinders. Get it going by 3pm and have a good run out to Mersa Matruh. All the way one sees Wop vehicles abandoned by our salvaging people and large stores of guns.

Friday 24th January 1941

Start off at dawn. The road is filthy and the car runs very badly. I cannot give enough praise to our supply people for the way they've kept going on these impossible roads and to the material and design of our vehicles. They have an incredible amount to stand up to.

The road is good for 20 miles then we have successfully mined it to Sidi Barrani where Musso's *Via Vittoria* [military road built in 1940 between Bardia in Italian Libya and Sidi Barrani in western Egypt] ends. I only reach Sollum where I spend the night. A hogshead of brandy has come in, which we tap. Alas, others come in later and I am kept awake 'til after 2am as I sleep on the mess room floor while the drunken crowd tap the cask.

Saturday 25th January 1941

Rise at 5.30am after a nearly sleepless night. Start off at 6.30am and get to Tobruk at 10.30am. The harbour and quays have been thoroughly wrecked, many ships sunk, all motorboats sabotaged and the lighters, though afloat, have charges in them. The Australians have been through the town with a fine tooth comb, anything they don't want they destroy. The sailors arrive later and take their share; bicycles, typewriters, sewing machines, tobacco, clothes all go.

Rifles and military equipment take second place in the looting. The accumulated stores are enormous – for some reason best known to the Wops they have not destroyed their ammo dumps and we now have hundreds of their guns.

Their bombs they have blown up in a great cavern and a large piece of hillside has gone as a result. A large oil dump is still burning. The cruiser *San Giorgio*[11] and a liner are still smouldering in the harbour and a flying boat lies there half submerged. There's a continual popping of grenades and rifles. Many of the men are drunk and completely out of control. All very dangerous.

I take over some very good offices and eat a grand dinner of Bovril, tinned tunny fish from Italy, Australian tongue and chipped Wop potatoes. I have a dear little room with good furniture right next door to my office. After dinner I discover a large unexploded bomb in the room the other side of my office!

Monday 27th January 1941
Ulster Prince comes in at 8am, empty for prisoners. Other ships follow and our port becomes a hive of activity; prisoners embarking, personnel and baggage coming off, sappers [Royal Engineers] working on the docks, mending quays, cranes etc and crowds of anxious, dust-covered people.

At 2.30pm a terrific dust storm starts accompanied by very heavy weather. Our rooms are filled with sand and a thick oil is sprayed all over the docks. Life is just as bloody as it can be. All shipping comes to a standstill as nothing much can be done.

Wednesday 29th January 1941
Work progressing with ships coming in and out. However hard we work we know they'll grouse at GHQ because the statistics they go by show a poor amount but only on the spot can one realise what difficulties there are.

In the afternoon I go out to El Adem, the Wop aeroplane cemetery – there are over eighty corpses lying about.

I have achieved 14 years of soldiering today. Never thought I'd bluff it for so long!

---

11. The Italian Cruiser *San Giorgio* was used as an anti-aircraft station at Tobruk but was forced to scuttle herself as the Allies started to occupy the port. She was subsequently used as an immobile repair ship.

Friday 31st January 1941

We live like animals, wake/eat at daylight, work all day, with no chance to think of anything beyond our work, and sleep like logs 'til the next dawn. We don't discuss or even mention the war. Our talk is petrol, supplies, lighters and transport. The mess is now ten officers and a nice crowd: Australians, New Zealanders, a Rhodesian, a Canadian and an Irishman.

At dusk, while standing on the steps of Navy House, we watch three planes come low over the harbour. Suddenly *Crista* disappears in a curtain of water. Only then did we realise the planes were not Blenheims. The rear gunner evidently knew she was a petrol ship as he fired a burst of tracer but got his aim wrong and hit a sunken ship. It was over far too quickly for anyone to think of taking shelter and made a thrilling spectacle. It was nerve-wracking as right in front of us was 48,000 gallons of petrol and over 50 tons of RAF bombs!

Tuesday 4th February 1941

Woken by a couple of bombs. We scramble down and endure 45 minutes of intense bombing. While the main raid is concentrated on the town and aerodrome on the far side of the harbour, we get several planes swooping down shooting tracer and dropping magnetic mines. I think there's no doubt it's a German attack.

Wednesday 5th February 1941

No air raid but at 7am one of the mines goes off almost getting *Rodi*. The mines are very powerful and shake the buildings as well as all of the ships very noticeably. Poor Cochrane, who has spent a lot of time with Duff trying to locate the mines at great risk to their lives, gets blown up while going out to pilot the *Rodi* off her mooring. A very nice type and a great loss to us.

An easterly wind makes the harbour very rough. I go out to *Bantria* and on to tie up some lighters on the far side. We keep a careful eye open for mines as yesterday at Sollum a water barge went over a mine and touched it off. Some New Zealanders, stevedores and 150 PoWs went sky high. Poor devils.

Saturday 8th February 1941

Adinda comes in at 8am and strikes two mines just where other ships have anchored.[12] She bursts into flame as the splash subsides and drifts on with

---

12. The Dutch tanker *Adinda* arrived in Tobruk carrying a cargo of aviation fuel, low grade petrol and lubrication oil from Alexandria. Seventeen Chinese crew were in the forecastle and were killed when her bow hit a magnetic mine. She was later towed to Alexandria to make her seaworthy before steaming to Bombay for permanent repairs.

flaming bows broadside into *Rodi*, who catches alight. Crew and stevedores jump overboard but many die in the burning petrol on the surface. A strong wind blows *Adinda* shore bound and we see many men dying in front of our eyes but cannot help. Some boats do some good but all we can do is clear the quay of flammable materials and care for the survivors. The loss of life must be big.

Mr Menzies,[13] Prime Minister of Australia, arrives here on a tour with General Blamey.[14] I meet them both at dinner where Colonel Godfrey introduces me. Am so badly dressed as all my clothes are soaked through after today's exploits.

I'm going to Benghazi tomorrow. Everyone makes very nice and undeserving comments about my departure and I feel really sorry to be leaving such a nice, friendly, cosmopolitan crowd.

Rather a blow not to receive any news from Cara and I've no idea if she's sailing or not. I've a feeling that she's not – pray God a wise decision.

Sunday 9th February 1941
Bill Wainman, who stayed the night with us, joins me for the drive up. At Gazala we break down and chug slowly over to a Hurricane fighter where a fitter takes the engine to pieces. It is 274 Squadron with seventy-six enemy to their credit confirmed and over eighty shot up on the ground. We can see the remains of over thirty Wop planes all around the aerodrome.

Monday 10th February 1941
Leave early, unshaven. Road remains good – as Harris, my batman, says, 'It's about all the Wops are good for.' Near Barce we drop down onto a wonderful fertile plain but the going is bad as the road has been mined in several places. After Barce we go on to Tocra and then follow the coast to Benghazi, which we reach around 2pm.

Troops have been in the town several days and the large civilian population are settling down under our rule. Colonel Stamer is town commander and I am two days late for my conference but excuses are accepted.

Benghazi port has been badly damaged and will take a lot of putting right. Air raid in the evening – a couple of 'shakers' and I am told later that mines have been laid.

---

13. Sir Robert Menzies (1894–1978), longest serving Prime Minister of Australia, in office 1939–41 and 1949–66.
14. Field Marshal Sir Thomas Blamey (1884–1951), the only Australian to attain the rank of field marshal.

Tuesday 11th February 1941

Rise early and recce the railway, dumps etc. The Aussies have made a frightful mess everywhere. Discover a big cylinder in the harbour with parachute attached. Report to naval authorities but when we go for a closer look discover it is empty but no one knows what it could have been. Several more are found as well as some enormous bombs half sticking out of the water.

We are now 800 miles from Cairo. Smaile flies back with a letter for Cara.

Wednesday 12th February 1941

Walk around the docks looking for an office. It's amazing what has been left lying about. If one had time and room, one could collect thousands of pounds worth of stuff here. I visit the cathedral. It's lovely inside and of exquisite workmanship with no sign of damage but on the outside one can see where several near misses have spattered it.

The civil population is becoming friendly – too friendly for me. I am afraid many of them are fifth columnists here.

We dine at the pub where one gets a good dinner and poor wine. A very heavy air raid spoils it somewhat. All the windows are blown in and we are knocked off our chairs by three magnetic mines which are laid ashore in error and explode. The blast is terrific.

Friday 14th February 1941

Have a motor accident in the evening. My truck is taken on the broadside and turned over – not a pleasant feeling. We are all rather shaken but no one seriously hurt. A remarkable escape as the truck was doing over 50mph.

Saturday 15th February 1941

Heavy raid from 5.30 to 7am. The last plane comes in broad daylight and drops a big stick within 100 yards of where I stand. It knocks out a whole row of Arab houses and kills nine. Very unpleasant and unnecessary.

John Cowley comes down from corps HQ and has gone over me as a lieutenant colonel. He has no practical knowledge beyond looting and takes away a truck load of furniture.

I fear the port will not be a success –the Navy aren't risking any of their ships unnecessarily these days and the RAF seem to have lost interest. If we can't keep Benghazi we'll have to withdraw to Tobruk but deny Benghazi to the enemy too.

Sunday 16th February 1941

A very heavy air raid lasts from 2.30am 'til daybreak. Another hospital hit and the CO, an Australian Colonel Cunningham, gets killed by a direct hit too. The wall of our pension is knocked down and we have to relocate to new quarters near the cathedral.

Spend all evening embarking prisoners. They include three Germans; one from a plane that force-landed 7 miles from home, he escaped while the Arabs murdered all the other airmen. He has the expression of a newly caged animal at the zoo. The other two are very arrogant young Huns, good looking men and one with an Iron Cross.

Monday 17th February 1941

Another air raid but feel very secure in the new shelter. A magnetic mine drops quite close and almost blows the candle out – even right down where we are.

Tuesday 18th February 1941

At 3.15pm we are given a very fine display of dive bombing by Ju88s [Junkers Ju88, twin-engined multipurpose combat aircraft]. Luckily *Coventry* was the escort ship and she has very powerful AA guns. Her fire was more than disconcerting even though they missed their targets.

The mine experts set off several acoustic mines during the afternoon. They have a terrific blast effect and send up great sheets of water.

We then have another bombing attack just after dark when the newly reopened railway is cut. The Hun seems determined to drive us out of here.

The evening passes off a little more cheerfully, possibly owing to the effects of absinthe.

Wednesday 19th February 1941

The Navy decides to pack up. Captain Poland is charming but lacks guts. I can see no reason why we shouldn't work the port – we've brought down eight planes in 6 days – three today alone with *Coventry*'s salvoes becoming more accurate.

At 3pm we have another dive bombing attack. Our native labour, instead of going to ground, stand about on the quay and cheer. I have become sick of this continual bombing. At night I have got into the habit of waking 15 minutes before they arrive – it must be subconscious hearing.

Thursday 20th February 1941

Spend the morning supervising the raising of Wop planes from the harbour. There are over twenty fighters in the water, some with petrol still in the tanks.

Depart in the afternoon on the back of a RAAF truck. They go like hell and one has to hold tight. Stay the night at Barce and meet a lot of old friends. It's a pleasant relief to go to bed with little fear of bombardment and with the prospect of getting back to Cairo and Cara. Receive a letter from her dated 1st February. She seems resigned to having the infant in Cairo.

Friday 21st February 1941

Due to leave at 9am but no transport turns up so eventually get away In a staff car at 1.15pm. We can see the countryside in sunshine and very lovely it looks. The corn is about 6 inches high and there are many Palestinian flowers.

We stop at Cyrene. The ruins of various temples still stand and are very magnificent. The old fortress sits on the edge of the escarpment and overlooks a wonderful bit of country. It's a very commanding position.

We get into Derna at 5.30pm. I get a bath, the first in exactly a month. It's a grand moment sinking into the hot water with a whisky and soda at my elbow. I had reached the stage where I scarcely noticed a flea biting me – I am covered with all sorts of bites, bruises and scratches.

Tomorrow we'll be back in desert conditions within half an hour of leaving here and I dread it. The country today has been lovely – green everywhere, great long-horned cattle, no dust, Greek and Roman remains and I even saw a partridge.

Saturday 22nd February 1941

Hawkins rings from Barce at 8am and I feel I must return to Benghazi as a project of mine has just been approved. In any case I had decided to do a recce of Apollonia as a possible port. The old port is not of much value these days but obviously in Greek and Roman days was used to capacity.[15]

On returning through Cyrene, I send the men for lunch while I examine further ruins which we had not seen yesterday. There is an entire town built into the side of a hill with a wonderful working water system. The amphitheatre faces north and I take the centre dress circle seat to take in the scenery. The old Greek was a great artist with the sea 12 miles distant being used to tremendous theatrical effect.

Get back to Barce at 4pm. Stay with Hawkins in a double-decker bed. He snores like a pig and has coughing fits every hour.

---

15. Apollonia was a thriving port when Libya (Cyrenaica) was part of the Roman Empire. Along with much of the southern and eastern Mediterranean coast, the port was destroyed by a huge tsunami in 365AD following a violent undersea earthquake near Crete. Large parts of the ancient port of Apollonia were left permanently submerged.

Sunday 23rd February 1941
Colonel Renton takes Hawkins and I back to Benghazi. The harbour is empty, most of the troops have left their guns and tanks and are beating it back east. I feel it won't be long before the Wop gets this place back. With a little initiative he could make a landing now without any opposition.

Tuesday 25th February 1941
Set off with Gibbs in his truck for Derna but it dies on us just before we arrive so get towed in. Late lunch and set off again at 3.30pm. Pick up Merton (*Daily Telegraph*) and Lumley (*Times*) who have broken down, a very nice couple.

Arrive into Tobruk in time for rather an intense air raid. See one ship hit and hear that *Terror* never arrived and that a destroyer picking up survivors was also sunk. Very sad.

Wednesday 26th February 1941
Rather pleased to be back as they are a nice, cheerful crowd here. Have a long day trying to pick up the threads again. It seems office work is becoming a menace. During my first time here none of us ever entered the office. Now it seems we're hardly on the quay!

Have several air raid alarms but no fireworks. It's hard to understand why we don't get a concentrated attack – we have such a lot of shipping passing through and yet such small defences. I fear we'll get hell with the next full moon.

Saturday 1st March 1941
Another wild night. A big swell has got up during the night and the harbour is a sorry spectacle. Our two valuable water lighters have disappeared, about 40 tons of ammunition sunk on a big lighter, about four others have broken adrift and one that had sunk never to be salvaged rose from its watery grave and cut clean through No 1 jetty! The transportation staff here lack nautical experience and tie up a 100 ton lighter with a rope one would not consider strong enough for a head rope. This is the second time we've had this calamity.

Give the men a talk on nerves. They are getting jumpy with all these air raids and alarms.

Monday 3rd March 1941
We hear that *Knight of Malta* has run aground 50 miles east of here. The passengers and crew abandon ship and have 12 miles to walk into Bardia. Not unfunny in normal circumstances but the loss of a ship is serious just

now. Things are boiling up fast in the Balkans and it won't be long before things start happening here. I'd love to be in it if only if it weren't for Cara worrying. I hear poor Angela has had her Hamilton killed in the Sudan and it was ten days before she heard of it. One of the very best, a great athlete and a real nice character.

I am to return to Cairo, probably for a fresh task (Turkey?). I am not going to work myself up over getting back to Cara for fear that once again I get turned back. I write to Cara by air but dare not mention my return.

I feel I've done a good job here; the real task is finished and now it's an office war with statistics and returns and other dull desk work. So now for fresh fields but I hope for a spell with Cara first.

Thursday 6th March 1941

My last day in Tobruk – I hope – not that I haven't enjoyed myself, as I have. I've not only met a lot of people that I've grown to like but I have had a lot of useful and interesting experiences.

We ship off about 500 officer prisoners, including one who, in voice and accent, seems an English gentleman. He used to hunt with the Pytchley and Fernie and we have several friends in common. I don't think any of these people have bitter feelings against us. Very different are four Hun airmen that I put out in the same boat – surly, obstinate swine and I felt like letting them take one more swim.

Farewell parties all round and finally feel I'm off.

Friday 7th March 1941

Leave at 7.30am by Valentia [Vickers Type 264 Valentia, biplane cargo aircraft] from El Adem and reach Abukir after 4 ½ hours of uneventful flying. Do a bit of office work in Alexandria then catch the afternoon train.

Cara meets me at the station and we are both overjoyed to be together again. She's looking extremely well and everyone seems to have been very kind to her in my absence. Ahmed has been a real old watchdog and tried to keep her amused. He is one of the rare type; loyal, honest and as reliable as a man can be.

Saturday 8th March 1941

Go into the office late. Get a very nice welcome from everyone and am greeted with a barrage of questions. Am told confidentially that I may get Cairo sub-area to reorganise and run. At least it would mean a base job 'til the infant arrives. In ordinary circumstances I would not jump at this but just now it's a good opportunity.

After tea I hear that Nigel has arrived in Cairo. That evening we open a bottle to celebrate and have a long talk. It's nearly 6 years since we met except for breakfast at Port Said in '36 when on his way to India and 2 days at The Malting just before the outbreak of the war. He's looking very well groomed now as an ensign in the Scots Guards.

Wednesday 12th March 1941
After a couple of days doing nothing but hanging about GHQ, I start my new job as DAQMG(M) Cairo sub-area. Find the new routine extremely dull. The staff are also dull and of poor calibre. I am certain I am not going to enjoy this job but am very much on the horns of a quandary. If I complain I'll be sent to the ends of the earth which I particularly want to avoid 'til after May for Cara's sake.

We dine with Reggie at Shepheard's.[16] Spot Brian in the corner with what is known as 'The Club'. She has passion written all over her face and I don't think her morals are particularly high. A good thing to have some of that sort around in wartime, especially in this country!

Tuesday 18th March 1941
Roosevelt, president of the USA, makes a remarkable speech which is almost declaration of war on Germany [*see* Appendix A]. Hitler is becoming a bit foxed. Italy has been beaten everywhere which has heartened Yugoslavia and Turkey, and Germany is not left with many possible schemes. The alternatives seem to be a Balkan thrust which will bring Yugoslavia in against her or an invasion of GB which must end in disaster.

Thursday 20th March 1941
Return to a very welcome letter from Mummy dated 19th January. An interesting letter as it's full of details of rationing etc: half a pound of meat per week, 4 ounces of bacon per man per week, no cheese, fish/fruit unobtainable, oatmeal and barley ad lib but chicken and eggs still available, for her at least. She seems to have saved a lot of jam, honey and potted eggs and gets the best out of the garden. Poor Mum – she doesn't grumble but they must be going through a rotten time at home.

London had a terrible raid again last night – all indiscriminate bombing from a great height and we seem to be bagging very few.[17]

---

16. The leading hotel in Cairo and one of the most celebrated hotels in the world from the middle of the nineteenth century until it burned down in 1952 in the Cairo Fire.
17. The Blitz, the sustained bombing offensive by the Luftwaffe against British industrial targets and cities, had started in September 1940. It continued until May 1941, when the German focus switched to merchant shipping. It is thought at least 40,000 British civilians were killed for the loss of 3,363 German aircrew.

Sunday 23rd March 1941
Go to the office at 9am for a short time and then collect Cara to take her to church as His Majesty has ordered it to be a day of national prayer. Cathedral very crowded.

Cara is now finding the extra weight very tiring and apart from her daily exercises is best not doing too much. She has been busy painting the cot that she has borrowed. So far most of the paint has gone on the pot.

Monday 24th March 1941
Go down to south Cairo to see flour being loaded (what a job for a cavalry officer!). Have a row with a man maltreating a horse so beat him up. He's the boss of the mills and has obviously been in trouble for this sort of thing before. We have a good hunt before catching him.

Friday 28th March 1941
Visit RAOC depot. If there's one place where one should not, but one can, forget there's a war on it's that depot. Little doves flutter about on great anti-aircraft guns – guns desperately needed in Greece and Cyrenaica but that have been left to slowly disappear in layers of sand and dust. There are 1,200 native workers to be seen sleeping in the shade of the trucks they should be loading with stores of all description, supervised by military staff that all seem absent on permanent holiday. Thus do we run a war …

Monday 31st March 1941
War news continues good – the naval engagement has resulted in three Wop cruisers and two Wop destroyers sunk with no loss to ourselves. The Wop is also packing up in Eritrea and Abyssinia far faster than we can keep up. Deserters and natives are now turning against the white troops and I would not be surprised to see that party end in the next ten days.[18]

Wednesday 2nd April 1941
Go straight to see Rex Hewer in the morning and hear I'm on an extremely interesting and equally secret job which is all very thrilling. Spend the day packing up at Abbassia as start afresh in Cairo tomorrow.

Lunch with the regiment – all on very fine form. See a lot of old friends and others I knew by sight to work with.

Altogether very pleased with life at the moment.

---

18. The Battle of Keren was fought from 5 February to 1 April. The town of Keren in Italian Eritrea was of vital strategic importance as the road and rail gateway to the colonial capital of Massawa and the Red Sea ports. British, Indian, Free French and Ethiopian troops eventually overcame the Italians, and within a week they had surrendered Eritrea.

Thursday 3rd April 1941
Start life in a new office with old friend Jerry Duke facing me. Nothing could be nicer. All the staff are especially handpicked and I discover the troop are too.

News from Libya is not too good but from everywhere else it's grand. How serious an attack from the west could be for us is difficult to foresee but it's high time we took action – or are we leading them into another trap?

We see a film in the evening of Marlene Dietrich entitled *Seven Sinners*. On leaving the cinema have the back bumper knocked into by a drunk taxi driver with two poor nurses on board. I give the man hell and we take the girls back to the Citadel. They inform us that Benghazi has been evacuated – pray heaven we've destroyed things better than the Wop did when he left.[19]

Sunday 6th April 1941
Germany has declared war on Jugoslavia[20] and Greece – events are now moving fast. We are in Addis Ababa but we'll have to shift it if we're to get troops back from there to assist in Europe or the Western Desert. Troop shifting is a bigger problem than people realise and shipping in wartime is not quickly or easily obtainable.

The canal area is now one long enormous camp. Churchill says in his speech today that we've got to maintain a maximum effort in 1942 but this looks more like a 10-year programme.

I leave the office early as the whole place is in a state of disintegration. I have been listed as 'special employment' which has raised some consternation among the crowd.

Friday 11th April 1941
There's been some terrible news from the Western Desert that O'Connor, Neame, Parry and Combe have been put in the bag by the Hun.

Have a long walk before dinner and drop in on the RAF mess. Meet many who are actually bombing the Hun from here. They all have their tails up and it's very cheering to see. They say our air force in Greece is stronger than the RAF was in France last May! We are daily and nightly putting in far heavier raids than we ever did six months ago.

---

19. The Allies had captured Benghazi from the Italians on 6 February 1941. On the same day Hitler ordered Lieutenant General Erwin Rommel to take over the Afrika Corps. He soon received a boost in the form of the powerful 5th Panzer Regiment joining the Corps and wasted little time capitalizing on this. In a series of battles Rommel consistently outmanoeuvred the British forces, recapturing 600 miles of desert and retaking Benghazi on 4 April. By 14 April he had reached the Egyptian border.
20. Operation Retribution was the German invasion of Yugoslavia in retaliation for the coup d'état that overthrew the government which had signed the Tripartite Pact. The pact, a defensive military alliance, was originally signed between Germany, Italy and Japan, and later by Hungary, Romania, Bulgaria, Yugoslavia and Slovakia.

Sunday 13th April 1941

Easter Sunday. Church at 11am. Very crowded but commander-in-chief not there which makes one realise the gravity of the situation. What anxious times we are living through – personally I feel the Western Desert show is only a flash in the pan and not to be taken too seriously.

Lunch with the judge. Hell of a good lunch with far too much to eat and drink. The little man in great form despite the fact he was going to a great friend's funeral as soon as we leave.

Have Nigel to dine in the evening, on very good form. He seems to be quite happy in his new job and we hear that he gets made up to a captain on Tuesday. Thoroughly deserved and it will give him a leg up when he goes back to the battalion.

Sunday 27th April 1941

Go off at 5am to meet a ship. Bitterly cold morning with a bad dust storm that rages all day – have to wrap up in my old Wop blanket from Benghazi.

The ship is bound for Tobruk but I feel sure she's for Davy Jones' locker as our protection from the air is not as good as it once was.

Churchill makes a situation speech [*see* Appendix A]. Not very exhilarating but the best that he can find he puts into it. So much better to be open about these things than just make them up like the Hun does.

Tuesday 29th April 1941

The Greek news is very bad. Only about 50% evacuated and over 8,000 vehicles lost. The shipping losses have been heavy too. I hear a German broadcast of Churchill's speech which is full of venom.

Wednesday 30th April 1941

Rather overworked at the moment but manage get to bathe in the afternoon. Clear, translucent, green water with no waves, rocks or jellyfish. The war suddenly seems 100 miles away. If only we could get this war over and settle down to a peaceful life again. No doubt one would have one's worries but not this perpetual shadow of the unknown future lurking in front of us.

Thursday 1st May 1941

The Axis have started a big attack on Tobruk. They are reported to have forty-four tanks into the perimeter and 200 outside. It must be uncomfortable there now and for Cara's sake I'm glad I was not left there. Old O'Shaughnessy[21] is probably doing sterling work ...

---

21. Major C. J. 'Shaugno' O'Shaughnessy MBE, MC, GM, MM (d. 1965) served in the First World War with distinction, earning the Military Medal, Croix de Guerre and a

Sunday 4th May 1941

Meet Biddy's brother and David Watts-Russell. The latter has just returned from an adventurous 24 hours on the roof of Sollum Barracks while in German occupation! He says the Hun is very windy – so would I [be] with the Coldstream Guards after my blood! One Coldstream corporal in a raid killed twelve Hun with his Tommy gun, two more with his butt and then came back with a prisoner over his shoulder!

Tuesday 6th May 1941

Hector Spear returns having left Tobruk on a destroyer. Everyone seems to have their tails up and not a bit downhearted although at the moment the Hun has complete air supremacy.

An awful sandstorm blows all day – the wind must be at gale velocity with large petrol tins and tents hurtling past your head. Visibility is four yards at most and the air scorches your flesh. Quite how the Hun is feeling up at the top I don't know but like to think it's hell for them.

Ring up Cara as receive a very depressed little note from her. Elizabeth Coke is now living with her and Nigel is keeping in the closest of touch. It's apparently 105° – poor Cara.

Friday 9th May 1941

A bad sandstorm has already started when I leave camp for the train at 7.30am. Have a most unpleasant journey to Cairo, missing my connection and arriving in at 5.30pm.

Cara looking so well and cheerful when I arrive home. Roger and Nigel also there and R takes me to one side to tell me he has intercepted a telegram to say Cara's father[22] has died. How am I to break this to her and when? It's ghastly and will be a terrible blow to her, being her last link to Australia. Her

Mention in Despatches. Throughout the siege of Tobruk the port was under constant attack, but he and his batman manned an improvised AA post with two salvaged Lewis guns. During one particularly heavy daytime raid a Hurricane pilot bailed out and landed in the harbour. At the height of the raid O'Shaughnessy rowed out into the harbour to pick up the wounded pilot, earning himself the George Medal. He was later awarded the Military Cross for his brave conduct throughout the siege. On leaving Tobruk he joined the SAS and served with them through to the end of the war.

22. Philip Charles Holmes-Hunt (1874–1941). Born in Warwickshire, the son of a gas engineer, Holmes-Hunt studied engineering and chemistry before starting work for his father. In 1902 he became assistant engineer to the Metropolitan Gas Co in Melbourne, Australia. He rose through the ranks to head the Metropolitan Gas Co and was the first president of the Australian Gas Institute. For many years he was a prominent figure in the gas industry in Australia, described as being 'extremely farsighted, amazingly energetic and well-preserved'.

Ma died before Cara could let her know she was pregnant and then Pop dies before she gives birth. This is indeed a tragedy.

Saturday 10th May 1941

A terribly hot day. See the doctor to ask about breaking news to Cara. Feel I can't keep it from her, living the lie and always with the fear of her finding out by other means. Determine to see she'll have a really happy day today and then I'll tell her tomorrow.

Lunch with Evie S in her flat at the top of the highest building in Cairo, drink at Shepheard's and then Nigel and Desmond come to dine. Cara is so gay tonight and pleased with life – I'm back with her, the baby is nicely placed and Pop has just increased her allowance. Tomorrow all this happiness is to be shattered.

Sunday 11th May 1941

Poor Cara. She's terribly cut up. I don't leave her all day, and as it's so very hot we don't leave the flat at all. We send Phie and Mummy cables.

Monday 12th May 1941

Christopher Miles Barne arrives. At about 4am Cara starts pains and though she's more than a fortnight early we have no doubt what is happening. Her pains become worse and frequent and at 5am we arrive at hospital. I leave at 6.30am thinking there's plenty of time but am rung after 8am to say he arrived at 8.05am. Both well and no complications.

I go round to see them and spend the rest of the time in a dream telephoning, writing and cabling. Everyone very friendly and charming and Cara's room is soon full of flowers.

He's a magnificent little chap, 6¼ lbs but fat as butter and with a lovely complexion. He has his wits about him and his eyes focus from the first moment. All the nurses say he's the prettiest baby they've had for a long time.

Tuesday 13th May 1941

Cara picked up and feeling more herself. The brat is very well behaved, is a good feeder and makes little noise.

Rudolf Hess,[23] Hitler's No 3, flies to England – whether for protection or to make some curious deal no one yet quite knows. The wireless and papers can talk of little else.

---

23. Rudolf Hess (1894–1987). Deputy Führer to Hitler from 1933 until 1941, when he flew solo to Scotland in an attempt to negotiate peace. He was captured, convicted of crimes against peace at the Nuremberg Trials and served a life sentence until his suicide.

Friday 16th May 1941

Cara not good today, in awful pain which causes some depression. Rather a tearful day, poor pet.

Get a cable from the Acting Prime Minister of Australia about Mr H-H's death and a bunch of other cables of condolences and congratulations.

Tuesday 20th May 1941

Have spent the last couple of days touting for a new job and eventually Charles T rings me up to say I've got it and start work at crackers tomorrow morning.

My routine is to see Cara in the hospital at 7.45am on my way to the office, in the afternoon and then on the way back from the office or after dinner. Cara still having fits of depression but looking much better. She has received a bunch of cables – fifteen in total – which cheer her up a lot.

Wednesday 21st May 1941

Report in at 8.30am. DAQMG ops are my companions and a very nice lot. Work spasmodic – today appears to be quiet but there is a lot of reading up for me to do to get into the picture.

The Hun started invading Crete by air yesterday.[24] I feel by sheer weight of numbers that he'll bring it off but at present the situation does not appear too serious. It seems to be a dress rehearsal for England! Alas we are short of players on our side and though it's only a rehearsal, the whole world is watching and will judge the results ...

Friday 23rd May 1941

Our chaps in Crete are fighting quite magnificently – but I can't see how they can hold out forever. Dear little Hammy and all that great Black Watch battalion will probably be wiped out –likewise Gilly and his new battalion. God help them all.

It's starting to heat up here again. There's not a breath of air and everything is horribly hot. With the french windows open it's like the open doors of a blast furnace and with them shut one feels like suffocating.

---

24. The Battle of Crete was the first significant airborne invasion in military history. Around 14,000 paratroopers landed on the island and met fierce resistance from British, Greek and ANZAC forces, aided by Cretan resistance fighters. Even so, the Germans managed to establish a foothold on the island, allowing them to land reinforcements. Within 10 days the Allied forces had withdrawn to the south coast, where over half the troops were able to be evacuated by the Royal Navy.

Saturday 24th May 1941

Empire Day. An inauspicious day to our lovely battlecruiser *Hood*,[25] sunk apparently by one lucky shot from *Bismarck* but I'll lay odds we get the bugger.

News from Crete not too bad but there must be a limit to the amount of time a mere handful can continue fighting without any form of respite.

Nigel stays the night with me (and pinches the bathroom soap!)

Tuesday 27th May 1941

Receive first airgraph letter from Mummy dated 3rd. Not bad and shows a level of interest is being taken in the mail scandal. Reply in same airgraph system by which one's original letter is photographed then reduced to the size of a first class stamp. This is then sent home as part of a film including everyone's letters, is enlarged and then sent out to addresses. In this way about 4 tons of mail is reduced to about 20lbs.

Friday 30th May 1941

Cara comes back for tea at the flat. She gets a terrific welcome from the staff. Ahmed insists on getting all the flowers and Morsi produces a most wonderful cake with 'A present from the cook to the new born' written in large letters across it and a Union Jack stuck in the middle! They are a very faithful couple and genuinely fond of us.

Take Cara back to the hospital at 5.30pm – she's been out quite long enough and had enough excitements for one day.

Sunday 1st June 1941

Hear Gilly is back from Crete but young Hamilton was killed. Freddie Graham and Bob L are also in the bag, I fear.

---

25. HMS *Hood*, HMS *Prince of Wales* and six destroyers intercepted *Bismarck* and *Prinz Eugen* as they were exiting the strait between Iceland and Greenland to attack Allied merchant shipping in the North Atlantic. Less than 10 minutes into the initial engagement, a shell from *Bismarck* struck *Hood* near an ammunition store, causing her to sink within 3 minutes. *Prince of Wales* continued to exchange fire with *Bismarck*, but malfunctions in her armaments systems meant she had to withdraw, allowing the Germans to claim a victory. After the battle, the damage *Bismarck* had suffered to her fuel tanks forced her to head to France for repairs. British forces lost contact with *Bismarck*, but an intercepted message on 25 May from Admiral Lutjens allowed them to triangulate her approximate position. She was located the following day, when the Royal Navy engaged and eventually sank her.

Monday 2nd June 1941

The big day. Cara and brat return home from hospital. He settles down quickly and makes very little noise. Nanny Downie looks like being a very good find, gentle but full of experience. Cara in seventh heaven and seems full of maternal instinct.

Thursday 5th June 1941

A very busy day in the office which makes life a great deal more amusing. Have several serious jobs to do and it means going round collecting information from the various services and branches without giving away what I have in mind.

Friday 6th June 1941

Duty officer. Sit in the general operations room for the afternoon and night. Perhaps it's rather vain but an interesting thought that for a few hours one really is in control of the whole war on this side of Europe! Signals of all sorts from everywhere come buzzing in all day and night. The more important ones have to go, if I think necessary, to BGS (Jock Whiteley)[26] or CGS (Arthur Smith)[27] or the chief [Wavell] himself.

At about 11pm I have to go and see the chief. He's stretched out on his sofa in the nicely furnished GOC's house and merely grunts at me. The poor little man has a great burden on his shoulders but there's no one more fitted to bear it. Just now the responsibility of the decision about entering Syria must be worrying him. The result can only be discovered by trial but I think we have no other course but to test the French opinion. I can't believe the Vichy government can bind these unhappy misguided Frogs.

Saturday 14th June 1941

My half day so from lunchtime 'til 9.30am tomorrow morning I am free.

Take Cara shopping after tea. The town is absolutely crowded – troops, troops, troops. Indian, South African, Australians, New Zealanders, Maoris, Jews, Arabs, French, Poles, Czechs, Greeks, sailors, airmen and nurses. It is indeed a strange sight. On the whole they are orderly but there's no doubt the police are kept pretty busy as they warm up a bit as the evening progresses. There are rows and brawls and molesting of civilians and stealing of cars for jaunts or to get back to their camps.

---

26. General Sir John Whiteley GBE, KCB, MC (1896–1970) was to become one of the key British staff officers leading the planning of Operation Overlord under Eisenhower.
27. Lieutenant General Sir Arthur Smith KCB, KBE, DSO, MC (1890–1977).

Sunday 15th June 1941

Am reading a most interesting German officer's diary from Tobruk. He must have been a very fine fellow. He has the greatest admiration for us and yet is quite determined to capture Tobruk. He is actually in four separate attacks, each of which is planned to take the town. Their casualties in one attack are 50%. On one occasion he makes a move across the open instead of the Italian lines in order to draw fire away from them as he considers they've been sufficiently hit!

We start a push in the Western Desert. Pray God it's a success – we need something to buck up the people back home. Unfortunately although it's been kept a good secret here, we now know the Hun Intelligence knew about it on the 11th.

Tuesday 17th June 1941

The Western Desert battle hasn't gone too well[28] and the chief is up there himself. Several hundred tanks are engaged in a pitched battle over a flat, featureless bit of unwanted desert. What an HG Wells scene! Our casualties are great but we believe theirs are greater.

Sunday 22nd June 1941

Christopher's christening goes off well. The archdeacon takes the service, Christopher behaves perfectly and godfathers Barne (Henry and Nigel) and godmother (Marion O-E as a proxy for Phie) do their stuff.

Russia and Germany are now at war[29] and our troops have entered Damascus. The town is in fervour over the former event and all think Hitler's defeat is imminent. Personally I doubt it.

Monday 23rd June 1941

The water for the last fortnight has had a filthy taste. At first I was not believed but now it has got into the soda and will shortly become noticeable in the beer (God help the NAAFI when the Australians find this out). I ring the waterworks to inform them that the African elephant has found a new graveyard in their reservoir but apparently it's algae.

---

28. Operation Battleaxe was designed to re-seize the initiative in the Western Desert and lift the siege of Tobruk. The British lost over half their tanks on the first day, and within three days the remaining units were withdrawing, narrowly avoiding a German encircling movement. Churchill was furious and blamed Wavell personally for the operation's failure.
29. Under the codename Operation Barbarossa, Germany invaded Russia on 22 June, breaking their non-aggression pact. Despite several intelligence reports that an invasion was imminent, Stalin had refused to believe Hitler would attack.

Friday 27th June 1941

Bob's birthday – and I never wrote to her for it as I have every year up to now. It is 8 years since we broke it off – or at least had it broken off for us. I am not sorry now and don't think she is either.

Tuesday 1st July 1941

The chief is leaving us. He goes to be Commander-in-Chief India. He definitely needs the change and a rest. Poor man, he's had a great burden on his shoulders these last 18 months. Auchinleck[30] is replacing him – as he replaces Auchinleck. On all sides one hears nothing but praise for Auchinleck but he has some troubles in front of him!

Monday 7th July 1941

What a long time ago it seems when we used to go for weekends at Peterhayes, gardening on a summer's evening, eating fruit and strolling in for a drink just as it becomes dusk … Such thoughts really make one homesick. Life will never be the same for any of us again; and what world will Christopher grow up in? Will he ever ride a peaceful countryside or spend hot, happy September days after partridges? I doubt it. After this war life will be a struggle for existence; no leisured classes, no army officer-cum-gentleman of leisure.

Tuesday 8th July 1941

We get a rough estimate of what Cara's father's estate was worth – very disappointing and when taxed and dutied and the trustees have had their whack there won't be much left for Cara and Phie. There is also the problem of what can be salved from the house. Cara would love to go through things before they're disposed of but is torn between the desire to stay with me as long as possible and the desire to put things straight in Australia.

Wednesday 9th July 1941

Russia sticking it out bravely against the Hun. I reckon another 10 days and the Russians will be able to deny the harvest to the Hun and in another 6 weeks will be able to stop them getting the oil going before spring. If they hold out 'til mid-October the Hun will have to sit down to a hard winter on short rations, little fuel, a lot of bombing and a war on two fronts. What a lovely prospect.

---

30. Field Marshal Sir Claude Auchinleck GCB, GCIE, CSI, DSO, OBE (1894–1981).

Tuesday 15th July 1941

War game starts. It's an exercise to test the staff and plans of DesForce, BTE and GHQ. Charles Gairdner,[31] a master of strategy, makes up the German plan – I rather dread what would happen if the plan fell into enemy hands! Egypt appears a ripe apple for the Hun but perhaps we are underestimating their difficulties in the desert.

Wednesday 16th July 1941

The war game goes on steadily all day. I attend the 'G' conference at 8.40am where there are five generals and very few under the rank of brigadier.

A bevy of South African girl clerks have arrived here. Every office (except ours!) has a few. They are beautifully turned out and I think there'll be a few romances started with the aid of the war atmosphere and the full sized Egyptian moon!

Thursday 17th July 1941

Cara's birthday. She cashes my birthday cheque and goes hay-wow. She's such a very economical person that it's a pleasure to see her going a bit extravagant. Considering the very luxurious way she was brought up it is amazing to see the distance she can make money go. There's no reason she should go without nice things like soap etc.

Friday 18th July 1941

Attend a monster conference presided over by the new commander-in-chief himself with Tedder[32] and eight other generals and air marshals in attendance. Not seen Auchinleck before – he's a fine looking man, quiet, strong and purposeful. Tedder has rather a puck-like face, large eyes and might be described as ascetic looking.

Thursday 24th July 1941

A very good captured Italian officer's diary is being published in serial form. I wonder if the publication of my diaries by Wop HQ would be of such an interest or whether my views on life would appear as warped or propaganda-led as this young officer's are to us?

---

31. Lieutenant General Sir Charles Gairdner (1898–1983), distinguished British Army officer who was later Governor of Western Australia (1951–63), then Governor of Tasmania (1963–8).
32. Marshal of the Royal Air Force Arthur Tedder, 1st Baron Tedder (1890–1967), Officer Commanding RAF Middle East Command. Later, Deputy Supreme Command of Operation Overlord, the invasion of France.

Saturday 26th July 1941
There's a taxi strike on as the Australians are alleged to have beaten four drivers to death for over-charging. They deserve a beating occasionally but I think the death penalty is a trifle high.

Monday 28th July 1941
Duty officer and we have an air raid during the night. It's only the second air raid when Cairo has used her guns and the second time I've been out of the flat. Poor Cara, it's very upsetting for her. Discover later that she obeyed my instructions and went down to the basement.

The hooter here is the worst part of the air raid. It makes a horrible noise and sets every child, dog and donkey to give tongue. It's like bedlam. To make it worse, the same happens with the all clear alert!

Wednesday 6th August 1941
We send off a parcel to Alan Orr-Ewing[33] who is a PoW in Germany. One just hopes it gets through to him.

Extremely hot and the office from 3 to 8pm is absolute hell. Sweat just pours from off our arms and faces – before dinner I can take my vest off and wring it out!

We dine in and I'm asleep before Cara finishes feeding Christopher. I am determined to keep his name from being shortened. Michael writes and suggests 'Kit'. 'Chris' is also an easy habit to fall into but they must be avoided at all costs.

Monday 11th August 1941
Cara gets a letter saying she's for evacuation this week unless she gets another medical certificate. Very worrying.

Tuesday 12th August 1941
Cara and I each go our own ways to get her off evacuation and ring simultaneously at midday to say we've both succeeded. Huge relief.

Thursday 14th August 1941
Duty officer and have long, dull day. In the evening have to take a letter to the chief for signature. Have whisky and soda with the chief and Lady

---

33. Dr Alan Orr-Ewing MC, PhD, RPF (1915–95), AMB's first cousin. He was awarded the MC before being captured near Dunkirk in 1940, spending the remainder of the war as a PoW. A serial escaper, he ended up being transferred to Colditz, from where he nearly escaped twice, managing to clear the castle before being recaptured. After the war he became a distinguished and pioneering forest geneticist in Canada.

Wavell who is still here. Auchinleck has a very fine face and is a very different type to Wavell. He doesn't have the same broad outlook and manner or the culture of Archie. I always think Wavell and Lady Wavell had ambassadorial manners with the Egyptians and French and I'm sure it did an enormous amount of good.

Friday 15th August 1941
Great excitement over Churchill and Roosevelt meeting in the mid-Atlantic. They announce an eight-point agreement[34] which looks black for Germany. I think war must be the next stop for the US to take.

Saturday 16th August 1941
Watch a demonstration trial of tanks against various obstacles. There's something awesome in seeing a man-made monster crush slowly and inexorably through a barricade of 78lb rail arranged in a crisscross manner, double banked and chained together. All the red hats of the Middle East present.

Go round to the stables after and very refreshing to smell dung and see a row of equine faces peering out from each box. All the old stables we occupied in '29 are now garages – I could hardly bear to look at them. What fun we had in those days but I suppose we had our worries – caught out in slacks at morning stables or overdrawn at the bank and committed to buy a new pony!

Saturday 23rd August 1941
Watch cricket in the afternoon. Wally Hammond[35] and about seven other Test players are playing and a crowd of 7–8,000 turn up to watch them. See Hammond knock up a century in double quick time and the whole game is played like country house cricket – plenty of dash and everyone out to enjoy themselves.

Monday 25th August 1941
Russia walks into Persia.[36] We were preparing to do the same but the action was meant to be joint – I don't believe non-game players have any sense of decency, let alone team spirit!

---

34. The two heads of state met in Newfoundland and issued a joint policy statement that became known as the Atlantic Charter. The statement specified the aims of the war including the disarmament of aggressor nations, no territorial changes against the wishes of the people, restoration of self-government and a reduction of trade restrictions.
35. Walter 'Wally' Hammond (1903–65), English middle-order batsman and captain. He scored 7,249 Test runs at an average of 58.45 and was considered second only to Bradman during his playing career.
36. Operation Countenance was the joint Anglo-Soviet invasion of Iran. Whilst Iran was neutral, the Allies believed the Shah was sympathetic to the German cause and felt

Angela Hamilton causing great chat as she got engaged to one of the CIH before he went to the desert and on his return he found her engaged to one of the KDG ...

Wednesday 27th August 1941
Christopher has first meal from a bottle and Cara gets terribly upset as she feels he's becoming less reliant on her. What complex things women are – far more so than we can ever realise.

Thursday 28th August 1941
Persian resistance ended. Well, we've conquered a country with one of the oldest histories in 3 days – quicker work than even the Hun managed for all his talk of Blitzkrieg. I hope it will have a good effect on Turkey.

Jack dines with us. He really is one of the most charming, genuine people I've ever known. It's a great tragedy he never became my brother-in-law. Poor Elizabeth will never recover her heart from him.

Tuesday 2nd September 1941
The local knocking shop in Alexandria, known as 'Mary's House', received a direct hit in the night – six officers killed and four wounded. All very unfortunate and discouraging to young officers!

We get disturbed by three alerts during the night. They drop some bombs on Abbassia but there is little damage.

Monday 8th September 1941
We all have to go through the gas chamber on the roof of GHQ. My mask was issued in 1934 and I don't think has ever been out of its case! I get my deserts in the chamber as the mask is useless.

Cara starts work again at the Information Bureau for 3 hours in the evening.

Wednesday 10th September 1941
The ambassador, Miles Lampson, is about 58 and has married for the second time. She is Italian and the same age as his daughter. They have just produced a son and there is great speculation as to his paternity. Shack, the doctor who brought him into the world, says it's the spitting image of its

---

they could not run the risk of the Iranian oil fields not being available to them. The attack was a surprise, with Russia invading from the north and Commonwealth forces invading from Iraq. The Shah was deposed by the Allies and replaced by his 22-year-old son, Mohammed Reza Pahlavi. He was to be the last Shah of Iran, overthrown in the revolution of 1979.

father but won't say any more ... Others are saying how delightful that Sir Miles should have had a gun in his own syndicate!

Sunday 14th September 1941
The German has started quite a big attack in the Western Desert. I am not perturbed by the situation but it's the same old story – they've moved first and now we must react to their plans.

Tuesday 16th September 1941
Heavy air raid in the night and I hear several heavy 'crumps'.

Poor Ahmed is in a terrible state as a stick of bombs only just missed his house. They have about 120 casualties in the native quarter – one bomb landed in the taxi rank and killed four drivers asleep in their cars. No doubt there will be a big evacuation today but trams and buses are all on strike for higher pay. With the butchers also on strike, the air raid really hasn't improved the mood of the town.

Wednesday 17th September 1941
Daddy was killed 24 years ago today. I can remember coming home from Wrentham having received the telegram from the Post Office and Mummy bravely insisting on driving and keeping news from us 'til we got home. My God what a waste of lives it was. To beat the Hun and then show such mercy that in 20 years he can rise again to an even greater strength and try to tear down the civilised world.

We must firmly resolve that the only end to this war must be the end of Germany forever. Germany can never have any place in a settled Europe.

Thursday 18th September 1941
I think I have fixed it for Cara to stay here 'til spring. Wonderful if it's true but I only hope we're not being stupid and endangering her and Christopher's lives. I don't think a German invasion of this country probable and shipping in the Red Sea is threatened as much as it ever will be.

Tuesday 23rd September 1941
Cara gets orders for evacuation which makes us both very depressed. It's bound to come some time so that the powers that be can save face. They can't admit they made a mistake when first ordering it and are determined to clear the whole lot out.

Sunday 28th September 1941
Nigel comes to lunch and goes doggo on the sofa immediately after; he doesn't rouse 'til 8pm! He and Cara get on very well now and are terribly funny together.

Feeling terribly optimistic about the war. I believe Finland will pack in, Russia will stabilise the war for Winston, Italy will pack in in the spring then Turkey will join us and after a few months of hammering there will be a revolt in Germany meaning by October the war will be over. Maybe I've had too much stout over lunch to cure my boil?

Thursday 2nd October 1941
Am off to Alexandria tomorrow on leave 'til Monday. We've been warned not to go as it's a full moon and they are expecting heavy raids but I'm not going to miss my leave! If the rest of this diary remains empty, gentle reader (if any), you will understand why ...

Friday 3rd – Sunday 5th October 1941
To much excitement, we set off on the 4.30pm train to Alexandria where we are met by Harry and Jack. There are occasional air raids and there is a 10pm curfew but life is as gay as I remember it in 1928. The Union Bar remains the centre of attraction and at a late hour we all move on to the Excelsior. It's officers only and everyone goes completely wild each night – jitterbugs being the dance of the day. Cara enjoys it all and is on sparkling form – after all it is our first weekend away for a year.

We don't do any bathing but sail in the harbour each afternoon after an enormous lunch at the RYC of Egypt. There's a lot of the fleet in and it's great fun sailing around it all. One of the big ships, *Ajax*, is an old friend of mine and has been in every important engagement of the war. There are also a number of British and Greek submarines which are most sinister looking. At sunset we see two going out. Apparently when they return after three weeks without contact with the outside world they come in flying the Jolly Roger and the appropriate number of flags of ships sunk!

Monday 6th October 1941
Return to Cairo feeling one hundred percent better and with pockets not quite so depleted as I'd expected – cost £15 all in.

Thursday 9th October 1941
Russia looks like collapsing very soon and the seriousness of the situation will depend on the completeness of her collapse.[37] If her Black Sea fleet and the Caucasus area hold on we should manage alright but I fear if they go Turkey might readjust her views and Japan, Spain and whoever else is left, other than USA, will feel Hitler is invincible.

---

37. The Battle of Moscow commenced on 2 October 1941 and was to last for over three months, until the Red Army's winter counter-offensive drove the Wehrmacht from Moscow.

Thursday 16th October 1941

Had to put Nigel to bed last night on the camp bed in the drawing room. He turned up very much worse for wear and then today he doesn't turn up for lunch 'til 3pm (we don't give him any) and on the verge of passing out again. He's behaved thoroughly badly to us and it's only the fact he's off to the desert and has a lot more in front of him than he realises, that I don't kick him out of the house. I just don't want to part in anger on this occasion if it might cause lasting unhappiness.

I hear after that the little brute then drank most of a bottle of whisky on the train up to Alexandria and passed out on the platform. If he goes on like this it will be hard to differentiate between him and some of the incurables whom one can only look upon with disgust.

Thursday 23rd October 1941

At 7.30pm I pulled back to the office to defend and justify some statements that I have made. Apparently the commander-in-chief of Mediterranean and Army don't agree with Barne and a big decision is dependent on the accuracy of my statement. I have an awfully vicious half an hour but eventually my opinion is vindicated. Thank God!

Saturday 1st November 1941

A new month and things seem much the same: a deadlock in the Western Desert, Turkey on the fence, USA and Japan not in the war yet, Russia valiantly holding out and the French cooperating more and more closely with the Germans.

This is the thirteenth November 1st that I've spent abroad although many of them are not regretted. At dinner I drink my customary glass of port and am scoffed at – but who cares? If they don't know the delights of foxhunting that is their loss.

Friday 14th November 1941

Another quiet day in the office. Hatch has a talk with me and suggests that my job here is becoming redundant. I agree but what troubles me is that at the moment there is no vacancy in the regiment and if I can get away here that is the only thing I want to do. If I must sit in an office then I'd rather be near Cara and see Christopher develop.

Wednesday 19th November 1941

The great news but still terribly hush-hush is the big advance into Cyrenaica [the eastern coastal region of Libya] on 17th. It started very well with a dust storm helping to hide our moves and then a cloudburst yesterday bogged down the Italian tanks. Rommel, their supreme commander, is supposed to be in Athens so we've fairly caught them with their trousers down. If only we could bring off this coup the repercussions throughout the world could be enormous. It's the first occasion when someone has taken the offensive against the Hun – pray God it works.

Thursday 20th November 1941

My 35th birthday. From today I start my decline, having reached half my allotted span. To prove my youth and agility I play a violent game of squash with Charles Oliver. I get beaten but only just.

Friday 21st November 1941

Terrific news filters back all day from the Western Desert. By evening we seemed to have destroyed 200 enemy tanks and got the remainder cornered. It's all gone much faster than expected and may well turn out to be one of the decisive moments of the war.

Sunday 23rd November 1941

A fairly good night as duty officer. The sitrep does not come in 'til 6.15am. The PM is anxiously awaiting it as he wants to make a statement. It's not so good, however, so suspect the statement might be off!

Bardia is in our hands but Tobruk has not broken out properly and the Hun have produced 100 tanks more than expected. However, it is good that they are inside our cordon and not taking up position in theirs.

Take the situation report round to Auchinleck and sit with him while he goes through it. He seems fairly satisfied. He does not seem at all weighed down by the enormous responsibility that is his. I should think he is very tough, very cool and level-headed.

Monday 24th November 1941

The great battle in the WD still rages. I would, no doubt, hate it if I were there but I feel equally miserable thinking of all those good chaps in a life and death struggle for my preservation. I am resolved to get back to the regiment.

Wednesday 26th November 1941

On the way to the office try get tickets for a film called *Lady Hamilton*. I would never go near a cinema if it wasn't for Cara. I think films have done more harm than any other invention in the last 50 years. They have bred discontent, fanned socialism, loosened morals, increased vice and criminal acts and, what irritates me most, have spread frightful American slang and twang.

Friday 28th November 1941

Tel El Keri shoot. Despite getting out of bed at 5.30am Cara thoroughly enjoys her time loading for me. There are an enormous amount of duck in and we shoot not more than 1,100. I get forty-eight and if I shot as well in the first hour as the last then I would have doubled that.

Back to the office in the evening but I feel bodily and mentally refreshed after my first day's outing in 2 years.

News of casualties from the WD are coming through and there are already several new widows amongst our friends. Thank God Cara is spared this time but I can't remain in this life of luxury while my friends are being sacrificed for me.

Monday 1st December 1941

Cara and I go up to meet the regiment coming through. Talk to Ronnie about coming back and he seems quite enthusiastic. We then motor down the line – over a mile long – and see many old friends. It's just grand seeing them all again but very sad in a way as Cara won't be seeing many of them again for a long time and some she may never see again. The regiment only comes second to me in her heart.

Tuesday 2nd December 1941

Spend the morning in the office winding up my affairs. Sorry to leave John and Franco – they've turned out to be pleasant and sterling characters.

Whilst Colonel Feilden, commandant of the RAC Base Depot, has no difficulty in me returning to duty, William rather pompously insists on my doing a full course beforehand. It is completely unnecessary but I start on Friday.

Sad news comes in of the total loss of HMAS *Sydney*[38] and crew off West Australia. There's worse news yet which has not been broken to the public as the Hun has not yet announced it. Unfortunately it is running around town as a rumour.

---

38. HMAS *Sydney* was sunk by German auxiliary cruiser *Kormoran* with a loss of all 645 hands. *Kormoran* was so badly damaged in the exchange that her captain was forced to scuttle her; 318 of her 399 crew were eventually captured.

Chapter 4

Rejoining the Royals

The end of 1941 saw a dramatic escalation of hostilities. On 7 December, without a declaration of war, the Japanese launched an astonishing attack on the US base at Pearl Harbor in Hawaii, killing 2,403 Americans, sinking and damaging many naval ships and destroying numerous aircraft. The shocked Americans declared war on Japan, and four days later Germany declared war on the USA.

Equally shocking to the British were the coordinated Japanese attacks on Malaya and Hong Kong. The British were caught off-guard by the experienced Japanese troops, many of whom were veterans of the Second Sino-Japanese War, which had started in 1937. Suddenly a European-based conflict really had become a world war.

Technological progress had finally caught up with the Royals, and they had started the transition from horses to armoured cars in September 1940. The regiment was divided into three squadrons of eighteen armoured cars each and then subdivided into patrols of three cars. Each car housed four soldiers: the commander sitting on the turret, two drivers and a wireless operator. With limited space available for storage, these cars were festooned with items (bedding, petrol cans, ammunition and luggage) strapped on to the hull.

The role of the cars was as reconnaissance patrols to gather intelligence on enemy positions, strength and movements, and to support the tank regiments in battle. Given that they were not designed to be a strike force, they were typically only armed with a 20mm gun, as well as small arms. To make matters worse, the first generations of armoured cars only had 9mm of armour plating and were particularly vulnerable to attack.

This reconnaissance force was to play a crucial role in the unstructured, often chaotic, desert warfare. The wide open spaces of the desert did not allow for defined defensive positions, as seen in mainland Europe, but made for a fluid battleground where armoured cars could roam many miles behind enemy positions. With frequent sandstorms and mirages it was often difficult to identify friend from foe, and accurate navigation was an essential skill.

Commanding the German forces in the Western Desert was Generalleutnant Erwin Rommel, popularly known as the 'Desert Fox'. Rommel had a glowing record from the First World War and his operational successes during the invasion of the Netherlands, Belgium and France helped seal his reputation as a master military strategist, deploying surprise and swift manoeuvres. During late November 1941 Rommel led a strong counter-attack in a push that became known as the 'dash to the wire' (the Egyptian border). It was at the beginning of this retreat that Major Barne rejoined the Royals.

*   *   *

Friday 5th December 1941
Attend my first course at 9am. Bill Pitt is running it and, as such, everything is chaos. Initially there's no truck to take us out to the desert and no sun compass and once this has been solved the instructor admits he has never seen a sun compass. Thankfully one of the lads has already done a course.

Saturday 6th December 1941
Trek around the countryside all morning to practise driving with a sun compass.

Have a Royals party in the evening to celebrate my acquiring a beret. A good crowd including Pitt-Rivers, whose father was in the regiment but is now interned as an ardent fascist,[1] and Peake, who is not at all pleased at me stealing a march on him. He's talked about getting back to the regiment for years and I secured it in three days.

Monday 8th December 1941
Don't hear 'til halfway through the morning that Japan has attacked USA and British possessions at dawn yesterday. They've sunk two of our cruisers and a Yank battleship. One only hopes their successes are initial ones and they'll soon be stopped. The experts only give them three months before their oil runs out.

---

1. George Pitt-Rivers (1890–1966), one of the wealthiest men in England during the interwar years and a noted anthropologist and eugenicist. He was interned in Brixton Prison from 1940 to 1942 as a Nazi sympathizer.

Saturday 13th December 1941

After couple of days in bed with filthy cold, return to work and spend the day on the Breda gun, a 20mm Wop gun that proved so good that we've started production. I've fired one in earnest in Tobruk but had no idea it was so complicated to strip.

Monday 15th December 1941

Start Driving and Maintenance under Sergeant Dover. I am alone on my course so we romp through it.

Cara works at the canteen all morning and ends up losing her voice.

Friday 19th December 1941

Confined to barracks as sector commander.

Stay in a bungalow where I once had the thrill of sitting in the drawing room and seeing (one couldn't help notice) my hostess disrobe entirely and then re-robe for dinner – and I've never seen a prettier figure! I often wonder if she meant for me to see her and I was just too young to realise.

Thursday 25th December 1941

Early church and reckon there must be 600 there.

Cara spends the morning at the canteen and then [we] have a very long, jolly lunch with Diana. Afterwards we have eight Royals and four others to tea and we all thoroughly enjoy ourselves.

We hear on the news that the Royals were the first British troops into Benghazi which fell yesterday.

Monday 29th December 1941

Cara pushed a truck of books around the hospital in the afternoon and then spends all evening working at the Information Bureau.

Poor Diana gets news that Roger is wounded, missing and believed to be a prisoner. She's in an awful state, of course.

Wednesday 31st December 1941

Well this is the end of another year. We celebrate it at Shepheard's. Everyone gets very boisterous and the dining room is broken up completely.

I feel the tide has now turned and from now on we can take the offensive. Hitler will have to wait to see what we do and each month of 1942 he will find it more difficult as his army gets fewer and the Luftwaffe dwindles away.

Stalin has been the hero of the last 6 months but Roosevelt must be the star of the next year. I think he can and will be.

At home, Christopher is the star and we thank God we have such a fine, healthy son. If anything happens to me, Cara will find everlasting comfort in him. God bless them both.

Thursday 1st January 1942
Start the year bright and early, but with a slightly sore head. Bobby picks me up at 6.30am and we go down to Laguna to shoot. A lovely day – too lovely for shooting – but we enjoy ourselves going from one small lake to another. We get fifteen, mostly pochard, and four snipe.

Get home at 6pm and hear that Reggie and Ronnie are coming in slightly wounded. Hope it's nothing too serious.

Diana comes to dinner. She's still very het up and will have a nervous breakdown if she doesn't steady up. She's as white as a sheet with great dark shadows under her eyes, poor dear. When she leaves she goes flat on her face, which has happened several times apparently. For Cara's sake I just hope nothing happens to me.

Friday 2nd January 1942
Hear the sad news that Reggie[2] has died of heart failure on his way in with a crushed arm. Curious that our first death in the field should be the commanding officer.

Friday 9th January 1942
Tony P rings in the evening to say he's in and can he dine. Of course, every Royal is welcome here and nothing pleases Cara more to feel that this is a centre they feel free to come to at any time. Tony looks very thin and worn and gets the story of Reggie off his chest. It seems the regiment must have had a very hard time.

Tuesday 13th January 1942
Get my marching orders – am to go off by train tomorrow night. Now I feel I've been stupid to have been so 'brave' and burnt my boats. However, after the war I shall be able to hold my head up amongst my friends whereas if I'd sat all the time at GHQ people would rightly look askance at me.

It's wretched for Cara but she sensibly sees my point of view.

Wednesday 14th January 1942
24 hours reprieve!

Geoffrey Wilson and two other Warwick Yeomanry give an enormous party in the evening. They take the reception rooms at some dago's flat. The dago daughters join in the party and Mama acts as a lady's cloakroom attendant!

---

2. Lieutenant Colonel Reginald Heyworth (1896–1940) died after a Stuka attack on 27 December.

Thursday 15th January 1942
The fatal day. When will Cara and I meet again and where? We are mercifully
kept busy all day as I have a lot of kit to collect and affairs to wind up.

We go to the cinema after tea but we are only there to keep our minds off
other things. There is just nobody braver than my Cara. She looks pale and
tired but up to the point of departure she shows no signs of breaking down
but she'll go to bed later and cry her little heart into her pillow.

Cara arrived at Haifa two years ago and the time we've had together have
been two of the happiest years.

Friday 16th January 1942
It's bloody to have to go by train but there are no cars available. Have an
extremely uncomfortable night but am thankful for the sheepskin coat. Get
to Amriya by 8am and have two hardboiled eggs but get no tea. At lunch we
are grateful to Cara for the cold teal and bread she's prepared.

There's a strong wind blowing all day, whipping up the sand continually.
All the old familiar sights along the way awaken many memories. In many
places there is actually water lying about from the heavy rains earlier in the
month. I've never seen so much greenery in the desert before.

Jumbo [Riddell] and I stay at the staging camp. Our tent is almost carried
away by the wind in the night and a jerboa [hopping desert rodent which
was the inspiration for the 7th Armoured Brigade's nickname, 'The Desert
Rats'] eats a lot of my chocolate. I hope the silver paper gives him violent
indigestion.

Saturday 17th January 1942
After expecting to be doomed to spending two days here, Jumbo finds an RA
convoy at 10am which is leaving in 20 minutes. We have a charming gunner
driver but the officers are bloody.

Doss down in the desert in the evening with a completely flat horizon in
every direction. The only interesting feature [is] two camels moving in leaps
and bounds across the landscape. The rear one is obviously male and feeling
the urge of spring – let's hope we all develop the offensive spirit this spring!

Sunday 18th January 1942
We have a peaceful night, broken only by a passing aeroplane and some
barking foxes. The morning is cold but not too bad and there is a lovely
dawn. Jumbo makes for a good companion as we are both interested in birds
and natural history in general.

Our convoy is late to start and slow on the move. We lose six more vehicles,
including one with some of my kit, and get to Bir Talata at 4pm. It is the most
dismal looking mound set in a great plain over which the wind continuously

whistles, blowing up sand. It seems to be a focal point for all convoys and there are lorries and bivouac tents dispersed as far as the eye can see.

Monday 19th January 1942

Pick up a convoy of 240 three-tonners, driven by New Zealanders but with a RE survey party to whom we attach ourselves. A high wind soon picks up and we cover 99 miles of filthy road under filthy conditions. My driver used to be a farrier in the North Island and dealt chiefly with race horses.

Arrive at Capuzzo at dusk and soon turns very cold. Turn in at 8.30pm as there is nothing else to do.

Tuesday 20th January 1942

Spend some time visiting the other vehicles left behind yesterday. Also see many relics of battle: several old tanks, German vehicles, Wop guns and the ground littered with junk.

Leave at 10.30am and get through to Tobruk by dark. Squeeze into the transit camp and very thankful for a hot meal and bed out of the wind. Everything is saturated in dust: bed, clothing, hair, teeth.

Wednesday 21st January 1942

Go to see the port which is surprisingly not very damaged. Navy House took a couple of rounds and the cold storage has been hit but otherwise things are the same. The church still stands but all the furniture from every house has gone. The buildings stand but roofless, doorless and windowless.

Thursday 22nd January 1942

A very disappointing day. We set off at 11am in a great hurry, go 10 miles and then stop for the night but always at short notice to go on. Our convoy is of all sorts: petrol, ammo, gunners and RN.

We talk to one of the petty officers. Since the last war he has been one of the chief divers in bringing up the German fleet at Scapa Flow.[3] He said most of the scrap was sold back to Germany – presumably to make *Bismarck*?

---

3. The scuttling of the German fleet took place on 21 June 1919 at Scapa Flow in Orkney. Fearing that the ships would be seized and distributed amongst the Allied powers, the German commander, Admiral Ludwig Von Reuter, gave the order to scuttle. In all, ten battleships, five battlecruisers, five cruisers and 32 destroyers were sunk. In 1923, after complaints about the sunken fleet causing a navigational hazard, the Admiralty started raising some of the ships and subsequently sold 26 of the sunken destroyers to an entrepreneur, Ernest Cox, for £250. Developing new salvage techniques powered using coal from one of the refloated vessels, Cox managed to lift twenty-four of the ships.

Friday 23rd January 1942

We continue taking the now famous Trigh El Abd, 'The Slave Route', right across to Msus. The dust when sitting in the back is awful – one gets a thick coating on one's lips and rims of eyelids, one's face has a yellow mask on it, earholes are filled and blowing one's nose produces thick mud. These RASC drivers do this day after day week in week out.

Water is understandably pretty short and 2 pints a day have to suffice.

Saturday 24th January 1942

Have an even more dusty and dirty road. At 4pm we get into Msus and immediately get a shaking from five Stuka[4] dive bombers. We soon have five Hurricanes up and we see them going into the distance weaving and wheeling in mortal dogfight.

Sunday 25th January 1942

Leave Msus and head out 4 miles south to find the regiment with the terrific noise of battle in the background. Suddenly we find ourselves amongst grey berets and all one's doubts and fears are dispelled. What confidence one gets amongst a well-disciplined crowd and to know everyone as a friend.

Alas our arrival coincides with a signal for withdrawal and as far the eye can see there are vehicles moving northward. In less than an hour Msus is in German hands. In our retirement we go over three land mines. No one is badly hurt but we have to set fire to one lorry when we abandon it. We see several large parties of our bombers, with escorts, coming back but I fear the situation is serious.

Make camp that night and see many brother officers, all looking fit, brown and so cheerful. Now I'm here I'm now cheerful but not yet brown. I am to take over A Squadron. Pray God I'm fit to take the responsibility and never let the regiment down.

Monday 26th January 1942

Spend an anxious night expecting to move or having a Jerry patrol bump into us but all remains quiet and cold.

Have a miserable day just waiting. We have an odd collection of people including a nice young 12L, Charles Burrell, whom we picked up after he hit a landmine.

Tuesday 27th January 1942

Burrell goes back to Tobruk and I stupidly don't give him my letter to Cara – damn!

---

4. Junkers 87, also known as the Stuka dive bomber. Easily recognized by their potential victims as they flew in close arrowhead formation and had a distinctive fixed undercarriage.

The South Africans move off and scare Sergeant Galland into abandoning a vehicle. I rashly send him out again to get it at dusk and 5 minutes later we are ordered to move 20 miles east. Thank heaven Galland works at super speed and I get him in before we get going.

Have a horrid trek in the rain over some desperate ground – sixty great vehicles lumbering over countryside that a horse would not look to take on in the dark. The men know their lives depend on keeping in the column and we only abandon one truck.

Wednesday 28th January 1942

Glorious fresh morning and we awake to find we are on some high ground with a very grand view. Even out in this uncharted spot one finds natives. They are all unafraid and one shows us a chit written by two escaped gunners who they befriended.

Thursday 29th January 1942

Complete 15 years of soldiering today – they have been happy years.

Quiet morning other than a certain amount of administration stuff. Manage to complete a full change of clothes, my first in a whole fortnight. Also manage a jolly good wash and shave.

Meet with Morley who says that Arthur Grendel was killed – terribly sad – and Cooper has been taken as prisoner.

Friday 30th January 1942

Jack rings up to ask the date which shows how monotonous the days are!

Sharp Stuka attack in the morning. We move just before dusk and do the last 17 miles in the dark on a bearing. More by luck than judgement I hit our 'point', a well, absolutely plum on.

We pass Mechili Fort, an old Italian stronghold surrounded by abandoned and broken aircraft and vehicles. What a life to have been posted here in peacetime, I can't believe we have anything as bad as this in the outposts of our Empire.

Monday 2nd February 1942

See a young Scots Guards just before we move and hear that Nigel has halted nine miles short of me. Very frustrating! However, he says he's well and happy.

We arrive at a bleak and desolate spot on the old slave route. There are no landmarks and no shelter from the biting wind which drives sand across the plain. It feels like one is being continually being rubbed with sandpaper.

Thursday 5th February 1942

No move ordered so have a grand wash and clean up. I ride Hawkins' motorbike out into the desert far enough to relieve nature. It's very bumpy and I wouldn't like to do a long distance on it. Two ravens come out to inspect me – out here one shouldn't move a yard out of camp without a compass.

In the evening go up to have a drink with Philip Fulden, Adrian Paton, Anthony Goodall and others who have arrived with a lot of armoured cars. They have a large parcel for me and four letters, including two from Cara. She is well and happy and there appears to be no signs of evacuation. Bless her, she's made a wonderful parcel for me with a great cake, six cans of beer, tinned butter, powdered milk, porridge oats, sugar, chocolate and dried fruit to fill in the gaps.

Sunday 8th February 1942

Attend the service and I'm sorry to say that the South Africans provide the majority of the congregation. The British troop is not a religious type, I fear.

I go up and see the others after dark. There is a large crowd and it's all very cheerful. They have a large and lovely dog called 'Rommel' who walked into their leaguer. Victor M captured a Hun staff car which contained an officer, a staff sergeant major, eight bottles of '34 Heidsieck, six bottles of brandy and a quantity of beer and provisions.

See Desmond H-R who has aged terribly in the last 6 months. He's no longer a light-hearted boy. I should think that troop leading in armoured cars is quite the hardest job in the regiment, permanently on the alert and with a very great responsibility.

Tuesday 10th February 1942

Situation in Singapore is very bad now with the Japanese already on the island.[5] Can't possibly let Cara go to Australia now.

One develops quite a feeling of confidence bowling over the desert in one's iron horse. One sits high on the turret lid and sees the horizon unroll before one. No doubt my personal feelings will be somewhat different when there is an enemy actually firing at me. I develop a sore bottom as appear to have sat on an upright bolt.

Wednesday 11th February 1942

Had all my leaguer dispersed widely at dawn as had a feeling we might be visited today. Sure enough at 8am four enemy fighters arrived but after circling around decided we were no target!

---

5. On 8 February the Japanese began an assault on Singapore. The battle lasted a week before the British capitulation, the largest surrender of British-led troops in history, with about 80,000 Commonwealth soldiers captured.

Peter Starkey arrives after lunch who has (mis)used two magazines of his Tommy gun, all his revolver rounds, several rifle rounds – to say nothing of the petrol or damage to his car – in the killing of one dorcas gazelle. It really has quite a nice head of 11 ¾ inches with a very good curl at the tips.

Have a game of football against the South Africans who are lying near us. Major Lindsay is my opposite number and is very friendly and cooperative!

Thursday 12th February 1942
After breakfast I go up to A Squadron to take over from Brian. John Bowlly will be my second-in-command and the troop leaders are Victor Whitworth, Desmond H-R, Freddie Fisher, Hugh Rocksavage[6] and Walter Scott.

Friday 13th February 1942
After lunch we move up to RHQ. I have to give my first set of orders. No doubt in time all these things will become routine but for the present it's rather alarming. From now on this not inconsiderable force is my care and responsibility. I earnestly pray that I will be given wisdom and courage to lead in the right way and be a credit to the regiment.

Saturday 14th February 1942
We go up to the line to relieve Harry. On the way we have a grand shoot at a Wop recce plane. It's low and slow and I see my tracer go right into it but it shows no effect. Our Breda gun loses its head and we are lucky not to be slaughtered by it. Speak most severely to Harland who was in charge of the gun.

Take over from Harry in the morning. We are left on our own in a big flat *wadi* with a certain amount of scrub in which we conceal our vehicles. Freddie, Hugh and Victor go forward to a line about 12 miles distant where they watch for enemy movements and I keep in constant touch with them on the wireless.

See one Hun Me110 [Messerschmitt Bf 110, twin-engined heavy fighter] strafe B Squadron on our right and am kept informed every 10 minutes of a Hun tank column moving down our way.

Tuesday 17th February 1942
Get orders to move again. I have to work out a plan, get all the cars on the wire, decide map references, put it into code, then give my orders and get packed up myself (I still have no servant). It's rather fun to climb into one's

---

6. Hugh Cholmondley, 6th Marquess of Cholmondley GCVO, MC, DL, styled Earl of Rocksavage (1919–90). Author of *A Day's March Nearer Home. Experiences with the Royals 1939–1945.*

turret and see cars scooting around as far as 15 miles away given on my verbal orders in a quiet voice from my car.

Everything works like clockwork. The troop on the horizon is waiting for me to move – will be my advance guard – another is scooting across the basin to take up position on my vulnerable flank and a third will whip in as soon as we move off.

Wednesday 18th February 1942
We are in a rather pleasant *wadi* but there is a cold wind and rain most of the day.

Sergeant Cook finds a snake which, strangely for a troop, he doesn't kill. He calls me to have a look at it. I put it down to a horned viper, a venomous looking beast about 16 inches long with a wide, flat head and horns over its eyes. Its back is pale buff with dirty dark stripes across its back but white underneath.

It stops raining and the sun comes out briefly before setting. The air is filled with a most aromatic smell from the thorn bushes. I sleep in the lee of a bush and go to sleep partly enjoying the scented air and partly wondering if the viper's partner will slither along to share the warmth of my flea bag.

Friday 20th February 1942
Wake up in the night and hear my radio operator tuning in to jazz in America. Hurl a rock at the car which puts a stop to that. The bloody man should be on constant watch in case one of my patrols wants anything in the night. This sort of thing is not good enough.

Saturday 21st February 1942
I have to send Harry out to look for two men who have been seen 66 miles away walking in. Our chances of finding them are slight but their chances of being found by the Hun are equally slight.

We have captured coffee for lunch. I'm not quite so sympathetic for the poor Hun any more – it's better than the coffee one gets at Shepheard's.

Harry gets back in the evening having seen nothing, not even a stranded vehicle.

Sunday 22nd February 1942
Freddie and Victor continue the search.

Three large Me199s come over in the morning – very noisy and sinister looking beasts. They don't see us, I hope. They return in the afternoon and this time make a threatening gesture which sends us to our guns but it comes to nought.

Monday 23rd February 1942
Roddy [Heathcote-Amory] arrives in the afternoon to be my 2i/c. Lovely to see him again but I shall equally be sorry to lose John. He brings a load of letters, including three from Cara. Nanny has had flu so Cara has had a bad time looking after Christopher. Otherwise she seems happy and there's no more talk of evacuating her. Wish I could get her somewhere cool just for the summer. She's in a different boat to anyone else as, separated from me, she really is alone in the world although she would never lack friends, of that I am sure.

Wednesday 25th February 1942
Desmond announces on the wireless that he has meat for me. I suspect prisoners but it turns out to be antelope. We can't work out what sort, it has horns like an impala but closer together and about 40 inches high, a rough very light coat, large cloven hooves and white markings under the eyes. Regardless, it should make good eating!

Morgan collects a Hun motorbike which the boys soon get working. Roddy goes out to a Wop mobile brothel (alas abandoned) and brings back a fine double seat from it.

All day long a Hun column has been upsetting our peace by being on the move. We don't particularly want to move from here as it's the best bivouac we've had with lovely bushes, shade and cover.

Friday 27th February 1942
Gosh one does feel well out here. It may be dull and dirty but I have never felt better and one never gets a man going sick.

John Leslie, the doctor, comes up to inspect some men with lice. They've had no change of clothes for 3 months and washing facilities have been nil. Lice are synonymous with wars and famine. There's certainly no famine here and most days the war feels a long way off.

Wednesday 4th March 1942
Bob comes up to relieve me. I get very het up as feel he should have been here earlier but apparently he thought he was due to take over tomorrow.

Have a sort of hurricane during the morning but nothing to what breaks on us at about 11pm. We have the most vivid lightning I have ever seen with torrential rain accompanied by gusts of wind of gale force. There is literally nowhere the rain does not enter, usually along with quantities of sand. It blows itself out in about 1½ hours but the drizzle continues 'til morning. I have never spent such a miserable night.

Thursday 5th March 1942

Wake up to a chilly dawn and have to get dressed in the rain into wet clothes while standing in a muddy pool. The salty pan by the camp is now a lake and all the cut bushes used as camouflage have blown away.

Say farewell to Bob at 9am – I feel certain he is going to move from this nice place. I can see it in his demeanour.

Rejoin the regiment by 10am and quickly get everything out to dry as the sun is now out. Spend the afternoon with Ronnie and Jack, as usual in great form. Get a small parcel from Cara: porridge oats and mustard. Very acceptable!

Friday 6th March 1942

As we leaguered with RHQ we have to disperse before daylight. Have my long anticipated bath using the bivvy as a screen, back of my chair as a bath mat and put some hot water in a bowl first to loosen all the interesting flora, fauna, lichens and fungi from my body. Once I'm finished, my car crew have a scrub.

Sunday 8th March 1942

A football comes up from B3 so we have two games in the afternoon. I've done 6 weeks today up here but the men have done over 3 months without a moment's relaxation.

Monday 9th March 1942

We were due to head off at 8.45am to relieve Harry but owing to an unfortunate mistake of Roddy's we don't get off 'til 9.15am. He really is terribly dreamy and forgetful. We have a very rough ride out and the last 8 miles we have to grind and bump over great boulders with the car swaying like a ship in rough seas. At such times it's hell to be sitting on the turret.

Take over from Harry and everything seems quiet despite the nearness of the enemy. They're so near we can count and report on the number of vehicles. We are on a horrible, bleak, open plateau with no features or bushes. I shall probably move but it's hard to know in which direction.

Tuesday 10th March 1942

Am now in direct touch with the enemy. Victor is the north patrol and all day long I get a stream of information chiefly about numbers and movements of enemy vehicles, where their guns are firing from and the smoke rising from Mechili Fort. He has also caught two Arabs. It is rather serious that unproved characters can move freely between our line and that of the opposition.

Wednesday 11th March 1942

Go off early to relieve Victor. Lovely cool, sunny day and within 2 miles arrive in a large area knee-deep in grass and flowers. The smell is heavenly – rather like the Sotterley bowling green on an early summer's day with Fred Delf going up and down on his mowing machine. I see larks courting, a bee-eater which we flush out is swooped on by a falcon, a marsh harrier, pharaoh's chicken [Egyptian vulture] and a large eagle.

On our way out we get a front row seat of the 12L relieving patrol being shelled. They have foolishly got up on to the skyline.

Desmond reports he is being chased by armoured cars so we try to join in. It turns out they are four Hun tanks with biggish guns. Two shell burst near us are surprising and unpleasant – we would not have been so keen to join if we knew what was coming! The Hun soon discover for themselves how filthy the going is and after dark they go back to their line where they remain, I hope.

Saturday 14th March 1942

Start the day early. Am woken at 1am to be shown flares all over the place combined with heavy gunning and bombing and an aircraft trying to perch on my aerial. I almost miss my breakfast as twelve enemy tanks debouch from Mechili and make a general nuisance of themselves all day.

It's really quite interesting back here, and by our new method, started last night, we are in direct touch with 12L Squadron HQ and the Free French guns, whose fire Hugh helps control. They knock out two but regret to say that both are recovered. Our little war goes on 'til 4pm. We have three cars out of action and at least two will have to be evacuated.

Sunday 15th March 1942

Daddy's birthday. He always paid tribute to his father by treating his birthday and the day of his death like a Sunday. Difficult in these days of rush.

Sergeant Cook paints my car to a camouflage design of mine. I am a great believer in camouflage and beat the division by several weeks as I insisted on digging in my HQ cars when stationary well before it became an order.

Monday 16th March 1942

Cold stormy day and our 'wars' start early again. Over thirty opposition tanks involved and we have another interesting day. I am kept pinned to the wireless and rather enjoy myself.

SQMS has sent up some goodies for us to divide up: eggs, potatoes, tinned veg, marmalade, jelly and jam. There's also a cake which we decide to divide into two and draw lots – Desmond and Freddie are the lucky ones.

Derek C has joined us from base. He is very young and green but I think will turn out alright. He goes out with Victor and as soon as he becomes proficient I intend on getting one officer back on leave as a regular system. This should allow me to get away in about 2 months, perhaps for Christopher's first birthday. Cara would love that.

Wednesday 18th March 1942
Victor sends in a South African pilot called Somerville who has walked 60 miles in after a forced landing. He's very young, very footsore and very appreciative of what we can do. We can only keep him one night and have to get him back on the morrow having sent word back to say he's safe and sound. His feet are in a terrible state and he's extremely tired but it's amazing to think that when his engine cut out he was able to manage a landing. He says there was not much left of his Hurricane.

Thursday 19th March 1942
Bob comes up to relieve us and we give him a good takeover, leaving later than planned. Harry gives the impression of trying to get away in time to see the first race but I hate leaving 'til everything is absolutely straight.

We have a bit of adventure on the way home with Hugh shooting a gazelle, our fitter bogging a truck for an hour and Ludford falling into a lake while trying to collect bath water for me.

We are all agog as the Msus party[7] is on. There will be much crying by those I am forced to leave behind as CO says three troops are sufficient. Operationally and sentimentally, though, I want to take all my troops.

Friday 20th March 1942
Ronnie agrees to my taking all my troops and we start preparations. Today is the first day of quite a big operation. Shrimp C is commanding a force so probably Nigel is on it too. Good luck to them all.

Saturday 21st March 1942
Seem to be kept on the run all day. At 1pm we send off Victor to recce an area where the RAF have reported a lot of vehicles driving with lights on at 2am in the middle of the Sahara! It turns out to be sunspots.

Call in at RHQ before bedding down to say farewell. Everything seems to be fixed and in order. Tomorrow we set off for one big adventure.

---

7. Raiding expedition behind enemy lines to recover tanks and other ordnance for parts or repair.

Sunday 22nd March 1942

Up well before light and before the sun comes up over the horizon we are well on our way. We are quite a big column and cover about 3 miles by 2 ½ miles when on the move.

See an old bull addax [large antelope, now critically endangered] in the early afternoon and turn it over to Roddy who slaughters it with a Tommy gun. Nothing to be proud of but we need the meat and the head will be of interest as they are rare beasts.

Find a great Mk 1 tank in the desert. At £1,000 per ton this alone makes our trip a paying concern (if we manage to get it back). The next find is a thermos bomb field right across our track, not so good. I decide against a night march. Blows a gale all night and it's icy cold. We all wear everything we've got.

Monday 23rd March 1942

Divide up at dawn into two parties. Hugh takes the second and bumps the enemy. Unfortunately he hasn't got sufficient guns otherwise might have had a nice shoot.

We find various things during the day – aircraft, guns, lorries and a truck with three bodies – not so nice. Later we bump the enemy on two sides so feel it's prudent to withdraw into the desert where we have manoeuvre room with all the thin skins.

It's unfortunate as we are under 5 miles from our objective but if you have a great eight-wheeled armoured car and its gun between you and your objective it's not so easy. We do a cast to the south-east and pick up some more stuff before dark. Everyone is more alert than I've ever seen them. We have an alarm at around 1.15am when a tyre that got heated during the day suddenly went up like a flare. There was panic and pandemonium for a few minutes! It's a good warning that if one of these tyres gets chucked into the back of a lorry it might easily cause a fire.

Very uncomfortable night but I don't mind as I had rather steeled myself to expect at least three nights without sleep.

Tuesday 24th March 1942

Have a filthy sandstorm. The heat soon becomes unbearable and the inside of the car feels red hot. We all take our turn at driving, mate-ing and sitting on the turret.

We don't quite make it back to HQ. It's not bad navigation having covered 230 miles of country with only a pocket compass and without a solitary landmark.

I feel very weary having not dared to relax a moment during the last 60 hours. Would give anything for one small can of cold beer tonight.

Wednesday 25th March 1942
Return to HQ directly after breakfast, very dirty and unshaven. Everyone thinks we are lucky not to be in the bag and to have got on as we have – the ordnance estimate is £12,000.

Thursday 26th March 1942
Sanderson sent down yesterday. He's not a good driver or a nice character; surly, bad tempered and a dirty footballer. He's a low type and not suitable as a squadron leader's driver. He wants to stay up in a fighting position but he quarrels with everyone which doesn't do when one lives cheek by jowl.

Letter from Ma dated 2nd March but she's not heard from me for ages. I am very sorry as I know she sets such store by our letters.

Walk down to watch some football in the afternoon. A great Wop bomber comes in very low, I think looking for a place to land. We gave it no option and a few accurate rounds from the Breda car sent it crashing into flames. The smoke was terrific and fresh cauliflowers were sent up one after the other by the bombs exploding. We found four bodies – one had blown out and the others were charred in the most nightmarish attitudes. All very gruesome.

Friday 27th March 1942
A Wop S79 bomber comes over looking for 'brother' but sadly I didn't have a gun. We then have Me110s over us all day, have never seen so many about before. Perhaps there was a big noise on board the bomber we shot down?

Saturday 28th March 1942
Weather definitely hotting up and flies are very bad here. We find a lot of waste food about, including a 7lb pot of jam, so one can understand why.

Victor spends the day looking for the Free French who were to meet him at a certain spot at 10am but he picks them up miles away 5 hours later. Hope they won't continue like this with me!

Tuesday 31st March 1942
The Free French Colonel de Rue and Le Commandant Amiel come round to visit me. They are mad keen and exceptionally charming. I'm sure with a little encouragement we'll get a lot out of them. The chief thing is that they have guns and we won't have to run away every time we see the Hun in a halfpenny truck.

An interesting point is that these French are all extremely pro-de Gaulle. They maintain that he is their sole leader and after the war is over if France is to resurrect itself that he must be their supreme dictator for a while. Civil war, they say, is their chief fear after the war and nothing but one strong leader can prevent this. They see de Gaulle as a truly great man.

Thursday 2nd April 1942

Hand over to 12L early and after the usual long period hanging about while troops go out and come in, leave at lunchtime. Say goodbye to Colonel de Rue and General Konig who seem really sad to be losing us.

Have a nasty sensation driving 6 miles along a ridge in full view of, and parallel to, the Hun line. Can see them all quite clearly and I must look like a tempting target to them.

Have a peaceful night with Victor although rather too close to Jerry to be comfortable! In armoured cars one must learn to get used to great wide open spaces and a lack of fence wire, trenches and mine fields between you and the opposition.

Sunday 5th April 1942

The echelon arrives in the afternoon and brings a real Easter present in the shape of two letters from Cara and some odds and ends. She has had a grand trip to Syria and great adventures returning, scrounging a lift in a troop train and got home 20 hours late. She must have been desperate as she thought I might have returned in her absence. Christopher has been running a temperature but is now better.

Monday 6th April 1942

Easter Racing today? As it happens we attend a real point-to-point.

We retire gently in the morning and get held up by the gunners going through us. A '110' then attacks us and keeps us occupied while some American Honey tanks, manned by Huns, charge my HQ.

We have to make a quick get-away. Lose the Breda car, petrol lorry and Lumper's car. We pick up all the crews except for Jennings and Emmet who have not been seen again. I hope they may yet appear.

The whole rout was accelerated by a good bit of shelling, some of it very accurate, and we were lucky to lose only three vehicles. It was all really rather exhilarating. It was useless to be frightened so one just drove on, bumping and swaying, watching the shell bursts. Actually one was very busy helping and cheering Sherratt, working the wireless and keeping an eye on all one's vehicles – plus Jerry.

Our drivers all did very well. They stopped where I did and everyone was out to help their neighbour rather than save his own skin. SSM Morgan deserves a special mention. In the evening I've never seen the chaps so cheerful and everyone has a funny story to recount.

Tuesday 7th April 1942

The morning starts quietly but deteriorates. We again retire, 13 miles this time. It is significant that there is no word on the BBC about Libya but suspect that a big push is expected at our main line and the spokesman is keeping quiet until the situation clarifies.

The Hun continues his harrying tactics from the air to support his advance. Wish to God that our RAF could become a cooperative force.

Thursday 9th April 1942
Morning starts with thick fog and everything is damp to make matters worse.

Get further forward and decide to do a dash up to the patrol's country. I'm sure one should do this occasionally. Find rather a lot going on and so don't stay long. Before lunch quite a good battle starts and eleven columns of black smoke are clearly visible from here. These are enemy vehicles destroyed by gunfire. Most satisfactory.

Friday 10th April 1942
Day starts ominously but by 11am the flap has died down. I don't see why we should retire from here but everyone looks at it as a certainty. In consequence I ensure everyone has all minefields marked and know the bearings and distances to go back. I don't think we are inquisitive enough and we never seem to go a yard beyond the demarcation line on the map. The Hun, on the other hand, is always putting feelers out here and there.

Saturday 11th April 1942
Walter returns from RHQ having got lost on the way in. He's just returned from a course in navigation!

Get a sitrep which reports that we are to be relieved tomorrow. I'd be sorry if it wasn't for Cara sitting in Cairo and I've got an awful feeling that we are probably going back to the 'wire'.

There's a considerable air battle above our heads. Some Stukas dive-bomb our gunners and are swooped on by SAAF. We go out to visit one wreck and it is unfortunate that the only one we visit should be a South African.

Orton has built himself a slit trench but when the bombs started falling he couldn't find it. We all find this extremely amusing!

Sunday 12th April 1942
Our spirits are low as we were expecting to be relived today but not a word from RHQ. We are in a rotten position, constantly in touch with the enemy and without the weaponry to hit back with. On the other hand if we were to have a heavy weapon we might be deployed in the role of tanks which would not suit us. This independent life in armoured cars suits us well; enough excitement and as little danger as war can allow. How different to Daddy's war – cold trenches, mud, immobility and strafe, strafe, strafe.

Listen to the news in the evening. The Japs are pushing on far into Burma and are now a direct threat to India. God knows how this will all end. If the Hun make a big push this way to join hands with the Japs I daren't think of the results – or what might happen to Cara. Perhaps we are being very short-sighted hanging on here and not going down to the safety and good climate of Kenya.

Monday 13th April 1942

We were expecting fireworks today but they never took place. Nigel called in at RHQ but of course we missed each other.

Tony Murray-Smith called in with his bevy of dummy tanks with skirts flapping like old ladies. They are very lifelike at a distance. How furious Rommel would be were he to round them up. I feel sure that a sense of humour is not amongst his attributes.

Have been reading Bagnold's *Libyan Sands*.[8] He paints a very graphic picture of the desert and so much of what he has done I have also done. He is now head of the Long Range Desert Patrols – very interesting work with a long waiting list of officers and men.

Tuesday 14th April 1942

I'm really getting rather worried over Roddy. He daily becomes more and more morose. He's terribly deaf now which I think is half the trouble but he's forgetful into the bargain. In peace, one doesn't mind but now it's all very awkward and such lapses may lead to grave consequences.

Saturday 18th April 1942

The padre makes us treat today as Easter and holds Holy Communion by my car. One's religious feelings are slightly shattered by the sight of the padre in crushed blackberry cream pyjamas setting up, placing his newly vacated bed as a communion rail!

Walter Scott is out every night getting star readings and working out our position. He's a very charming fellow and full of old fashioned ideas. Am trying to help him do a tour with LRDG, 6 months of real useful experience.

I've been determined for so long to have a *shamiana* [Indian ceremonial tent] and I've never been more grateful for the chance pick-up of some poles and an old tent. It has given me 12 x 10 foot of shade, especially important

---

8. Brigadier Ralph Bagnold FRS, OBE (1896–1990), the founder and first commander of the Long Range Desert Group and a pioneer in desert exploration. The LRDG was tasked with deep penetration behind enemy lines, covert reconnaissance and raiding parties.

during this enforced drought. My canvas basin stands in the corner but I won't touch a drop of it until sunset, not even a soft one. In the evening I get through a large mug of whisky and water and then two of lime juice and water.

Sunday 19th April 1942
The news seems to have undergone a change lately. It really looks as if the Hun was beginning to worry over the opening of a second front. Our policy is now obviously to show our determination to crush Germany before dealing with Japan. It's a toss-up whether they can keep going all out at Malta long enough to starve us out.[9] That is their only hope – if they give in now all that effort will have been wasted.

Monday 20th April 1942
All spend a quiet day under my makeshift tent. We're disturbed only by a Kittyhawk [Curtiss P-40 Warhawk, American single-seater fighter plane] tumbling out of the sky with a crash, and long after the pilot comes floating down on a parachute. Poor devil had engine trouble but is fine.

Tuesday 21st April 1942
We move to Mersa Luch, 84 miles of the worst going in Africa. We're close to the sea and hidden amongst the sand dunes.

We are to sit here but the men can go in to Cairo for leave. The only sop is that the 11th have gone to Persia so are unlikely to see Cairo at all again this war. It might so easily have been us which would have left Cara in a hopeless situation. As it is I am still considering whether her position now isn't rather tricky.

Friday 24th April 1942
In the morning we see a convoy bound for Tobruk heavily escorted by cruiser, destroyers and an air defence umbrella. May they arrive and discharge safely.

Have to take Trooper Duncan up before the commanding officer. He's a real plausible rogue who deserves all he gets. He generally just keeps within the law but when away from the regiment goes out of his way to spoil our good name.

Walk along the beach with Walter in the afternoon. It's bliss to walk on unmarked sand with no wheel tracks or footprints. The light and colours are

---

9. Malta was a key base in the Mediterranean for the Allies; Churchill described it as an 'unsinkable aircraft carrier'. The besieged island was one of the most intensively bombed areas in the war, subjected to over 3,000 raids during a two-year blockade.

wonderful. We walk barefoot and hatless and return with a great appetite for dinner.

We have a hysterical dinner party and Walter becomes devilishly silly trying to trip up Geoffrey with petrol cans everywhere he goes. We end up in almost hysterical giggles! Poor old Quart gets stinking and passes out soon after the end of the meal. My subalterns carry him out feet first to cool off and after a short while [he] is found to have disappeared!

Tuesday 28th April 1942

Walk around the lagoon with Jumbo and find a lovely wild *wadi* with the most marvellous wild birds. We have a great stalk so as to get up to some waders and get close enough to watch some snipe feeding. We see a peregrine stir up every bird on the lagoon, a harrier with young, a pair of golden oriole and a black-headed wagtail which is equally brilliant. I haven't enjoyed an afternoon as much in a long time.

See the emptied convoy returning from Tobruk – extremely satisfying to see the ships intact after all the banging and roaring of guns and bombs that welcomed their arrival.

Thursday 30th April 1942

By 11am the day can only be described as having become impossible. A hot, dry wind raises all the dust in the desert meaning the sun is not visible all day. The wind leaves the day as dry as a bag of flour and one feels all the drink in Cairo would leave little impression.

HRH Duke of Gloucester has kicked up a fuss and insisted he must visit us. The visit is shortened to tea and then tea is shortened to a meet up on the main road with a tent. Eventually all is cancelled by the weather. Lucky he did not turn up as the best we could produce was hot lemonade and stale biscuits!

Poor Tony P is in a terrible state as he got lost this morning and would have missed HRH if he'd turned up. A lifetime's chance of meeting royalty when CO! He would not admit to anything afterwards but Jack got the story out of Harry.

Friday 1st May 1942

Thankfully it's a finer day as we have General Ritchie,[10] our army commander, coming to lunch. Neil Ritchie behaves charmingly and naturally. A remark worth recording is that the Hun has lost world air superiority. He's also very 'pro-Royals' and gave us a good pat on the back.

---

10. General Sir Neil Ritchie GBE, KCB, DSO, MC, KStJ (1897–1983) commanded the British Eighth Army, November 1941 to June 1942.

Saturday 2nd May 1942

Get mail from Ma. Granny [Hon Mabel Addington, 1853–1942] has died, poor old dear. One of the greatest and kindest and bravest characters this generation will ever know. We were all very genuinely devoted to her.

Sunday 3rd May 1942

I think this is the first royal visit since George V and Mary in 1926! HRH Duke of Gloucester arrives to inspect the whole regiment and is presented to all the officers. The squadron turnout is extremely good considering the means at our disposal for cleaning up. The men fully appreciate the honour and at the end give him a good cheer.

Tuesday 5th May 1942

Squadron leaders' conference. Promotions, decorations and awards to be put in. Would like recognition for each troop leader but can't select one in particular as all good. Put up SSM Morgan for a Mention. He's done excellent work since I've been up, full of calm courage and intelligence above the average.

Wednesday 6th May 1942

Start for Cairo on leave. Lunch at Sidi Barrani and spend the night at Dabaa.

Thursday 7th May 1942

Get off at 6.45am and make Cairo for lunchtime. Meet Cara in the little blue car at the Shell Petrol Corner. Intense excitement!

Have a long bath, shave and shampoo. Lunch at about 2.30pm then we go out to get my hair cut. We then go to Shepheard's where we form the usual Royals group. There is a mass of people around, lots one knows and lots of new faces.

Friday 8th May 1942

Get up very late to a civilised breakfast. The sight of a nice white table cloth, clean cups and neatly laid cutlery is breakfast in itself.

Dine at Shepheard's. The new drink hours are a curse – no ordering after 10pm and all drinks finished by 10.30pm. The only ones who mind are the ones in from the desert – anyone living here is either too blasé to go out or has their own private supply.

Sunday 10th May 1942

In the afternoon we take Christopher to the zoo. He takes the most incredible interest in animals. His sight is very good and is seemingly fascinated by the animals and birds. Very satisfactory.

Tuesday 12th May 1942
Christopher's first birthday.

It's a very important occasion and a very happy day for Cara. We have a lot to be thankful for; Cara, so far, has been spared the horrors of war, is near me, in a nice home with a perfect nanny, faithful servants and perhaps the greatest blessing of all, a host of real friends.

Christopher really is the whole world to her and is worthy of her. He's not very big but is strong and of great vitality with the most cheerful face one could wish for. All other children look stodgy and expressionless beside him.

Friday 15th May 1942
Despite being our last day we don't spoil it by being miserable – we're far too old campaigners for that.

Dash out to do some last minute shopping – cases of beer, oranges, grapefruit etc. as CT says there's so much room in the car. Wait for CT 'til 11.30am then start ringing round after him. Eventually find him at the bar in Shepheard's quite unable to explain anything. I go home for lunch in disgust and order him to ring me when he's sobered up.

The sod then turns up with two cars both laden with black beret soldiery and no room for anything at all, even kit. Am I angry?! He really is one of the worst, dumbest staff officers one could ever meet.

Eventually make Amriya where we stay the night.

Saturday 16th May 1942
We're all bitten to hell by sand flies all night long.

Make Capuzzo and there seems to be a bit of a flap on. The Hun has moved one of his Panzer divisions down on to our southern flank. Hope they like the sand down there!

See Nigel on the road going the opposite way in a truck but can't catch him.

Sunday 17th May 1942
Spend a quiet and comfortable night in a tent with two others. Water very scarce indeed and we shave, wash and clean our teeth with one small mug full each.

Eventually get back to our old seaside resort at 5pm. There is absolute chaos in the camp as we have had to find two composite squadrons to help the flap now in progress. Some say it's a German flap, others that Winnie has ordered it so that we can use Benghazi and other landing grounds to relieve Malta.

Monday 18th May 1942
I head off to take over the squadron. We take two trucks and have quite an interesting drive to Bin el Gobi past the scene of some very heavy tank fighting.

Arrive just in time for supper. Ludford has erected a fine shelter which becomes a mess tent after we've eaten. There's a new moon that goes down very red and a little bombing to the north but otherwise all is very still.

Tuesday 19th May 1942
Take over from Roddy. Afraid he hasn't done much except take my servant and make himself very comfortable.

The betting is 11-4 on the Huns attacking before the end of the month. I feel it's so obvious that either our intelligence has shown its first signs of intelligence or it's a 'blind' working in conjunction with some other big operation, possible an attack on Syria.

Wednesday 20th May 1942
Wake up early to find a jerboa and his wife in my tent. At first they are very timid but as the bustle around the tent increases so they grow in confidence and come in and out fearlessly.

We move further south, taking the jerboas, Mr and Mrs Hunca Munca, in a cake tin.

Thursday 21st May 1942
The betting is now 3-1 on an attack but I don't think it can be successful as we seem fairly strong here. It's the first time that the Hun will try his strength against a prepared British position and I feel either he doesn't know our strength or else he's synchronising this with some other big move. I also feel convinced our air force has been saving up something pretty brutal.

Read out a pretty strong letter from the brigadier calling to all and sundry to rise up and smite the enemy that is at our gate.

Saturday 23rd May 1942
A very hot day and there's a considerable flap on. We have to stand to at 5am but it comes to nought.

Have an awful sweaty afternoon in my lean-to marking maps and preparing codes. At about 6pm a wall of dust slowly approaches us from the north. It's as thick as pea soup and object after object is swallowed up by it. The air remains perfectly still 'til it's only 20 foot away and then we are plunged into a tornado. I luckily have collected up all the map books and papers we had on the table but we have a damn struggle to keep our tent from being blown away.

Sunday 24th May 1942
Move up to 'battle' position. Not very exciting really as it's miles behind the line.

We go down to the El Adem escarpment. It's a very precipitous road, obviously made by the Hun. The road creeps down the side of a great gorge. All rather impressive.

Brigade have a hold-up so we sit alone upfront. I am now convinced that this cannot be a suitable role for us and am determined to see the brigade in the morning.

Monday 25th May 1942
Day dawns as a great covey of our bombers sweeps over us on their way to deal out death. Very inspiring and a good bolster to morale. Our chaps have not seen us in the air for a long time.

Go off at 8.30am to see brigade and win my point.

In the evening I manage to find Nigel. His HQ is just the other side of the track from me, 800 foot at most! He sups with me. Looks very well and happy.

Tuesday 26th May 1942
There has been fairly intense bombing all night and it continues after daylight. Don't know if this is a prelude to an attack or the opposition has got windy and hopes to disturb and dislocate communications.

Wednesday 27th May 1942
The mornings are still cold and dewy and getting up at 5.30am is not pleasant. At about 8am we get the first warning of enemy movements. After a quick shift around of cars and crews we go off to the south to take up the line. The day becomes a dreary scurry to avoid being shot or captured.

Corps and division HQ are overrun while still in bed and great flocks of three-tonners swan around like sheep being chased by a dog. We see them surrendering in their hundreds and our famous Grant tanks falling to the enemy in the rout.

We get down one escarpment where no car ever built could be thought capable of descending. A Hun tank follows us and goes arse over tip, rolling the whole way down.

We rejoin the regiment at 10.30pm after a long trek over some awful ground. Everyone is dead beat but I believe the situation is not as bad as thought. I hate to think of my little Cara as she will now have days of anxiety. I wish I was single at moments like this – I'm not worth all the worry she will be going through.

Thursday 28th May 1942

Day dawns and I send out patrols before daylight. Shave in record time and cast aside my natural modesty and squat about 50 yards from the squadron!

We sit around doing nothing until the afternoon when we move 4 miles and see quite a lot of activity. In the late afternoon another armoured brigade and motor brigade come through in battle formation to take on the Hun's 90 Light Division. We later learnt the Hun fled and we only managed to hit their tail.

Freddie collected two Hun prisoners. We also arrest a very unpleasant officer on the grounds of being fifth column. He turns out to be a 12L MO named Patton. As he had been in the Wop air force in Spain I feel we were justified.

Have a magnificent view of seventeen Stukas diving on the desert – thankfully just missing Corporal Jones. There has been a lot of Hun ammo wasted on the regiment.

Friday 29th May 1942

Our air force seems to be going all out. There is not a minute during the day during which one does not see or hear our planes.

Hear that Sergeant Donahue was killed by bombing yesterday and a nice mess waiter, Pollington, shot by ground strafers. We have the unpleasant task of burying several enemy corpses. It's usually hard to obtain identity but most Hun seem to carry a mass of photographs which may be of value to Intelligence.

Pick up three British officers who have escaped from the Hun. Nice chaps.

Saturday 30th May 1942

Move up again to the front as my troops are given a most awful job, really an RTR job. We find a proper battle raging and we aren't able to get in nohow. I'm not sorry. In these cars it is quite bad enough hanging around the edge.

Move in the evening and this time end up in what we come to term Stuka Valley. Have a rotten night as Jerry is doing indiscriminate bombing. I move the squadron up off the track after dark which has possibly saved some casualties.

We see the 110s against the moon or on occasion very low against the sky and only hope their aim is bad. The battle has turned very much against them and they are becoming rather desperate.

Sunday 31st May 1942

A great basket of grapefruit suddenly appears from Cara. How she gets these things to me I can't think – she's marvellous. As marvellous is the honesty of all the people who handle the open basket and I don't believe anyone removes one.

Leaguer in a most dangerous place right out in front. The Hun is just as windy and spends the night popping off bangers and fireworks of all sorts.

Monday 1st June 1942

Nigel appears driving across the desert just as we are eating lunch. He is taking some ammo out to the guns. We give him a drink and some grapefruit. The boy looks well and happy but I don't envy their time in the Box.[11] They are a target for every gun and plane in North Africa.

I take the squadron back for the night to north-east of the Box. I felt rather insecure the night before and I think the men realised it. I want them fresh and fit in case we get the chance of a dash across to the coast to the south of Benghazi.

Tuesday 2nd June 1942

A sandstorm of great severity interferes with everything all day and sleepy flies try to take refuge behind my ears and in my moustache. As soon as it gets cool our tanks go in but not very successfully. I should think everyone's morale is low after a day like this.

I've discovered that I only really sleep soundly for 2 hours and after that am semi-conscious. I can now happily go through a full day with no more than a couple of hour's heavy sleep.

Wednesday 3rd June 1942

We find an enormous Stuka bomb just beside our leaguer. Our tame sapper, Bunny Henwood, is mad keen to touch it off. It goes off with a terrific bang and showers of shit fall all around us even though we are 200 yards away, leaving a great crater 6 foot deep and 15 foot across.

Have an abortive hunt for divisional HQ in the evening where I am urgently required. Get back very late, very cross and very tired. I subsequently learnt that the general failed to find it himself 'til 2am – and only then using fireworks.

Speak rather candidly to Roddy over his lack of cooperation and manner of passive resistance. I think his nerves are partly the trouble.

---

11. Knightsbridge Box was a strategic strongpoint 16 miles west of Tobruk designed for all-round defence with dug-in infantry manning anti-tank guns. It was so called because it was chiefly held by the Guards regiments.

Friday 5th June 1942

Our big attack starts at 3am. It starts me out of bed as I have no knowledge that it was coming off. Our gunners put up a long, continuous thunder and the sky is bright with flashes and tracers.

At dawn I am summoned to HQ and the plan is divulged. In the event of our exploiting the attack, A Squadron is to lead the field. It may be very exciting and it is certainly 'flirting with the bag'.

By 3pm it is obvious that the Hun has started a game to which we must conform before we can make him play ball with us. At sunset he comes forward. He keeps us on tenterhooks all night as he has pushed his tanks right forward in small parties right into our midst.

Saturday 6th June 1942

The night is brightened up by fireworks and I'm up most of the night as I get the guard to wake me for any unusual activity.

We watch our echelons get a nasty turn from a big tank formation. Later they turn and give us a few shots so we pop over the edge of the lower escarpment. They overrun a small box and pray God that Knightsbridge holds out. Nigel is in there.

The situation clears up at noon and we have personally benefited by finding a much snugger, quieter campsite. We are well protected by a minefield and will get a good view of any enemy movement towards us. The greatest asset of all is an unlimited supply of water as the attendant authorities have fled from the pipehead leaving us in full possession.

Sunday 7th June 1942

Rise at 6am after the longest sleep I've had since this battle began. The morning is looking quiet so have an all over wash and change. Ludford manages to wash some of my clothes. He's a good man and turns his hand to anything. He is always cheerful but his one dread is that I'll send him back to B3 when things are happening.

Bob comes through us to take position on our right. Roddy makes a bog of orders and nearly causes a shemozzle. Luckily we discover in time and manage to save the situation. He's never tried to learn anything of a military matter (his own profession) and is more ignorant than a civilian in many respects. One day I'll be asked if I can recommend him for a squadron and it will cause a proper upset when I say 'no'.

Monday 8th June 1942

Still in our cosy spot. We get closely observed from the air and have Stukas twice in the neighbourhood but they don't touch us. We have a shoot as they are returning.

The only complaint one gets out here is a burnt nose. It never seems to get properly weathered but continually burns and peels then one picks it and it bleeds; the reason is usually one's peak shadows the nose but these berets give no protection.

Wednesday 10th June 1942
Wedding anniversary. Had hoped to be in the Delta for today but luckily had arranged for Ahmed to put a bunch of flowers on the table at breakfast with a note for 'my lady' in the event of my absence. That should cheer the old girl up as she must be going through a rotten time.

Thursday 11th June 1942
In the afternoon we hear the Hun has started an advance in the south. We hear rumours that Hacheim has fallen. If this is so then he has been very quick in pushing forward again.

As I started writing this, twenty-seven large Junkers came over and I looked up to see a shower of bombs coming down. There was no time to do anything so Gallagher and I sat at the bottom of the car. We had three near misses and got covered by dust.

Sergeant Peach is most unlucky and gets an almost direct hit. He dies in a few minutes. Out of eighty-odd men, fate has selected one of the best and nicest of our NCOs. He was Hugh's sergeant and a real friend of his.

Thank heaven I am not afraid. I am sure it is a thing that is either born in one or is without. I can watch shelling or see bombs falling without turning a hair. In this case I merely think to myself how very lucky I'm not being killed on my wedding anniversary and how very foolish Roddy and Desmond look with their noses pressed hard into the ground!

Friday 12th June 1942
The Hun starts his day with a most determined continuation to his advance.

Ludford brings in two little desert hedge-pigs. They are far nicer than our English variety with great big ears and a wriggly nose. They are not a bit shy and curl up when you pick them up but soon uncurl and wriggle around. One goes off – alas he's a cripple with only three legs – but the other settles herself in under a wheel next to us. She reminds me of Linda because every time I move she opens up one little eye to see what I'm up to.

We withdraw towards Tobruk in the afternoon. It's terribly depressing and one feels that, though we knew the Hun was stronger, our hearts contained more courage. Now it seems that we are not so fit and have exhausted ourselves earlier than the opposition. Well, all is by no means lost and should we get beat (tactically), the enemy will not be in a position to take great

advantage of it. I can picture myself in Tobruk for the summer and the line
back again on the wire.

Saturday 13th June 1942
Quiet night. The Hun makes the desert like Folkestone Front when he's
done a lot of movement by day. He sends up every type and hue of Very
light. Why we don't go in and rattle his leaguers I can't think. The strong
northerly wind starts blowing up sand at 11am which I think may be in our
favour. The main battle still rages around Knightsbridge – let's hope old
Nigel is alright.

At supper time some enemy tanks clamber down the escarpment where
we had blown a pass. They nearly get in amongst us and I have a very
undignified exit with my clutch of soft skinned vehicles. The severest blow
is that of the loss of our supper.

Go over to RHQ after dark who also had a scrambled exit. See Ronnie and
Jack but neither in any form whatsoever. In fact they are both unplayable.

Sunday 14th June 1942
Fierce fighting continues all day. The Hun take advantage of the passage
down the escarpment and we are forced to withdraw from the Knightsbridge
position. The Guards come out of it in the most orderly manner.

Thomas Dykes and Ronald Orr-Ewing get overrun on the Rigel Ridge
and some Scots Guards prisoners are seen to be made to march in front of
enemy tanks to cover their further advance. Briggs gives his guns the only
possible order and I hope one day will get the chance to do the same to them.

Hitler has given out that Free French prisoners are to be treated as
irregulars. De Gaulle replied that he'll treat an equal number of Hun
prisoners in the same manner.

We get slightly involved in the Acroma battle and eventually withdraw to
the Tobruk lodge gates. After dark we get orders to lead division right back
beyond the frontier. This is soon changed to the El Adem front. We march
all night in the most orderly withdrawal one could imagine. Victor gets a
bomb nearly on him at sunset and later goes up on a mine. He is shaken but
ok. Hepworth had his teeth blown out and Machin has bad foot injuries.

Monday 15th June 1942
Breakfast by the old Wop PoW cage. There are crowds of people everywhere
and our air force are prominent once again. Everyone showing signs of great
strain after 20 days of fighting but no signs that this is a RETREAT.

To me, it's heaven to be getting out into open country once again. I've
had an awful caged feeling behind minefields and walled in by the sea and

Tobruk. Tobruk, I am sure, remains impregnable and there is no reason they should cut the main road. We can still harass from the south-east. Their armour must be getting very worn while ours should be strengthened soon. Our tank losses must have been very heavy.

Sherratt rejoins me and tomorrow will be my driver again. I've now got Partington as my spare operator and consider my team absolutely first class.

Tuesday 16th June 1942
Woken with fresh orders at 2am and 5am which ends what was meant to be a good night's sleep.

Derek and Desmond go off and contact enemy at once. We get a couple of mystery shells – someone evidently didn't like the look of us! We now only have three armoured cars and five thin skins left. Roddy has tied a German Breda gun on to his car.

Get mixed up in a tank battle at sunset and lose my supper once again. Regiment orders us to move back by 8 miles so we have a trek in the dark. Desmond puts a car down a slit trench and breaks the two front springs.

See a Messerschmitt shot down at very close range. It comes in at very low range, ground-strafing, when it suddenly banks to one side and hits a wing on the ground. It skids about 50 yards and then disappears in flame and a pall of black smoke.

All day the RAF has kept up a continuous local strafe with good effect. See at least nineteen vehicles burnt out and twenty made useless.

Wednesday 17th June 1942
Come into leaguer with RHQ. At last we've come into some good going and great wide open spaces. Jerry is now gently shepherding us back towards the frontier – perhaps we have a little surprise waiting for him there.

We spend a quiet day but always on short notice for another move. The move comes just before dark and we cruise back 14 miles in comfort.

Thursday 18th June 1942
Waterloo Day. I wish we had some Waterloo troop stock here now. We think really the tank men are the same stout-hearted lot but the officers are not so good and General Messervy[12] is paralytic. Our only ray of sunshine is

---

12. General Sir Frank Messervy KCSI, KBE, CB, DSO & Bar (1893–1974), the only British Indian Army officer to command a division during the war. He was captured on 27 May 1942 but removed all insignia and managed to bluff the Germans into believing he was a batman, escaping the following day. He seemed to know little about tanks and was not considered a great success in commanding armoured divisions.

Herbert Lumsden[13] who is now resting and should join soon. We will have fresh men and vehicles against tired Hun who will have had a long march with little maintenance.

Callum Renton[14] is to our south with a very fine mortar brigade and he's a proper fighter. One of his night patrols came in to report they'd raided a leaguer and set fire to a petrol lorry.

'What did you do then? said Renton.

'Came home', said the satisfied Platoon Commander.

'Damn fool!' says Renton. 'Why didn't you stay on to kill the men putting out the fire?'

Saturday 20th June 1942

Move south to a prominent well. Find we have anticipated regimental orders as they come in half an hour later adjusting the line. This saves us another move.

Flies here are awful. The well is such a landmark that thousands of parties must have spent the night here and such places become very unsanitary.

Derek gets chased again by four tanks. We have him on the wireless and have a good laugh. He does very well and does not lose sight of them. The Breda keeps up a good rate of fire and he comes home with a bad wheel wobble.

Sunday 21st June 1942

Arrange to move after breakfast, partly because of flies and partly to be better placed in relation to my patrols. Our departure is hastened by the approach of six tanks!

The day turns out to be even hotter than Friday and I spend the afternoon stripped to my waist under my umbrella. In the worst of the heat, three lorries turn up with the startling and awful news that Tobruk unconditionally surrendered at 10am. This is a truly terrible blow and may lead to serious consequences. The Guards Brigade is in there and I can't believe they'd have surrendered. Poor old Nigel – he's certainly seen more high spots in this war than his regular brothers.

---

13. Lieutenant General Herbert Lumsden CB, DSO & Bar, MC (1897–1945). Praised for his command of his regiment in the retreat to Dunkirk, Lumsden rose through the ranks quickly until a disagreement with Montgomery regarding tactics in October 1942 resulted in his dismissal. He was sent to the Pacific as Churchill's special military representative to the US Army and killed by a Japanese kamikaze plane in January 1945, becoming the most senior British Army combat casualty of the war.

14. Major General James Renton CB, DSO, OBE (1898–1972). He lost an arm leading the Rifle Brigade at the Battle of Sidi Saleh in 1941.

Monday 22nd June 1942

Move back into the regimental reserve. Go in to see Ronnie. They are all very upset by this Tobruk tragedy and say it's definitely a balls-up. Frank Messervy has had the sack and Callum Renton now has the division.

Tuesday 23rd June 1942

We wake to find a large German column has arrived in the night and leaguered close beside us. We have to hop it quick and go over the wire back into Egypt once more. Trek back further in the late afternoon and am much depressed by the sight of large dumps being blown up as far back as Hamra. There is a great pall of smoke across the sky and the RE must be having the time of their lives with unlimited explosives.

The news is far from cheery; an unsatisfactory statement on Libya by Auchinleck, our losses in the Mediterranean in the middle of the month and a critical moment reached at Sevastopol.

Harry put up a grand show today. Routed three tanks, took some prisoners, destroyed eight vehicles and sent in some valuable information. Alas, tonight he has lost touch with two patrols and we fear they are prisoners.

Wednesday 24th June 1942

One of the hottest and longest days I can remember. Our short spell of 'reserve' is over and we take the field again in place of B Squadron.

The Hun seems to travel at night or in the cool of the early morning. We fight madly and have to to use the heat of the day or depth of night for retiring and reorganising. Everyone is getting heartily sick of this and I'm sure we'd all like to go in and have a real crack rather than this unspirited withdrawal. At best we can only say we have taken a polite interest in German movements!

Thursday 25th June 1942

We wake once again under bad conditions. A German column gets a flying start at us and is 5 miles ahead by the time light breaks. We just avoid getting caught up in a scrap or being taken prisoners and have a long, fast trek back.

It's very exciting as there's a lot of enemy about and one has to make big decisions very quickly; fire, or run or lie low. It gives one a very queer feeling that at any moment one might be popped in the bag. We put a Hun officer in the bag, he might have been rather a nice fellow if of any other nationality.

We get a new line just before dark as the Hun had got round our flank where the 13L had meant to be. The 13L just disappeared like smoke and then we were promised the KDGs but they failed to appear at all. We are rather left sitting in enemy territory so put on an officer's guard – we each do two one-hour watches.

End the day very badly. Freddie breaks down while under enemy fire and has to be towed out. Then all my batteries run flat and luckily Bob is near so tag on to him. We are also very short of petrol, a new sensation for me as we've always been so well supplied previously.

Friday 26th June 1942

Come into reserve at noon. Have a third bloody night, moving, listening and watching flares and lights of all sorts. I am really quite inured now to the fact that any night now we may get shot up by a friend or foe and put in the bag.

Herbert Lumsden looks in on his return with a reformed division. There are big changes happening – Auchinleck is taking over the Eighth Army, Herbert to have command of all armour, Richards at last got the sack and could only say, 'Oh, I thought I was doing so well?', Fisher from 12L to get the brigade, George to command 12L as Peter Burn in the bag, Tony P to command KDGs and Harry goes up to 2i/c. This will leave me as senior squadron leader.

It's a poor time for a big change around. There's no doubt we are just starting the last chukka [period of a polo game] but are several goals down. We'll only turn this around if we can get into extra time but that means we've got to do all the scoring now.

Saturday 27th June 1942

Have one of the most peaceful nights for over a month. However the peaceful morning is soon shattered by a hot engagement not very far from us. We have front row seats but eventually have to retire. The attack on Matruh seems to have begun and the Hun suddenly realise that the time factor is important to them.

Sunday 28th June 1942

Peaceful night. Start off back after breakfast and suddenly find we are being hunted. We have an awful scurry over awful country. Desmond stays in the rear and does a bit of gunning. We do 24 miles in near record time and everyone and every vehicle completes the course. En route we set fire to a great many abandoned vehicles that had been left to the Hun. Apparently they would be very short of lorries and petrol if it were not for kind friends leaving things behind. In certain cases the culprits should be court-martialled.

Get a parcel and letter from Cara. She doesn't seem to worry much about the situation up here but of course her letter is written before Tobruk fell.

Monday 29th June 1942

Poor old Nigel's birthday. I am sure he's very much in Mummy's thoughts but feel sure she would be much more worried if she knew the facts. I just hope that he is alright.

Have a bad day. It starts with being chased by an eight-wheeler. He comes out of the early morning mist and everyone in the place panics but manages to get away. We then collect two three-tonners, two large charging engines, a very smart saloon and a 25-pounder with full ammo!

Go back some way for the night. Morgan goes to collect the rations etc then runs into a German column and gets away only with the men and one car. We are completely out of touch with anybody but can only surmise that RHQ bumped into the same column.

Tuesday 30th June 1942

Gain touch with RHQ but have at least one Panzer division between us and home.

Eventually collect my patrols and Morgan who does well in finding his way back and then we have to decide how to get home. The problem soon resolves itself as Brigadier Hugo Garmoyle, who has risen very quickly, appears. He has Charles Wood with him and all very pleasant. We join together but soon run into the Hun in the mist. We take quite a lot of prisoners and lorries and my patrols prove very useful to the tanks.

Start a night march but owing to steep escarpments and bad going we give it up.

Wednesday 1st July 1942 [The First Battle of El Alamein 1–27 July 1942]

Get in 2 hour's good sleep then hang about for hours in the cold northerly wind. Move off at 5.45am but instead of going north then east we turn about and go south then east. The idea being to get behind the Alamein line which we hope is held in strength and from there as a base to strike hard and push him back. It's one of the biggest gambles in our history in letting the Hun get so close to the Delta but he is now fully extended and we should be able to do a lot of damage to the much vaunted 21st Panzer Division before driving him back.

We trek round through weird countryside of deep *wadis* with steep-sided, flat-topped hills. Suddenly we find ourselves in the midst of the greatest army one could imagine. We are 'home'. Owing to the heat haze we have trouble finding our regimental HQ and while waiting to be re-diverted we sit on a ridge looking out on a great plain teaming with vehicles with a tank battle in progress. Our planes roar overhead and the gunfire raises fountains of dust with each burst.

We find everyone rather disconsolate as there is talk of falling back to another line. This is, of course, nonsense. We have fallen back and back because this is the first, last and only line between here and Kirkuk [Iraq] with both flanks blocked. If we can't hold and then defeat the Hun here then we must give up the Middle East.

The CO seems to think we've done well to get back. What pleases me most is that I've brought every man back and the only car we've lost is one that was on tow and needed heavy repairs.

Thursday 2nd July 1942

We rise after a wonderful night's rest. We have a great clean-up of ourselves and vehicles. Morale is being rapidly restored and as the day goes on the situation seems to improve as troops of all sorts come pouring in. I think we here are facing the main German thrust.

An Indian brigade left twenty-four 25-pounders and forty-eight 6-pounders complete for the Hun. Frank A went in with his regiment to help restore the situation but got killed. We lose yet another of our better young soldiers.

Friday 3rd July 1942

Set off to relieve B Squadron. The going is awful and our vehicles get constantly stuck in the sand, needing cars with four-wheel drive to pull them out. Thank heaven we did not have to do a retirement across this.

Take over a very bleak bit of desert. This area is a New Zealand stronghold, real tough types who are mad keen to have a crack at the Hun again.

Saturday 4th July 1942

This may have been the turning point in the battle. Yesterday the New Zealanders stripped Ariete of all its guns and brought in a lot of prisoners. Our armoured division destroyed nineteen tanks and the RAF claimed over thirty enemy aircraft. The Hun has 240 miles to bring supplies and reinforcements to our 50 miles.

Today we waded into a leaguer and executed great damage with the artillery. By the evening we had 800 Hun with their hands up. We move 9 miles forward in the evening with optimism.

Sunday 5th July 1942

In the late morning we get ordered back to reserve as we are taking up a new area and getting five new cars which means some reorganisation.

Jack gives me a note from Cara dated 1st July. She is off tomorrow for Johannesburg. My feelings are mixed. It's a great relief if things become strained again but an awful feeling that it may now be years before we meet again. She has got everything organised down to the last button, bless her: guns, furniture, finance, kit etc.

Monday 6th July 1942
Cara sails today. I write my first overseas letter to her since November 1939. It's been well worth her coming out. I've been quite the luckiest man in the regiment and everything seems to have gone just right for us.

Tuesday 7th July 1942
We return to the line. Hugh gets a Daimler. They really look as though they were designed as armoured cars and have a cracking good gun with which we'll be able to see off any German eight-wheeler.

Get another letter from Cara and gather that Nigel may be safe and sound in Alexandria. She has received a note from him which must have been written since Tobruk fell.

Operationally it's been one of the quietest days we've had in a long time but things will be brewing up. Rommel can't keep a large force doing nothing at the end of 240 miles of precarious line of command.

Wednesday 8th July 1942
Am summoned to RHQ after dark and told to join Briggs [Major General Raymond Briggs CB, DSO, 1895–1985] who now has a composite brigade. We are going forward.

It's a comforting and satisfying experience lying in bed before going to sleep, or if one wakes during the night, to hear our bombers going over. One can hear the flashes and feel the rumble as they deliver their cargoes on Rommel's doorstep. It's so much better than that miserable period when our air seemed non-existent and Arsehole Charlie used to swan around making the nights horrible.

Thursday 9th July 1942
Desmond and I swan forth to join Briggs. He's a real charmer and when I say au revoir in the evening he says with a smile, 'Oh you'll come back. You all come back to me squadron-by-squadron and each of you is just as delightful as the last.' With most people one would confer that to be balls but not with Briggs.

Saturday 11th July 1942
We get bombed after lunch with one casualty. The raid seems more designed to ruin the afternoon siesta than anything else and the bomb that might have done most damage didn't explode. It landed by the tail of one of our cars,

bounced underneath knocking the axle out of position. Later the occupants return with bandaged hands (cuts received in scrambling out!) and drive the car off the bomb which is left as a memorial.

Ronnie is told he has got a DSO. A frightfully good show and richly deserved. I wish Jack could have got an MC but feel sure that will come.

Monday 13th July 1942
Receive a bunch of mail – four airgraphs and three postcards. Mummy seems fairly happy – the garden and summer take her mind off things but naturally she worries terribly about all of us.

We go up in the afternoon to relieve C Squadron, now commanded by William. He looks too frightful in a great topee and Indian army blue shirt. Blast him, he's the blackhead in the otherwise clear complexion of the regiment.

Tuesday 14th July 1942
Visit the front in the evening. The whole vast rolling desert is covered with vehicles or remains of vehicles, tanks, guns, lorries, trucks and armoured cars.

At dark we join up with Brigadier Fisher who used to be 12L. He's very friendly and we have a lot in common. Trevor Moorhouse is also there. I last saw him 13 years ago when he and I fought over Diana. They're now separated.

Thursday 16th July 1942
Return at sunset to our leaguer and Derek brings a 12L patrol back for the night. It is officered by an absolute boy who admits to only being out here for a month. It's absurd that a lad like that should be entrusted to produce intelligence for the Eighth Army. We don't think anyone is capable of doing this accurately in less than 3 months and for some time thereafter his word is taken with a degree of suspicion. It is no wonder our information is valued up here.

Friday 17th July 1942
Cara's birthday, bless her.

Another long day at battle HQ. We seem to be doing quite well but things are slow and one is never quite sure what Rommel keeps up his sleeve.

Harry pops in dressed up as the CO of 4 CLY and in great form. Also see Tubby Cooper who is getting command of the Gloucester Yeomanry, a very good appointment. It appears that these appointments are being made by senior officers in the field who know what they are doing without favour or affection. It's refreshing after old MS Fogey who works by paper and the whisperings of friends over late night drinks.

Saturday 18th July 1942

Brian relieves us 'after breakfast' which in his mind means 'before lunch'. He seems very much more cheerful again.

Harry comes in to brigade HQ as he is taking over from the Greys who seem to have had unnecessary casualties and are being taken out of the line 'til they are more experienced.

Sunday 19th July 1942

Get up very late indeed but don't suspect it does anyone any harm. Have a long day of office work, interviewing people and reorganising. There seems to be no end of reorganisation required as each casualty or change generally involves three or four others as in a crossword puzzle. This is all because of our lack of trained reserves.

I've got these ruddy boils on my neck again. They are not serious, only unpleasant, and it's very hard to stop oneself from picking them.

Go to RHQ after dark and sit talking 'til late. Desmond and Jack are a more united pair of brothers than any I know. I think there's a certain amount of big-brother-worship from Desmond's side but he's no ordinary character either.

Monday 20th July 1942

The morning starts with a fighter coming in low and fast. It's a nasty feeling to be woken up by apparent sudden death screaming down at one at 400mph. However, all is well.

Philip Fielden rejoins us. He has been in hospital with severe burns. His car got hit by a Messerschmitt when Dunn got killed.

Tuesday 21st July 1942

Out of the line to relieve C Squadron.

John Curry has taken over the brigade as nice Brigadier Briggs got wounded yesterday along with Gott and Herbert.

Wednesday 22nd July 1942

We are supposed to have started an attack during the night and we've all been saying, 'Little beginnings have great endings', but as the day wore on it became less and less like developing. Admittedly we knock out over fifteen tanks but we make little progress and our own toll from mines is pretty severe. I lose two cars, Hugh's and Derek's, but thankfully the crews are fine.

Thursday 23rd July 1942

Muffkins comes up with the echelon. I am always at a loss when having to make conversation with him – he really has nothing to say for himself, is grossly stupid and extremely self-satisfied. I dread the time when he comes to replace Desmond, who himself is intelligent, cheerful, full of energy and sympathetic to a womanly degree.

Write to Cara. I'm beginning to feel a little uneasy. Surely there should be a cable by now? On the other hand nothing should go wrong on that trip down the eastern seaboard of Africa.

There's a big raid on the leaguer next to us after tea. Twenty-two Stukas and eighty-eight bombers hit the 10H next door. They are rather tightly packed and the whole place soon becomes buried in smoke, sand and dust. Eventually when it dies down only one man has a cut face. The bombs were very big but just buried themselves in the ground. Remarkably not one of them scored a direct hit.

Friday 24th July 1942

Chief item of interest is that Derek has managed to hit another mine! It can only be attributed to the most appalling luck. We're patrolling an old minefield that we have crossed and recrossed many times- he just happens to find the one that was never removed. No one is hurt and the car is taken back on suspended tow.

There's a big air battle bang over our heads. Four 109s take on sixteen Spitfires and I'm sorry to say they run rings around our chaps. One Spitfire is knocked out and the pilot, a NZ sergeant, lands in our leaguer by parachute. In no time the most enormous crowd of sensation-hunters and busybodies has collected. It can only be likened to a fall at a point-to-point.

Monday 27th July 1942

Arrive at dawn at the now famous Ruweisat Ridge [a prominent part of the defensive line during the Battles of El Alamein]. There are many burnt-out German tanks, a most satisfying sight.

We sit all day just out of range and watch air battles and shelling. The Hun is using a very large gun which has a double explosion, half black and half white. It's amazing to watch but rather less formidable than it appears.

The Hun appears (temporarily?) to have run out of Stukas and we are bothered almost continually by 109s who strafe and drop bombs from a high level. They seem to be able to climb higher than us and certainly have the legs on us as they get added speed from the dive.

Move again after dark and spend most of the night on the move. There's a lovely full moon, a perfect temperature and sufficient humidity to keep the dust down. Moving behind a brigade is always very slow work and tiring for the drivers.

Tuesday 28th July 1942

Met a Scots Guards officer last night who thinks Nigel is at Mena. Poor chap, if so, as they are not given much rest there.

We are in the 'A Box' and it seems to be pretty much impregnable. The going is bad and we have made use of every feature of the landscape, filling every gap with minefields and wire. The Hun would be running into a brick wall if they tried to come through here. He must not, however, be given the opportunity to do that or to build his own brick wall for us.

A party goes down to bathe after lunch and I rather stupidly stay behind to do some writing and sleeping.

Wednesday 29th July 1942

We settle down to a day's peace but at 12.45pm we are told to move by 1pm. Had just got the gin out to celebrate Walker's birthday so lunch was very much curtailed.

We had a spot of bother last night as two men, Hammond and Hunter, got blind drunk on rum and then, as bad luck would have it, had to move Walker's car. They both get 28 days which is the CO's maximum. I have read in a Hun intelligence report that they'd get 18 months for the same thing.

Friday 31st July 1942

Rommel promised Hitler he'd be in Suez by today so we've scored a moral victory if nothing else! It would appear we are going to have a rest here.

Sunday 2nd August 1942

The site we have taken over from B Squadron is filthy and the flies are quite awful. They hang over one in swarms and one has to brush them off one's face and food. If dysentery was to break out then the whole army would go down flat – but let's hope it would get to the Hun lines as well! I don't know if the flies are worse than in previous years but the desert has never held more troops and on the Ruweisat Ridge there are a lot of unburied corpses. A flies' paradise!

Brigade moves back in the afternoon without any warning. I go over later in a rage and they are very apologetic.

Monday 3rd August 1942

Harry arrives in a jeep having been blown up by a landmine, to the detriment of his face and hands. He's absolutely stone deaf and discharging from his ears. It's remarkable he wasn't killed. At the end of the day I get Roscoe to send Harry to see a proper doctor.

The situation seems very static. Rommel, no doubt, is reinforcing like hell and I think intends on making a big push in conjunction with something else, possibly on the Levant.

Tuesday 4th August 1942

Do another recce, heading out as a fleet of jeeps. We must be the most strange-looking sight like desert fleas hopping over the ground at great pace.

The desert looks rather pleasant in the early morning light. The ridge, on which we are shortly expecting to fight to the death to lose or save Egypt, is a lovely rich russet brown colour. The depression fades away into the distance and one or two big hills stand out in a most beguiling manner.

Saturday 8th August 1942

Veriod goes off to collect canteen stores and goodies. We are running rather short of beer and there is no doubt that this is more appreciated than anything. I suspect that many who have never touched a drop of beer in their lives are now gulping it down with relish.

Sunday 9th August 1942

Bob comes in after tea and brings definite news of Winnie's visit and believes Sir Archie[15] is here also. He also brings the sad news [that] Strafer[16] has been shot down. We are incredibly unlucky with our higher commanders but also awfully stupid. Apparently he was in a normal, unescorted mail plane.

Monday 10th August 1942

Am informed by RHQ that the 18th is definitely the earliest at which we can expect to be relieved. Very disappointing as we sit here day after day doing very little except some more training.

Given the German attack is expected on about the 15th, the chances are we'll be too involved to be relieved.

---

15. Archibald Sinclair, 1st Viscount Thurso KT, CMG, PC (1890–1970), Secretary of State for Air 1940–5. His first task was to help build up the RAF in preparation for the Battle of Britain. Towards the end of the war he was often at odds with Churchill, despite being a lifelong friend, arguing against bombing raids on German cities with no strategic significance, notably Dresden.
16. Lieutenant General William 'Strafer' Gott CB, CBE, DSO & Bar, MC (1897–1942) was en route to Cairo to take up his appointment as commander of the Eighth Army, succeeding Auchinleck, when his plane was shot down.

Wednesday 12th August 1942

Tony Crosby comes back from Cairo with news that my flat is occupied by the wife of a Greys' officer. Must find out terms etc as soon as I get back but apparently all done through official channels, i.e. the judge.

He was also full of news of Winnie, Wavell and Alan B's visit as well as reinforcements. All this sort of news is like water to the desert traveller.

The news is generally much more cheerful this evening. Russia seems to have steadied the German advance and India seems to have been taken firmly in hand. The USA is also becoming more and more in the picture in the Pacific.

Thursday 13th August 1942

We are killing flies literally in thousands. As our great 'Q' has failed to give us anything official we have made our own traps of tins with gauze on top of soapy water, and by evening these traps are quite black with dead flies. I strongly suspect this is what brings in the scorpions as I have seen several of their transparent white bodies filled with a dark substance.

Hear over the air that Cara has officially arrived safely and that Nigel has been in hospital but is now alright.

Friday 14th August 1942

Have a practice stand-to in the morning and a big brigade conference at 6pm. Mark Roddick has arrived to take over from Roscoe but doesn't recognise me owing to the size of my moustache. I really can't help it – a nail file is my only weapon against it and I can't do much with that!

Saturday 15th August 1942

There is an alarm in the early morning but nothing comes of it. I dare say we will have a good many more in the coming days as the Intelligence people have predicted a German attack any time after today. Well, we can't do more than keep on the alert. I reckon that at any time of the day or night I could have the whole squadron on the move in 15 minutes from the time the telephone rings. Personally I don't think an attack likely before the next full moon.

Heard a lovely bit of advice today, perfect for a godchild: 'Never hunt south of the Thames, never lay the odds and never travel sober at night.'

Sunday 16th August 1942

Bob calls in with the astounding news that Monty, our old divisional commander from Haifa, is now army commander. Monty and Cyril were deadly enemies so feel we will no longer remain the 'blue-eyed boys'.[17]

Jimmy very kindly looks in at tea time to say Patsy had written to say Cara had arrived. I'm afraid the passage down the Red Sea was quite a strain but she is now picking up. Patsy was delivered of a daughter on 19th July, just about the time of Cara's arrival. That means in the bungalow are Cara, Patsy, four children and two nannies. God help 'em, I must try to get Cara to Kenya.

Attend Renton's conference outlining future policy and plans. It's very interesting and cheering. Things start picking up noticeably from tonight and then after another four days we should be able to hold any attack. After another 8 weeks we should be in a good position to then take the offensive. This will suit us as our refit and spell of rest should be complete and we'll be fresh and ready for anything.

Monday 17th August 1942

I am beginning to form a really hopeful outlook to the war. Here we are with any luck capable of holding any thrust into Egypt, Russia is not yet overrun and only ten weeks from winter, England potentially capable of an invasion, USA not yet thrown in her weight and the RAF growing so fast that by next spring we should be able to bomb or fight anywhere. On their side, Japan is fast switching to the defensive, Italy is no longer a nation and the German losses in Russia must be appalling – far beyond anything even Hitler dared think of.

Wednesday 19th August 1942

William arrives at first light, and give him a very good handover with everything he asks for and more – including the fly traps!

---

17. Field Marshal Bernard Montgomery, 1st Viscount Montgomery of Alamein, KG GCB DSO PC DL (1887-1976). As a young infantry captain in the First World War, Montgomery had earned a reputation for bravery and leadership. By the beginning of the Second World War he was a junior general and demonstrated his ability to remain calm under intense pressure during the retreat to Dunkirk, withdrawing with minimal casualties. After Dunkirk he had been passed over repeatedly for command in the field and at the age of 55 most people felt he had risen as far as he was going to go. However, the chief of the Imperial General Staff, General Alan Brooke, recognised Montgomery's flinty qualities and argued with Churchill that only he had the steely temperament and strategic vision that had thus far been lacking in the desert generals. Despite reservations about Montgomery's prickly character and unorthodox methods, Churchill relented and sent for 'Monty'.

We are away by 9am and by 7.30pm we arrive at Khatatba. Although we were up at 5am and have had a very long march, we manage to keep up a real party spirit 'til well after midnight.

Thursday 20th August 1942
Awake rather thick in the head and stiff-necked. Have an awful day of sorting things out, paying the men, issuing clothing etc and then have to attend a lengthy squadron leaders conference on promotion. There are many vacancies to be filled but we are at a period of very low ebb and some of the appointments are not particularly suitable. We do, however, have some first class younger fellows coming on.

Friday 21st August 1942
Before breakfast I give a harangue, a pat on the back for past work and an insight into the future of A Squadron. Afterwards the first leave party, thirty-six strong, heads off.

I intend to spend the morning on personal correspondence but in the end am pinned to the office seat. I have promised Cara a letter every day we are here but there's also a mass of other affairs to be managed. Send her a cable to say I am well and back.

Sunday 23rd August 1942
Ronnie and I leave early on the Delta Road for Cairo. The first sight of greenery and water is very lovely and refreshing. The gardens at the Barrage look unbelievably luscious, despite being full of Polish armoured cars. See a child run over by a bus and we stop to help – the bus doesn't. It's horrible.

Go to visit Nigel at the hospital. He is very miserable with an enormous neck from swollen tonsils. Ahmed has been coming in daily to administer and is very surprised to see me.

Mary Readman invites me to stay at my flat. Take her to church after tea and the place is packed, with hardly any women in the crowd of troops. Dine at the club at my old table. An air alarm goes after dinner which hastens my retirement for an early night.

Grand night in our very comfortable bed. It is the first time I'd slept between sheets or pulled a plug in quite some time. I'd give the world for Cara to be here now.

Tuesday 25th August 1942
Return with Ronnie and Jack to the camp but very little to do but doze and write some letters.

Have to take Barrett in to see the CO over family matters. Poor man has a wanton wife who is not content with four children by her own husband but now has one more and a miscarriage by someone else and is selling their home.

Dodie and I dash back to Cairo. Spend the afternoon with Nigel who is far from well and going to be operated on tomorrow. He's got quinsy and is thoroughly uncomfortable and in very low spirits.

Russian news is far from encouraging and I think Rommel intends on launching an attack in the next few days.

Tuesday 1st September 1942

Leave ends today. Have a bad morning at the dentist. He's certainly very good but has a filthy Gyppo assistant in whom one has little faith. The dentist (Gerson) puts a platinum crown on one tooth and then leaves the filling of another to his assistant. I don't stand for that for long – I don't pay £9 for a man to put his garlic-reeking hands down my mouth.

Ludford and SSM come round at 4pm to pick me up. I decide that, though I've enjoyed my leave, it's not done me any good. I feel unsatisfied and made me want Cara back more than ever as I see how lonely one can be without her.

Well, there's a good battle begun again in the Western Desert so perchance I'll soon forget all this. I expect to see great excitement when I return but the camp is undisturbed and the mess is empty, mostly because most officers are out playing rounders!

Wednesday 2nd September 1942

I have two new officers, Stone and Weil, both around 33 years of age and with very definite formed minds. I don't think either holds much of an opinion of the regular soldier and thinks he could run the war much better on a civil firm basis. Maybe they are right and it's my ambition not to develop fixed ideas but to listen to and try to visualise things from every point of view.

Three years of war completed today.

Thursday 3rd September 1942

Geoffrey M goes into hospital today for Gyppy tummy. It's been coming for some time and I think he's contributed to it by being so highly strung. Just now he's having a love affair with a young woman, whom he has told he is in love with, but can't marry as she is his 'social inferior'. She's a clever and most determined young lady and very much in love with him. Because she has let him play ball with her I fear there may be serious repercussions.

I have taken on a new lease of life with parades from 7am to 7pm as well as drill, gunnery, wireless operating, car maintenance. I am also busy interviewing NCOs, disposing of undesirables and looking for fresh blood. I believe I could be quite a good soldier if I set my mind to it – I love my squadron and enjoy getting to know the men and all their complex problems.

Friday 4th September 1942

Nasty hot sandy day. The news from the front is most cheering.[18] We seem to have the whip hand and the RAF have had an amazing run of successes. Our position is just as the doctor ordered; we hold all the commanding features and are on three sides of all the German and Wop forces that matter (15th and 21st Panzer, 90th Light, Ariete and Littorio). It would appear that unless Monty makes some supreme blunder we should mop up the whole lot. Pray God we can as it would prove a most decisive factor in the length of this war.

Sunday 6th September 1942

Take over from Brian. It's an awful effort getting the squadron out of the camp and extracting the troops from barrack life and camp routine.

Our HQ site is on the edge of the Wadi Natrun. This great *wadi* lies at my feet and in the evening light the hills and allies take on exciting shapes while the monasteries, black and foreboding all day, suddenly take on shape and colour. Further up the salt lakes glisten in the sunlight and the palm groves and rush swamps are a brilliant green.

Brian leaves me with four Daimlers to play with. They are not much good on their own as they can neither get out of sand not help pull another out.

Tuesday 8th September 1942

Start reorganising squadron for Humbers [armoured cars with a heavy and a light Besa machine gun]. We hear in the afternoon that C Squadron are returning from the line tomorrow but are not being replaced by 'B'.

Saturday 12th September 1942

Take over six more Humbers. From them I shall select mine as I'll want certain modifications. I have also to find a driver to replace Sherratt who has proved himself a star turn on the Daimler.

---

18. The Battle of Alam el Halfa, 30 August–5 September 1942. Rommel attempted to envelop the British Eighth Army from the south, but Montgomery had been forewarned of Rommel's tactics after Bletchley Park had decoded a message with the battle plan. Montgomery left a gap in the southern sector and kept his tanks stationary (a new tactic) high on the Alam el Halfa ridge, where they were able to deflect the attack. This was an important moment in the desert campaign and paved the way for success at El Alamein.

Tuesday 15th September 1942

Jack Arthur gives a lecture on the last battle. Poor Jack has no vocabulary at all and gets terribly tongue-tied. He battles on and takes 90 minutes to say what a good lecturer could say in half the time. I do, however, think that Jack is a good type and probably a first class CO.

Raymond Briggs, now our division commander, comes to dine. He chatters hard from the time he arrives until midnight. His hands are never still and he gesticulates madly and incessantly. He has no qualms in criticising senior officers to us which I never think is a good trait.

Friday 18th September 1942

Get a letter from Cara in Salisbury [now Harare]. She seems to have found the ideal house and is wild with excitement. It sounds perfect and, if she and Daphne share, not too expensive. The airline runs directly to Salisbury so I shall have door-to-door service if ever I get any leave.

Saturday 19th September 1942

The papers announce that Nigel has the MC. I don't expect we'll ever hear why (from him) but I think it was for his part in the Knightsbridge battle.[19] Jolly good show!

The Sherman [tank] is becoming a common bird around here so in our next encounter Jerry will get another nasty surprise – and for once the men using these toys will have had some chance to train with them.

There's an impressive display of seventy-two bombers with attendant fighters in the morning. We cannot make out what they are doing in such force but it makes for a grand sight.

Sunday 20th September 1942

There's hardly a soul in the mess. Everyone is in Cairo or Alex having a last fling before we go back into the dust and heat and glare and boredom of the desert. Actually the weather is now very pleasant and the dust storm gets later and shorter every day. The moon is fast reaching full and I think its wane may bring big moves.

---

19. The citation read: 'This officer was commanding a platoon during an attack made by his company on an enemy position at Tacua plateau on July 15th, 1942. After the attack had been held up, his company commander killed, another officer killed and another wounded, Lieutenant Barne showed initiative and courage in leading his platoon round the flank of the enemy position, crossing an area covered by enemy machine guns and under fire from our own 25-pounders. It was largely due to this officer's determination to close with the enemy that the attack was successful. Twenty-nine Germans were taken prisoner and four anti-tank guns, with other equipment, were captured.'

Stalingrad still clings to freedom in the most titanic battle ever recorded.[20] Even if the Hun enters it before the rains come I do not believe now that it will do him any good. I think when the ground becomes bogged there that a large portion of the Luftwaffe may be diverted here.

Monday 21st September 1942
Get a letter from Cara dated 13th. She seems busy getting ready for the move to Salisbury and has a big plan to get to Cairo as a South Rhodesian VAD. I only hope she's not letting herself in for a packet of trouble!

Tuesday 22nd September 1942
All the usual commotion for the departure – increased by our new corps making a bog of our orders. The new cars certainly run beautifully and are very comfortable. We do 108 miles and after order, counter-order and Brian taking the wrong turn we eventually land up not far from where we started.

Get a number of cars stuck through inexperience but put a Humber on sand trays and it comes out like a cork from a bottle.

Friday 25th September 1942
There's a heavy mist in the morning and a very heavy dew which leaves everything dripping and all clothing damp and clammy. It's a good test for the new cars and wirelesses but everything seems to start easily.

Another afternoon of practice shooting and the guns are all going well – with the exception of Derek's. He always seems to be unlucky and have the dud car or incompetent crew but it gives us something to laugh at.

A big cannonade starts at 10pm. We find, with some concern, that we are really not that far from the front after all!

Receive a letter from Nigel who goes to Syria on Saturday.

Tuesday 29th September 1942
Have a shoot-off to decide who will represent the squadron in the colonel's competition. The standard is extremely high and at 1,200 yards every team hits a half page of the *Bystander* [magazine] set on some petrol tins.

Jack comes over to say that Ronnie has been made 2i/c to Bill in 4th Armoured Brigade. I have been dreading this for many weeks as it means I either get kicked out or go 2i/c to the regiment. I have no ambitions beyond commanding A Squadron.

---

20. At the Battle of Stalingrad (23 August 1942–2 February 1943) it is estimated that the Russians lost over 1.1m men, against 627,000 German losses.

We all go to HQ after dinner. Everyone is there and in great form. Hugh starts the singing – he is naturally musical but also a great mimic. He keeps us all rocking with laughter 'til very late. We end up having to carry the colonel to his tent!

Wednesday 30th September 1942

Ronnie departs at 9am. I get the squadron formed in a line and he drives down. Owing to error I am at the wrong end of the line and fail to lead a cheer so he drives off in awful silence. He has been an ideal CO; unmoved by anything, unprejudiced and always fair and just in his decisions. We hear that Tony [Pepys] has got command and that Ronnie is to be a full colonel.

Saturday 3rd October 1942

Have another of the dust storms like the one in May when we had a great wall of sand slowly advance on us. I'm told in some cases the infantry thought it was a gas attack and sounded the alarms!

Wednesday 7th October 1942

A big scheme starts today. We have a conference at 5.30am but no one seems to know anything definite. I am detached to the 8th Armoured Brigade and get no specific orders at all. As usually happens, one uses common sense and tries to arrive at the right place at the right time and by dark we join a large collection of people, vehicles and guns.

There's no moon at all and the night is made up of a hideous roar of every kind of vehicle in every kind of direction. It all seems to go smoothly and one can see that this is a dress rehearsal for something very much greater and more serious.

Thursday 8th October 1942

We are sent off before light on a job that could easily be done by the tank's own recce. It would be maddening to have all our cars knocked out on a minefield and then when we are required on our real job find there are no Royals left to go forward.

Friday 9th October 1942

Return to our desert home by 9am. Tony comes over to see me about future policy. I'm to be 2i/c in name but stay with A Squadron. Teddy will come up and act as 2i/c 'til it can be seen how fit he is and learn his way. Thereafter, I will go as 2i/c and we are agreed that if we get on each other's nerves I shall get a staff job until my turn comes to command. Out here one is apt to get on one another's nerves which may affect the regiment and we are all keen to avoid this at all costs.

Sunday 11th October 1942

A willow warbler has made our mess his home. He hops around picking up flies off the table and floor and has no hesitation [in] sitting upon us.

I open Cara's South African ham for dinner as rations were not good. I reluctantly open my reserve beer crate as Jack and Eddie come to dinner. Jack gets absolutely stinking but is in great form.

There are all the signs and portents of war in a big way in the near future. I think we've all learned a lot on our period of training but are still not totally confident in the new cars. It seems that when things do go wrong it is always something more serious than my fitter can deal with.

Wednesday 14th October 1942

One of the most lovely sunrises I have ever seen. A mass of little fleecy clouds turn to a wonderful rich red 'til the whole sky is afire.

Muffkins is coming up to take over the squadron as Teddy is not fit. I am now 2i/c. It's horrid leaving the squadron and I've grown far more attached than I ever would ever have thought possible – what's more it's a rather bitter pill to be handing it over to Geoffrey of all people.

We play the 4th South African Regiment at football after tea. They are a most delightful crowd and play a good game, being noticeably fitter than us. They win 3-1.

Friday 16th October 1942

Geoffrey comes over after breakfast. He looks magnificent with his MC medal. They say he suffered a crick in his neck from admiring it but he seems to have got over it now. Spend the morning handing over.

In the afternoon we have an awful sandstorm. I sit in the back of my truck and for over half an hour in the mid-afternoon it is too dark to read. Outside the air is a thick dark yellow like London in November at its worst. An occasional petrol tin comes crashing past and the flies become worse than usual as they try to hibernate in one's clothing.

Saturday 17th October 1942

At dawn it clears but as soon as the sun is fully up the winds picks up to gale force and picks up the fast drying sand. By 10am we are in the middle of a raging sandstorm again.

I take the jeep to go round the cars saying goodbye and am almost blinded by the driving particles of sand. See all senior NCOs and various friends. Lunch at HQ and now must sit and wait for orders. I hope to goodness they are not long in coming.

The storm dies down in the evening. Ludford and I bed down in the open. The temperature has dropped about 15° and the fur coats are back out.

Sunday 18th October 1942

We get orders at 'crackers'. Everything is cut and dried so it does not entail much panic. Just before we start I receive a lilo mattress that Cara has been saying is on the way for a long time. It could not have arrived at a more opportune moment.

Ludford starts the march in deepest misery as the truck is not what he was expecting to have as a 2i/c's driver. By time of arrival he is wreathed in smiles as he realises that, not only does it go well, but frolics through the thick sand.

Tuesday 20th October 1942

Tony goes to a talk by Monty and comes back after dark with his tail right up. I remarked to Tony, on seeing Geoffrey Roberts, that he looked even thinner and smaller than ever. Tony replied that Geoffrey said he'd seen me and had said how much I'd thickened out recently!

Wednesday 21st October 1942

Have an all over bath. Don't quite know when I'll get another.

We are all very busy doing nothing; marking up maps, reading orders, titivating the cars etc but it's clear something is brewing. The Wops have announced that there is an attack impending. There is – and I have full confidence we shall surprise and perturb the opposition no end. But there will have to be a lot of bloodshed and we're going to have to take some knocks before we can break them.

It's a funny feeling waiting for this battle, rather like waiting to get mounted before a big race. We don't discuss it much and are very superficial in our conversation. Everyone is very much at the top of the wave as our superiority in every way is obvious and we have leaders whom we know will not fail us or withdraw or, worst of all, change plans to conform to the enemy's.

The air have been hammering them for several days and it's grand to see these great machines coming and going. We sit after dark drinking a glass of port and talk 'til late. There are several bombers flying overhead and a Hun one comes over very low indeed.

Thursday 22nd October 1942

A quiet day and Tony is away again. In the evening I have to move the regiment up to the assembly area. As there's wireless silence, I don't do much in the way of commanding and it all goes very smoothly. The moon is very full and the march is done under almost daylight conditions.

I leave Ludford behind with the truck and most of my kit. Goodness knows when I'll see him again.

Chapter 5

El Alamein

By the late summer of 1942 the Allies were in trouble; the U-boat blockade of Britain was severely affecting supplies and morale, the Russians were on the back foot against the Germans having lost huge tracts of territory and suffered unimaginable numbers of casualties, and the Japanese were dominating the battlefields of Asia. The war in the deserts of northern Africa became pivotal. Apart from the psychological blow of surrendering the strategic colony of Egypt, the implications for Allied shipping of losing the canal and allowing the Germans access to the oil fields of the Middle East could well have been enough to sway the outcome of the war.

Over six long months, the Commonwealth forces had been forced to retreat over a thousand miles in the Western Desert, falling back on the Alamein Line. This was a thirty mile stretch of desert with the Mediterranean to the north and the Qattara Depression, a sea of soft, impenetrable sand, to the south. Only 150 miles west of Cairo, it was the final defensive line if Egypt was to be held.

The promotion (however circuitous) of Montgomery to command the Eighth Army seemed to have a transformative effect on his troops. 'Monty' had been Major Barne's old divisional commander in Palestine and was a divisive figure. Not shy of pushing himself forward, he was once described as 'quick as a ferret and about as likeable'. On assuming command he immediately made efforts to visit his troops as often as possible and instil in them his own determination and fighting spirit.

The Second Battle of El Alamein was to become one of the defining battles of the Second World War, the culmination of an extended North African campaign and the final arm-wrestle between two well-matched, experienced armies led by two charismatic master strategists. Unlike the European theatres of war, the Western Desert provided an equitable

Elizabeth, Nigel, Michael and
Anthony, 1919.

Sotterley Hall, Suffolk.

Royals team pig-sticking in Panigaon, India, April 1934.

Cara Holmes–Hunt and
other members of the
'fishing fleet', 1935.

Anthony and Cara's wedding, 10 June 1937.

The Royals returning from a raid, Caesarea, Palestine, November 1938.

In Palestine, 1938.

Refugees arriving into Haifa, August 1939.

Anthony Barne on his first day of running Haifa port, 22 November 1939.

Anthony and Cara skiing at Cedars, Lebanon, February 1940.

Climbing the Pyramid of Khafre with Lin Showers, 26 October 1940.

The tanker *Adinda* after striking a mine off Tobruk, 8 February 1941.

Nigel and Anthony, Cairo, April 1941.

Anthony Barne's Marmon-Herrington armoured car camouflaged in the Western Desert, February 1942.

Christopher's christening, Cairo, 22 June 1941. Back: Captain Langham, AMB, Archdeacon Johnson. Front: Judge Barne, Marion Orr-Ewing, Cara, Nanny Downie.

Humphrey Lloyd ('HWLL') and Ronnie Joy, commanding officers of the Royals, December 1941–September 1942 and January 1943–February 1945 respectively, 1938.

EIGHTH ARMY

Personal Message from the
ARMY COMMANDER

1—When I assumed command of the Eighth Army I said that the mandate was to destroy ROMMEL and his Army, and that it would be done as soon as we were ready.

2—We are ready NOW.

The battle which is now about to begin will be one of the decisive battles of history. It will be the turning point of the war. The eyes of the whole world will be on us, watching anxiously which way the battle will swing.

We can give them their answer at once, "It will swing our way."

3—We have first-class equipment; good tanks; good anti-tank guns; plenty of artillery and plenty of ammunition; and we are backed up by the finest air striking force in the world.

All that is necessary is that each one of us, every officer and man, should enter this battle with the determination to see it through — to fight and to kill — and finally, to win.

If we all do this there can be only one result — together we will hit the enemy for "six," right out of North Africa.

4—The sooner we win this battle, which will be the turning point of this war, the sooner we shall all get back home to our families.

5—Therefore, let every officer and man enter the battle with a stout heart, and with the determination to do his duty so long as he has breath in his body.

AND LET NO MAN SURRENDER SO LONG AS HE IS UNWOUNDED AND CAN FIGHT.

Let us all pray that "the Lord mighty in battle" will give us the victory.

B. L. MONTGOMERY,
Lieutenant-General, G.O.C.-in-C., Eighth Army.

MIDDLE EAST FORCES,
23-10-42.

Montgomery's pep talk on the eve of the Battle of El Alamein, 23 October 1942.

Mitchell bombers on their way to bomb the Mareth Line, Tunisia, March 1943.

Crashed aeroplane in Ndola, Northern Rhodesia, 28 July 1943.

Major General Vehbi Kocagüney at
El Alamein, 22 September 1943.

The 4th Hussars drawn up for inspection by Churchill, 3 December 1943.

Churchill addressing the troops of the 4th Hussars, 3 December 1943.

Churchill inspecting his regiment. Anthony Barne is walking behind with Lieutenant General Stone, 3 December 1943.

Bobby Kidd saying goodbye to Churchill with Field Marshal Alexander to the right, Loreto Aerodrome, 25 August 1944.

Regimental battle HQ on the Gothic Line, September 1944.

Anthony Barne's tank, *Dauntless*, at a liberated Italian farm, 13 April 1945.

Dr Ranier and other war criminals in front of the body of Gruppenführer Globočnik, 31 May 1945.

The 4th Hussars' 'private' lake near Paternion, Austria, with amphibious jeep and Anthony Barne's tent pitched by the Humber, May 1945.

Churchill painting at Lake Como, September 1945.

Sailing in the Solent.

Anthony and Cara at Christopher's wedding, 1976.

battleground unhampered by civilians or towns and unrestricted by rivers and mountains.

Montgomery was well aware that Rommel's forces were running out of fuel and supplies, given the huge distance any reinforcements had to travel to reach El Alamein. His plan was to launch a main attack from the north of the line (where the Royals were under the 10th Armoured Division) with a diversionary attack to the south. It was hoped the attack in the north would enable the Allies to clear two corridors through the 5-mile-deep minefield known as the 'Devil's Garden', allowing tanks to move in and consolidate their position. The attack began with the largest artillery bombardment that had ever been mounted by the British army, with 900 guns firing at the German lines to allow the infantry and engineers to begin clearing the paths.

*　　*　　*

Friday 23rd and Saturday 24th October 1942

Tony goes round the squadrons to give them a little pep talk and to explain the plan. Monty wants everyone in his army to have an intelligent idea of what is happening and I'm sure he's right. We move off at 9.30pm on the Great Adventure. By midnight we are within an unpleasantly close proximity of the guns.

I've never heard anything like it and hope I never do again. The whole universe quakes and shakes with a continuous barrage of 25-pounders, sounding like rolled drums. On top of that there are the bigger guns with their roar and bark. Over us come the medium shells sounding like a plane coming in to land. All along one horizon there is the continual flicker of gun flash. The car develops a nasty smell like a stale fart. Even a normal man feels like he is driving in to his death. Before daylight, however, one has got used to it and all day long the shells roar over us and drop amongst us but we have lost our first fear of them.

The attack goes fairly well, rather slower than was expected and with not a great many prisoners to show for it. We lose a very nice Sergeant Wiley from C Squadron when his car runs into a well-placed anti-tank gun. There are no survivors.

We knock out a good number of tanks and guns during the day but by sunset the drive has gone out of the attack. Rommel has once again been very clever but we'll get him yet. The RAF have worked hard all day and we are free from attack but lose several of our fighters and bombers.

Feel pretty weary by dark and doss straight down. Manage to get in two good hours before the battery opens up on continuous fire for the rest of the night. I defy anyone to sleep 100 yards in front of eight 25-pound guns!

Sunday 25th October 1942
We have a good day on the whole. Some Hun and Wop prisoners come in to give themselves up. I do hope that no British PoW would look so bedraggled and dejected as they do.

See the first signs of German Air Force in the evening when thirty-three Stukas appear. They get nowhere and three Hurricanes and our anti-aircraft guns drive them off.

We have a long wait after dark 'til we move. All rather sleepy but one can't doss down here. Battling is very tiring as one is constantly on one's toes.

Monday 26th October 1942
Reach a new pitch at 2am. The Hun bombs us with a nasty new type of anti-personnel and oil incendiary bombs. Luckily they're not very effective.

Spend the day sitting doing nothing amongst a vast assembly of vehicles. An occasional 109 comes over with a load of bombs which he drops and then dashes on. Our anti-aircraft defence is ineffective, undisciplined and a complete waste of time and material. They don't seem to spot a plane 'til it's past and then open fire when it is heading out of range, continuing for a further 5 minutes in a baffled rage.

Tuesday 27th October 1942
Another disturbed night but no damage – except to Adrian who skins his cheek when diving under his car! Seem to be stuck here for another day.

Sergeant Prior accidentally kills himself when cleaning the big Besa. He shot himself right through the chest while pulling himself up on to the car. He was a very nice chap and will be a definite loss.

Wednesday 28th October 1942
Tony and I head forward in our cars to be with Division HQ. It's right through the Hun minefields and in sight of enemy tanks. We receive a certain amount of shelling but nothing to what is going on out here.

Our RAF are now excelling themselves. They come in six times with eighteen bombers each time and give proper stick to a concentration of enemy tanks. I wouldn't be in the German Army for all the world – nor would one or two Huns as they walk in during the night.

Have a nasty creeping barrage of 105s advance on us. Just at the *moment critique* they seem to knock off for lunch but it's a mean thing and the next salvo would have caught us.

Get a mail which included two letters from Cara, one with photographs of her and Christopher. She has had real hell from a dentist – two wisdom teeth out, one in three parts and needed her jaw drilling to remove it! She has more guts than three average men.

Thursday 29th October 1942
We moved back a little last night and the rest of the regiment came up to join us. At one point during the night the barrage was particularly intense; 25-pounders going like hell with 60-pounders more intermittent and seemingly urging on their little brothers. It has the most extraordinary effect.

We have front row seats for the occasional Stuka raid. They only dare come once or twice a day now and there's no more fancy diving. They just drop their bombs and run for it with negligible effect.

Friday 30th October 1942
Nigel suddenly turns up about 11am looking most awfully well and happy. He has arrived up here as ADC to Oliver Leese[1] (30 Corps), just hope he's well enough to stick it out. He likes his new job and boss. With effect from today we are under Leese so shall probably see more of Nigel. We have a long chat and I have a number of letters to show him.

By lunchtime the day becomes enshrouded in thick dust and we have a perfectly bloody afternoon. The worst of it is the horrid, fat sleepy flies who come to drink on our lips as we sleep open mouthed.

There's a grand barrage of guns at 10pm. We learn afterwards that somehow we had discovered where Rommel was spending the night so decided to keep him awake! It failed to keep me awake – nor did a mass of bombers who strafed the next door battery. One is getting completely immune to the noise.

We get orders for the most amazing show. Tony and I get into a stuffy ambulance to plot and plan. More of this when it's less secret.

Saturday 31st October 1942
Plotting and planning gets me to corps HQ by 8.30am. Meet BGS – Cooney by name, who remembers me from Mersa Matrum in '36. Herbert Lumsden, now corps commander, gives me 10 minutes of his valuable time. He is very easy to talk to and puts one immediately at ease yet one does not lose one's respect for him. It's a happy knack and necessary in a big man.

Get back late and Tony heads off to see the army commander. I am left to move the regiment back about 12 miles.

---

1. Lieutenant General Sir Oliver Leese, 3rd Baronet, KCB, CBE, DSO (1894–1978).

Sunday 1st November 1943

Malcolm W-M comes up on business and returns after 30 minutes with a cable to say that Grizel[2] has been lost at sea. What comfort is there for a man on such an occasion? I greatly fear that Mary R's little daughter must have gone down too. It's an awful tragedy. Poor Malcolm.

Tonight we are off on a marauding expedition behind enemy lines. Only A and C Squadron go through, much to the disappointment of the remainder. They may, of course, be completely written off if the army can't break the Hun within a week but I personally think they're on a good wicket. To them everything is the enemy and they can shoot at anybody but no one can shoot at them until they've recognised them as unfriendly. The four South Africans are coming too on our right. The whole crux is the breakthrough.

Have a very noisy night right up at the front. We scoop holes in the ground and doze 'til midnight. I manage a glass of port in honour of the day.

Monday 2nd November 1943

A and C Squadrons go through before daylight. I stand at the gap and wave them farewell. By 8am we hear of their safe passage. At dawn we retire from our perilous position for a mile.

In the late afternoon my car has the narrowest squeak of its existence. About thirty Stukas come over us with no evil intent to us. The Spitfires get amongst them and one of the Stukas jettisons its bombs, one of which is a 500-pounder which lands 10 yards in front of my car. Luckily it doesn't explode on impact but politely waits twenty seconds to let us get under the car. I get a half pound brick on my forehead and Wright gets a 10lb rock on his leg and is carted off in an ambulance.

During the day various car crews walk in. They have had to abandon their vehicles for various reasons and many come in with prisoners too. They have all done sensible things with their cars to avoid them getting in to enemy hands.

---

2. Lady Grizel Boyle (1913–42), wife of Malcolm Wolfe-Murray (1908–85), was killed when the passenger ship *Laconia* was sunk by a U-boat in the Atlantic en route to Canada. The ship was carrying 136 crew, 348 passengers, 1,809 Italian PoWs and 160 Polish guards. After the attack, the U-boat commander was surprised to hear Italian voices amongst the survivors and started rescue operations, sending an uncoded message to all vessels in the vicinity to assist with the promise to cease hostilities. He was joined by other U-boats, all flying the Red Cross flag, and spent three days picking up survivors. The U-boats were subsequently spotted by an American bomber who was ordered to attack, forcing the U-boats to submerge immediately. A French warship was soon on the scene to conclude the rescue operation. In total, the master, ninety-seven crew, 133 passengers, 1,194 PoWs and thirty-three Polish guards were lost. The event led to Grand Admiral Dönitz issuing the controversial 'Laconia Order' forbidding efforts to save survivors of stricken ships.

Tuesday 3rd November 1943

The two squadrons are doing frightfully well. They have bagged all manner of things and have been chased by tanks, air and guns but without avail. We sit gathering information of what Jack and Roddy are doing and swelling in reflected glory. There is no doubt we are writing some of the greatest pages in our regimental history.[3]

Tonight we are getting Victor and Peter to lead two squadrons of 4SA through a gap the infantry are making to harass the enemy still further in the rear.

Wednesday 4th November 1942

The breakthrough seems to have started and the main force has been ejected from its positions.[4] Some armoured forces are going through tonight to try to cut off and harass the enemy.

Thursday 5th November 1942

Start off bright and early and by noon we have crossed the SA Rahman Road. See a mass of destroyed trucks and the pockmarks from the artillery barrage. The Hun in the south borrowed all the Wop transport saying they'd send it back for them but we are already through and they've left 6,000 Wops behind, now in our hands. We see some of them in a long straggly black line, scarcely with any escort!

We advance all afternoon catching odd convoys and columns and burning vehicles. It's a pity, I think, as some of them look like decent vehicles. Tanks are a different matter as we seem to be able to make use of their arms and armour.

All around us are columns of smoke from burning tanks and lines of prisoners coming in. The whole atmosphere feels different now with everyone on their toes and longing to get on. The Arabs are suddenly very thick on the ground and seem (?) very pleased to see us.

Brian goes out in front of us and soon runs into some Wops. He soon gets fifteen vehicles with hardly any opposition.

Poor Victor W, who led both parties through, got shot by one of his PoWs. Thank heaven his troop had no scruples and made the whole group pay the penalty. Henry W and Sergeant Gauntly have also been shot but not seriously.

---

3. The two squadrons are said to have destroyed 181 vehicles, twenty Breda guns, seventeen anti-tank guns, three tanks, three field guns, one armoured troop-carrier and an aeroplane.
4. By 2 November Rommel knew he was beaten. Hitler ordered the Afrika Korps to continue fighting, but Rommel refused to obey. On 4 November, short of fuel and and having lost over 25,000 troops, he started his retreat.

We bring in a South African pilot called Faura, three New Zealanders who have been prisoners and a very nasty Nazi officer who is universally disliked. He is a tall, fair man with thick-lensed glasses and might have been a London bank clerk to look at, but his manner is absolutely bloody.

One of the finest feelings today has been the sudden feeling of getting elbow room. We're now back out in the desert without any confines. All is now silent with no mines or guns or vehicles swarming through our leaguer.

Friday 6th November 1942

The work goes on with more and more columns rounded up and brought in. Only on the coast is there any organised resistance but we can always find a flank so every time they stop to fight we can round them and put them in the bag. We get Fulgore from divisional HQ, General Fartino (the big noise), Colonel Poffa and Major Veranda. Are such names really possible?!

The German stragglers are mostly Luftwaffe who have been shot down and not got back in time. One is a 14-year-old fighter pilot, an absolutely mad little devil as he is not old enough to have fear.

Saturday 7th November 1942

After some more destruction, albeit on a reduced scale, we move on. We find one car of C Squadron that has been missing for 3 days!

There has been rain to the west of us and I get stuck twice. The ground is a sheet of water and it's very heavy going. The weather has also changed and it's turned bitterly cold.

We are now just above my old station of Fuka. The Hun is now further back and with any luck is stuck in the mud and will have no choice but to stand and meet us. The more we can come to grips and get round him, the more will fall into the bag and the sooner the war can end.

Sunday 8th November 1942

A heavenly day. Everything is a rush of excitement and we have orders to go on to the frontier. Tony doesn't seem too keen as he is more anxious to have a quiet day for reorganisation and maintenance. We are rather short of cars but certainly not inoperative. He can be a very stubborn man.

The BBC announce American landings on the north and west coasts of Africa.[5] The News lasts for 30 minutes and interest in the Eighth Army seems to have fallen well into second place. I believe we have been the stooges with no other job than to open the ball. We'll never catch the Hun

---

5. Operation Torch was the joint British and American invasion of French North Africa. Three amphibious task forces landed simultaneously with the aim of capturing Casablanca, Oran and Algiers.

now and it will be level pegging to see who gets to Tripoli first; the Hun, the Americans or us!

We are all madly excited by the news as this looks like big business. We are not considering the Vichy French feelings at all which is a very good thing.

Monday 9th November 1942

Start off early and the going is still deep. We waste 4 hours just getting cars out of the mud. The flow of traffic is terrific; big guns, little guns, ambulances, transporters, tanks, RAF and a continual flow of lorries with petrol. The air is dense with our bombers and fighters.

We make the Sita track by dark and feel safe lighting fires as there's not a German plane that dares take the air. There are crashed aircraft everywhere along with broken up vehicles and guns. There must be very little of the main German force left. And now they are retreating into the arms of the Yanks who are crossing Tunisia to meet them. This is a big step towards the end of the war.

I have lost Sherratt. He has gone as a car commander in A Squadron. I would not have stopped him, even if I could. He deserves to get on. I've had him for almost a year and one could not want for a better driver.

My new man is Brudenell, a nice little chubby chap from Derbyshire. He has lots of common sense and a good eye for the country.

Tuesday 10th November 1942

We start before daylight and crack on all day. By evening we are almost on the frontier wire but are a rather depleted party. We wait at odd intervals for stragglers, delaying our arrival at Tobruk which we've had orders to harass. The 4th SA are already doing it and are getting stick from the air which just proves our nuisance value. I think the Hun is now going all out to delay us while he evacuates everything he can from Benghazi. There is no point going back to Tripoli if the US are coming along from Tunis and any delay in evacuation means endangering sea communications further.

Listen to old Winnie on the BBC. He is quite magnificent in his choice of words. This, he says, is not the beginning of the end but the end of the beginning [*see* Appendix A]. I think he's just about right.

Wednesday 11th November 1942

There's a mass of enemy about and there's no doubt we're going at a great pace to cut off every Hun in North Africa. I should not be surprised at all if we and an Armoured Brigade were ordered directly on to Benghazi. I just wish we had a few more cars.

At 2pm we cross the frontier.

The news is fast and furious. Hitler has occupied 'unoccupied France' and we are forging ahead all over North Africa. German losses here are 34,000 and Wops 25,000 to date – as well as 1,000 guns and 500 tanks. They are going to ring the church bells at home on Sunday. How thrilled Mama will be – she'll be pulling the rope herself!

Friday 13th November 1942
We start off at 6.15am to catch up with the brigade. The Hun is completely on the run but we see Mark employing the whole brigade to catch three or four wretched men who have been left behind to make noises and delay us. It's pitiful and drives us wild – no wonder we take so long to win a war.

We pass Knightsbridge and other places that would have been of interest a few months ago. I'd no idea we'd left so much behind. There are Grants by the dozen and all sorts of other vehicles strewn around the place. We find a newly burnt-out German armoured car which bears no comparison to our cars. I get a fly net and sherry glass out of it.

Saturday 14th November 1942
Bitterly cold wind but get an all over wash and very necessary it was too! I am soon filthy again.

Desmond goes into Tobruk for a meeting and comes back with a big load of Wop and Hun rations: Norwegian biscuits, Naples tomatoes, Marmite and curry powder.

Monday 16th November 1942
Get our orders to continue and we are off to Msus and beyond. Wretched day with a bitterly cold wind and rain. Sitting nine foot up with no protection at all one wears every garment one can lay one's hands on!

We manage over 80 miles. On the first leg we pass the tank mortuary where our tank brigade lost itself in May on a minefield in the faint, but valiant, hope of relieving the 150 Brigade which was lost in the 'Cauldron'.

Tuesday 17th November 1942
My stomach has been upset for a few days now so I take two of the famous Army Number Nines![6] I starve all day which doesn't improve my temper.

We reach Msus around 5pm and see a lot of sandgrouse, ravens and kestrels, the first signs of life for 200 miles. The *wadi* has the most lovely-looking green bushes but on closer inspection one finds they are forbidding and unappetising, even for goats and camels.

---

6. Laxative pills which gave rise to the bingo call 'Doctor's order, number nine!'

Wednesday 18th November 1942

Number Nines live up to the great and historic army traditions. I have a very disturbed night and am convinced they contain more explosive than two Stuka bombs!

We move at dawn for about 8 miles south. Get some trouble from the air but we treat it with contempt in these cars. A 109 shoots me up while talking with Tony. We stand to leeward and don't even break our conversation. Our planes arrive some time later and from then on we don't see another enemy aircraft.

Friday 20th November 1942

Tony P is getting rather like an old man with his favourite daughter with Teddy G. I'm getting rather worried over my position. If I have a row with him I'll go backwards and sit as a captain under Pitt until some C3 job is discovered for me 'til the end of the war. It's only a matter of time before a row breaks out, unless Teddy goes sick. It's all rather worrying.

We move down to Antelat which the Hun hasn't bothered to hold this year. The defences are half completed as they left as soon as we started working around their flank. Desmond gets bitten by a camel tick in a place where no nice camel tick should be! He says it's very painful and walks wide all day.

The 11th Hussars have entered Benghazi. The BBC have been storing this up as headline news.

It's my birthday but we've left all the goodies and drink on the other car so we can't celebrate. In fact, it's almost a day of fasting.

Sunday 22nd November 1942

We put in an attack on Agedabya. I had been betting they'd have evacuated during the night but it seems they haven't and put up quite a lot of resistance all day.

We are going back a few miles for a refit. This means we will remain upfront and go on with the war up here. It's the best possible thing that could happen to us. I've no hesitation in saying that if one's got to fight then one might as well fight where it's easiest.

Monday 23rd November 1942

The Hun evacuated Agedabya last night. Tony and Teddy go over to have a look and hit a mine on the way back. We eventually learn that Tony has a nasty foot injury and Teddy is badly shaken. The foot has a nasty bleed in the afternoon and Tony has a blood transfusion. John thinks he might lose his foot but it's by no means certain. Teddy is going back by air tomorrow to look after Tony. Poor Tony, he's only had 6 weeks of command, having looked forward to it for 18 years, and now he may be off the road for good.

It's weeks since I've had any mail. Rations are very good here although water is increasingly scarce. The Wops have used some of the wells as lavatories – what charming people!

Tuesday 24th November 1942

I go up at first light to see Tony and Teddy before they depart [AMB now becomes an acting lieutenant colonel]. Tony is in very good heart but full of dope and is a horrid colour under his tan. Teddy seems not as good as yesterday but nothing serious.

Desmond and I go up to division before tea. We say cheerfully that we ought to be in time for the evening strafe and, by Jove, we are … Twelve 109s come in and give us hell. We get in the ACV vehicle which has a dozen hits on it and then the bomb rolls over the roof and lands outside, bouncing like an empty beer bottle. It settles and then, while I watch it, it explodes filling the car with gas but nothing else. Three are killed and five wounded, including poor Sam Maxwell who gets two bullets in the leg.

As soon as I get home we get a Wop strafing which is much less effective.

Wednesday 25th November 1942

There seems to be a party on for us so I go down to meet the divisional commander, John Harding,[7] and we then all go on to Agedabya to meet the corps commander. The first person to arrive is Nigel! After business Sir Oliver goes up the road and leaves Nigel and I to talk. Sir Oliver is charming and Nigel obviously gets on very well with him. He wears knickerbockers and has rather an old-fashioned appearance.

The village is filthy dirty and very knocked about by the shelling. There are mines and booby traps everywhere. I see three mines go off in the time I am there.

We are due to probe the Agheila defences. I think air is going to be the chief annoyance as they seem to be getting stronger by the day. Ours hasn't come out in force yet and may not do so in time to reap the benefit.

We move up another 10 miles. See the rear division strafed just after we move, killing Simms and wounding poor Sergeant Windsor. Luckily John L is down there and renders medical aid.

---

7. Field Marshal Allan Francis 'John' Harding, 1st Baron Harding of Petherton, GCB, CBE, DSO & two Bars, MC (1896–1989).

Friday 27th November 1942

Have a conference to arrange the column and everyone meets everyone else. Taken all round one could not hope for a nicer or more 'English' looking collection. I have no doubt we'll pull together well as a team.

We get off at 11.30am after various delays and avoid a Stuka attack by 10 minutes. Get forward to Mersa Brega where we are almost through the Hun lines. From all accounts, we are not going to get all our tasks completed but we are determined to make a proper nuisance of ourselves.

Receive a letter from Cara in the evening dated 12th November. It was flown up by a Rhodesian who is not on this column.

Saturday 28th November 1942

Brian sends patrols off early and we follow once the extra petrol has arrived. I carry on with the recce party. We decide on a position for a fortified base and then call up the rest of the column.

Before we are all settled we get a 109 attack. They drop a lot of bombs, mostly unexploded. One goes clean through the side of a quad without exploding. Roddy and I find a stick beside us and scramble out on hands and knees. Very undignified!

Despite the attack, our only casualty of the day was due to a mine.

Sunday 29th November 1942

Go up to see Jumbo and then get bombed by Macchis and four 109s for 20 minutes. Jumbo sticks it out 'til near the end when a petrol can catches fire so has to bail out. It's like a nightmare. I'm close by but powerless to help. These new 109s flash by time and time again so close by that I could chuck my beret at them.

In the afternoon we have another visit from fourteen Stukas but do no damage at all. The secret of our luck is partly down to wide dispersion and also due to feeling safe when in our cars.

We sit up late (10pm) to listen to Churchill. He tries to impress on us that though the news is good now on every front we must not relax our efforts [as support for the war at home flagged, Churchill called the Allies' position in North Africa 'not a seat but a springboard'.] We have shown our courage in bad times and we must now show it in the period when things appear well. Relaxation might well spell disaster.

Monday 30th November 1942

Day of repairs and maintenance.

We have one attack with one bomb landing within 10 foot of Brian's car. Thankfully there's little damage – our luck so far has been unbelievable.

Tony P has apparently asked that Humphrey Lloyd[8] should get command. I am surprised that he should let personal prejudice come into the matter. Perhaps the drugs have affected him more than one would think.

Tuesday 1st December 1942

Talk to General Harding before daylight about command. I think he understands my point of view and is certainly very charming about it. He spends the day in front of my patrols. He is undoubtedly brave and is just the type that should be leading troops in the desert. He lives hard with no shelter at night and survives on cold bully, biscuits and water.

Our replenishing echelon comes up under George. He gets strafed (as he did yesterday) and loses some vehicles. He was so spread, though, that he didn't know his tail was being shot up!

Roddy hits a thermos mine. Adrian is rather shocked and one wheel is slightly damaged but nothing more. There are a mass of these about and, as they were laid last year, are now hard to see. Bloody little things! I see a sapper foolishly pick one up and [he] soon dies with two wounded.

Wednesday 2nd December 1942

We have a slow start with people sticking all over the place. Get hell from the air all day from Stukas and 109s. Strath from B Squadron is killed and some of our other chaps are wounded. We also lose rather a lot of vehicles but without proper anti-aircraft or RAF one must expect this. We manage to bring down two 109s, much to everyone's satisfaction.

Poor Robert Wingfield-Digby, sitting on the front of his Daimler, takes most of the force of a thermal bomb explosion in the seat of his pants. He has horrid great pieces torn out of the back of his thighs. Whilst painful, thankfully it's not too serious, but he has to be evacuated.

As we've lost a number of essential vehicles, petrol supplies and wirelesses I decide to turn for home tomorrow. We've made a very complete recce of the ground and enemy positions. Our presence here has been deeply resented but I feel we are not strong enough to go further and will do no more good by sitting out in this desolate spot. We are further west than anyone else and, except for the RAF, as near to Tripoli as any Crown forces have been during the war.

---

8. Lieutenant Colonel Humphrey Lloyd (1903–90). At this stage he was away from the Royals commanding the Yorkshire Hussars, a yeomanry regiment, which had been stationed in Palestine for the first three years of the war. Hereafter he is often referred to as 'HWLL'.

Thursday 3rd December 1942

Having accomplished our task we set off for home. We strike better going and make good progress.

On arrival at base we get orders first to remain and then to get back to 4AB by 4pm tomorrow. All very tricky and to try and clear the matter I go off to try and reach division that night. I get benighted, lose my escort and have to spend a very miserable night by the roadside. Luckily I have some bedding but no wireless.

It starts to pour with rain at 11pm and goes on most of the night. A stream of water runs off the jeep tarpaulin and cascades via my pillow into the intimate depths of my flea bag. I don't discover it 'til there's a pool the size of Lake Chad.

Friday 4th December 1942

Start off at 6am on the darkest, coldest, wettest of days I can remember. Our clothes dry on us in the icy blast as we drive on.

Reach division by 6.30am. The general is just up and I get a satisfactory interview. There's an enormous amount of work to be done and changes to be made. Tomorrow I am sending Roddy with a party to collect twenty-five cars from our old friends at 4SA. When they return and Brian is back we should just about get a week to reorganise ourselves.

Saturday 5th December 1942

Bitterly cold last night, as cold as any night I can remember. Sleep with everything on that I own and even then I'm cold!

Go up to see Ronnie and discuss the situation about Humphrey. He's very noncommittal, chiefly as he hasn't been bothered to think about it. Tell Victor and Dodie who are flabbergasted. It's very hard for me to do anything as the personal side looms too large – not that I have any self-interests really and I'm fully aware of my limitations.

The air is full of 'Spits' and 'Kitties'. I think there are a lot of new pilots taking the skies as they are forever stunting over our heads. As every gallon of petrol arrives here at a great cost of labour, their *joie de vivre* becomes hard to watch.

Sunday 6th December 1942

At 1pm I go up for an interview with the divisional commander. Find Roscoe in command. He'll be an ideal leader for this expedition of ours: full of guts, shrewd, determined and to the point.

See Harding later in the day. He sees my point of view and has promised to take no action 'til this battle is over. I offer to hand over to Brian but, thank heaven, the gesture is not accepted. I think it was realised that it was only made to demonstrate I am acting in the interests of the regiment and not my own.

Monday 7th December 1942
Seem to be hard at it all day. Write solidly all morning and then spend an afternoon interspersed with interviews and discussions with Dodie, Brian and Victor. If I ever have command I am quite sure that it's important to keep the 2i/c and squadron leaders fully in the picture and get their views. There is no point being a dictator as there's plenty of things that a squadron leader knows about better than a commanding officer.

Ronnie comes to dine. He, and everyone else, has received a bunch of mail. All our minds therefore are rather concentrated on the letters that burn holes in our pockets. By the end of dinner no one can resist just opening one or two to see the contents. Half an hour later and everyone has unashamedly got down to solid letter reading. I get six from Cara, all written in a real happy vein.

Tuesday 8th December 1942
Get told to move. We've just got settled down with the promise of a complete undisturbed week with people dispersed, vessels stripped and messes going etc. This will delay us 2 days but no one seems to care or realise it.

Start off at 1.15pm and are kept hanging about doing a 25-mile march in 4 hours. As soon as we get in Roscoe tells me there's a flap on and we may have to move at short notice, whatever our state.

Hold a squadron leaders conference and tell them first that HWLL may be coming but 'til then I want their loyal cooperation. I also have to let them know that all present appointments may prove to be temporary. I think the present officers we have here have much the same ideas and are more progressively minded than their predecessors. That is one of the reasons I don't want HWLL.[9]

Wednesday 9th December 1942
As we are so far out and in virgin country there is an extraordinary, muffled silence. At night, one wakes up with the feeling that there must be a thick fog. I've never known such dark, clear nights in the desert as we are having now.

---

9. In his memoirs, AMB wrote: 'Tony P, hoping to get command again, plotted to get Humphrey Lloyd, who was senior to both of us, out to command. This was against all the squadron leader's wishes as it meant that all promotion would be delayed and our best junior officers would go off to command other regiments.'

I dine with A Squadron and have a terribly funny evening. Brian is given a bottle of rye whiskey which he consumes and when finished it's the signal for him to say goodnight. He's highly amusing but a very cynical old bird and I'm not sure a terribly good influence on the younger chaps. Eddie and Derek are both young enough to be rudely shocked by his attitude to sex.

At the end of the evening I have a mile to come home. Am very grateful to find it but can't see it 'til I'm within 15 yards. I come to the conclusion that it's an act of God if one can find one's tent after dinner! Bob recently had to get his wireless going and request a tracer to be sent up to guide him home.

Friday 11th December 1942

Have Sergeant Wilkinson on my car. He's an awfully nice chap and will always be remembered as the band boy in Meerut who was in love with the brigadier's daughter. A sad case of unrequited love.

Roscoe dines with us. It turns into a filthy wet, windy, cold evening. C Squadron are having their Christmas dinner as they feel they may not get it later on! They come to outside our mess through the heavy rain and, as tight as ticks, sing hearty carols to us.

B Squadron go to the cinema show at brigade but the lorry never makes it back and the men spend an awful night in the open. There's not even a tarpaulin for them, poor devils.

Saturday 12th December 1942

Go to conference at noon and told that everything has been brought forward by 48 hours and that we are to move at once. General Freyberg[10] comes along to meet us as we will now be under his command. Harding comes to say farewell.

The conference is abandoned with no plan given and only brief orders. I decide to set off with two of the three squadrons with Jack to follow on at first light.

We are all agog as to why this sudden move. If our presence really is unknown then, when discovered, we should give Rommel a rude shock. No enemy plane, as far as we know, has been near this area.

---

10. Lieutenant General Bernard Freyberg, 1st Baron Freyberg, VC, GCMG, KCB, KBE, DSO & three Bars (1889–1963). Freyberg had a distinguished record in the First World War, taking part in the beach landings at Gallipoli, becoming the youngest general in the British Army and then serving on the Western Front, where he won the Victoria Cross and three DSOs. During the Second World War he commanded the New Zealand Expeditionary Force and later served as Governor-General of New Zealand 1946–52.

Sunday 13th December 1942
Move on at daylight. It's a free-for-all rush for this big *wadi* which is only crossable at certain points. There are two New Zealand brigades also in the race and Lugs somewhere behind with his tanks. It's not unlike the rush for the first fence at Aintree.

We leaguer near brigade in the evening and I go over to see Roscoe and Freyberg. Everyone is in great heart as to how this thing has started. At first one felt the whole thing was far too rushed and likely to end in failure but we are now on the road and must appear a formidable force.

Monday 14th December 1942
We cross the Marada track which has a wire fence 'defending' it from the east. I've never seen such a waste of time and material.

The petrol lorry turns up just as I'm in despair with only 6 gallons left. I had the uncomfortable job of saying at the conference that we'd soon become immobile and was told we'd have to be left behind!

Do a night march. All goes extremely well and manage in 2 hours what we were expecting to do in five. We are all hoping for big things tomorrow.

Tuesday 15th December 1942
General Freyberg arrives at 7am, just before first light, and finds fires blazing everywhere. His white anger is quite frightening and for a full 5 minutes he is completely out of control. He went off and stood alone to regain control and then comes back and is back to normal. In actual fact, I do not believe it mattered.

We march on 'til 2pm and cross into Tripolitania,[11] the first British unit ever to enter that country. There is a very feeble attempt by the Hun to cut the road but nothing definitive is done. We are now back up to strength but gnash our teeth in fury that we are wasting a fine flanking movement. The cork is obviously not in the bottle and tonight the Hun are pouring out of the bag to safety.

Wednesday 16th December 1942
Last night we had a lot of enemy on the move. C Squadron find a column which Roscoe decides to hunt. As soon as we start we get news of another bigger column but we are already committed. We have a poor hunt killing two tanks and several lorries. It's just like a bad day's hunting at the end of the season.

---

11. One of the three administrative districts within Italian Libya, and a separate colony 1927–34.

This afternoon I saw a great red dog fox which gave me these whimsical homesick thoughts.

Thursday 17th December 1942

Gather a lot of good information about Nofilia which turns out to be rather strongly held. The Greys have a good scrap but poor Mark Bodley gets a 50mm straight through him and is killed. Very bad luck. Lugs and Massy R are also wounded.

The New Zealanders again bog it and do not manage to block the road. We are quite certain the Hun will again slip out after dark, leaving us to find a mass of mines and empty trenches in the morning.

Friday 18th December 1942

Move on early. B Squadron go through the village and meet a mass of mines. The enemy is 50 miles back along the road by now.

I catch up with brigade and get at least ten orders and counter-orders. It all starts from the top as Freyberg changes his mind every 10 minutes so by the time the orders filter down to us everything is in disorder.

Eventually hack along west and settle down for 48 hours (they say). I don't think it's a bad idea provided they stick to it. We are now on the 17th parallel of longitude. By Cairo time the sun sets just after 6pm and rises just before 8am. It's bitterly cold at night and even on the move by day one wants to wear all one's clothes.

A curious habit is starting whereby officers drink their whisky neat from the bottle. This is supposedly due to the water shortage but I suspect that one or two officers find it tasty that way.

Sunday 20th December 1942

It's a miserable day with no shelter from the wind and dust. It makes my paperwork extremely difficult.

Read a German diary. The diarist starts off by saying, 'First impressions of North Africa – frightful'. I agree completely and wonder what his later impressions were. His chief complaints seem to be about rations, lack of water, sleeping in the open and our bombing. I can't disagree about any of these but do not understand how he could expect to sleep anywhere else. Except for the native village in Agedabya, I haven't seen a building or slept under cover since I left Cairo in early September.

Go to brigade after dark and see Roscoe. Have had some trouble getting Roddy and Jack's awards through. What was headline news in October has now faded into an incident during a period of excitements. It's frustrating as owing to operations we've never before been able to get these citations in before.

Monday 21st December 1942

Am summoned for an interview at 9am. Have a cold shave and rush off. Find all COs are going to meet the corps commander. Travel with Bob [commanding officer of the KDGs] who is becoming a real and dangerous rival.

Monty, himself, is present and Bob and I have to give an account of our doings. We jockey madly for position and try to minimise the doings of others. I score the last point by getting Monty to put 'ROYALS' with a large red arrow pointing right off the map and he wipes out KDGs.

Monty is in great form and puffed with self-pride. He's aged a lot and changed from the sour little brute we knew to a more charming, smiling exterior. I heard someone say, 'Monty only got as far as this by efficiency' which is pretty damning. There's no doubt he'll be a quarrelsome old man in a few years.

Wednesday 23rd December 1942

Head off to visit the patrol line with John Harding. We cover an enormous amount of ground – he seems to be in the habit of doing about 100 miles a day.

At Gasr Bu Hadi we see a mass of gazelle, bustards and a great flock of sandgrouse. As we arrive a little tank comes out of the fort, gets behind a ridge and fires off a few rounds. It then dashes back behind the shelter of a wall like a goldfish going into the weeds. We go on and look over the enemy positions which are all over a *wadi*. There's not much there, a few lorries and dug-in positions. We are not even shot at.

Get in before dark, by the grace of God, as otherwise would have been benighted. I think Harding is rather impressed by my navigation which is sheer good luck! Harding tells me I've been put in for (temporary) command. I am not a little thrilled. I shall put on my extra pips on Christmas Day. The last Colonel Barne commanded the 12L.

Thursday 24th December 1942

The general slept with us last night so we have to up betimes as he's always on early moves. We head off at 9am over the most lovely going at 25mph. We run straight into a herd of gazelle. I break the line, get in the jeep and we go after them. Ludford drives me well, but madly, and I get a nice young doe with my revolver using the only round I put into it. Liver and bacon for breakfast tomorrow, boys! Fresh meat is always a luxury here.

Roddy takes the fort in a most unorthodox manner. He drives up in his armoured car after knocking out the anti-tank gun. He is shot at with rifles, revolver, hand grenades but is forced to retire when his gun jams. The enemy seems so discomforted that they evacuate. We find a lot of blood and spent cases but the great thing is that they are hustled out without destroying the well or its pumps.

Roscoe comes up and spends the afternoon with us. He informs me that Humphrey Lloyd will definitely be getting command and, I suppose, is just awaiting the opportunity to step in. I feel just as flat as this ruddy bit of desert we are sitting on.

Friday 25th December 1942

After sunrise a heavy fog falls like a blanket. Nine Me109s fly directly over us but don't seem to see us.

I have to go to brigade and, as the regiment is the only unit in touch with the enemy, it is my party! I wear my colonel's badge for the first time. At the end of the discussion on how to take Sirte, Adrian announces, 'Sirte is in our hands' and I feel very proud.

Victor arrives back from a recce to Sirte and says it is a dear little Wop town with villas and gardens etc but the Hun has systematically blown up every home. There can be no military reason for such wanton destruction. The two Arabs who help us both get legs blown off by booby traps and we have great trouble getting them back. Poor devils.

The Eighth Army has been liberally treated with pork and I consider it a great feat for getting it up to us. Together with our rum ration and gazelle meat we are more than satisfied. The pork is excellent and I get King to brew up the rum into a punch which the men enjoy. I get a letter and calendar from Ma.

The gunners come over after dark. We hear the King's speech, a good simple homely talk but very stirring.

Sunday 27th December 1942

Move on in the morning and regain touch with the enemy who spirits himself back in the most amazing way as soon as we approach. One is inclined to believe that he is leading us up the garden path. The KDGs are now up with us and we are beginning to get a bit suspicious of their information which seems a bit dressed up for the shop window.

In the evening we eat a gazelle haunch that has been hanging from the mudguard for 5 days. It is black and quite horrid to look at but when cooked up is perfectly excellent – very tender and gamey. The black exterior gives it a form of crackling, I think it's the flies eggs that have been laid in it! I also consume my first bottle of beer for a very long time. It is most welcome.

Monday 28th December 1942

Spend first part of the morning having an all over wash. Get into clean clothes, including one of the new issue shirts which is of a jolly good material.

Once again the enemy have debunked during the night and so we have to move on. We go round to the south and pass through some rather fine scenery including a little place in a great gorge with a white mosque, burial ground and two good wells.

Tuesday 29th December 1942

Jumbo does a very good day's work. He has Sergeant Lay with him and [they] form a good combination. They knock out a Hun armoured car, a 10 ton lorry and a fully laden petrol lorry. It makes a fine column of smoke.

Kenneth goes off on a recce to the south and captures a couple of Wops. He brings in a lot of information, on which we move in the evening. We have a good Stuka attack just before we leave. It is the first for a long time but does little damage.

We go down a side *wadi* for the night. It is quite awesome with high escarpments and flat tops. I really don't believe that anyone but our own chaps (and possibly the 11th Hussars) could do what we do. If the infantry or guns go anywhere they always scream for us to lead them and on any column we always command.

Wednesday 30th December 1942

At dawn Stukas come in for brigade for over 20 minutes. Thank heaven we're not there. Strong air attention goes on for the forenoon and at 1pm six of our fighters catch six 109s. It's quite pathetic the way our Kitties play with the 109s at low altitude. I see three 109s literally blown to pieces in the air and another comes down. It's a most refreshing sight.

We have a certain amount of warring all day. Jack gets to Bungem at 11am and finds the fort in flames. The enemy has destroyed everything there and retreated south.

Thursday 31st December 1942

C Squadron get embroiled in a battle with eight enemy armoured cars. Hogarth takes them on and destroys two. He has to abandon his car, however, and the other gets hit too. I have to send in reinforcements.

The *wadi* in which we are living leads into a much larger *wadi*, a sort of dead Isis pouring nothing into a lifeless Thames. The land has a tired, defeated look as if it gave up living a million years ago and is now resigned to midday frying. But of course it is impressive in an oppressive way. Sitting in the *wadi*, the surrounding banks feel like mountain ranges, their tops pressed flat by the gigantic palm of wind erosion.

Through centuries Nature has decided that the land should support no life. In 1943 the Eighth Army has decided it should.

Friday 1st January 1943

As C Squadron had an engagement yesterday and have two wounded, I take John and his ambulance out at first light to collect them. I have to go on a recce in any case and be back at brigade by 10am. It's all a bit of a rush.

Am fighting to get the regiment out of the line for a bit to rest and re-equip. Take Roscoe on a recce in the afternoon. He is in very good form and clearly the Royals' stock is very high for the moment.

Saturday 2nd January 1943

We hear the 11th Hussars are coming up tomorrow to take over. We've been in the line now for over 10 weeks and certainly do need some respite. Our car strength is lower than 50% and, of those, a further 50% are on their last legs. People don't seem to realise that every vehicle here has to do over 1,500 miles before it even reaches the front line.

Monday 4th January 1943

Roscoe, Ronnie and Geoffrey Bull, the new brigade major, all come up to say goodbye. Very complimentary.

We have the most wretched drive back as the wind lifts the sand and almost cuts one's skin and bruises one's eyeballs. Desmond and I go into division on arrival and have tea with General Harding. All very friendly.

We get a good fug up in the tent and play poker after dinner. I don't know when I last had such a cheerful evening.

Tuesday 5th January 1943

Glorious idle morning and shave in bed after sunrise from the shelter of my tent. Write solidly 'til lunch in the office lorry which is well placed to collect the sun and shelter the wind.

After lunch hold discussions with all officers on the composition of the regiment if we go on to the Continent. I have a squadron leaders' conference on some small points followed by a bath. It's not quite a bath truthfully but it's an all-over in a basin of hot water.

Wednesday 6th January 1943

Have to be back at division to make a report on recent recces, all highly secret.

Move on to corps where we get orders to spend the night. People could simply not be more charming – Nigel is half the reason, having been a definite hit there, and the word 'ROYALS' on the shoulder is the other half.

Go around all the people that can help us get on the road again and end up having a full hour with Sir Oliver. He lives in great luxury and Nigel lives in a penthouse against his caravan. His commode is absolutely full of whisky!

Monty has his caravan about 100 feet away. Nigel has marked out a track so that Leese won't lose his way by night!

We get twenty Macchis strafing us in the afternoon. No one this far back has ever seen Wop fighters before.

Thursday 7th January 1943

Return across country calling in at division. Monty comes to see us after lunch with Harding. He motors round and inspects the men of HQ, B3, C, B, A in turn. He talks to every officer and about one man in three. It's very informal and I was very impressed by the men's bearing and the way they answered his questions. They all spoke up and gave good intelligent answers. He kept reminding us that we'd be needed very soon and were our cars pointing the right way?

Each squadron gave him three cheers as he drove off. The cheers were spontaneous and enthusiastic and he was visibly touched by it.

We get strafed after he leaves and poor Thomas of A Squadron gets killed, with another three wounded.

Friday 8th January 1943

This would be a quiet spot if it were not for the RAF. We are in a direct line between the Hun and our new fighter aerodromes. The result is a constant hum which keeps us with one eye cocked skywards in case it's an Me109 returning to do some strafing.

One Spitfire crashes in the leaguer. The pilot bales out but the machine comes down in a headlong dive and breaks into a thousand small fragments. Even the engine is split in two.

Julian is going round collecting officers' shopping lists. There is a travelling officers' shop available near here. Our wants are many and varied since it's over three months that we've had any chance of renewing our wardrobes and things don't last very long here. I need boots, shoes, socks, handkerchiefs, goggles, a table, a chair (my old Indian one got bumped out of the truck) and a new valise.

Sunday 10th January 1943

Rush up to corps to be at the talk to all commanders at noon. Monty tells us all the dope, it's just a pity one cannot record it. He gives us the greatest confidence and we all leave with our tails up.

One doesn't need particularly good sight to see that things are happening. Our air is like bees in May and the road is stiff with tanks coming up on transporters. It really all does make for a thrilling sight. Oliver says that everyone knows what is happening, including the Germans and Cairo, but the great secret is the date and direction of the attack.

Five cars come up for us today and we're due to get eleven more tomorrow. Then it's a gamble if we can get enough rest before the big day ...

Wednesday 13th January 1943

The squadron leaders and I go up to brigade for the divisional commander to give a talk. Harding puts it very well and the brigade operation order is very well written. The regiment, less B Squadron, come up to almost the same place we were before and A and C are to take over from the 11th H.

We've benefited enormously by our rest and refit. With luck we should get B up tomorrow and start this battle as strong as we've ever been.

Thursday 14th January 1943

I move HQ to join C Squadron but remain myself to collect guns, sappers, provost etc and to meet the divisional commander who is coming up at 2pm.

Well, the next week is going to see a concrete milestone towards the end of the war. Monty didn't promise but he prophesied the 20th or 21st as the probable date we'd be in Tripoli. But the best laid plans of mice and men ... Come what may, it won't be later than the end of January.

Friday 15th January 1943

The big push starts at 7.15am, very cold and dark. There's not a sound at all from the north which is very strange.

We get a bad start as we are 15 miles of poor going behind the starting line. Roddy gets on well but Jack is held up by heavy fire. We struggle on with our unwieldy tail and by dark are just short of Fascia.

We go down one of the worst escarpments I've ever seen in the semi-darkness. I'm sure in broad daylight it would have looked too steep to attempt. Remarkably we have no accidents which says a lot for our drivers.

Saturday 16th January 1943

Move on again, still leading the advance. We take Fascia and head on north then west across some really awful going. We move through a rather fine *wadi*. The bottom is cultivated and there is a strong smell from the mass of wild flowers.

Roddy gets ambushed higher up in the *wadi* but gets the better of the attacking party. Brigade close up on us in the afternoon – a position they love and we hate as it cramps our style entirely.

Brigade spend the night with us. We have a cold meal as there are fears that fires may bring enemy aircraft. The whole atmosphere stinks of safety first instead of old school 'cavalry dash'. Given a troop of guns we could have been in Beni Ulid tonight.

Sunday 17th January 1943

Delighted to find real frost on the ground in the few places where there was some moisture on the surface. It really is bitterly cold.

We lead on down the *wadi* and debouch on to the Bir Tala plain. One can see for miles in all directions. After waiting for many hours for brigade, we reach the road outside Beni Ulid.

The advance is not without adventure as we, at last, have a troop of guns and have three small engagements. The road is full of enemy vehicles and we have another engagement at sunset. The 60th arrive and help us block the road. There is then an after-dark engagement lasting 3 hours in which we come off best.

We are now going into reserve. I think it's ideal timing so as to let the KDGs do some work for the next couple of days and then we'll persuade the brigadier to ship us in for the final race into Tripoli.

Monday 18th January 1943

KDGs take over from us but not until we've made it into Beni Ulid. We count twelve abandoned tanks, including a Mark IV Special and a Mark III Special, after hustling the enemy last night. We keep getting reports from C and B Squadron 'til after noon, thus wiping the eye of the KDGs. Very satisfactory after the way they treated us at Nofilia.

As we are now the rearguard we spend the rest of the day idling in the hot sun in a *wadi* bed. At about 4pm we are dozing when Humphrey Lloyd bursts in. He is wearing colonel's crowns and our grey beret! We are absolutely flabbergasted and Humphrey is not a little embarrassed. I just cannot put my feelings on paper.

Tuesday 19th January 1943

Start off at 7.30am to close up on brigade. We go through Beni Ulid which looks like a film set. There is a castle on a hill then the road winds down the escarpment into a great canyon of olive trees with ancient, crumbling stone houses along both sides.

Humphrey is going to be quite impossible and I can see I shan't last long. He contradicts everything one says and tries to boss everyone and everything. Wintle never did have a very high opinion of him and I don't think he was far wrong. He seems obsessed with the idea that the regiment has gone to the dogs and is trying pompously to go against old customs. He understood that treating brother officers to drinks had become a habit and was to cease forthwith! I made sure I took a jolly good dollop from his bottle!

Thursday 21st January 1943

Head along the road at dawn to see the situation and am greeted with a salvo! Roscoe tries to get us to return to the rear of brigade but I am anxious to avoid that – given four guns I'd be through Garian in no time. From a high point we can see Tripoli burning briskly. The road here leads through some really precipitous country and, as usual, the Wops have made a fine 'scenic' road through it all in cutting s-bends across embankments and across cliff faces.

Humphrey is complaining a lot about pains in his back. How fortunate it would be if he found this life too much for him. I really think he is finding he is not welcome and to all intents and purposes he is a stranger. Only four officers and a handful of NCOs remember him and it is a great disappointment to many to have another officer in over their heads.

Friday 22nd January 1943

Jack still hasn't got Garian so we decide to leave the high ground. I go ahead to see the brigadier but miss the axis and find myself ahead of the Greys as they make an attack on Azizia. I only discover my mistake when shells start falling about me!

Saturday 23rd January 1943

We move on at 6.30am. There's still quite a good moon which enables us to get over some very bad country.

I go out to see Roddy and take some sappers out. He has been sent out especially to search for rations as we are now very short. I find a good dump and send a lorry out to collect it all. Also find 2,000 12-bore cartridges – they are over £2 per hundred in Cairo! Discover a crashed Liberator [B-24 Liberator, American heavy bomber], a very sad spectacle. I collect the official USAAF numbers. The name *The Lovely Irene* still remains on an unblemished piece of fuselage.

It has been reported that our troops have entered Tripoli today. It's all rather of an anticlimax somehow. We move on up into the hills where we intend to remain until relieved. This is the end of the hunt, and the end of the period of my command!

Sunday 24th January 1943
Attend church at 11am but Roscoe comes halfway through so I have to leave. He has come to say farewell as he is taking over 8th AB. Newton-King of 4th SAs is taking over, a second pass-over for poor Ronnie.

Two Arabs walk in at daylight with news of two Yank airmen. Go up to Jefren and a bunch of Wogs meet me with a Yank called Bishop. They have looked after him very well. The natives we have met are all amazingly intelligent, well informed and most importantly anti-Wop!

Monday 25th January 1943
Go into brigade with Humphrey on various matters. Muffkins there is growing a moustache and looks awful. The new brigadier comes in closely followed by the new divisional commander who turns out to be Bobby Erskine, late BGS to Monty.

A situation develops as guns, info etc are put under me. All very unnecessary as we next hear that Brian has knocked out two eight-wheeler cars and is moving on. We all go up the road to see what is happening and the situation as to who is in command becomes mixed. I had already offered to give up but Humphrey refused to take it on.

Tuesday 26th January 1943
We move at crackers, bitterly cold but fine. Reach a nice village in the foothills with a definite frost on the ground. The natives are very hospitable and we get a few eggs and a lot of sweet, crisp carrots.

There's a big mail in. Receive five from Cara and four from Ma including a lovely pair of socks. Ma's last letter was written on her 61st birthday – it seems incredible to think she can be so old. I suppose one never really thinks of one's mother as old. Cara seems intensely happy. Thank God she's so settled and has Christopher to keep her from brooding.

Wednesday 27th January 1943
I go up to Brian who is starting a battle. He does awfully well but eventually it gets a bit hot for him so I call up C Squadron and take control myself. I stay there 'til sunset having laid my plans for the continuation of the battle tomorrow, providing the Hun hasn't been frightened off already. I then have a 42-mile hack back home, getting a puncture en route.

Peter Lee collects five Huns who had bailed out of their eight-wheeler and he disarms over fifty Libyan soldiers who are riding along the Tunisian border. I also collect a few. They are coming in from the outlying country mounted on ill-bred Southern European nags. The saddlery is very Algerian, cloth covered with Moorish stirrups.

I've done 16 years' service today and from tomorrow – or some near date – will be completely without command.

Friday 29th January 1943
The best breakfast for years: fried eggs, American bacon on toast, coffee, then brown bread and marmalade, eaten on grass, off plates in a palm grove beside a little pool of the clearest water I've seen since I last looked a gin square in the face.

Go up to the village to interview the sheikh. The village is centred around a circular 'fort' that turns out to be a granary. Inside there are four stories of little windows all set askew like a child's picture-book house. I take Trooper Williamson who talks Italian having been a waiter in Italy. We get a most friendly reception.

Saturday 30th January 1943
My truck comes up and I go in to Tripoli taking Peter Lee who is off on a LRDG swan. The main road is magnificent but Jerry, in his retreat, has blown it at frequent intervals, which makes the journey pretty uncomfortable for those sections.

Ring Nigel to say I'm coming for the night. I'm very lucky to find him in as he joins the brigade at dawn. We have a very giggly time with Burgundy over dinner followed by a bottle of Drambuie.

Sunday 31st January 1943
Rise very late (for me) having slept in a shelter close to the chief's caravan. Attend a victory parade and church service. It's a fine setting and the 11th Hussars manage to seize and hold the full stage. Runners-up are the Highland Division who are all kilted and in bonnets.

I go around the port. The damage, partly by bombing and partly by Hun demolition, is terrific. The Hun has sunk at least five ships in the harbour mouth and many barges filled with concrete. Movements and Transportation have done wonders and are already landing over 1,000 tons per day.

Join a crowd entering a house thinking it's a place of interest before finding it's a queue for a brothel – the inmates must be working overtime! I'm rather revolted by the sight. It's ORs only but I expect there are officers behaving equally badly round the corner.

Tuesday 2nd February 1943
I always wake early here just to enjoy the exquisite pleasure of watching the first shafts of light strike the palms. At first wakening each leaf is clearly arched black against the sky as sharp as any needle could produce on copper

plate and then the sun jumps up and the effect is like coloured lights being switched on.

Go up to brigade, taking Brian, for a tactical exercise. It's not very instructive nor does it bring much out. It does allow Brian and I to have a long talk over the general state of affairs though. Jack has now put in to go off for a job so things must be serious. If only HWLL would realise how much people resent his butting in and his foolish attitude I'm sure he could soon settle in. Someone has got to talk to him but I am not in a position to do so myself.

Wednesday 3rd February 1943
KDGs take over at first light and we go back 30 miles to the same nice spot we were at on 23rd. Take pot shots with the Luger all the way along the roadside. It's childish but these days one's general outlook is childish. I think we are all terrible weary. I, for one, feel it very much and it's noticeable now with a good many others. When one gets out of the line and relaxes a little, one feels absolutely worn out. Just now I'd give anything to have 48 hours in a comfy bed in a house.

HWLL goes off to Tripoli for a couple of days. He jokingly asks me to hold the fort and 'hold off the mutiny'. I wonder if he is becoming aware of the feeling of unrest in the regiment?

Thursday 4th February 1943
Visit Jack during the morning and find him very bolshie. It would appear that everyone is bolshie. There's never been such an unhappy atmosphere of general distrust and gloom so long as I can remember.

HWLL returns from Tripoli. Have a talk with him and am rather blunt in my speech and stick to the point. He writhes a bit but it's doing good. I cannot see any chance of his doing a graceful withdrawal as a man of brain or thinner skin would do.

Friday 5th February 1943
Hold a squadron leaders' conference and the atmosphere is rather electric and HWLL looks visibly nervous as to the outcome. When everyone is gone except Brian and Roddy, I nail him down and we get some definite policy out of him that no more outsiders shall return unless there's a real vacancy. It is obvious now that HWLL realises the regiment has been running fairly smoothly for the last 10 years despite his absence.

I do hope that people will come together and return to that old happy life. Someone once asked me, 'Do you still keep up that lovely habit of all joining up at HQ after dark and enliven the desert with your laughter?' The answer at the moment is sadly 'no'. I don't think anyone has come for a friendly visit for a fortnight and laughter is seldom heard now.

Sunday 7th February 1943

Go off into Tripoli on leave. See various officers after dinner and watch rather a good raid on the harbour. They pick up the plane in the lights and give it hell.

Monday 8th February 1943

Rise at 6am on a cold and wet morning. Drive down to the aerodrome in the dark. Quite how I missed a head-on collision with a camel and then a staff car I simply don't know.

Travel in a Lockheed Lodestar in which I now write this. It's very comfortable and, so far, has been a textbook flight. The plane is a civil one though when we left there were fighters streaming out on operations.

We get into Cairo at 5pm. The last bit of the flight was interesting, right over Knightsbridge and the El Alamein line where I could pick out many details from my time there. We come along the Nile Delta very low and it's a pleasant sight with luscious green palms, native villages and men, women, camels, donkeys teeming about.

Tuesday 9th February 1943

Go to GHQ in the morning about a passage to Rhodesia and am stunned to hear they are almost unobtainable. Cable Cara who, I know, will be miserable. Lunch alone which is the best thing in my present mood. God, it is sickening … I'd taken it all so much for granted.

Thursday 11th February 1943

Spend the morning in GHQ doing some work and seeing old friends, including BJ. He has gone completely to the dogs and keeps a Dago mistress (who was also an officer's mistress in the last war) and is fast killing himself on Canadian rye.

Friday 12th February 1943

Wonderful lunch with the judge of stuffed artichokes, devilled goose, mince pies with red wine and the inevitable brandy. Golding, the lawyer, comes in at the end of lunch to talk 'shop' about the flat lease. He's the most pleasant elderly European Jew but don't glean much from him as feel my pockets are not full enough for him.

Rush off to the club to see Babe who starts telling me how grateful we should to him for getting HWLL back to us. I tell him exactly how we all feel and put it pretty bluntly.

Tuesday 16th February 1943

Get my movement order – I fly back tomorrow. Try to get some more rations but NAAFI now only issues foodstuffs against a ration ticket. Things are obviously getting short now. The bars are also short of drink despite opening hours of 12.30–2pm and 6–10pm. The war will not be able to last much longer at that sort of rate.

Visit the judge in the evening and make arrangements for the disposal of the flat on Mary's departure. I fear I am being far too philanthropic by keeping it going just for her.

Wednesday 17th February 1943

Leave at 5.45am. My baggage is 40lb overweight but manage to laugh it off. Don't laugh later when we have great difficulty leaving the ground. These Lockheeds crash very easily if over- or wrongly loaded!

Have an easy, quick flight (8 hours) but ground transport on arrival is non-existent. Meet up with Tim who kindly puts me up in his mess for the night.

Thursday 18th February 1943

Have enjoyed a really good night. I feel it may take a long time to learn to sleep really soundly indoors again. All this week I've never awoken feeling really refreshed.

Get a jeep to corps and hear that we have moved on miles and miles. Hop in an RASC staff car in Tripoli and get to Sabratha for lunch. The road is packed with vehicles and the troops all look so well and happy in comparison to the Cairo crowd.

Get a further lift in a lorry of fresh bread – the smell is simply heavenly. However, the afternoon clouds over and the wind gets up. Soon sand blows like a veil across the road and life becomes bloody, despite the smell from the back of the lorry!

Bed down literally on the Tunis frontier against a wheel for a long night of profound discomfort.

Friday 19th February 1943

It's still blowing a gale of sand at dawn and the light reveals a dreadful landscape of desolate, wind-blown tents with 'Beware Mines' signs everywhere.

Have a very good breakfast with Major Raper. They have an old Wop seven-tonner as a mess. It is beautifully fitted out and very well organised.

Saturday 20th February 1943

Spud turns up after lunch and I have the pleasant feeling on first seeing a grey beret again. Get back to the regiment, less A Squadron who are in the line, at about 6pm.

HWLL has settled in a bit but has definitely not got full command of the situation. He's over forty, very unfit and getting grossly fat. Not right for an armoured car regimental commander.

Wednesday 24th February 1943
HWLL has gone off for the day for the army commander's lecture. A signal came in last night to say the lecture was cancelled but was never handed in. The result is that HWLL leaves at 6am and drives 10 miles for no reason. How we all laughed!

Teddy got a hen from a native, a stupid looking bird that won't lay eggs. It's a toss-up whether it dies before it's killed or lays an egg in an effort to preserve its life. Life in the near future looks dull for the hen and for me.

Very good news from the other side of Tunisia. The Yanks and 6th Division have pushed the Hun right back and given him a good knock.

Thursday 25th February 1943
What a difference surroundings make. Here I am breakfasting in the delicate shade of an olive tree with the sweet smell of figs about one. It makes one's mind feel settled and rested.

Later I walk about 5 miles into the hills. There's a good deal of gunning and, in fact, a spent bullet or splinter whistles past me. Even so, it's lovely and peaceful. I put up a pair of partridges whose whirring makes me think of Linda.

Saturday 27th February 1943
The canteen returns with a load of NAAFI stores, including nine bottles of whisky. Brian comes in after dinner and drinks most of our share but repays us by keeping us amused all evening.

We are under orders to move tomorrow and will be direct under 7th Armoured Division.

Sunday 28th February 1943
Several of us not feeling quite as good as such a lovely spring day deserves. Brian is still extremely tight and completely unaware of what occurred last night.

Move after noon to a filthy piece of scrub-covered sand dune. It blows a gale and visibility drops to 100 yards but as my eyes are full of shit I can only take other people's word for it!

HWLL won't allow tents or shelters and we are having to stand to before dawn and sunset. It is like the old El Alamein days but the weather is less amenable. Our chiefs are clearly expecting a flap before we start our attack.

There's a good deal of movement in this direction and they've broken off battle around Kassarine. I personally think it's a defensive measure, not offensive.

Monday 1st March 1943
We are shelled in the afternoon. At the first shell a Fourth-of-July-like display of Very lights is shot up and then as the shelling continues the aircraft get up like a good flush of pheasants. It's an amazing sight. The shelling goes on intermittently all night but a large percentage of the shells are duds.

Tuesday 2nd March 1943
Spend the morning doing some work at B3. The two Hun guns are turned on RHQ just before I arrive and thank God I miss the bombardment. They all look a bit shaken.

John returns from A Squadron where he spent the night. He has evacuated poor SSM Morgan who is getting worse headaches than ever.

Wednesday 3rd March 1943
Jack comes in. It's the first time I've seen him since 7th February which shows how one can be close to people in one's own unit without seeing them for long stretches.

Thursday 4th March 1943
I recce a new position after breakfast as we are fast getting crowded out by the New Zealand division. We find a nice grove of olives, palms and late flowering peaches. There is also a glorious scent from a yellow blaze of charlock.

We see seven Spits rise from the neighbouring landing ground – they seem to have no particular purpose and are on no set course. Suddenly four 109s dash in and a mass of flak goes up preventing any bombs dropping on the LG. Before one has time to blink the Spits are on their tails and bring three of them down. It's an exhilarating sight and makes one more credible of the RAF story today of a convoy of twenty-two Jap ships completely wiped out except for one destroyer which escaped and another escort ship crippled but not sunk.

HWLL summoned to brigade after dark and comes back in a passion of rage over some signal procedure that went wrong. I have a stand-up row with him and go to bed still furious. I still see no solution to the problem of getting the poor old regiment back into shape. At the moment we are at sixes and sevens and far from happy.

Friday 5th March 1943

HWLL starts the day by trying to keep the row going. He threatens not to recommend me for command – luckily I have some unsolicited testimonials and do not think anyone would pay much attention to him as he's completely ignorant of the regiment.

Saturday 6th March 1943

The long expected attack starts at day break and produces no surprises or results. It's one of the noisiest battles any of us have experienced. The two big guns lob shells over at short intervals all day and each one makes a noise like a London bus coming directly at one. Luckily many of the shells seem to be duds. At one moment we count eight duds to five that go off with a sickening crash.

The air activity is terrific and the anti-aircraft fire from both sides is far more intense than ever before. Our aircraft keep up a constant stream of offensive patrols and we see several 109s shot down.

I ring Peter to ask the cause of the machine gun fire we can hear. He replies, 'Oh, only an angry German tank firing in the general direction of the Eighth Army!'

We don't hear much of what else is happening in other parts of the line but by our own and 12L reports, we make a tally of thirty-six tanks destroyed. The actual figure given later is thirty-one.

Sunday 7th March 1943

A very noisy night of artillery fire all night with Big Bertha at intervals. It also drizzles most of the night. There is more sustained air activity today. We see the Fw190 [Focke-Wulf Fw 190 Würger, a single-seat fighter] for the first time and see two 109s brought down in a fair fight before lunch. Another nearly knocks off our hats but we don't actually see it hit the deck.

The enemy has withdrawn to his old positions leaving a number of knocked-out tanks in front of our positions. There are various estimates but I believe the forty-two, as given by the RE, to be the most likely.

Get two letters from Cara dated 18th and 19th February. She's very upset about the HWLL situation here. I suppose I shouldn't burden her with these affairs but if I don't write to her about it I have no means of getting these things off my chest.

Monday 8th March 1943

Lunch with Jack and have a discussion. It's clear I'm a disturbing influence here but if I go Teddy won't be considered for command and an outsider would have to be brought in. That is the worst option of all. I shall have to leave if I get the chance of a good job in two or three months. In the meantime, HWLL will just have to stick it. By June anything may have happened in these uncertain times.

Wednesday 10th March 1943
After visiting division HQ I go to see Nigel. He seems extremely well and in good spirits. He's not particularly happy as an intelligence officer but he's much happier doing that than a staff job.

Walk around the leaguer all afternoon. The men are surprisingly clean and tidy in their habits – very different from most units and gunners in particular. The French and Italian are the dirtiest campaigners. They leave everything on the surface and one always finds a swarm of flies where they have camped, even in winter.

The complete lack of alcohol is getting us all down. One's conversation after dinner is unnatural and serious.

Friday 12th March 1943
I find a bottle of Kümmel I brought up in May last year. Victor and I go to A Squadron after dinner and have a very convivial evening. Our conversation becomes seditious and libellous at times. We look at our watches and find it after 1am. The moon is down so we grope our way home along ploughed fields to our respective trucks. Ludford helps us with his loud snoring.

Saturday 13th March 1943
As we were expecting to move tomorrow I wrote my normal Sunday letters in the morning. Basil comes back from a padre's conference to say the 11H have orders to take the same bit of line we were due to take over. We therefore gracefully climb down and prepare to stay here a few days longer.

Monday 15th March 1943
After an early breakfast Jack, John, Adrian and I start off on a shooting expedition We find a *jheel* [pond or marsh] which looks promising. Sadly it contains nothing more than six old spoonbill, some heron and large egrets.

As the day is yet young and we are near Goffer we take a ferry on to Gerba Island and lunch at the Grand Hotel. Am introduced to Mr Guido Pariente and find him the most charming and intelligent man. Have a long talk with him and he gives us all a glass of Cointreau which goes down 'like cream on a satin bedspread'.

He tells us lots of interesting news – how pro-Axis the Arabs are, how short of shipping in the Mediterranean the Axis are, how his son has joined the *Bataillon du Pacifique* [a Free French unit formed in French Polynesia in 1940], of the strike on growing vegetables due to the new tariffs, the shortage of flour etc.

We also meet the French recruiting officer who is with a most attractive young lady. She is about 6 months gone, not to a German, I hope. They seem to have taken everything worth taking on this island.

Wednesday 17th March 1943
King has come back and took over my car today. He came back of his own accord and looks pleased to be back. I am very happy to have him back. We also have had more cars delivered and arguably have more than we require.

Head to Boughrara in the morning where there are the remains of a temple, houses and a jetty. For some reason flowers always seem more profuse amongst ruins and this place is no exception to the rule. Whilst looking around I could see through a great carved pair of pillars the blue bay and a Spitfire comes across. It dives down to the sea and looses its cannons, whipping up a line of white spray. An absolutely thrilling sight.

We move on at 11.30am, an odd time for a peace march; the morning is spoilt as we are packing up, the afternoon is spoilt as we are making camp and in the middle the midday brew is made impossible. We are moving south to join up with our old Brigade again.

Thursday 18th March 1943
The QM gives me a new cardigan. I've been wearing my old one since we arrived in Palestine in 1938. Those jerseys were made of a wonderful material.

It blows much harder than I've ever known all night long. I keep beautifully warm and lie awake wallowing in the luxury of my new cardigan. If the Hun has been laying mines in quantity then we're going to have a very sticky time as there will be no trace left of mine, tank, men or their vehicles. The Guards had a very sticky time a few nights ago and the Grenadiers suffered heavily. Luckily Nigel and co were in reserve.

Saturday 20th March 1943
Wake to a lovely morning, fresh and cool with a clear sky. All the hills stand out as if cut out of cardboard. Every little detail can be seen as if painted on the scene.

We have a few bombs and ground strafing in the night but not sufficient to keep one awake. The big attack is strangely quiet and the day becomes a bit of an anti-climax. Our current job is one of 'telephone girls' as we have such a large number of wireless sets.

Get a letter from, and write one each, to Ma and Cara. How very important one's letters are, the sole connection between oneself and a sane world. I am sure some of these matrimonial troubles are caused by slackness in writing or possible incapacity for expression in paper. How can one live for years away from one's wife and expect her to remain the same on return if all connections have been severed. One might as well have been dead, and the dead can't be mourned forever.

Monday 22nd March 1943

The war news continues to be good. Everyone is very full of Winston's speech [*see* Appendix A]. He spoke at great length about post-war policy having started by denouncing those who were discussing it. He purposefully put us all back a pace by thinking the war might last another 18 to 30 months. I am sure there are many who require sobering up and to be kept at full work.

Tuesday 23rd March 1943

As things haven't made much progress on the coast it is decided to scrap the original plan. We are now left on the shelf and I'm afraid will be out of the war until the fall of Tunis. Rather disappointing. Bob has stolen all the thunder for the KDGs and deserves all the praise that he will surely get.

We rarely see an enemy plane and only occasionally hear one after dark. They drop a few bombs which are of nuisance value only. I am convinced that their output of planes and arms is now on the downward trajectory and ours is still rising.

The outcry for a second front seems to have temporarily stalled but I don't think we can delay it very much longer. Next month's moon may well herald its opening.

Friday 26th March 1943

It's now one week since we last saw an enemy plane. I don't think there's *lebensraum* for them now! When one sees our air strength growing daily and realises it's only a small proportion of the United Nations air strength then it is awesome to think of the cataclysm that is about to befall the Axis forces.

I grow more and more to dislike the wireless. People like Victor and Adrian can't sit in the mess without some frightful American crooning full blast. It forms a sort of background that they can't do without even though they are only semi-conscious of it.

Sunday 28th March 1943

I cut out new maps to put on my board so that I can follow what is happening north of Gabes. If, 6 months ago, a member of the Eighth Army had been interested in this part of the world, he would have been considered mad!

Hugh returns from leave about a fortnight overdue. The others have failed to get air passages and having to come by sea! He comes in in the evening and surprises us all by having a whisky. Previously he's always been teetotal. I think he's beginning to find his feet and discover the pleasures of life. There's no knowing what he's been up to in Cairo ...

Tuesday 30th March 1943

Ronnie takes Jack, Roddy and I out to shoot a *jheel*. It's a nice bit of marsh and covered in duck but they aren't very tame. We get four and return to flight it after tea. Unfortunately the duck come in very late but it's gloriously peaceful standing in the gathering gloom with all the familiar marsh sounds of snipe calling and the beats of wings overhead.

The German cartridges I've been using are very strong. I can pull down duck from a greater height than I'd have thought of lifting my gun to. I now have a bruised shoulder.

Friday 2nd April 1943

Our prospects for getting back into the war don't seem rosy although we are better for cars than we have ever been. We are being given nothing but sufficient rations to live on but I can see we're going to get very bored. Fleas abound and the flies are getting worse; both are very bad for our tempers!

Meet a charming old tramp who owns (or says he owns) the garden we're living in. He fought in France in the last war and is full of interesting chat. He's very pro de Gaulle, France and England. I intend to use him as a means to get fish and eggs shortly!

Dodie dines with us but it is not a cheerful meal. Philip F has just returned with news that Jumbo's ship was torpedoed and all but six men perished. Jumbo Riddell will be a sad loss to the regiment. He was very young although had been with us for about 3 years. He was made prisoner in Syria in June 1941 and released when the armistice was signed. He got an MC and was always a fearless and cool troop leader. He was a great naturalist and got endless pleasure in finding odds forms of life in even the most arid desert. He was always cheerful, never grumbled and a most charming companion.

Monday 5th April 1943

All officers go to a talk on our recent battle. It is most frightfully interesting but strangely enough only highlights enemy mistakes and how lucky we were. The Guards brigade destroyed all their own tanks with six-pounder fire. They were badly sited and the guns do not seem to have supported each other. Lessons to be learnt.

Visit an LG. The Yanks, SA and RAF are there with Mitchells, Kitties and Baltimores. It is a magnificent sight, hundreds of great planes and everything very calm. It's hard to believe that one of the greatest air offensives ever was going on from here.

The next attack on the Gabes Gap line starts tonight but, alas, we are not in it. We're behind everything. On my way in this morning I even saw nurses going forward in front of us.

Tuesday 6th April 1943

The new offensive [the Battle of Wadi Akarit] starts at dawn. It looks like an Eighth Army offensive while the First Army and US sit back. It seems strange considering that we have had 1,700 miles at least to get here and our line of communication must be very much the longer.

News comes in in dribs and drabs all day: 2,000 prisoners, all objectives reached, 5,000 prisoners, 4CLY safely over the bridgehead, 7,000 prisoners, NZs moving forward, 90L forming up for a counter-attack and so on.

Our light bombers have been busier than I've ever seen them, heading off laden with devices for the destruction of the Nazis. This stream of death will be kept up night and day until Tunis is ours and then still stronger 'til the end of the war. The tip of Tunisia must be an inferno.

I've started a new drink to safeguard the whisky. We have gin with a couple of drops of Worcester sauce. It's really quite palatable.

Wednesday 7th April 1943

Another day of heavenly weather and nothing to do but pick up bits of news from visitors. A football team is sent down, and I am forced to watch it as an officer. Adams comes with them. He's an extremely interesting fellow to speak to. He tells me that a Liberty ship loaded with Shermans came into Tripoli when he was there and that the ship had had its keel laid only 2 months previously![12]

Dine with Dodie to see the film *Desert Victory*. Quite a good film, very well served up but a bit amateur in style. It might look better on a proper screen I suppose. About 700 of us sit on one bank of a *wadi* on a glorious starlit night and see our daily lives for the last 18 months depicted for us.

HWLL also dines. His attitude is fast becoming unbearable. We are moving tomorrow but he doesn't tell me and when I ask him he says, 'Yes, to Ben Gardene' which is 50 miles back. John L is also there and says, 'No, we're going to Gabes' which is forward – the way the whole regiment wants to move. It struck me as very odd.

We seem to have the Hun on the run again but Rommel is a cunning sod, he never retreats in disorder but manages to reform some definite line. He hasn't got many left now to fall back on and soon his only option will be annihilation or capitulation.

---

12. Liberty ships were built in the United States from 1941. The record for construction was less than five days, with an average building time of 30 days during peak production.

Thursday 8th April 1943

We moved forward up through the Mareth Line to just south of Gabes. The Mareth Line looks a pretty tough proposition and I think would have proved a costly venture to break frontally. I follow from behind having seen the regiment through the starting gate. It's a new experience telling people to 'close up' instead of 'open out'. Our air has become so terrific that dispersal has become less important than speed and density of traffic along the roads.

Friday 9th April 1943

We go past Gabes, a nice looking village, but miss going in as we are the military bypass. I don't think the Hun even took the town road but we seem to have caught him out a great deal on the bypass.

We go through the newly pierced Akarit Line. The infantry are busy clearing it up. It was a great performance breaking through and one has a hankering to be in one show of that sort.

Roddy gets evacuated by air and Teddy takes over C Squadron. John thinks Roddy has kidney trouble.

Saturday 10th April 1943

Start off at 6am on a cold, cloudy morning. Drive all day over fields of corn and end up at a French farm. Two days ago we were bemoaning our fate that we were left out of battle. Tonight we are leading the Eighth Army with no one in front of us but the Hun who are legging it north.

We are a little disturbed at dusk by some bombers. These are the first enemy planes we have seen for weeks. One flare is dropped directly over us and it gives one a very naked feeling. It lands almost in B Squadron's petrol lorry! We also get a delayed action stick between us and B Squadron. Victor is a bag of nerves. Considering he's never been hit, it seems absurd and born from affectation.

We have a laugh that only an hour prior to the bombing I was consoling the old lady farmer in my best French that never again would she have to hear the sounds of war!

Sunday 11th April 1943

Drive on after breakfast, sticking to the roads now. It's most heavenly country now and I've never seen such a profusion of colour – great areas of yellow daisies, red poppies, dark green unripened wheat and pink, white and purple gladioli.

We spend the afternoon in a most horrible grove where the Germans have been. The filthy condition of the ground is quite incredible and it's amazing how they've escaped being wiped out from some ghastly epidemic.

The Queen speaks at 7pm on our wireless – a good pep talk to mothers and wives!

Monday 12th April 1943

Have to go back a bit to go forward on the other side of the lake, thereby losing our front rank position. The whole manoeuvre is a waste of time and petrol as it gets us nowhere. By evening we are only 3 miles further north and 20 miles further west. We end up close to Kairouan which fell this morning.

Tuesday 13th April 1943

We start off at sparrows. After 2 miles we stop and don't move on 'til 10am. We eventually get to Karouan where we join forces with the First Army. We see a lot of Americans but they appear to be taking the war very lightly and spend their time sightseeing. They all wear great helmets and have masses of kit but no guts to use it at all.

We drive on through Kairouan, a large walled city of mosque, and the inhabitants cheer, clap and make V signs to us. We are now back with 7th Armoured Division and in 10 Corps again.

Wednesday 14th April 1943

HWLL puts my name in for a tactical course starting on 10th May in Gaza. I feel it would be a nice change but I'd be sorry to miss the fall of Tunis. I'm also not sure that HWLL doesn't have some ulterior motive but at the moment his hands are rather tied as we are so short of officers.

Thursday 15th April 1943

We move up 10 miles which brings us into sight of some magnificent ranges of hills to the north and west. On the lower slopes we can see the dust of enemy movement.

Everybody spends the day bargaining madly for eggs or hens. Some claim to get six eggs for nine cigarettes, others that one egg costs ten cigs. Personally, I can get three eggs for a packet of ten.

We buy a hen for the car. She's a nice friendly creature and we call her Elizabeth. I doubt, though, she'll lay eggs. For an old pair of size six gym shoes we get another hen, an aged spinster we think who has maintained her virginity through her impressive sprinting powers. She's fit as can be and carries no spare flesh – we find this out while trying to eat her.

Friday 16th April 1943

Have a long talk with Victor. He's going to refuse to continue as adjutant, chiefly owing to HWLL being so impossible to deal with and the fact the

RHQ is far from a happy family. I quite realise that I'm partly responsible for this but I (and others) find HWLL is not open to reasonable argument. He hides a wooden stupidity under a cloak of short-tempered abruptness and rudeness. I never attempt to argue with him any more – one could always win him round if necessary and for the present it is better to bide one's time and let him wallow in the mess he is making.

We have a regimental sweepstake on the end of fighting in Tunisia. I take tickets for 1st, 9th and 12th May. The general opinion is the end of May is more likely.

Saturday 17th April 1943

Spend the morning writing letters, including one to Jumbo's father. I hope hereafter I'll be too busy to write right up to the end of the war in Africa.

The sun sets tonight behind the western barrier of hills and makes the perfect child's drawing of a sunset. The hills rise in layers one behind the other and each crest is darkly outlined against the next one further and higher. The sun sends out rays peculiar to infantile drawings or the Japanese ensign.

David R comes up with two prisoners, one of whom is given twenty-eight days field punishment for shooting at a dog in the leaguer and then assaulting a man. He rather frightens the CO by saying he'll write to his MP demanding justice and says he'll give the Royals a 'good write-up'.

Monday 19th April 1943

At lunch we hear the stunning news that Desmond H-R was killed by a shell while on a visit to A Squadron. Jack was one of the first on the scene. It's all too tragic and I cannot believe that we'll never see him again. He'll leave a very large gap in our ranks. His quick wit, first class brain, humour and captivating charm will always be remembered by us. Basil and HWLL go up to A Squadron in the afternoon to bury him. Poor Jack must be in an awful state and I feel I could help him if I were there.

The battle for the Enfidaville line starts tonight. Our part is very minor – or so it would appear if all goes according to plan.

Tuesday 20th April 1943

The battle seems to be going alright but will take several days before a conclusion is reached. Beyond getting up at 5am and the extra traffic on the wireless and telephone, we do not have much sense that there's a big battle in progress. I see Lightnings [Lockheed P-38 Lightnings, US fighters with a distinctive twin-boom chassis] for the first time, four of them escorting Mitchells back to the First Army's landing grounds. They look strange and ungainly but no doubt in a few years there will be masses of planes built to that sort of design.

I still can hardly believe that Desmond is no longer with us. He's been almost a younger brother to me and I'm lost without him. I think we understood each other perfectly. He was so alive and sympathetic to one's mood.

Thursday 22nd April 1943

Go off at 6am to B3. It does one the power of good to get into some decent country. When we get over the first range of hills it turns glorious with every colour visible except green. The corn would appear to be a bumper crop, the animals look well and the natives happy and prosperous. To see poplars or aspens with their leaves turning and shaking in the breeze moves one's heart like only a touching poem or wonderful piece of music can.

Friday 23rd April 1943

We start off early getting to Souk El Arab at 9am. It's a very attractive town with shady streets and lilac and acacia in bloom. Get a fill-up of stores so have managed to draw two weeks of rations but have drawn a blank with beer.

I've never seen the air so thick before with the USAF working overtime with their Boston Bombers.

Saturday 24th April 1943

Unfortunately a day of low cloud and drizzle. We try the direct route through the mountains but the roads are horribly greasy and we slide all over the place. We pass through most of the French XIX Corps lines. The animals all look cold, wet and miserable having recently come from Morocco by rail. The men are living (and looking) as we did our first winter in Palestine when camping out was new to us.

Later in the morning we get held up while the road is blasted. While the men have a brew-up I go down to a rushing stream for a wash. I don't want to go in as it's so cold but little-by-little as I strip and wash in patches I get nearer to it and eventually plunge in. Feel tons better for it but would have liked the sun out to dry me.

Return to HQ in the afternoon. Hear Kenneth E has been wounded again. My car is now mended which I put most of the way down a well on Thursday! HWLL doesn't seem pleased to see me back. What a life.

Sunday 25th April 1943

Go to early service and attendance is, as usual, very small.

Jack comes in in the morning having been relieved by Teddy. He ensconces himself in a cactus thicket about a mile away. I walk over in the afternoon to see him. There is no doubt Desmond's death has affected him very much. It has been an awful shock as well as a blow to him. I've always loved seeing Jack and Desmond together. They were so proud and fond of each other and looked after each other's interests in a way few brothers do.

I think my course at the tactical school must be 'off' as it's getting rather late in the day to pack up and be there in time.

Thursday 29th April 1943
See a lot of French troops on the road looking like a drunken party returning from a football match. They are terribly scruffy looking, badly disciplined and poorly equipped. Such troops would be of much greater use if they were put into road mending.

Do a deal with Trooper Pragwell for a gun he picked off a German dump at Fuka. I give him £10 for it. The gun is a Jeffrey's and the owner was/is 'P Sterricker' – I must make enquiries about him. It's quite a nice gun, a little rusted but all complete.

Friday 30th April 1943
Rejoin RHQ before breakfast at the outskirts of Djebibina. Am told I'm off tomorrow on my course. It's very short notice but typical of the army to leave everything to the last minute.

Saturday 1st May 1943
Back to the B3 after breakfast to hand everything over and then set out for army HQ. It takes a lot of finding and well over 100 miles to get there. Am advised to get to Tripoli to catch a plane. The roads are good and there's very little traffic but I have a long drive in front of me. Get as far as I can before dark.

Sunday 2nd May 1943
Start off at 6am after a showery night and one that was rather troubled by a plague of earwigs. It's a childish superstition, I know, but I could not get rid of the thought that they'd get into my ears. I find about forty under my pillow in the morning ...

The further we go the more the country turns hotter and drier. We find a stream running at Mareth and while the kettle boils Ludford and I go in for a wash. It's quite heavenly. The stream is perfectly clear with a sandy bed and rose pink oleanders everywhere. The only thing missing was a lovely young nymph!

Push on all afternoon and by dark we are over the frontier and within 100 miles of Tripoli.

Monday 3rd May 1943

Start at 5.30am and breakfast at Sabratha where there are some wonderful ruins I want to look at. A *khamseen* has started which is pretty bloody. Manage to book my plane for the 5th.

See O'Shaughnessy in whose mess I drink. It's an old fascist propaganda HQ full of pictures of lovely nude women, Balbo[13] and Musso! Balbo's propeller hangs under his picture. I believe he really was a fine man.

Meet Eddie in the street marching at the head of a large number of drafts who have just arrived. Why can't HWLL be open and tell us that he's sent for him. I had heard it originally through Ludford and David heard it from his wireless operator.

Tuesday 4th May 1943

The standard of officer joining now is incredibly low. At breakfast one out of three boasted any table manners, the second said pardon and the third looked like he was addicted to self-abuse. These statistics were formed on careful perusal of about 150 2nd and 1st lieutenants.

Wednesday 5th May 1943

Depart at 7.30am by Douglas. It holds twenty-eight and a pile of luggage. We stop for half an hour at Benghazi which is very hot and then arrive into Cairo at 16.40pm at the same LG I left on 17th February.

Get into my flat by 6pm and Ahmed is delighted to see me. Have just enough time for a bath and change before a big party given by James Hanbury. The drink flows freely – enjoy myself thoroughly and behave pretty badly.

There are a number of wives about still who are not ungenerous with their favours – not that I avail myself but one could. I feel thankful Cara is not here. It's not a nice life and chaps come in from the desert with only one idea really.

Friday 7th May 1943

Visit the bank and put some money into Christopher's account. More importantly I also have to sort out poor Desmond's finances for Jack.

Go on to Abbassia and get most of what I want done. Oliver Leese has a word with me about some secret and exciting news concerning our future. One only needs half an eye on a map to realise that big things are on the horizon.

Dine with the judge and remain talking (one-sided) until Tunis and Bizerta fall at 3am on the 8th.

---

13. Italo Balbo (1896–1940), a leading Fascist who served as Italy's Marshal of the Air Force, Governor-General of Libya and commander-in-chief of Italian North Africa. He was killed on 28 June 1940 when the Italian anti-aircraft batteries outside Tobruk misidentified his aircraft as a British fighter.

Sunday 9th May 1943

Terribly hot morning and not feeling my best. Have a proper fight to get on my train. It's terribly crowded and they try to stop me because I haven't booked. I am not deterred and though many others give up I eventually find myself in possession of a corner seat.

The chief item of interest (for all the world to see) are the trains of wagons laden with tanks and carriers. If that's not a pointer I don't know what is. It's very interesting to see how my (?) planning has borne fruit. There is a maze of new lines everywhere, a new bridge over the canal and acres of new sidings.

Monday 10th May 1943

Arrive [in Gaza] at 5am, stiff all over and not having slept a wink. Get a bit of breakfast in a good mess with a paper full of news of the falls of Tunis and Bizerta.

Tuesday 11th May 1943

Rise at 6am and go off hacking. Have an old troop horse and old troop saddle but it's seventh heaven to have a ride again.

We work 8.30am–1.15pm then 2–7pm. It's a long day really when one hasn't been doing that sort of thing. Have a signal demonstration in the afternoon, including pigeons. My bird is reputed to be very fierce so I undertake to seize and hold it but it flutters through my hands to a nearby rooftop whence it is stoned off. It flies around for a long time then points towards Jerusalem, beginning speculation the signal officer was sending a message booking a room at the KD [King David Hotel].

Wednesday 12th May 1943

The demonstrations are very well put on, although rather too realistic at times; mines go off at one's feet or screaming Very cartridges are shot off behind one to get the war effect.

It's Christopher's second birthday today and no doubt he's being given a great time by his doting mother. I feel sure it will never be her fault if he's spoilt – she's got her head screwed on too firmly.

Today is the end of organised resistance in Tunisia. A very great event in the war and a big step towards a successful end. The very sudden collapse and capture of Von Arnim[14] seems full of omen to me. Without being overly optimistic one can't help feeling the collapse of Germany will be equally

---

14. Generaloberst Hans-Jürgen von Arnim (1889–1962), highly respected general and recipient of the Knight's Cross of the Iron Cross. Having taken part in the invasion of the Soviet Union, Von Arnim was appointed commander of the Fifth Panzer Army under Rommel. On 12 May 1943 he surrendered to British forces and spent the next four years interned at Camp Clinton, Mississippi.

sudden. The great loads of bombs now being dropped nightly on Germany is not going to help their morale.

Thursday 13th May 1943

We go to gas school and are sent through clouds of every known gas. We choke and splutter and tears roll out of our smarting eyes. We then form up in a queue and have mustard gas put on our arms and then form a rather more enthusiastic queue to get the stuff for removing it!

Saturday 15th May 1943

Everyone itching to get away for their weekend leave, mostly to Tel Aviv but a few to Jerusalem either sightseeing or partying, like Hugh, Tony B and I. We have a hair-raising drive in a big Jewish taxi. The driver keeps dropping off to sleep. It's pretty shocking, especially on the hill road and does nothing for our nerves!

We get a big double room, bathroom and dressing room for the three of us and order cold soda and sandwiches pending our return. Run into all sorts of old friends and potential friends. At closing time a large party has gathered round and come up to our rooms – Michael Hogan and two MTC girls, Billy Grazebrook with two WREN girls, John Readman and others. The MTC is, I'm afraid, a sort of mobile brothel organisation full of charming ladies but not above reproach. The party breaks up at 2am in disorder but we have enjoyed ourselves and that means a lot in these miserable days. How perfect it would have been if Cara would have been there.

Sunday 16th May 1943

We all wake up feeling slightly the worse for wear. Tony is still intoxicated and gives us a good laugh. Mary R unfortunately comes in when he's chasing the waiter who has removed breakfast before he's eaten it. We are all three in the one bed and as the maid has already been in she thinks we've all slept together!

Motor down in the evening. Tony sleeps and Hugh and I chat all the way. He's a very easy person to converse with and has a glorious sense of humour. Dine in the mess and go to bed feeling that I could have 'done' another party.

Wednesday 19th May 1943

Jumbo,[15] now C-in-C Middle East, comes to our attack discussion which goes on all morning. Cooke-Hurle (Cheshires) and I supply all the model answers and what is more we argue Brigadier Findlay round to our way of thinking twice.

---

15. Field Marshal Henry 'Jumbo' Wilson, 1st Baron Wilson, GCB GBE DSO (1881–1964). Wilson was Churchill's choice to succeed Auchinleck as commander of the Eighth Army in August 1942 before Brooke convinced him that only Montgomery had the necessary qualities to beat Rommel.

Dine with Morton. I think he's very strong-minded and has completely given up drink. He's out to get on and I don't think intends on staying here as an instructor. We talk regimental gossip 'til a late hour. I discover that the 'good report' on me that I've heard of and thought was a regimental one was really a hell of a report by Roscoe on me as CO. Both Bones and Peter W had seen it and remarked on it. There seems to be more pro–Barne-ists behind the scenes!

Thursday 20th May 1943
Have a good outdoor scheme on the Beersheba Road. The country is a mass of camels under loads the size of haystacks. The things one sees now both on the roads, the railways and at these specialist camps make one want to know more of the grand plan. There's no doubt to my mind the direction the wind will soon be blowing.

I find a nice mail from Cara when I get in. She's very perturbed at the change of address, thinking the worst has happened.

Saturday 22nd May 1943
Having got a note from Andrews in the short morning break to say he can't give us transport to Jerusalem I decide to give up all thoughts of getting away. The train times don't fit and lorry-hopping is not in my line but old Hugh, fuller than ever of enthusiasm, gathers me up. With Richard Thornton we sit on our bags at the roadside 'til we get a lorry going our way. By easy stages and scrambling with Indians, Jews, ATS girls, NCO's, officers and all, we reach Jerusalem in three stages. What is more we get a room with a bath.

Sunday 23rd May 1943
Feel distinctly better than this time last week! We walk the streets all morning. I buy four pipes, pipe-cleaners and an Anglo–Italian dictionary (on spec!).

We have lunch with Henry Hunloke MP at his flat. The Jewish Agency have him fourth on the list for bumping off! He's very interesting and genuine, I think. He talks of staying out here after the war as he feels bitten by the country and believes it will become a centre of world interest.

After lunch we see *Mrs Miniver*, a most excellent film based on the book. We all blub horribly. I don't know why it should be so moving – I really felt quite ashamed of myself but found the other two in the same plight!

We return by taxi –very extravagant at £6.

Monday 24th May 1943
Ride a most charming horse at 6.30am. It's a lovely, cool fresh morning and grand to be out. There's a smell of mimosa in the air. It's my favourite smell and brings back happy memories of the old hot weather pig-sticking days.

Mountain warfare is the subject for the next few days.

Thursday 27th May 1943
Have a lot of work in hand – a TEWT discussion to prepare, a model answer on armoured cars to work out and my own lecture due tomorrow evening. There is definitely an end-of-term spirit developing and everyone is friendlier than they were a week ago.

Morton comes in after dinner to say goodbye. I think he's rather pinning his faith on me as future CO and to get him back to the regiment when the time comes. He's a stronger man than I'd thought. He seems to have managed to knock off the drink to a very great extent.

Friday 28th May 1943
Out all morning but the scheme is entirely ruined by a plague of small midges which settle all over one and, if given a chance, burrow under one's hair and bite shockingly. My arms and back of my neck are a mass of poisoned lumps.

I give my talk on probing the Mersa Brega line and it seems to go down very well. Many unexpected people come and thank me, including Brigadier Martin, the commandant. He's very friendly and I feel it's a good thing that he's seen I've been here.

As it's the last night of the course we drink long, deep and late. It's so stupid as we're bound to feel like death in the morning.

Saturday 29th May 1943
Sure enough we wake feeling very poorly and are dragged out to see a parachute jump display. Only one platoon comes down but one can only imagine the effect of a whole battalion or more falling from the skies.

Charles Spenser (12L) gives a talk on Tripoli–Tunis operations and puts it over very well. The commandant then gives his farewell speech. It's such a good talk delivered almost as a sermon, quietly and to the point but avoiding the pure military point of view. He urged us to prepare for the unknown, the value of discipline, avoidance of waste and the need for knowing more than we need to. All these points will be over the whole great army stretching from Persia to Tunisia and which will, I hope, germinate and eventually bear fruit.

Leave in the evening and have booked a sleeper so travel in comfort.

Monday 31st May 1943
Return to Cairo. I hear Jack is down so make haste to contact and meet him to dine at Shepheard's. He has got over Desmond's death well and recovered a lot of his form. He's very busy re-equipping A Squadron (Monty asked for our best squadron).

To bed at midnight feeling exhausted and rather disturbed. I hear all my heavy baggage has been sent down. No one seems to know why but evidently HWLL is making an attempt at getting rid of me.

Wednesday 2nd June 1943
Go up to Abbassia with my future still surrounded in mystery. Have lunch with the Kinmonts and Shrimp Coghill, military secretary to Monty. Have a talk with him and he swears any changes in my circumstances did not originate at the Eighth Army end! Advises me to see MS GHQ and offers to help.

Dine with Jack and Roddy at Shepheard's and sit 'til late. There's a large mixed crowd of young South Africans who do a very amusing native dance on the floor once the band packs up. They get great rhythm into it and one suspects some of the song is obscene! I don't think their morals are very high in any case.

Thursday 3rd June 1943
Visit Colonel Fraser, the MS. He seems very friendly and listens patiently to my story but seems equally mystified. The upshot is I am to go back on Saturday morning.

My baggage arrives down from Abbassia looking awful and full of filthy, worn-out clothes and boots. Looking at it from a clean flat in Cairo, one wonders how one even wore it even though I have lived in it for longer than I care remember. What a shock Cara would have had if this had been dumped on her had I been killed. I fear that there are many poor mothers and wives who do have such bundles thrust on them. Thank God we keep it all in the regiment for those who lose kit. Frankly, it has no value outside the desert anyway.

Monday 7th June 1943
HWLL due to arrive today so I decide to clear out and let Jack discover the form. I don't want to have a first class row for nothing.

Hear that I won £52.10 in the regimental sweepstake on the end of the North African Campaign but on one of the last days a direct hit from one of our own bombers (US probably) on the RSM's car destroyed the whole lot and killed the driver!

Tuesday 8th June 1943
Lunch with Jack and then go on to Shepheard's to see HWLL. He starts off rather lamely as to why he's done all this without a word to me and then brightens up and says he's sacked me as I'm temperamentally unsuited and disloyal and then tells me a few unnecessary lies which I can easily refute. I let him drivel on as he gets redder and hotter and his eyes narrow 'til they appear to be one eye on the bridge of his nose. I don't argue but let him finish. He then starts apologising for it all so I leave him. He's in an awful state as he doesn't quite know what cards I have on him or how I'm going to play them.

Well I can't go back now and I don't think I want to. I feel more depressed than ever I've done in my life before. I'm mentally and physically at a low ebb. Thank God I've got my two Cs otherwise I really believe that the large expanse of the Nile flowing past my window could be an invitation I could easily accept.

I suppose, at last, I must face up to it that I'm a failure in life...

Chapter 6

The Wilderness

Wednesday 9th June 1943

Mooch round GHQ looking for a job. Miles Wood, who used to be in planning with me, puts me on to civil affairs so I go out to Mena where the staff school is. Bones D is the commandant and cheers me up a lot. He offers me a G2 job. I shall have to decide by Sunday and, if I accept, must burn all other boats and hold it for six months. In his opinion the war will be over by then and we'll be in Europe but my job might entail me hanging on as a local administrator for many more months.

Thursday 10th June 1943

Our sixth anniversary and our third apart.

Have a large drinking party, first with Ben W and Toc Elton and then with Jack, Peter Palmer, Donal McCorquadale and others. John Henderson and John Postern, Monty's ADC, are also there. They tell us how they almost got DTs in London. Monty paid their four day Claridge's bill of £80 without turning a hair! They were welcomed as saviours of the empire and made the most of it apparently!

Saturday 12th June 1943

Go to GHQ in the morning. Meet Monty on the steps and exchange civilities. He's a funny little man and looks like a cock sparrow. He wore desert boots, short shirt sleeves, an Australian blue jersey and his beret with two badges on it.

Fraser offers me brigade major to a static brigade in Malta or Liaison Officer to GHQ or a transfer to another regiment. He's not very enthusiastic on Bones' offer.

Monday 14th June 1943

Interview with John Currie in the evening. He's not committal but is sympathetic and I think will write a sympathetic letter to attach to the proceedings. A sharp counter-attack to HWLL is necessary.

Wednesday 16th June 1943

Make a plan to get down to Rhodesia. See General Norman who is not only sympathetic but volunteers to assist and pulls strings to get me priority passage.

Tuesday 22nd June 1943
Tram into town to see if there's anything 'round the corner' to get a priority passage. Am told prospects are rosy.

Lunch at the club and find Charles Cooper there – just exactly like the old Charles. He managed to drive the train down from Suez and buggered up all the brakes – and then, of course, he went feet first and asked Jack how Desmond was. It was simply awful, as painful a moment as one could experience.

Friday 25th June 1943
The judge receives a cable from Cara asking if she can get in touch with me to get approval for her to fly up for 2 months. Poor poppet – she obviously realises I'm not getting her letters. I don't know how/why my letters are being held up.

Spend the morning and evening in GHQ trying to see General Theron and Norman but everyone seems to be out when one wants them. Eventually see General Theron's lady secretary and nearly cry on her to stress my point. Theron comes in in the evening and won't promise me a seat before the end of July. I am polite and grateful but, of course, it's of no use to me at the moment.

Monday 28th June 1943
Off early to the consul who passes me on to the Ministry of the Interior regarding Cara's entry permit. They then pass me on to BTE who pass me on to GHQ who send me back to BTE.

AG12 is still under McCandlish who turned wives out [and] who still sits smugly in his comfortable office during the day and then spends his evenings dancing with the girls he condescends to leave here for his pleasure. AG12 seem to glory in their power to stop husbands and wives meeting, but loose women, enthusiastic amateurs, dancing girls, mistresses etc are all fully approved. Sadly I lose my temper and burn my boats. I can never go back to AG12 now but at least they know what I think of them.

Bowen Jones also not optimistic over an air passage for me so I feel I've reached a dead end. I think I'm passed caring now. I just feel flat.

Tuesday 29th June 1943
Nigel's birthday – I think he must be 34. How very old we are all getting. It's high time he was married and I think if there hadn't been this war he'd have married Esther White. Now, alas, tired of waiting she married a sailor.

Wednesday 30th June 1943
The end of a miserable month doing nothing, expecting nothing and waiting for nothing. With everyone I meet I have to hide my real feelings and my candid view on things. If it goes on much longer I'll go mad.

Thursday 1st July 1943
A chance word I had with Rex Hewer in the Department of Movement seems to have done some good. BJ (perhaps dangerously) puts pen to paper asking me to go down to Bulawayo by the UD7 officially.

Saturday 3rd July 1943
Go in to GHQ and meet Ellsworth who is not responsive and insists on hearing from General Moorshead. Am told to return in one hour. Fidget for an hour. Return to hear a favourable result. I nearly swoon! God, what a relief!

Dash everywhere at once, send flowers, cables, letters, notes, cancel engagements, pack, tip, kiss, shake hands, drink, sweat, drink some more and finally set off with SAAF pilots Pienaar and Nordern to Luxor. I have such a feeling of joy and relief, it's like I'm a completely different person.

Sunday 4th July 1943
Set off at 5.30am. The aircraft is still hot from yesterday and we move off without any fuss or bother. A few years ago such a flight would be considered a great adventure now they all take it as a matter of routine.

We land at West Halfa before it has had time to hot up and then again at West Sedna (really Khartoum). The heat is terrific – thank God I'm not stationed there. The next stop is Malakal where we stay the night in a most modern establishment. The whole thing is netted with a fine-mesh gauze which keeps out anything down to sandfly. It looks like a building at the zoo.

Walk down the Nile bank in the hopes of seeing some natives fishing but only find one, complete with spear and headdress but little else. To my dismay he asks for 'backsheesh'. How civilisation is defiling and ruining the whole world ...

Monday 5th July 1943
Off again at 6am having slept like a log in the most wonderfully comfortable linen sheets. Reach Juba by 9 where we get a cup of tea. The landing ground is very primitive and set in the jungle where we see giraffe, buck and one lioness. We go so low one can pick out the elephant tracks and fly below the hawks and vultures.

On to Kisumu, a lovely little town against the Victoria Lake. One realises what a vast continent this is having travelled for hour after hour at 150mph over what appears to be the same spot. We have a very hard landing and blow a rear tyre. As we had to go straight on to make Dodoma or else stay for the night, the decision is made for us. Stay at Kisumu Hotel, a nice enough pub where we have a cold lunch and play snooker.

Tuesday 6th July 1943
Start off at break of day. It's bitterly cold and owing to cloud formation we have to fly at 10,000 feet thus missing out on seeing any game on the Ngorongoro Crater. Stop at Dodoma for a magnificent breakfast and then on to Kassama. We eventually arrive at Ndola at about 5pm. It's a lovely little spot. All the way my heart has been singing *tomorrow tomorrow* and now I can hardly believe it that it really is tomorrow I see Cara.

Wednesday 7th July 1943
Wake up with the feeling that something wonderful will happen today. Daylight arrives with a sharp frost and I shave in cold water. The natives are all tucked up from the cold but it's like champagne to me.

We take off at 7am, crossing the Zambezi, and arrive at Bulawayo in one hop at 11.25am. As we circle round I see Cara on the landing ground waiting for me – what other woman could manage such miracles. I've sent one cable saying I might be in Bulawayo on Wednesday and here she is at the other end of Africa, awaiting my arrival and with a taxi waiting. It's a great reunion.

After lunch we meet Colonel Brady, Cara's 'Godfather' out here who seems to do everything for Cara and Daphne. Bulawayo is a fine place and very well laid out. Rhodes stipulated that the streets should be wide enough for a twin span of oxen and this foresight has made car parking and double ways of traffic possible. Horses seem rare but one sees a number of carts and donkeys. The place is overflowing with RAF. Many, no doubt, will settle after the war as they are allowed to bring their families.

Friday 9th July 1943
There's a sharp frost when we wake up and the country looks heavenly. All the *veldt* grass is the colour of ripe corn and there are many more features and trees than we'd seen at last light near Bulawayo.

We are driven out to the house which is quite delightful; beautifully sited, prettily and sensibly furnished and with a lovely garden. It's quite amazing how these four women (Cara, Daphne and the two nannies) have managed. Everything is in apple-pie order, Cara has made the garden very productive, the cook produces first class meals, they are all great friends and there seems to be no flaw or friction other than the awful loneliness and dullness of life.

I meet my son, Christopher, now two years and two months. He's a lovely fair-haired, rosy-cheeked little boy, not a great talker but very receptive and thoughtful. He looks the picture of health.

At sunset a fire is lit, the curtains drawn and the lights put on. There are drinks on the side table and a wireless playing English music. Prue, the Great Dane, sprawls in front of the fire while Nanny can be heard bathing

Christopher, and Cara and I play backgammon. It all looks so snug and homely I feel I'm living in a dream. I suppose when we go back to this sort of life in England we'll grumble and say it's dull. May I look back and remember this period if I ever feel that way inclined!

Saturday 10th July 1943

Finish breakfast at 10am and spend the morning playing in the garden with Christopher. We are now great pals and we have a great laugh. He has an impish little face and a great sense of humour but not very good at concentrating on one thing for long. He understands an awful lot but is terribly lazy about talking.

On the 11 o'clock news we hear that the invasion of Sicily started at 3am this morning. This is a week earlier than I'd predicted as I thought a full moon would be necessary. All seems to be going well.

Tuesday 13th July 1943

Cara not at all well in the morning but insists on coming with me to see a farm belonging to Townsend. En route we see a troop of baboons and run into a heavy locust storm. It's just like a snow storm.

The farm is old and well established and the Townsends are a charming young couple with three lovely kids. It's all just as one would expect a farm to be in the colonies. We have tea at 11am on the stoop followed by sherry and a great lunch, obviously from a bottomless store cupboard.

Friday 16th July 1943

After breakfast we shop; the bank is open for the first time since I arrived. I have three Gyppy five-pound notes to change and have to certify they are 'free from the taint of the enemy'.

I could never live in this country, attractive as it is, owing to the complete lack of game. The earlier settlers seem to have shot it out completely.

Sunday 18th July 1943

Muck about the house and garden in the morning and do some packing whilst the telephone seems to be going continually. We have a farewell drink with the Dudgeons, our nearest and nicest neighbours. The garden is most awfully attractive and full of every variety of flower and shrub.

Say goodbye to Nanny and Christopher at 5pm. He, of course, doesn't realise that I'm going. I'm very glad I've had these 10 days with him, it may impress itself on his subconscious memory. God knows when I'm going to see him again but with the war going well on all fronts I feel it may well easily be within the year.

Nanny has apparently much appreciated my visit. Poor dear, she leads a very dull life but no duller than those back in England. She lives in a first class climate with unlimited meat, veg and dairy produce and has a married sister within a mile.

Cara and I leave at 6.30pm by the mail train.

Monday 19th July 1943

Wake at 6am absolutely frozen. Get in at 7am and go to the Grand Hotel. I am loosed into a tiny bathroom with my baggage, towel and a mirror. I think I'd rather have had unlimited space and one mug of water.

Go to the shops and am lucky to get four Kodak films which are getting increasingly unobtainable. I've used five since I've been here just on Christopher and the house.

Our train moves off again at 2pm. The country is lovely now with all the scrub taking on autumnal tints. It's not the most exciting landscape being flat with just scrub and low trees. Game being non-existent one gives up looking out of the window except at stations.

Tuesday 20th July 1943

After a cold and rather uncomfortable night we reach Victoria Falls at dawn. The first thing one hears as the train stops is the roar of water.

The hotel is modern and extremely comfortable but the visitors are the most amazing collection of old trouts that we've ever seen. Where they've all come from I can't think but it does show that all the young are away serving King and Country.

Walk down to the falls after tea and do the 'Rain Walk'. One walks parallel to the lip of the falls for about ¾ mile and yet only 100 foot distant. Between us and lip is a chasm about 250 foot deep from which a continual stream of vapour and spray rises like steam from a pot. The noise is incredible, like a vibrating roar, and only at intervals can one see the bottom.

Wednesday 21st July 1943

In virtue of being in uniform we get an officer from the North Rhodesian soldiery to take us down to the 'Palm Grove', now out of bounds as from there there is a big bridge from where the copper is brought out which is of vital importance. The Palm Grove is the nearest thing I've seen to tropical jungle with palms, ferns and creepers with stems as thick as one's leg and all sorts of things hanging down from the branches. The whirlpool at the bottom is in a narrow channel through which the whole waters of the Zambezi flow after coming over the falls. A woman fell in here a little while ago and her body was only picked out of the cauldron over a fortnight later.

Thursday 22nd July 1943

After lunch we take a Canadian canoe over to Cataract Island. The island is now very overgrown and covered with 'rootlings'. We come straight onto a great pig and by the grace of God he has a getaway without having to come through us. Another 30 yards and we'd have cornered him with a chasm on both sides which could have led to a nasty accident. It was a great experience for Cara who adores seeing wild animals.

Friday 23rd July 1943

Our last day here and possibly our last day together in Rhodesia. I should think we must look like a honeymoon couple here.

Saturday 24th July 1943

Breakfast on the train and arrive at Bulawayo 40 minutes late. We have a sickening feeling in our tummies as we are to hear in the hotel if I have to rush to get the plane in the morning or wait several days.

Joy of joys – we find Pienaar went through yesterday and Nordern has also gone. I may be here for a week but will have to take it day-by-day.

Sunday 25th July 1943

No signs of a plane and we can't go to church as Cara doesn't have a hat. Bulawayo is a dull town but especially so on a weekend!

Monday 26th July 1943

The great news today is that Mussolini has resigned.[1] No doubt Hitler has given him a task which even the Italian cabinet won't accept. It seems the worm is turning at last and no doubt on the fall of Sicily Italy will capitulate. They must realise that they stand to be blasted from the face of the earth if they continue resistance. Let's hope that we can recover the many prisoners held in Italy and also put many thousand Hun soldiers and Gestapo into the bag.

Tuesday 27th July 1943

Nanny really is first class; she has got herself organised in less than 24 hours and on to the train. At 8.20am we meet her and Christopher at the station. The young man is in fine form, full of spirit and looking extremely well.

---

1. The German military presence in Italy had turned public opinion against Mussolini. Following the first bombing raids on Rome and Allied landings on Sicily in July 1943, the King removed Mussolini from office and had him arrested. Two months later, he was rescued by German paratroopers and made puppet ruler of the 'Italian Social Republic'.

Wednesday 28th July 1943
See 150 Rhodesian soldiers return from the Middle East. They march down from the station at 6.30am with a native band from Salisbury and look very fine indeed. Christopher enjoys the spectacle enormously.

Cara has prophesied that I'd be going today and we are kept on tenterhooks with everything packed until noon when I am rung up and told they have room for me. Cara and I have one of our, now customary, goodbyes with no scene … it's just as if I'm going up by train to Diss for the day. It has been the most wonderful 3 weeks (to the day) and made the world of difference to the both of us.

Our first and last stop is Ndola. We land far too fast with a passenger having control (Major Villiers DFC) and swing off the runway.[2] We crash into a drainage ditch at about 60mph. We all pile out but luckily the plane doesn't catch fire. The upshot is the Savoia 74 is a complete write-off and we are now stuck here until such time a relief plane comes.

Thursday 29th July 1943
We were four in a single room opening straight on to the street so when I am invited to move to the mess I accept without hesitation. It's very picturesque with thatched whitewashed huts and great ant heaps as high as the buildings dotted around. We are just south of the Copper Belt and 22 miles from the Belgian Congo border.

Eisenhower has broadcast terms to Italy although don't quite know what they are as the wireless is so bad.

Saturday 31st July 1943
Another aircraft has pranged one stop back. It means there is now another crowd awaiting a relief plane. Just hope they don't get priority.

It looks as if there is going to be a row over the crashing of our plane. Villiers has been ordered to return and a court is assembling on Tuesday. Why the station commander let him go away I can't fathom.

Tuesday 3rd August 1943
Start off by native bus to visit the copper mines. The road is through thick jungle, not unlike the Mysore bison jungle, but without a sign of any game.

The mines are the largest in the belt and produce 250 tons of pure copper per diem. We have an intro so are taken around in a lordly fashion. We see the ten-ton crusher which crushes the hardest and largest rock as one's

2. In his memoirs AMB adds, 'We crashed on the way back as the two pilots fought (literally) as to who was to land the plane.'

teeth would crush snipe bones. The smelting plant is awesome in the size of machinery and the heat coming from the furnaces.

Wednesday 4th August 1943
Start off at the crack of dawn on a beautiful new Douglas DC6 and reach Kassama in 1 hour 45 minutes. Then on to Tabora in 2 hours 25 minutes. The new runway has been placed across the normal direction of the wind so we have to strap in before landing. Thankfully our pilot avoids an accident but he feels his load is too heavy and I get chucked out. It turns out I wasn't on the official list in the first place and I was 'surplus cargo'.

It's the most desolate feeling being in one of the wildest, most inaccessible places in central Africa, knowing no one, with not much money and already well overdue for leave!

Go down to the local pub – an awful place run by an Austrian Jew out to squeeze the last cent out of everyone. The town was meant to be the Hun capital of German East Africa but was never completed.

Thursday 5th August 1943
Start off the day with hell's own row with the manager. The food is filthy, the servants useless, the service non-existent, accommodation slummy and prices exorbitant. There's a big Wop internment camp close by where they live like kings.

Walk about the cemetery. There's an old German corner, a Belgian memorial to 1916/17, a few British war graves and then an Italian portion (filling up nicely) with very handsome headstones and a Wop at work caring for it all.

We hear the Eighth Army has gone through Catania and, along with the RAF and Navy, are massacring the enemy retreating along the coast road. Also hear the Russians have occupied Orel. Indeed the war is going well, it's just frustrating not to be part of it.

Friday 6th August 1943
Apparently the hotel was built as a pavilion for the German crown prince when he came on tour before the last war and then made into an officers' club (or brothel). It's very well designed and spaciously built but successive Greek managers have given the place an air of decay and poverty.

Tabora was apparently a collecting place for the big slave columns from Central Africa to Dar es Salaam. There are hundreds of great old mango trees and the fruit was collected and eaten by the slaves on their way to the coast. The route can be traced the whole way by a struggling wood of mangoes grown from the stones scattered by the poor blacks.

Meet Major and Mrs Norton in the evening, the nicest of a poor selection. I hear you ask on the coast, 'Are you married or do you come from Kenya?'

Sunday 8th August 1943
Hear an aircraft at breakfast but take no notice as no signal has come in for me. At 10am Hartley turns up and says my plane is waiting. Have a rush pack and dash out to the landing ground. Duncan, the Anson pilot, is rather snotty as I'm late but all is fine. He's a first class pilot and we get in to Nairobi at 12.45pm.

The pubs are full but I get a room at the New Stanley. At bar opening time the place packs absolutely full. Where all these officers and NCOs come from beats me. It seems there are plenty of NCOs wearing officer's clothing, lounging about smoking cigars. They look like they live on about £800 a year but with no business connections.

Monday 9th August 1943
Dine and dance at the '400', a most amusing place with good food, good band, decent sort of people, plenty of drink and cheap with it all. The best looking girl there turns out to be Robin's girl, Diana Billyard-Leake. They call her the 'dumb blonde' but I gather she's not all that dumb. I think she and her husband have parted company.

Thursday 12th August 1943
Wake feeling like death after no dinner and one brandy too many. There's nowhere to get breakfast as it's so early and I finally have a plane to catch. Stop at Juba and Malakal but still can't get any food!

After 8 hours of bumpy flight we arrive at West Sedna where we stay a most uncomfortable night.

Friday 13th August 1943
Start off again at 6am to arrive back to Cairo at 2pm. The heat seems awful but there is a hearty meal waiting for me and Roddy who, thankfully, says I'm not under arrest or anything awful! Jack seems ok – I've been rather worried about him and A Squadron.

Saturday 14th August 1943
Mussolini reported drowned but I don't believe it.

Visit GHQ. It seems jobs are scarce. Armour looks like coming into second place in European fighting and soon armoured car regiments will face being disbanded.

Wednesday 18th August 1943

One is woken in the morning by the Wop prison bugles next door. The sky is leaden with low mist and there's no wind. It's not actually hot yet and one lies in bed under a sheet and blanket (donned about 3am) and thinks about how bloody the heat is going to be and how long until one reaches the blissful moment when it cools below sweating point.

In GHQ all morning. I gather my future is being considered. I'd much rather it was decided for me than I should have to select. I know there is a chance of a G2 vacancy in Nairobi.

Monday 23rd August 1943

Run into Victor Blundell, just back from Sicily. He tells me Jack was killed in a motor accident on Friday. It really is too frightful if true and I can't believe it's not true. How could people start such a story?

My God, it's as though the Hamilton-Russell family are cursed and yet there was never a family as loved, respected and honoured in such a wide circle. I don't suppose Jack has said or done a mean thing in his whole life. He's never had anyone, except the King's enemies, wish him harm. He had all the points that make an English gentleman: kind, generous, brave, sympathetic, honest, cheerful and loyal. I am proud to have been counted amongst his close friends. Cara will be heartbroken. Poor Lady Boyne has now lost three sons, a daughter-in-law, husband and granddaughter all in this reign. There's only Dick, the little Lord B and James Hamilton-Russell left.

Tuesday 24th August 1943

Attend a lecture by 3CLY on Sicily. It's not bad but there seems insufficient meat for a lecture. He gave us a gloomy picture of armoured fighting vehicles in close country and rather bore out my theory that tanks will now be subordinate and in support of the infantry. The exceptions might be for specialised places like the big plain of Lombardy or up the Danube valley but when we reach either of these localities I expect organised resistance will have ended.

All through the lecture one's mind is reverting back to Jack constantly.

Friday 27th August 1943

Old Cripps, our most excellent gentleman's gentleman, makes a speech of commiseration ending up saying how they would have all liked to see me remain as commanding officer. It's very embarrassing but soothing. I also have a charming letter from Teddy who is about to go home. It makes one feel a little less of an outcast.

Monday 30th August 1943
See Colonel Fraser at 11am. He's not at all forthcoming and says my future is under discussion at the highest level and the delay is entirely at the protection of my interests. I think I would be ill-advised to keep pestering so will just have to wait. I don't think he's a dependable type with shifty eyes and trembling hands.

There's a terrific rumour afoot that all who were out here prior to 1st November 1939 have the right to go home. This would affect the regiment enormously. I, for one, shall stay out here of course.

Friday 3rd September 1943
The Eighth Army lands in Italy proper. Everything appears to be going according to our plan. I have had a bet of £4 to £6 with Anthony Goodall that the war in Europe will end on or before 31st December 1943. I only hope I am not being unduly optimistic.

Saturday 4th September 1943
I gather that HWLL is pushing David Rogers out for unnecessary use of his jeep and for staying up too late after dinner! Not that Teapot will worry much, if at all, but one wonders what conditions in the regiment can be like now! Such things have never happened to us before – they always took place in other regiments and we used to raise our eyebrows and smuggishly thank God that such things never befall us.

Sunday 5th September 1943
Meet Lin Showers at the Club. We spend a quiet afternoon on chaise longues watching the cricket. The more I see of the man the more I like him and would welcome him as a brother-in-law. What a little silly Lysbeth is!

Wednesday 8th September 1943
Am summoned to GHQ to take on a job as bear-leader [the escort of a young man of rank] to General Vehbi Kokaguney[3] of the neutral state of Turkey. He arrives on Friday and there is a certain amount of organisation to be done. He ranks as a distinguished visitor of the commander-in-chief.

Italy unconditionally surrenders and Russia drives the Germans out of the Don basin and captures Stalino. Things should go like hot cakes now for a month. I wouldn't mind doubling my bet with Anthony!

---

3. Major General Kocaguney (1881–1950). A much decorated soldier, he was elected to the Grand National Assembly in 1946 and remained a member until his death.

Thursday 9th September 1943

The Italian surrender is being fairly splashed around.[4] It certainly is a very long step towards the end. We must now rush troops up into north Italy thence we can threaten the whole of German-occupied Europe and make the Hun retire from the Balkans.

I think we are very near an invasion of France now. There will be an immense air strength freed from North Africa for the main target.

Friday 10th September 1943

Dress up all smart to meet General Kokaguney and his staff officer. An awful scruffy little old apparition appears from the carriage complete with luggage typical of the east: cardboard boxes, old suitcases tied with cord, a hurricane lamp and a *dhurrie* [thick Indian rug]. The old man has 35 years of service and is very kind-looking.

I take them to Mena to have breakfast but they are aching to get at the shops – shooting sticks being their priority!

Saturday 11th September 1943

Pick up Vehbi at 9am but he's not ready and goes off to the hotel barber for a shave. We start off by shopping – he tells me he has £1,500 to spend! We buy sheets, shirts, socks, scent, suitcases, shoes, cloth etc. Each item is examined as though an attempt is being made to pass off bad stuff on him but never keeps his attention fixed for a minute.

Tuesday 14th September 1943

To the artillery school. Another very interesting day but not appreciated by my Turk. We go out on the ranges and at the end the General asks his 'clever' questions of the students to try and impress upon them how smart he is.

Wednesday 15th September 1943

Go all around the workshops and find it most amazingly interesting. We see a shop full of 500 Shermans, new secret weapons, guns, armoured cars etc. In one shed we see three-ton lorries being stripped and overhauled. They turn them out at ten lorries per shed per diem. All the heads of department are big men in the same trade at home in peace time. They know their job brilliantly and avoid wasting time, material and labour in a way the army cannot begin to understand.

---

4. An armistice was agreed on 3 September 1943 and made public five days later. It was signed by generals from both sides at an Allied military camp at Cassibile in Sicily and approved by both King Victor Emmanuel III and Prime Minister Pietro Badoglio. After its publication, Germany retaliated by attacking Italian forces in Italy, France and the Balkans. The Italians were quickly defeated and northern Italy was occupied by German troops.

Thursday 16th September 1943

Have a gentle morning down at the camouflage school. Travelling around in our large saloon we see a lot of what's on the move. American vehicles are still coming in in their thousands – each American soldier has his own camp bed and enough equipment to fill the back of a jeep and they still think they're roughing it!

The Turk seems convinced we are an army of fornicators. I must say that every second car on the road has one or more wild female in uniform, generally hatless and squeezed in by the driver.

Tuesday 21st September 1943

Visit the anti-aircraft practice camp and watch a demonstration of all sizes of gun. Then see Tough Tactics demonstration of men climbing out of wells, through barbed wire and unarmed combat. It is most impressive and at last it appears we have learnt to be thorough in our fighting. It's bestially cruel but so are the enemy and one must learn to compete.

Wednesday 22nd September 1943

Out to Alamein. One gets a good idea of how featureless and barren the country is. What a wonderful thing it was to be able to fight it out on a ground where no civilians, buildings or land could be destroyed. There's a lot of wire up showing the way between minefields. We find one Wop corpse partially underground and a lot of graves but my driver tells us the majority as far as Msus have been brought in.

There are literally thousands of tanks formed up in rows in an enormous car park. A year ago we were just hanging on to Egypt with our stocks at a low ebb. Now Egypt is right out of the war but with a surplus of everything in the way of war material.

Friday 24th September 1943

See Bobby Kidd who tells me he has sacked FHB and wants me to come as his 2i/c. It's a genuine offer and I'm very honoured and pleased. I believe I could make the grade but must think it over.

Roddy brings down my mail. Nigel has cracked his skull and missed the landing in Italy. Michael has gone and started Peg on another infant. It must be the 'anguish of farewell' as it's due in November and I think the Scots Guards went out in February! Poor Cara will be very jealous.

Saturday 25th September 1943

Make the big decision to extract the Royals' eagle from my cap and replace it with Winston Churchill's Queen's 4th Hussars' badge. Have an interview with General Charles Norman and by 11am it's all decided. I think it's my only hope of getting back into the war but it may be some time before we see some fighting. I am to get a relief bear-leader sent up to Tel Aviv.

We make the train but not very easily. It's a filthy 1908 German Pulman coach with no ventilation or fan. It's as hot a journey as I've ever undertaken and I lie there starko with bed bugs coming out at regular intervals to make a meal.

Sunday 26th September 1943
Crawl out of the train at Lydda at 6.30am feeling frightful. Take Johnny Turk shopping and then to visit Jaffa port but he's most unsatisfactory to take sightseeing.

The blackout here is intense. Take a walk at sunset along the front. Sodom and Gomorrah must have been quite respectable places compared to this. Everywhere expectant women (mostly in uniform) are accosting rampant men. The bars are thronged with mixed customers swallowing the filthy local gin and the beach is a writhing mass of bodies. The Turk is thrilled. He thinks it's the most wonderful town he has ever visited.

Thursday 30th September 1943
Today is a Jewish and Arab holiday and the war is off in Palestine for 3 days. The General hasn't kept the fast but is keeping the feast. We buy him two kilos of grapes and he eats the first kilo in the time I take to have one small bunch.

The sea is oily smooth with dark *khamseen* clouds hanging over the horizon. The beach is thronged with black-coated, hatted and whiskered Jews and curious old ladies in clothes of central Europe and Russia. They stand as close as possible to the sea praying and reading the Hebraic Bible whilst swaying and nodding in rhythm with their speech. The young generation do folk dances in the street or march in formations singing. It is probable that the young people are taught to look upon patriotism and the Jewish religion as the same thing.

A few disdainful Arabs walk through all these celebrations and a mile away, in old Jaffa city, guns fire periodically in celebration of the Moslem Bayram feast.

Saturday 2nd October 1943
I say farewell to my general. Not everyone can boast of being kissed by a general in his pyjamas. He has grown extremely attached to me – and I to him in a queer sort of way.

I'm now 3,000 feet up. My plane is an old four-engined de Havilland. I suspect our outside starboard engine is a bitch. It's stalled once and I'm now watching it carefully. It's cooler up here and over the sea becomes pleasantly chilly. I've had the secret mail pushed on to me but sadly there are no lovely blonde spies on board.

Chapter 7

The 4th Hussars

The 4th Queen's Own Hussars was a cavalry regiment with a history dating back to 1685, 24 years after the formation of the Royals. It had a distinguished record, having seen action in most of the major engagements in the three centuries since its inception. The regiment had been mechanized in 1936 and posted to the Middle East in 1940 where they found themselves fighting in the Greek campaign. They were put in a hopeless position, fighting a rearguard action at the Corinth Canal to allow time for Allied forces to retreat to the Peloponnese. Vastly outnumbered, they lost all their senior officers and over 400 men as prisoners of war.

After the disastrous events in Greece, the regiment was forced to look elsewhere for the seniority and experience required to lead it. They recruited a Royal Dragoon, Bobby Kidd, to become their commanding officer. Kidd, short in stature and with a light touch on the reins of command, was to re-form the regiment in Cairo in 1942 and lead them through the second half of the Western Desert campaign.

Whilst the regiment was being reconstituted in Egypt, a request was sent to its most illustrious alumnus to become honorary colonel. Winston Churchill was commissioned as a second lieutenant in the 4th Hussars in 1895, serving with them in India before becoming a war correspondent in India and then during the Boer War. Churchill's patronage was deeply important to a regiment that had lost so many key personnel, and he, in turn, closely followed their progress through the war.

* * *

Sunday 3rd October 1943
Spend morning at GHQ saying goodbye and getting £3 cheque for services rendered with the Turk. Drive down to Beni Yusef in time for

lunch. Only the squadron leaders know what I've come for. Talk with Bobby most of the afternoon and evening. Have a really good heart-to-heart with all cards on the table. It looks like a job just learning the names of the thirty-seven officers.

Am given a servant called Bosworth, a nice, clean, well-spoken young man. I hope it's only temporary and that I'll get Ludford back.

Tuesday 5th October 1943
Have a morning talk with Pitt QM, Reed RSM and John Vaughan PRI and PMC. Find my old Troop Corporal Wilson is here. We are delighted to see each other. He was a great boxer and it's stood him in good stead since. He has twice been captured and got away both times.

Friday 8th October 1943
Bobby and I go down to watch the practice of wireless sets. The tanks have a much more formidable and unwieldy group than the armoured cars used to have. I am wholly bewildered.

In the evening join Kenneth Grant who has Michael Lycett staying. The Greys have just kicked out Michael as being 'woolly' and he's very despondent. I give him all the hard won experience and advice that I can.

We then pub crawl and finish too late to get the last bus home so collect Margaret Duff and go to the Auberge des Pyramides. It's a delightful spot with charming company. The King of Greece sits at one table with Mrs B-J and two scruffy Dagos. The King of Egypt sits not far away looking just frightful with a couple of bodyguards.

Thursday 14th October 1943
The Warwickshire Yeomanry entertain me for the morning. It's all extremely good for me to get this 'breaking-in' to tank life. I now no longer climb into and down into the bowels of a tank like a complete novice and by picking everyone's brain have developed ideas of my own.

Hear Guards casualties in Italy have been very heavy. So far as I know Nigel hasn't gone out there yet.

Friday 15th October 1943
Charles takes me out in a Sherman. They take a lot of getting used to – owing to its weight and size everything takes much longer to happen. It's the story of the dinosaur that took 5 minutes for a pain in the tail to register in the brain and 5 more minutes for the order 'swish tail and kill prodder' to be enforced. The conclusion is to gear down one's mind as it does no good to try and act too quickly. It's a wonderful feeling of implacable power.

Friday 22nd October 1943
Bobby is off in Algiers so I'm left as CO of the 4th Hussars. I hope my duties won't involve any big decisions over the next few days.

Ludford arrives in the evening having flown from Italy yesterday. I am overjoyed as he's a great tower of strength to me and we are real friends. It's great to see his great red marrow of a grinning face. He's so full of talk from Italy that I have trouble getting away from him!

Monday 25th October 1943
Visit police barracks about one of our officers and an SSM reported drunk, sick and incapable clasped in each other's arms on the streets in Cairo. Then have more shocks – an officer presenting dud cheques and a private soldier wanting an interview as an officer is currently living with his wife in the Continental Hotel. The officer, Hugh Stewart, has already been kicked out of the Guards for being mixed up in a divorce case. He was supposed to have proposed to three different girls during one weekend in Alexandria! I've confined them all to the camp area until Bobby's return.

Today is Balaclava Day,[1] a big day for the 4H and we get an extra issue of beer. We eat a good dinner at the mess and I have to make a speech and present a cup. We end up at the sergeants' mess where we sit talking 'til midnight. They are a cheerful crowd, perhaps not as decorous as the Royals but it's a nice friendly atmosphere and officers mingle freely, perhaps too freely, with the sergeants.

Wednesday 27th October 1943
I have a much more settled feeling now and beginning to know the people. The effect of giving four chaps detention is that I'm considered a bit of a tartar, a good thing as it's easier to soften down than it is to tighten up.

Much relieved that Bobby is back. We have a long talk about the incidents and he's very upset. He already knows about the Stewart case as it's the talk of civilian Cairo. The woman has two very nice children – Stewart has completely broken up a happy home. The question is whether he should be asked to resign his commission or be court-martialled, the only charge being presenting cheques that are not honoured.

Friday 29th October 1943
Take my tank out with the whole of HQ. Soon get accustomed to it and find it a pleasant ride. I have introduced many dodges in my tank from

---

1. Anniversary of the Battle of Balaclava in 1854 during the Crimean War. The 4th Hussars were one of the cavalry regiments which took part in the ill-fated Charge of the Light Brigade.

my experience in armoured cars. I have a stool to stand on, extra boxes for storage and a fitting to carry my bed roll.

Bobby is knee-deep in interviewing these blasted officers. No wonder Bobby wanted a 2i/c from outside. I don't think there's anyone above captain who could be a suitable CO. It's going to loom large as a problem if, and when, my turn comes to command.

Sunday 31st October 1943
I drink my customary glass (or three) of port to 'foxhunting'. How many years have I had to drink it abroad and think of the lucky buggers at home while we have little chance of seeing a red coat for another season?

Tuesday 9th November 1943
We have a sand table discussion with squadron leaders. Bobby and I don't altogether agree but on a perfectly friendly basis. In this new role I keep emphasising the whole layout is more like our old armoured car methods but Bobby is loath to break away from his old tank training methods.

Tuesday 11th November 1943
We all wear local-made paper poppies. I suppose soon we'll have some other emblem for remembrance of the end of yet another war. There's the annual fuss about officers' dress but I never let it affect me. As soon as we are back in battle one can wear anything – but are we ever going to get back into battle?

Saturday 13th November 1943
Race in the afternoon but very crowded. See Patsy Hogan who has the lowdown on the Syrian troubles which have just started and have shown up the French in their true colours.[2] I hope this makes us treat the Frogs as mercenary troops with no better status.

Tuesday 16th November 1943
There is a note in the paper that Mena House was closing to the public for 'important talks'. We can only interpret this as a Churchill–Stalin–Roosevelt meeting. In which case Winnie will obviously visit us on one of his by-days. There are all sorts of preparations going on with soldiers digging in the cultivation, cables being laid and the houses around Mena becoming military beehives.

---

2. With the French mandate over Syria coming to an end, elections were held on 8 November 1943. The French responded by arresting the elected President and Prime Minister, to international condemnation.

Saturday 20th November 1943

It seems we may be wanted to provide extra mobile guards for the big talks, now openly admitted and likely to start next week. From the amount of preparation it is fairly obvious where FDR is going and where WC will be put up but Old Joe [Stalin] and the Generalissimo [Chiang Kai-shek, Chairman of the National Government of China] still have a veil of secrecy over their quartering.

I throw a party for my birthday and lay on a damn fine spread. The only upset of the evening was Mary R and Eileen B making a set on Bobby and nearly debagging him. He recovered his braces but lost his temper and lashed out as hard as he could, his face distorted with rage like a cornered rat. It's all very unfortunate but I restored order by sitting on Mary's head on the sofa to try and laugh it off. The party breaks up around midnight and all the 4H head on to go drinking scotch 'til 3am.

Well, I'm now 37. I'm told I don't look it and am sure I don't behave like it.

Sunday 21st November 1943

Don't wake 'til 7.30am and rise feeling remarkably well. Read the paper and a few poems out of an anthology of war verse.

Head back with the truck to get things ready. WC has arrived and everyone is now expecting the hell of an air attack; high-level, low-level, paratroopers, gliders, glider bombs and the secret weapon. At night wild dogs set off the trip wires and shrapnel mines go off. Someone then looses off some rounds which wakes everyone else so they shoot too to show they are awake!

Monday 22nd November 1943

Bobby and I go in to the Mena. Chiang Kai Shek and Madam have arrived. He wears a long yellow robe and complains as they are not allowed to take long country walks. In addition, he likes to sit in silent solitude and contemplate which is impossible with this many people around.

WC has arrived in a difficult mood too. When shown his air raid shelter he insists he'll watch any air raid from the roof!

Tuesday 23rd November 1943

They say Old Joe isn't coming but the rest are here and lots of people have seen – or imagine they've seen – the big shots.

I spend a hot afternoon with RSM Reed measuring out a parade ground on the Fayoum Road. A tank regiment requires an enormous amount of room and a good approach from the rear to avoid churning up the ground in front.

Wednesday 24th November 1943

Represent Bobby at an early morning conference at Mena. We sit around the outdoor dance floor in white wicker chairs still wet with dew. See Winnie come out for a breath of air and walk around the garden – he's not smoking a cigar.

Get quite a lot of work done. Find I'm thoroughly settled now and my presence recognised.

Thursday 25th November 1943

Am told to go into Cairo again to represent the zone commander at a US Thanksgiving Service at the Cathedral. It is packed with distinguished visitors: Dill, Cunningham (now First Sea Lord), Alan Brooke, Louis Mountbatten, Major General Bob Laycock, Portal (air chief) and many lesser fry that in normal times one would stare at. There's a tense atmosphere, everyone waiting and hoping that a portly figure and another in a bath chair might appear. Sadly as the organ strikes up the first hymn the great fat figure of Killearn[3] remains as the King's representative and senior figure present.

Friday 26th November 1943

Berlin is getting the most awful pounding from the air. One shouldn't gloat about it but one can't help feeling cheered as it's such a tangible and effective effort toward shortening the war. When people cheer in the mess or applaud in the cinemas when the news is broadcast, it doesn't mean they take any joy in the frightful suffering, misery and hardships that the Hun civilian population must be enduring.

Sunday 28th November 1943

A large draft has arrived. Bobby inspects them and makes his normal little speech. They are odds and sods collected from 8thH, SA Bde, 5th & 6th RTR etc but don't look too bad. Poor devils, it must be hell always changing cap badges.

Thursday 2nd December 1943

Get a very cheerful letter from Nigel. He has been wounded in the bottom and balls but recovering well. He's had a very near shave. Out of six in his company, the one mortar bomb killed three and wounded three.

After I go to bed the message comes through that the parade will be 1100 hours tomorrow.

---

3. Miles Lampson, 1st Baron Killearn (1880–1964), British ambassador to Egypt and the Sudan.

Friday 3rd December 1943

The parade looks very fine indeed: a row of great tanks 250 yards in length with the scout cars in front, pennants fluttering from the wireless masts and 635 men lined up in new battle dress with yellow lanyards.

The old man arrives on the tick. He has his son, Randolph, daughter, Sarah, General Stone and two ADCs with him. He walks around very slowly with a horde of cameras following him, clicking and whirring. I walk with Stone, just behind, so hear and see everything.

Churchill has got an amazingly agile brain and, despite his bulk, excesses and age, still seems a young man. He has fine, silky fair hair and an enormous back but with no waist. He wears a gaberdine, 4thH badges and three rows of medals.

He makes a speech from a mobile rostrum that we've prepared. It's a far better speech than ever he's broadcast or delivered in Parliament. Later in the tent when drinking sherry he says a lot of things he shouldn't to a group of subalterns. Afterwards he asks Bobby to ensure that it goes no further until published in the press. There is no doubt the man is inspired and has the most magnetic personality. He has the shrewdest little eyes that miss nothing and are full of humour and kindness.

We have a hectic rush to mount our tanks for a march past as he wishes to see us on the move. It is completely unrehearsed and I have to give orders and lead as Bobby remains at the Premier's side. All goes well.

We decide it's been an excellent show with no hitches except when the Old Man lost his sherry. We had to get another glass in his hand pretty quick!

Dine in Cairo and return to camp at 1am drunk but triumphant. A red letter day.

Sunday 5th December 1943

Pick up Hoot at 6.45am. It's a grand day with a cold wind but sunny. In places the mosquitoes are like a swarm of bees following a queen and there's a constant cloud around us. The result is, with the mossies and swallows coming to feed on the mossies, it's hard to see the snipe get up. We still manage thirty-three snipe and one teal.

Bath and have a drink with Stonor at Casey's Villa. Am asked not to make a noise as Roosevelt has arrived and is having a special talk with the PM in the room below!

Stonor is very interesting about the PM. He said his speech for us, and all his speeches, are prepared in advance. He often tries out phrases and bits of speeches in conversations to see how it sounds. All of his telephone conversations are recorded. It also appears that every cigar stub is collected by someone as a souvenir.

Monday 6th December 1943

The PM has issued a rocket as we were not wearing the Africa Star[4] on his parade. The ribbon, as announced in Parliament, is in the country but issue has been held up. Now Brigadier Elseworthy has come down in person to render a certificate that all ribbons have been sewn on by 1800 tonight. A team of seamsters have been sent down to do this.

Apparently the PM was thrilled by his visit and talked of nothing else for the rest of the day. As a result of that and the ribbon fiasco, everyone is now tired of the name '4th Hussars'.

Tuesday 7th December 1943

We are now very be-medalled. We got warning in the middle of the night to get ready for a guard of honour for President Inonu of Turkey. We parade at 8.15am looking very smart indeed.

The PM and president are arm-in-arm and everyone is sure Turkey will be in the war by Christmas. I am not sure how much it matters. The papers are so full of all these meetings these days that the operational war has been completely squeezed out of the front page.

Letter from Ma. Michael has had another son, born on 25th November. They have a fine family now.

Wednesday 8th December 1943

Bobby has gone off shooting and I'm left to hold the fort and entertain Randolph Churchill at lunch. To my horror, at 1.30pm, with Randolph not having arrived, an orderly comes up with the message that Sarah is coming too. I bustle everyone into lunch and get the table decently set. She is charming and worth two of Randolph; very simple, gay, natural and not unattractive. We sew a ribbon on to Randolph's coat and drink a glass of port to him and it.

Friday 17th December 1943

Go the cinema and see ourselves with Winston. I look so imposing that I don't recognise myself. A lot of people have sweetly made nice references to Bobby and I. Old Philip Kaye says he's been twice to see me and thereby gets a second whisky out of me!

Monday 20th December 1943

After a week of the most lousy cold Leigh, the doctor, writes me a chit to get me admitted to hospital. I am only in because I feel my only hope of curing

---

4. Campaign medal for British and Commonwealth soldiers serving in North Africa between 10 June 1940 and 12 May 1943.

this cold is with a rest in warmth with proper attention. They call it 'acute sinusitis'.

Tuesday 21st December 1943
Quiet day being given inhalations every 2 hours. The sisters are very neglectful and sometimes don't appear at all or else leave one for an hour with head beneath a towel.

Receive a long letter from Nigel dated 16th December. He seems to be doing very well and is along the coast from Algiers.

We get a good number of letters to censor. Most of them are very badly expressed. I don't know whether it's lack of any other subject or if they really are keen on films but every one of them has some allusion to the film of the week.

Saturday 25th December 1943
We find Lady Killearn has been round in the night distributing stockings to all patients. The Christmas Stocking Fund must have been well subscribed to as we get a big bag containing wallet, comb, hair grease, diary, sweets and a gold medallion. The poor sisters get nothing.

Leave at 11am completely cured other than the pints of orange mucous my nose is still discharging.

Monday 27th December 1943
There's a cable in to the regiment starting 'Pray give all ranks ...' The Old Man really does have a delightful way of expressing himself.

Friday 31st December 1943
Well I suppose I should review the year for my own benefit, press style:

Start 1943 commanding the Royal Dragoons in battle, end as 2i/c of 4th Queens Own Hussars under as peaceful conditions as exist anywhere in the world these days. I've flown the length of Africa and seen Cara and Christopher. I've had 3 months unemployed which might have been a good deal more miserable if I'd been less lucky with my friends. I gave up the flat where Christopher was formed, lost two of the nicest friends any man could want and discovered the hypocrisy and insincerity of a brother officer. I've certainly grown a little fatter and look a little older. To be quite candid, I think in this year I passed my zenith and am now on the decline. Perhaps more exercise and less ale this coming year might keep me in 'solstice'.

Monday 3rd January 1944
John V comes to me with an amazing story of how Austin, recently kicked out, has come back here drunk and slept in his old troop tent with his

men. Bobby wants him court-martialled, I want him mentally examined! There seems lots to worry over including Peter C's stupidity and Pat W's continuous absence. Things are brewing for trouble.

Tuesday 4th January 1944
Dine tête-à-tête with Eddie. He is wanting to get married. He has no definite girl in mind but feels it should be done. I feel one has to be very careful in giving advice as he is taking it and himself very seriously.

I also find out he has an intense hatred of HWLL. Have to be very careful in what I say – it would be so easy to let oneself go to a kindred spirit but it would be a bad thing. I gather the regiment is on the high seas for home but HWLL has gone by plane.

Thursday 6th January 1944
Bobby tells me 'they' have asked for a special report on me. I'm not allowed to see it but he says that it's a 'smacker' that he's written, that he's frightfully pleased with all I've been to him and that he strongly recommends me for command. I feel I may I get it by the middle of the year all being well (and the war not over – but I'd rather have the war over).

It's really bitterly cold at night now. I had forgotten how cold nights could be although I'll never forget one January night in 1928 in India crawling round the sewage farm near Kanka on a scheme. My God, it was the coldest night I can remember.

Friday 7th January 1944
At sunset there's a strange column of smoke and a glare underneath it followed by two brightly lighted cars cruising about after it. I send the orderly officer out to investigate. He reports that he ran into King Peter of Jugoslavia celebrating Greek Christmas by driving a jeep around with a flare tied on the back. Apparently he found once he set off he couldn't stop for risk of setting the car on fire!

Tuesday 11th January 1944
Out in jeep and Humber first visiting A Squadron and then out on a recce to look at the ground for a scheme this weekend. We go right up to Katta along the edge of the cultivation. We cut in across the desert to the road. It must be the same route as I took in 1929 on what was considered a great adventure. I navigated and my eyes never left the compass – and great was the triumph when we came out bang opposite the station. Now we don't even bother to take a compass and in a jeep the chances of sticking are really negligible. All was virgin gravel then, today the whole surface is crisscrossed with tracks.

We get home to the bombshell that we've got to send off 400 men straight away. I don't think it's possible. Bobby goes into GHQ in the evening to fight it – and wins. He is very clear-headed, determined and quietly expressive when he argues.

Saturday 15th January 1944
Head out into the chilly desert to the west. After a period into the teeth of a bitter wind we leaguer for the night. I sleep on my new bed in my car – it's just like a bunk on a train.

Sunday 16th January 1944
Though it's bitterly cold we all rather enjoy this taste of the old life that we knew so well. I'd forgotten the strange silence and amazing stillness of the desert. Rain patters for a while and is stilled. The wind continues to race across the desert wastes but makes no sound. There are no sharp corners to whistle around, no trees to sough (lovely word) and no bushes or grass to rustle and whisper.

Monday 17th January 1944
Our tanks are all named now. A Squadron has place names famous in the British Army annals beginning with A (*Assaye, Arra, Alamein* etc). B Squadron have Ps (*Pride, Prejudice, Prodigal* etc) and C Squadron have English towns beginning with C (*Canterbury, Chichester* etc). In HQ we have *Daring* (mine), *Defiant, Dauntless* and *Doughty*.

The turret of a tank is quite the coldest place to stand when the engine is running. There is an awful down-draught of icy cold air sucked into the engine.

Tuesday 18th January 1944
We move home by road, a long dark column of tanks stretching 2 miles amongst the desert dust. We come up Mena Hills, past the Pyramids and out again on to the desert. It's such a strange sight the modern tank against such a backdrop – rather sacrilegious in a way. What right have we to go disturbing the past like this and what worse things will the future produce?

Sunday 23rd January 1944
Yesterday morning the Fifth Army made a landing just south of Rome.[5] This should hasten things up.

---

5. On 22 January the Allies had landed 36,000 soldiers and 3,200 vehicles on reclaimed marshland around the city of Anzio. The plan relied on surprise and speed to establish a foothold and so that the invaders would not get bogged down in the soft ground. The initial landings were virtually uncontested and within a day a patrol jeep had made it to the outskirts of Rome. The Allies failed to capitalize on their early success, however, allowing the Germans to form a defensive ring around the beachhead.

Monday 24th January 1944
Rather a curious letter has come in 'directing' Bobby to tell me that my report is considered satisfactory and to draw my attention to the fact that my tact was not 100%. He also asks that I withdraw my appeal against HWLL! What do they take me for? I may be tactless but I can't see why I should ruin my future to ease the situation for HWLL.

Wednesday 2nd February 1944
Visit AMS and find George K in. He is all dressed up in his red tabs and breathes heavily through his large moustache. He rather confesses he doesn't know a thing about the job but is ardent in his advice that I should drop my appeal against Humphrey's report. He puts it that Bobby's good report cancels out HWLL's so I end up all square. If I appeal and it's turned down (and he seems to think the Army Council are bound to support the commanding officer) then he seems to think that I shall be worse off.

Sunday 6th February 1944
Get a biggish mail. One from Ma contains the shocking news that Michael has been relieved of command of his battalion. It will just about break him with his sensitive nature. As Ma says, it's not pity that he'll want from us just unspoken sympathetic understanding. I have heard he did most awfully well in Tunisia.

Cara's letter is rather worrying. She's very het up over my trying to dissuade her from moving up to Cairo. Her little heart is set on it and, having made all the arrangements, my disagreement comes as rather a shock. We just don't know when we will move on from here though.

The war is not looking too bright (temporarily). Turkey has refused to play[6] and the Anzio bridgehead is going through a very sticky time. Pray God they are not pushed back to the sea.

Monday 21st February 1944
Spend the entire day in camp growing more and more depressed. It seems fairly definite that our move is postponed for some time. It's an awful blow and huge anticlimax. As our tanks have done their full training–track mileage it leaves us with nothing to do. No doubt the officers and men will all get very bored and into trouble.

It's quite obvious we are earmarked for something but at present our shipping has more urgent demands.

---

6. Having spent the war as a neutral state, Turkey was to declare war on Germany and Japan on 23 February 1945, but no Turkish troops saw combat.

Sunday 27th February 1944

I'm getting very sensitive to bugs. I can tell at first nip, even when asleep, that I'm under attack and can usually catch them. The men get bitten quite frequently by rats. They have all had their typhoid inoculation but it's not very pleasant. Thankfully rats don't seem to include our areas in their visiting rounds.

This is now my 15th spring abroad. Not that there is a real spring here, it just goes straight through to hot weather. The symptoms are very strong today, the trees and flowers look jaded, the ground suddenly appears dusty and the sky is a different colour. Then there is the scent of the mimosa and other shrubs of hot climates.

Tuesday 7th March 1944

A signal arrives (not even addressed to us and brought in by chance) to say we are to move completely to Burg el Arab at the weekend. This leads to cancelling every sort of thing.

Saturday 11th March 1944

Bobby and I go to the station to see how loading is progressing. There is an impressive array of tanks lined up and the first train leaves at 9am.

Half way through lunch we get a vague telephone message to say the move is off. It's utter chaos.

Monday 13th March 1944

Take out HQ tanks to have a shoot. Their big 75s are amazingly accurate and powerful. What fun we'd have had in the old days in the desert with them. We'd never have had to run away at the approach of an enemy column and would have caused them to treble the strength of their patrols.

Friday 17th March 1944

Call in at Miss Grey at the BTE and hear that Cara has been permitted to return. My concern is if we're going to sit for two months outside Cairo then I won't see an awful lot of her.

Russia has driven the Hun right back in southern Russia and has actually crossed the border into Roumania. We may well consider the time ripe to exert a squeeze in Greece and elsewhere.

Wednesday 22nd March 1944

Judge rings me up to say he has a cable from Cara asking me to get her priority on a flying boat. I go to GHQ but am met with the usual brick wall.

Lunch with the judge who is not looking at all well. I try to dissuade him from a gin but he says he's feeling of a scientific bent and feels for the good of humanity one must experiment. He goes on to carry out three experiments!

Thursday 23rd March 1944

Peter M tells me very confidentially that he's been appointed AAG demobilisation. Naturally 'de-mob' is a dangerous word to throw to the public but it's a wonderful sign of the times. I still feel that the end may come very suddenly and before winter although it's not presently obvious how that can be brought about. The Hun is obviously relying on the Second Front failing in which case he could offer to parley for terms.

Lose about £3 at poker. It's not been a lucky month for me.

Sunday 26th March 1944

Drive to Cairo to go to church. A nice service, not too crowded and an excellent sermon.

Quite by chance I bump into Alasdair Gordon just back from Italy. He has a note from Nigel and all the news. He is back with the 2nd Battalion and will be going home shortly. All very good – they must have had a bloody good time.

The PM makes a very long broadcast [*see* Appendix A]. He's very optimistic but with the occasional word of warning. As usual it's an all-embracing review. Japan, in his opinion, is not going to be such a hard nut to crack as he thought a year ago. He tires a bit towards the end but his customary vigour and enthusiasm return for his concluding remarks. Wonderful man.

Tuesday 28th March 1944

The move is on again and Carlton goes off with the first train load of tanks at lunchtime. GHQ then make the decision to cancel it in the evening. Carlton reaches Benha when the train is turned around and comes back arriving 2am Wednesday. We were being moved as certain staff officers thought there were too many 4H at the club and could do with roughing it a bit.

Friday 31st March 1944

I go to GHQ to see BJ about Cara coming up. He has little hope to offer. Pick up a cable from her at the judge's house. She is proceeding to Durban, no doubt as previously arranged, and will try to get on a plane there.

Tuesday 4th April 1944

Brigadier Chrystal rings up in person ordering us to stand by for a local armed move. In 10 minutes the place is a beehive. I've never seen the men so cheerful – they think there's a chance of some action! We are supposed to raise 350 men and four tanks in one hour but on examination find it's going to be very difficult. We have troops in Fayoum and in Sidi Bishar as well as out on schemes.

We are kept standing to all day and in the evening we take over 300 scruffy-looking Dagoes who shut themselves in a house and refuse to come out. It's all over some silly political business. Why they weren't left in the house I can't think – we don't want them here. We have an officer guard with fifty men to watch them.

Thursday 6th April 1944
We've been told to be unobtrusive in our guarding but this is nonsense. Either we guard them properly, meaning curfew sunset to sunrise, double sentry posts, roll calls, or we take no responsibility at all. I gather they are all communistic Greeks.[7]

Friday 7th April 1944
My old back is hurting a good deal after two squash matches. It has always been a threat since I broke it pig-sticking at Meerut.

The RSM's servant, Moore, was picked up by the tram terminus early this morning with his head battered in. He died in the evening without regaining consciousness. A very unpleasant incident but not unique in this country.

Tuesday 11th April 1944
The Greek flap has become a proper nuisance. Our patrols are picking up the odd Greek from Alexandria where apparently we are at last taking stern measures and issuing the Greek Brigade with an ultimatum to lay down arms or ...

Get great news from Elizabeth. She is engaged to Lin Showers. Can't think of anything that could please me more. She sounds terribly happy now she has made her mind up. It has taken a long time – Lin has been running after her for at least 10 years! He's recovering very well apparently and will soon be out of hospital. Mummy will be so pleased.

Wednesday 12th April 1944
The Greek situation is pretty acute. About 4,000 are dug in at Burg el Arab, fully equipped and trained by the US, and four of our destroyers manned by Greeks are holding out in Alexandria harbour! It's all pretty tricky. A whole brigade of ours and two cruisers are sitting containing their forces. Meanwhile we are keeping up a cordon around Cairo and guarding HM's and the PM's houses.

---

7. A mutiny had broken out in the Greek armed forces in protest at the lack of representation of the National Resistance Organisation, controlled by the Communists, within the Greek government-in-exile. The revolt began from five Greek battleships based in Alexandria.

Friday 14th April 1944

Get a clue over the phone that our embarkation date has been fixed.

The same morning I get a cable from Cara saying she's still trying to get up here. If I stop her I'll probably find I'm stuck here 'til mid-May but won't know until after 24th. If she does start I doubt I'd be able to stop her en route. We are in an awful fix.

Thursday 20th April 1944

The big move is definitely on but everything in way of orders, plans and details is most indefinite. I think there is every chance of us being on the high seas before the month is out.

The judge comes to see me with a cable from Cara in Durban saying she might be able to fly. With a very heavy heart I go round to Marconi House and have to say it's impossible as I'll be long gone before she could arrive. Between us we must have spent £16–18 on this visit in cablegrams.

Friday 21st April 1944

To the bank in the morning. Everyone seems to know we are going. Wilkinson, the manager, rises to say goodbye and I ask why. He says he's seen so many 4H officers visiting that he can see no other point of view! It's a nice bank (Barclays) with charming management.

Bobby and I seem to be drifting apart. He seems to avoid me – and everyone else – these days. He appears in office and punctually at meals, shovels down a mass of food and then disappears straight off to his hut.

Saturday 22nd April 1944

Ludford comes in at dawn to say he's off. He has most of my kit in the car. My room looks large and bare with only a bed and some old whisky boxes for furniture. By 8am every vehicle has gone and we are left, about 300 strong, to move by rail at 24 hours' notice. Most of the troops think we're bound for Italy but a few old faithful are still banking on the UK!

I have no feelings at all about leaving this place. I've had some happy times but for some time I've been restless to get back into the theatre of war. Now we're off and good luck to us all.

Tuesday 25th April 1944

We move off by lorry at 12.30am. It's a pitch black night. This is movements at their maddest. We've been told the train goes at 3am but others have been told it's 5am. By 8am we are only at Cairo Main Station and approach Suez at 2pm. We are switched to one of the jetties that I helped plan.

Get a cup of tea and a bun and then embark on the MV *Rena del Pacifica*, a fine looking ship. Since we had no orders and are last on we get the bum end of everything. There are emergency situation notices everywhere, blackout precautions already in full force and any normal comforts completely absent. Curiously enough, none of the woodwork, and this ship has more than any other ship I've seen, has been stripped out. She wouldn't take long to burn out.

Thursday 27th April 1944
We sail at 1100 hours after a very cursory ship's inspection. We anchor in the Great Bitter Lake at 3pm and sit in a red hot southerly breeze.

We have some very scruffy Wop officers on board. There's not one I'd have as a lance corporal in the 4th Hussars. If they showed that they'd suddenly realised that Italy was wrongly governed and their mission was to return to fight for freedom then we'd feel friendly towards them. They've so obviously got out of their PoW cages on false pretences and are only anxious to get ensconced as barbers, ice cream merchants or the like in a safe part of southern Italy.

Friday 28th April 1944
Sail at 1030 and anchor again at Timsah. There's a lot of shipping both ways in the canal and we meet a large convoy going south. We reach Port Said at dusk. It's stiff with ships. They say we are part of the biggest convoy ever to leave Egypt.

Spend the night at Port Said. It's funny to think of the other nights I've spent here. Smuggling the regimental wine ashore in Oct '27, meeting Nigel at 4am on his way out in '35, nights with Jack in '36 preparing for the regiment to come home, meeting Cara on her way out in '38 and finally that strange night less than a year ago. It's played an important part of my life. The same stage scenery for many scenes and each can be connected by the frail, faltering, erratic thread of the life of AMB.

Saturday 29th April 1944
We sail after lunch, four large modern liners with an escort of 'L' Class destroyers. Let us hope I never see Egypt again. Not because I hated my years there but because I am sure I can be happier in England and want to be settled. Except for the year after we got married, I have lived a gypsy's life. I have never had everything unpacked or slept in the same real bed for long.

It soon cools down once we are out of sight of land. We only get fresh water for one hour after daylight and before dark.

Wednesday 3rd May 1944
There's a haze which rather spoils our view of Mount Etna clothed in snow. It's a heavenly sunny day with everything wonderfully peaceful. Lots of

birds visit us: a big flock of turtle doves, a nightingale, swallows, quail and a red-backed shrike.

As we disembark tomorrow there's a good deal of activity and preparation onboard.

It's exactly a year since I left the Royals. Let's hope a year hence I'll either be back with my regiment again or a civilian.

Chapter 8

Mainland Europe

The 4th Hussars disembarked at Taranto almost halfway through the Italian campaign that had started with the invasion of Sicily in July 1943. Their arrival coincided with the Allies finally breaking through the Gustav Line after four gruelling battles fought over several months. The resourceful German commander, Kesselring, had spent the previous six months building a series of formidable defensive lines across the narrow Italian peninsula. The Gustav Line was the most southerly, shielded by a mountain range and dominated by an elevated Benedictine monastery at Monte Cassino, giving the German defenders a clear view over the valley's mouth.

The Germans were to fight determined rearguard actions as they retreated north, until they eventually regrouped behind the imposing Gothic Line. Here the topography was perfect for defence as the mountains which form the backbone of Italy run close to the coast, leaving only a narrow plain crossed by a seemingly endless series of rivers. To make life more challenging for the Allies, the Germans had the benefit of choosing the most advantageous positions to hold, often giving themselves a bird's eye view over their attackers.

For soldiers who had fought in the North African campaign, the war in Italy was completely unrecognizable. In Africa, the battlefield was vast with few features of any note. In Italy, the war was much more visually dramatic. Towns and cities bore the catastrophic scars of recent shelling, and bodies were strewn liberally at the bottlenecks of bridges and road networks.

With the forthcoming D-Day landings and invasion of France in June taking priority, six Allied divisions had been removed from Italy to support the landings in southern France. As a result, the summer of 1944 saw some tough but unsuccessful fighting in the mountains against a resolute and well-prepared German army. In August 1944 General Alexander decided to switch the attack to the eastern flank of the Gothic

Line in an attempt to make use of the narrow coastal plain. This was to be the opportunity to get back into the action that the 4th Hussars had been waiting for.

*   *   *

Thursday 4th May 1944

We look very critically at the shore of Europe. It looks nice from the sea but then what place doesn't? The magnificent harbour of Taranto is full of Wop battleships. I count over sixteen destroyers, three cruisers and a monitor.

We land at Tosi wharf and then march 3 miles in the boiling sun to Tuker Camp. The town is filthy and full of slothful Wops. I don't know why we don't impress their labour. The countryside is very like Tunisia with almond trees and olive trees sat in luscious grass fields.

The camp is enormous but well organised. We are fed, 5,000 men, at a communal kitchen set in a farmyard. Tomorrow we'll break away on our own. There is blackout at 7.45pm and we head to bed at dark.

Saturday 6th May 1944

A very pleasant sort of day. Water is scarce and there are no local provisions or transport. Bobby issues an order that a very tempting bean field is not to be stripped. He and I rush out with haversacks and fill them before the order becomes effective!

Take a walk in the evening. It's lovely countryside and find a great variety of flowers down a rocky ravine. It might as easily be Palestine or Tunisia as Italy.

Lose a lot of money to Kenneth Hedley. He is an amazingly lucky backgammon player but I admit he has skill too. He's a bad loser and a very conceited young man. Being the only OE and the best games player in the regiment seems to be too much for him. A pity as he is not without his good points.

Sunday 7th May 1944

Our doctor finds a prostitute running a business in a cave at the back of the camp. Her old mother was stood outside collecting the money – 3d a time in the morning and 6d after lunch! Doc said he'd never seen anyone so revolting or anything so sordid in all his experience. I don't think our troops were going there that much but there are a lot of old Dagoes about.

Wednesday 10th May 1944

As we all have our own mess vehicles we have split into five messes. The food is good with varied rations and a certain amount of local vegetables and wine. The temperature is perfect and one can sit idly in a deck chair in the shade. How long can such existence last? These are the halcyon days before the final storm.

Ludford arrives in the afternoon with all my kit complete. This is more than I could even hope for even though I have the greatest of faith in him.

Receive two excellent, cheerful letters from Cara. She seems thoroughly settled and content for the time being.

Thursday 11th May 1944

I am sure I'll get a court martial soon for my attitude to these beastly Wops. The Wop navy is in town in force and walk four abreast on the pavement making everyone else walk in the gutter. No self-respecting man can accept that – after all, they are a conquered people. As such, I use my oak stick to great effect. A good prod in the base of the belly soon effects a break in their line.

Saturday 13th May 1944

At 9am I leave on a recce, really a jaunt around southern Italy at HM's expense. I take Ludford, our bedrolls, rations, the drink box and a book.

The country between Martina and Fasano is fascinating. At the top of a range of hills all the houses are built like fairy story witches' houses; long low buildings with crooked doors and windows and surmounted by a roof consisting of a series of cones.

At Bari I visit a mass of people in the hope of getting a villa as an officer's mess. Everyone seems to want the same thing and the place is already grossly overpopulated.

I go on to Barletta still in search of a villa. Ludford and I settle down in an orchard nearby for the night.

Sunday 14th May 1944

I am awoken at dawn by the convent bell at 5.30am. Surely no one rises at this hour on the Sabbath? It's these wretched people who have made religion their life being ostentatious about their godliness.

We drive through lovely countryside for a heavenly hour, have breakfast of fresh eggs in a by-lane and then on through some lovely old towns of Canosa, Minervino, Spinazola and Gravina where I meet many of our new division. They are in a palace that used to belong to a very high ranking fascist. The fascist has fled to Rome so we feel everything is officially 'booty'.

We go on to our future camp site at Altamura which is very attractive and will be described in due course. At 5pm we start for home after a couple of the most enjoyable days possible.

Monday 15th May 1944

We hold a trial of Sherman and Honey over terraced and stone-wall country. It's most impressive to watch a tank take on a 5ft 6 stone wall. Quite slowly it pushes against it, breaks the surface and then the tracks grip and it heaves its great body up into the next field leaving a slope of rubble and a cloud of dust.

A terrifying sight is the same tank coming down over a terraced drop. With half the tank sticking out over the edge, it seems poised and then starts toppling before falling on its nose. Like a good horse, it recovers itself, the tracks grip and it gets straight into its stride again. The troops are all very impressed.

Wednesday 17th May 1944

The Fifth and Eighth Army news is good and we seem to be breaking through the Gustav Line. I hope we're in time for the big breakthrough which will be what they call the Adolph Hitler Line.[1]

Saturday 20th May 1944

Every now and again one meets an old friend in this wild country. We call those from home 'Inglesi' and they refer to those with the Africa Star as still having sand in their hair!

I go in to HQ and find my old friend Hopkins is Head of Movements in Taranto. I first taught him the job in 1940! I suppose I'd be a full colonel now if I'd stuck the boredom of staff work.

The news is good. The Eighth Army have been switched over and taken Cassino. The so-called Gustav Line is broken and we've turned the flank of the Adolph Hitler Line. This is a big thing as it's the Italian equivalent of the last war's Hindenburg Line. I am told we'll be in Rome in a fortnight.

Tuesday 23rd May 1944

Have an uneventful run through to Naples through hundreds of square miles of magnificent corn rippling in the breeze. We pass through Salerno where the roads are bad and all houses bear pockmarks from the fighting and many are totally demolished.

Naples is awful – every other sign is about VD. The girls are good-looking in an ostentatious way and have a brazen look.

Because Naples is out of bounds for leave we go out to Sorrento via a terribly narrow and twisty road. I am in a house in the town. It's 50 lira for

---

1. A fall-back line behind the southern third of the Gustav Line, to be used if Monte Cassino was overrun.

the bed and I think for the same amount I could have had either the blonde or brunette daughter thrown in!

Wednesday 24th May 1944
In the morning Ludford goes to collect the car and finds my bedroll, blankets, lilo etc all missing. I'd heard the locals were pretty efficient thieves but this beats everything. Blast their bloody eyes.

Drive up to Benevento through lovely rich farmland of corn fields studded with olive and fruit trees. Eat lunch up a side track to the sound of cuckoos, nightingales and warblers. Return to Bari late, tired and angry at losing my bedroll. We have driven 633 miles in 72 hours.

Friday 26th May 1944
Pay a visit to B Squadron after dinner. John O, in the chair at the end of the table, keeps the party at his normal 'madly gay' level. Peter Q, our South African, is extremely popular. I keep thinking what a wonderful thing it is to mix the colonials up so that they can go home after the war and speak enthusiastically and sincerely about the Empire relations. I've never known a case where a colonial hasn't been fully converted and we also find what grand chaps they are.

Monday 29th May 1944
We have a small air raid in the evening which interferes with my backgammon as we have to turn the lights out. The AA defence is poxy with searchlights worse than the Egyptian Army and some very unimpressive gunning.

Go off tomorrow for an attachment with the Derby Yeomanry in the line.

Friday 2nd June 1944
Lunch at division as our cars arrive late. It turns out one has broken its steering arm – a good job it happened now and not on the mountain roads. Eventually reach Foggia at around 4pm where we stay in a scruffy hotel run by the army. All around us are desolate bombed buildings. It's impossible to sleep as the flies pour in in their hundreds and settle all over one.

Saturday 3rd June 1944
At 7.30am we start again but my car won't pull so we stop for repairs. On the road again at 11am and lunch by a babbling brook. The Poles are resting and bivouacked all along the road.

Reach Naples pretty exhausted at 7pm having driven 500 miles and not slept in 36 hours.

Sunday 4th June 1944

Rise to find the jeep with a flat tyre which we change ourselves. Ludford and I then pile everything onboard and finally ourselves. We go off to war down a great tarmac highway lined with plane trees, flourishing crops and not a sign of conflict. Near Cassino we suddenly find it. Everything looks like Death has been residing here. The ground has a charred look – brown, battered and scarred.We lunch amid derelict vehicles and gun pits in a poplar copse over looked by the ruins of now-famous monastery. There is a stream of aircraft going both directions passing overhead. It pours with rain and there's some shooting in the locality.

It seems the DY are in reserve and we have just passed through them. They are due to march through the night, take up the lead and are routed on Turin via Tivoli, Rome and Teani.

They come through 2 hours late and I join the march. We plod up an awful mountain road 'til 11pm. I am stuck between a badly pulling and backfiring Harry[2] and a great Sherman which looms out of the dark at furious speed every time I get halted. I expect to get squashed flat at any moment.

Monday 5th June 1944

Everything seems to be in a right muddle. Divisional Commander Evelegh is an infantry soldier and has little knowledge of armour. As a result we are right in the rear instead of being pushed up front for a fast run.

We sit impatiently awaiting orders. It should be a good moment to chat and learn their methods but they are not very forthcoming as they are chomping at the bit.

We move at 1800 hours and continue slowly all night. By the full moon we can see the enormous havoc the RAF have wrought. There are great bomb craters everywhere, some big enough to bury three Shermans in. They seem to have their fair share of direct hits with nine great Panthers scattered by the roadside along with a mass of other vehicles.

It rains all night and everyone is wet and annoyed. We are all wanting to get on but division don't seem to have a clue how to do it. After travelling all night I find to my disgust we've only travelled 17 miles and have lost touch with the enemy.

Tuesday 6th June 1944

At 8am the really thrilling news comes (from a German source) that the invasion[3] has started. At 10am Eisenhower confirms this personally and by

---

2. Light Tank Mk VIII known as the 'Harry Hopkins' after Roosevelt's chief diplomatic advisor.
3. Operation Neptune, the Allied landing of 156,000 men in Normandy, the largest seaborne invasion in history and the beginning of Operation Overlord, the Allied campaign to

11am it's in the headlines of the news. Pray God it goes well and it puts an end to this war this autumn.

We move on slowly and at 2.30pm we find Rome coming into sight. Curiously enough we follow the road that I had noticed 5 years ago when flying in. I also see the high tension wire that almost finished us off! We don't enter the city but bypass it.

There seems to have been a lot of fighting in the outskirts. There are a number of dead about and many animals in that strange, ungainly posture; legs straight, stiff and wide apart. It's not very pleasant.

An unfortunate detour leads us right under the barrels of a battery of 155s just as they begin to loose off. The blast is truly terrific. At one stage in the afternoon we halt in convoy and I find myself alongside a Hun with most of his head missing. Someone puts a map over the gap.

We bivvy in a nice field outside the city. In 21 hours on the road we have moved 28 miles. Even with the heavies firing directly over us, it won't stop me from sleeping.

Wednesday 7th June 1944
We spend most of the day in the Campagna. At every clock hour we crowd round the wireless to hear the second front news. Old Winston apparently wanted to be present at the invasion on a battleship. He was dissuaded but, my God, what spirit he has!

We move at 4pm for 4 miles and billet in a house and garden. The Hun has systematically looted every house in the area and most of the things they couldn't take they have destroyed.

If a Hun soldier beckoned to a native, he or she came running and trembling. With us they are cheeky and even ready to argue. I've no sympathy for the Wop but I trust that one day the Hun will get his well-deserved reward for what he has done to civilisation.

The bodies of six prominent anti-fascists were found in a field near here. They'd have been taken from Rome and shot.

Thursday 8th June 1944
After breakfast George Trollope takes me up for a post-mortem of the tanks knocked out yesterday. It's all extremely interesting stuff. He appears very young to be a squadron leader but he knows his job. When four Hun were looting one of our tanks, he saw a German section fire a mortar at the tank and kill three of their own.

We leave the DY to head back south after lunch. The roads are packed with vehicles in great endless queues moving in each direction. We pass St

---

reclaim Western Europe. By the end of August more than two million Allied troops were to be fighting in France.

Peter's, the Pantheon, the Colosseum and masses of other historic places I know nothing of. It really is a beautiful city even with the streets filled with tanks, transporters, lorries and every other type of vehicle. Wop flags fly everywhere but no doubt the Swastika was flying in German days.

Friday 9th June 1944
Take a snap of Cassino but it's the end of the film and a new one means unpacking the whole jeep. General Alexander[4] said, 'Let Cassino be erased' and by God and the RAF, it certainly is erased. Where buildings stood there are now merely depressions filled with water.

Saturday 10th June 1944
Up at 5.30am and ponder a while as it's our wedding anniversary. No doubt Cara is doing the same.

We make good time and get to Oakland Camp by noon. I must have covered over 1,000 miles and the jeep packs up just outside the camp!

Some of the tanks are already painted green but it it's too dark I think. Nothing much seems to be happening – I'm beginning to wonder if we are ever going to get back into the war.

Go to bed early as there's little else to do. Am in bed at 10.15pm when one of our South African neighbours sounds 'Abide with me' on the cornet. It's really rather atmospheric and I approve. Shortly after one of the Highland regiments pipes a Lament in reply.

Monday 12th June 1944
Have a lecture on the second front by Bobby after lunch. He got a lot of the facts from Cochrane who did some of the planning. It's really very interesting and I know is of great value to the men.

---

4. Field Marshal Harold Alexander, 1st Earl Alexander of Tunis, KG, GCB, OM, GCMG, CSI, DSO, MC, CD, PC (1891–1969). Alexander rose through the ranks during the First World War, finishing as a 27-year-old colonel, winning an MC at Loos and a DSO at the Somme for 'being the life and soul of the attack ... holding trenches held in spite of heavy machine gun fire.' He led the 1st Division to France in September 1939 and left the beach at Dunkirk on the last destroyer after ensuring the successful evacuation of British troops. In January 1942 he was sent to Burma to repel the Japanese invasion but was forced to retreat to India. After returning to the UK he was posted as commander-in-chief of Middle East Command in August 1942 to replace Auchinleck and presided over Montgomery's victories in the Western Desert. He then commanded Allied forces during the invasion of Sicily and the Italian campaign. Following the war, he was Governor General of Canada 1946–52.

Bobby and I then dash off to a sand table exercise on tanks and infantry cooperating. Brigadier David Dawnay[5] of 21 Armoured Brigade is the star turn at the exercise. They say he's the best tank commander that we possess.

Tuesday 13th June 1944

Bobby and I spend the morning in the countryside on a recce. We find a piece of the original Appian Way [*Via Appia* linking Rome to Brindisi and dating back to 312 BC] probably never before desecrated by car. There is golden corn being reaped on either side as our jeep pushes through shoulder-high thistles.

We come upon a great old cherry tree, planted from a stone from Caesar's lips, no doubt. It is laden with lovely fruit brazenly, not coyly hid. We startle a long-legged girl who is up the tree stealing its treasure and on our approach she flees for dear life. In order not to lose her booty she gathers it in her skirt with her hem clutched to her chest, leaving us a view of more maiden than modesty!

Friday 16th June 1944

To our north, South African tanks are firing over one corner of the camp with shells falling close to the east. To the south, our own tanks are firing south-west over another corner of the camp. The margin of safety, whilst sufficient, would not be considered anything like enough in peacetime. Maybe this will help our men become staunch to fire.

Saturday 17th June 1944

All the senior officers of the division have to attend a VD lecture given by an eminent venereologist. It makes one's flesh creep and wonder how one has ever retained a clean and healthy nether man. It appears that this is the home of the disease.

It used to be called Neapolitan Sickness and every woman I see now I assume is a prostitute and unclean. We are told many work thirty men in a single shift and by their proceeds keep their house and family going! Since we invaded this country, ten percent of our Army lie in hospital using up precious drugs, occupying valuable time, and all as a result of a few moments when all else goes hang.

Sunday 18th June 1944

My office is full of red caps all day. Our chaps have had a brawl with them and, as some rather serious allegations have been made, a full enquiry has started. It may last several days judging by the crowd of witnesses.

---

5. Major General Sir David Dawnay KCVO, CB, DSO (1903–71), an Olympic polo player before the war and later commandant of Sandhurst.

Monday 19th June 1944

Gusty cold morning. Amazing to think that in southern Italy on a mid-June day one should need overcoats.

The Hun is now using glider bombs on England, launched from a cradle they have a range of 150 miles.[6] I reckon all of England in a semi-circle from Kings Lynn–Oxford–Corfe is in danger of untargeted, promiscuous savagery.

Wednesday 21st June 1944

B Squadron on a scheme all day and we go out to supervise. There is a huge amount of rain. We call it 'Hitler's weather' as every time the Hun pull out for a long run our forward troops get held up by bad weather and the air strafing is handicapped.

Monday 26th June 1944

The same old scheme again with C Squadron but it's far from a success. Peter Crichton seems to ignore all the training policy, has no knowledge of tactics or where his troops are and has no control. He is quite unsuited to take a squadron into the field in my opinion. To make it worse he argues every point and gives the impression that the CO is a bloody fool and is impertinent to criticise him. He is so conceited and full of misplaced self-assurance that argument is useless. It's a big step to sack a squadron leader now but I feel it should be done.

Sunday 2nd July 1944

It seems Peter C has handed in his notice and is adamant about going. Thank Heaven he is. I fear I shall be dragged into this to give my opinion to the general. I only hope I can be moderate in my views as I feel very strongly on the subject.

Thursday 6th July 1944

Hear we've been given a fortnight's leave and a quick follow-up to say we've got to produce a transport column. Given eighty drivers are already away and leaving guards at the camp, it doesn't look as if many will get this leave!

---

6. The Germans launched V-1 flying bombs, also known as doodlebugs, from 13 June 1944 until 27 March 1945. Designed for terror bombing, they killed over 5,000 people and injured a further 16,000. The V-1s were shortly to be superseded by the V-2 rocket, carrying more explosive with a longer range and greater accuracy.

Friday 7th July 1944

Bobby calls up the squadron leaders and tells them of the Crichton situation, explaining his point of view. Peter is going today and in an awful state having taken it very badly.

Spend the evening in conference with Bobby who is completely exhausted after a week of crisis. I am trying to make him take some leave. The trouble is Mary is in London with her dying father and the flying bombs are coming in pretty fast. The PM made a statement on them. They are getting serious with 150 every 24 hours and an average of one death per bomb. All of this is not helping secure his peace of mind.

Sunday 9th July 1944

Almost everyone is away. Bobby, Smith and I with six followers take our lunch and go down to the sea. We take a chance on a spot that looks good and little frequented. It turns out to be the best beach – nay the only beach we've found yet. The water is warm and sulphate blue and the sand silvery hot. We stay 'til after 5pm and return in the cooler evening air. Even Bobby came into the water and enjoyed it.

Monday 10th July 1944

The rumour is that Stalin has announced that he'll be in Berlin in 800 hours (33 days) and that at the Tehran Conference he stated that Russia would police Germany for two generations, lay eight selected cities waste and have the Dardanelles.

Tuesday 11th July 1944

Ludford is off on Monday. He really has been the ideal gentleman's gentleman and I shall miss him. I've got very little time to find a new servant. Hawksworth and Flowers eventually come in to the final. H is John D's driver; young, enthusiastic and pleasant. F is older and more staid but with no experience of valeting. The decision is taken out of my hands as HQ say they couldn't replace F. This suits me and H takes over on Thursday.

Friday 21st July 1944

Everyone very cheerful. Someone has tried to blow up Hitler with a stick of dynamite[7] and France, Russia and Italy are all progressing well.

---

7. On 20 July 1944, conspirators led by Claus von Stauffenberg attempted to blow up Hitler inside the Wolf's Lair, his field headquarters in East Prussia. Hitler suffered only minor injuries and the military coup d'état that followed failed within five hours. The ringleaders, including von Stauffenberg, were shot the following day. The attempt was used as an excuse by the Gestapo to arrest more than 7,000 people, of whom they executed 4,980.

The only person not cheerful is Bobby. His father-in-law has finally died, a merciful relief as this means Mary can leave the flying bomb area, but to add to his woes his sister has had a heart attack.

It is astounding the way the battle-scarred country is sprouting. The scorched trees have come to life and the dust has been cleared off the bushes. There are trees cut off at the roots by shellfire which are now growing back up again.

Tuesday 25th July 1944
Make a dash for Taranto. It's full to bursting with two divisions of French troops and there are two Yank battleships in, a mass of shipping and a number of landing craft tucked away in odd corners. It looks as if something may be happening somewhere soon.

Our own future has also been disclosed but it is still TOP SECRET.

Friday 28th July 1944
After listening to the 8am news, Ronnie Pitt and I set off for our new campsite on the other side of Italy. While it's cool one can travel fast and we reach Foggia in 3 hours. By midday we're up in the hills and stop by a spring for lunch. We move on to Benevento and then follow the Calore river up a winding gorge, strike across the Volturno and then to Alife where we are to meet division at 1700 hours.

We have a casual conference, typical of this division. I refuse to make myself affable to them as things are better as they are – they are frightened of us and generally give us what we want.

Our camp site is virgin and very pleasant. We are the only ones up off the river bed. We camp in a wood on a hillside amongst the songs and cooing of thrushes and turtle doves. I surprise a green woodpecker feeding on over-ripe pears.

Saturday 29th July 1944
We recce the area which the Hun, of course, has done his best to destroy. Go up to Piedmonte, a funny little old Alpine town. It was the flank to the Adolf Hitler line. It looks like a formidable place to take. Even now, in high summer, the Volturno is a big stream.

We have bacon and eggs for breakfast and the choice of melon, peaches or grapes, still cold and glistening with dew. The peasants are a new type to me. We are the first English soldiers they've seen and are delighted. They all say '*buon giorno*', touch their caps and bring us little presents when we come past.

Monday 31st July 1944

I hate it when I have nothing to do. There was a time when I thought it'd be idyllic but now I'm not sure. Perhaps it's because one feels that everyone else is working so hard elsewhere.

General Galloway suddenly announces that he'll be coming at 5pm to see all squadron leaders. We can't think what for. He turns up at 4.35pm and apologises for being late! Everyone is quickly summoned and he announces he's been boarded sick and is going home. I think he'll be a loss – not that we've seen much of him but he's older and more experienced that most. Neither he nor anyone else knows who is coming in lieu. I only hope it's not a gunner – we have enough on this staff hence the lack of humour and efficiency.

Friday 4th August 1944

The Bishop of Lichfield comes for a visit. We have a very informal talk mixing home news with religion, post-war construction and politics. He is a most charming, gentle person and never finishes a sentence or comes to the point. He seems to be thoroughly enjoying himself but one can't help wondering what possible good he can be doing.

Saturday 5th August 1944

Go in to Bari to collect some photographs. They've been done abominably – some of them are irreplaceable such as Rome full of Yanks the second day after it fell and the destruction at Cassino.

Sunday 6th August 1944

Signal at breakfast to say our move has been postponed. Later it's cancelled and a new destination and date given! Can no one high up ever make up their mind or stick to a decision?

Ian Vogel gives us a most unconvincing talk on the divisional warfare scheme. To make matters worse he doesn't know many of the facts and figures. I'm all in favour of the command idea of everyone out to help everyone else but a conglomeration of men and units like this division will never coagulate after the war. The units are not intimate enough or sufficiently confident in each other.

Tuesday 8th August 1944

Ronnie Pitt has returned during the night. Division's first order was for him to go, the second to return and the third cancelling both and go direct to Ortona. He gives us the news[8] which is magnificent and then we push off,

---

8. The 1st Armoured Division were ordered to move to Ortona with a view to becoming operational soonest.

never to see southern Italy again I hope. Not that I haven't enjoyed my time but I've always had an uncomfortable feeling that history was being made without me lending a hand.

I drive all day along up the east coast. It is going across the grain and so we are continuously either rising from or sweeping into a river bed. Lovely views keep opening to one, either of high ranges of hills or glimpses of the sea framed by hillsides.

By 6pm we have done 243 miles. Division had said the distance was 182 miles and we were to meet the town major. He says they've left and set up a report centre. Search for it for an hour finding four other officers and a telephone operator also looking for it. We are all tired and angry.

We drive a further 4 miles north and find a delightful spot on a cliff over the sea. While Hawksworth cooks my dinner I run down and have a glorious swim. Return and eat a good dinner in my dressing gown washed down with whisky. Watching the sun set over the high mountain ranges to the west I feel I can forgive division!

Wednesday 9th August 1944
Go into Ortona and find the plans have been altered again. The regiment will, after all, move to Alife. I intend to stay here 'til someone makes up their bloody mind! Return to my campsite as I can find none better, save one where mines are still thick on the ground. Bathe and laze the morning through.

Thursday 10th August 1944
Am summoned urgently to division. We are told to get to Ancona. We all knew this was coming and could have ambled up gently in the morning – now we have to rush to get there in daylight. The coast roads are full with Poles, Wop army (an awful indisciplined crowd) and Canadians. Though the signs are blacked out I spot what they are so I now know the form. It seems we're in for a party!

Every bridge – and there are many – has been blown and so diversions are frequent. It's very pleasant country, well cultivated with nice gardens and houses.

I stay on a farm with Kenneth Hedley who has a detachment here guarding dummy tanks on one of the deception schemes. I think it's a double fox. They make pretend our division is coming here so ostentatiously that it is quite obvious we aren't coming and then we get orders to go elsewhere 'til finally when everything is totally disorganised they'll rehash the whole plot. The bad effect on troop morale and loss of confidence in one's leaders must far outweigh any good done in outwitting the enemy.

Saturday 12th August 1944

I decide to decamp to a very attractive large villa on the hill called Palazzino Antonelli. I take what would be the dining room as a bedroom and keep the big drawing room as a mess for when the others arrive.

Victor and two gunners come to drink. My opinion of gunners is not altered during the course of the evening but the level of the whisky is!

Tuesday 15th August 1944

The roads are crammed all day with men, guns and supplies all rushing northwards. We've got to be quick if we're to see anything more of the war. A French army has landed in south France I gather and so far has met with no opposition.[9]

Friday 18th August 1944

It's a vile day with a north-easterly wind whipping up the sea and rain storms. There's pretty good turmoil. The advance party hasn't arrived and no one knows when the regiment is expected.

Drive down to Ortona to try and meet and them and have a look at every vehicle in case it's someone with news from the regiment. Return in Bobby's car at snail's pace – even driving a car he deadens it. He seems incapable of having any dash or party spirit these days.

Late in the afternoon the regiment start arriving. Hugh Young also turns up with various other div staff all with orders, counter orders and announcements.

My house is now full of people with wireless blaring, petrol cooker roaring and cars coming and going. I've managed to retain my room and have the garden to myself at night. I don't think we'll be here very long but I've had a very pleasant time.

From the news I think the war will end by November. The Yank armoured columns are on the outskirts of Paris already.

Sunday 20th August 1944

The whole morning is taken up getting ready for a visit by Oliver Leese, the army commander. There's a hot sun and no wind and OL is 40 mins late. One man passes out and everyone else has quite noticeably sweated through their tunic and trousers! We had a very smart parade ready but he tells us to

---

9. Operation Dragoon, the Allied invasion of southern France, was originally designed to be executed in conjunction with the landings in Normandy, but a lack of resources led to it being postponed. The primary goal was to secure a number of strategic Mediterranean ports. The initial invasion by 151,000 men met with limited resistance and the Germans swiftly withdrew to establish a new defensive line at Dijon.

break, form a circle and sit. So much for the hours of preparation and long stand in the sun!

He talks very frankly, tells us how the war is going on all fronts and a bit about the future. This is a pep talk as well as a welcome back to the Eighth Army. There is no doubt that an all-out effort is required from us all for a decisive result in this theatre. He described it as the biggest battle the Eighth Army has ever been in. We are stronger now than ever with sixteen divisions and a strength of 460,000 men.

Wednesday 23rd August 1944

All our tracks have now arrived. Bobby goes off early for one of those talks that in Monty's day one knew well to precede a battle. It's now common knowledge down to squadron leaders and we are delighted as the form looks good and a job after our own hearts. The cry is 'in Germany before the year is out' and I've no doubt that we'll do it.

At 11.45am we get a flash announcement to say Paris has been freed. To celebrate, the BBC plays the Marseillaise, a recording of the Notre Dame bells and the Can Can! Curiously enough it's what I'd suggested they should play but only jokingly!

Guy W has a very near escape when guiding a tank into place. He gets crushed between two Shermans and the one on the move stalls its engine, holding him pinned. He then has the anguish of waiting to see if the driver can reverse first without even coming a fraction of an inch forward. He manages but Guy is suffering from shock and a cracked sternum.

Thursday 24th August 1944

Busy plotting for war. D day is not far off but doesn't affect us for several days.

The corps commander[10] visits us. He has a funny way of talking to one but is obviously competent and has a lot of experience in armour. He brings a message to say the PM is coming for lunch tomorrow – entirely a 4H party and no one else concerned in any way.

We allocate jobs to everyone and spend the day organising the mess, hanging curtains, collecting furniture, scrounging food and laying on cooks, waiters etc.

At dusk we are told he can only give us 45 minutes on the landing ground where we are to meet him.

---

10. General Sir Charles Keightley GCB, GBE, DSO, DL (1901–74), the youngest corps commander in the British Army during the war.

Friday 25th August 1944

Bobby and I spend a long morning going through the plans. We have a break for an hour for lunch which we spend doing a recce of the LG. Back just in time to continue conference having had no lunch and then back to LG at 4pm to finish the organisation.

At 4.30pm a mass of Spitfires arrive from every point of the compass and whirl around the sky. Soon a large graceful Douglas, Alexander's *Stardust*, comes in over Loreto accompanied by yet more Spits. After a perfect landing the PM appears in our uniform but looking a little queer with a squashed hat and tie loosely tied over a gaping shirt. He walks around the men and meets every officer. I walk behind with the commander-in-chief, Alexander, a most charming individual, quiet and simple. Randolph also appears limping after his crash.[11]

The PM then makes a speech from the usual jeep. He speaks with great feeling and dwells a good deal on repatriation and post-war conditions. He gets three of the heartiest cheers and then comes over to tea under some trees. Of course just as I was calling up the parade a ruddy Spit lands and half the regiment don't hear my command!

Tea goes well. He has whisky and Alexander sticks to tea. Alexander talks much more optimistically and much more indiscreetly than the PM. The PM seems very much more frail and has trouble getting in and out of the jeep. He insists on crossing a most frightful anti-tank ditch 10 foot deep and 12 foot wide, sitting on his bottom and sliding down before anyone could stop him. Bobby and I scramble out in time to seize a hand each and pull him up. I also strive for a medal by pulling up Alexander!

The PM very much has the air of a man who has achieved his task. He seems quieter, more settled and satisfied. It's hard to realise that tonight the last and greatest battle in the Eighth Army history[12] is starting and that the two instigators can sit peacefully chatting to young officers as if they hadn't a care in the world!

In a week we've met our division and corps commanders, commander-in-chief and the Prime Minister – surely a record!

---

11. Major Randolph Churchill MBE (1911–68), MP for Preston 1940–45 and Churchill's only son. On 26 July he survived a plane crash when his Dakota stalled at 400ft and crashed in flames. He suffered spinal and knee injuries, but the crew and his servant died. Also unscathed after the crash was the novelist Evelyn Waugh, who described Churchill as 'a bore – with no intellectual invention or agility. He has a childlike retentive memory, and repetition takes the place of thought. He has set himself very low aims and has not the self-control to pursue them steadfastly.'

12. Operation Olive, the British attempt to break through the Gothic Line, started on 25 August 1944.

Monday 28th August 1944

We are quite ready for battle and this wait is annoying. I think we are all looking forward to it greatly – I know I am. I am not worried about death – that seems remote – but I don't want to be maimed. I've had a good life and there's nothing I haven't had a try at.

Tuesday 29th August 1944

I wake at 5am and can't get back to sleep so get in a jeep and go down to the sea. There's not a ripple and as I step into the sea an inquisitive red-eyed sun slowly raises itself over the horizon. I swim a mile, run a mile and put on pants to see what the local fishermen are catching (swordfish, red mullet and crabs).

Feel frightfully energetic all day and spend the afternoon collecting RE stores for the forthcoming operation. We expect extensive demolitions and the terrain will hold us up more than the Germans so we are trying to be self-contained in bridging material for the first twenty-to-thirty obstacles. Baulks and cribs are wired on to all our tanks.

The BBC announce that WC has arrived home and visited his old regiment in Italy.

Wednesday 30th August 1944

Fit up my maps and go through latest intelligence reports, topological details and air photos etc. Though we are all set I am beginning to doubt the original plan coming to fruition. The Hun is falling back in perfect order and making extensive demolitions so that we'll have to start all over again at the Gothic Line. This is exactly what would have saved the Hun at Alamein – his tactics evidently are gained by experience. We'll now have to re-concentrate, move up dumps, repair roads, bridges etc whilst wasting valuable time.

We hear late that we're off tomorrow.

Thursday 31st August 1944

The tanks go tonight and then wheels on the 2nd. As we are completely ready everything seems quiet and normal. Mentally we are all wildly excited and cheerful.

We have got a very nice Wop officer attached, Captain Philippo Senni. He is a regular cavalry officer, ADC to the Italian king, educated at Oxford and is very well spoken.

I'm sorry to be leaving Pallazzino as we've been very comfortable there. From tomorrow my tank will be my home. We've all antied up for the mess lorry to go back and stock up on wine and spirits. I personally gave £15 but I am sure that we are about to leave behind the land of plenty and we won't see any of the good things in life for the rest of the war or, indeed, for a year after the war has ended.

We're up all night moving the tanks up by moonlight. They look most awe-inspiring crashing through fences and vineyards with little gleaming eyes, belching smoke and dust. One feels there is nothing that could arrest their progress.

Friday 1st September 1944

A nice fresh morning. Today I should be out in the stubbles shooting with Linda – I shall be next year. Now I'm in a vineyard with Spitfires roaring over us. There's a lot of gunnery in the night which belies the 'no opposition' tale of yesterday.

Saturday 2nd September 1944

We move from 4pm 'til 5am, stopping once for a brew. The track allotted to us is not less than 1:4 in several places. It speaks for the modern engine that it can pull 30 tons almost from a standstill. The dust is terrible and one soon looks like the miller of Dee. It is not uncomfortable riding in a tank but it is a great strain and very tiring on the driver. My gallant Corporal Patrick refuses to have any relief and drives very well the whole way. Just before daylight at 5.30am we arrive at corps and meet up with Bobby.

Sunday 3rd September 1944

We are due to move off at 6am but we haven't sufficient fuel. Division have once again bogged it. We take the opportunity to settle down for a sleep. I get to bed at 6am and at 6.05am I'm awakened by Bobby and loud explosions. I thought at first we were being shelled but it's our boys getting some practice in (about 60 foot off). As they are unlikely to 'examine bore' before firing Bobby deems it necessary to move.

Set off at 1130 with John V in the lead. He bellies two Shermans and can't get across country so is counted out. John O then takes over and eventually ends with his nose stuck. They find an uncrossable river so it is not until evening that our patrols reach their objective. Things have not gone right and as a consequence we are a bit discouraged.

I am hauled 20 miles back against dense traffic and equally dense dust to a division conference. Hear there that our leading patrols have done their stuff so all is well. I brew up and then start back at 11pm. It's quite chilly and I have to sit on the roof to guide Sergeant Taylor. At about 1am I pick up the regiment on the march quite by chance. They get halted on a river bank and manage to turn one tank completely over.

I do a recce with Kenneth H and find a different route. It's rather eerie going off alone in a strange country, for all one knows still occupied by enemy and strewn with mines. Our minds are set at rest by a Hun plane dropping a shower of incendiaries and one heavy bomb on us. It makes a very pretty display for some time. We continue 'til just before dawn when we catch up with some very tired infantry.

Monday 4th September 1944

I put on my tin hat and jeep up to find out the form. The country looks like a nice rolling plain and opposition seems slight. We put C Squadron upfront to help and everyone is terribly excited as this is the first day of the season for us. Alas the infantry attack peters out and as daylight grows so does the opposition.

By 2pm there's a very large scale battle in progress. In fact the 4H have the whole of the 26 Panzer Division forming up as a defence line in front of them. Their shelling and mortaring is heavy and unpleasant. A Squadron have two killed by a shell and we are very lucky in HQ as the near misses always arrive on the wrong side of the tank or when we were inside.

In the late afternoon I go to see how Brigadier Goodchild and the 2nd Armoured Brigade are getting on. Have an extremely unpleasant run both ways and am lucky not to be hit. I ask myself several times if the journey is really necessary.

We are busy 'til nearly midnight and despite having had no sleep for 60 hours, and very little for the previous nights, I am feeling very well and, except for occasional short periods, not a bit sleepy. I manage to sleep moderately well for about 5 hours with only two disturbances.

Tuesday 5th September 1944

The opposition is still heavy but division keep telling us that Coriano is not held so we'll have to send in patrols. Bobby, rather against his will, sends in Tim. They get in but on coming out get very knocked about. Two Honeys are knocked out and two are missing. Two men are killed outright and another two wounded. Poor Tim has lost a leg and both hands. We hope he will be mercifully released from what would never be life to him again. I had grown to like him very much.

A and B Squadrons do most awfully well all day and the information coming in is well up to Royals' standard. The great advantage here being that we can report up to the limit of visibility and shoot nearly as far with effect.

B Squadron take ten prisoners from the Panzer division. They are supposed to be their crack troops but I've never seen a more miserable bunch of runts, badly clothed, no kit, pale and emaciated. The oldest of them can't be much more than 20 years and the youngest 15 years old. The farm in which we took them is littered with dead, testifying to our and the gunners' good shooting.

Lloyd, our EME, gets hit on his way to us. I'm afraid he's lost a hand and gets one in the tummy. This shelling is the devil. We are the only people through the Gothic Line so our flank is fully exposed and dominated from the hills. They even managed a good observed shoot at our HQ. Our casualties were very high but our information has been first class.

In bed by 11pm, human endurance seems to have reached its limit! I've never been so dopey before. I was awoken three times in the night and each time was quite incoherent.

Wednesday 6th September 1944

Woken at 5am and have to be shaken out of bed. We left a troop out last night with a tank with a track blown by a mine. Early in the morning the troop gets ambushed and John O went down himself to help extricate Sergeant Hatton. We lose more tanks and several men are wounded.

The 2nd Armoured Brigade are very slow in their advance and are strongly counter-attacked. With considerable support from dive-bombing Spits and from us the counter is broken up. They take three more PoWs, one seems quite keen to talk. Musso has been down here with Kesselring[13] to inspect the defences. He was wearing khaki and said that the war would never go further up Italy than the present line. He then inspected some women and gave them 500 lira each!

In a very few days we've become real veterans. People no longer look up when the guns fire or start when a shell drops. It has been as noisy a battle as the first few days of El Alamein but thank God the only air so far has been ours except once when a 109 attacked an RA recce plane. It is shot down before it can do any damage.

Receive a letter from Ma. How it got here I can't imagine. She's very optimistic about the end of the war. Things are certainly moving apace. We are in Antwerp and Luxembourg. The Russians have declared war on Bulgaria and they immediately ask for an armistice – surely the world's shortest war!

Thursday 7th September 1944

We wake up to pouring rain. The ground we are in is thick clay and many vehicles will get stuck. It is stickier than Suffolk clay and one's feet get so

---

13. Generalfeldmarschall Albert Kesselring (1865–1960), one of most decorated and highly rated of the German commanders. Whilst respected by his Allied opponents for his military achievements, and nicknamed 'Smiling Albert' within the German forces for his warm demeanour, his record was marred by the brutality he showed Italian resistance fighters over the last two years of the war. At the Nuremberg Trials he was sentenced to death by firing squad (considered more honourable than hanging) but, following support from previous adversaries, including Churchill and Alexander, he was released from prison in 1952.

bogged one cannot move easily. Patrick and co produce a good breakfast and to cheer the sodden scene I open my one and only pot of strawberry jam.

I fear high command (above division) have not lost the war here but have temporarily failed to win it by lack of forethought and general slowness. When we first came up there was little in front of us and 24 hours previously there was nothing here at all. The battle isn't going at all to plan. We collect some Hun deserters who say they've been told to hang on at all costs and soon masses of Luftwaffe and a new secret weapon will come to relieve them. These chaps obviously didn't believe it!

Friday 8th September 1944

The rain has stopped and the ground dries pretty quickly. Brigadier Goodbody visits us. He's very friendly but a gunner. Our CRA, Jones, a complete nincompoop, has been sacked. Let's hope more of the staff will follow.

The 60th with us are a poor lot. We're all very incensed with them as they'll not attack any place until we announce it's totally unoccupied. One such place being a farm where Henry Hall and Sergeant Cope entered, took ten PoWs but the 60th wouldn't take it on as a native had said it's occupied by the '*Tedeschi*' [Italian for 'Germans'].

Saturday 9th September 1944

Feel rotten all day and am very short with poor Bobby. He won't decentralise or take anyone's word for anything. He pops up even when a shell bursts and reports it back to division. All the 4H lack experience of war but don't realise it. They think that the few days they had at El Alamein (in a very minor role) and after the breakthrough when they were in the rear (certainly of the Royals) that there's nothing for them to learn about war. We are actually very well trained but just terribly green.

Go to bed in the evening with a feverish cold. The doc gives me four pills but I have a real sweaty night. My head is aching and the continual roar of gun explosions and bursting shells drives me nearly frantic. In addition we get bombed and strafed all night and the Canadians answer back with every available weapon.

Saturday 10th September 1944

Have a filthy night and was a bit delirious at times. I hope I'll never be sick in more squalid surroundings – a pit against a tank with an awning over me.

The only relieving feature of the day is quite a good mail – Cara, Michael, Ma, two *Punches* and a *Country Life*.

The canteen comes up with half a bottle of beer per man. There's an ugly rumour that there'll be no whisky ration for another month. I'm alright having three in hand still. I've been going very steady with it – one tot a night, usually in my tea. It makes even the worst tea taste quite reasonable.

Monday 11th September 1944

The day starts very badly with a report from outside that one of our jeeps has gone over a mine killing one officer and wounding another. We hear Sergeant Hatton and Sergeant Mitchell have also been killed and Peter Woods and Bobby wounded. Tim, I am thankful to say, has died – life would have been no fun for him.

CO is in a very bad temper over our losses; they were entirely unnecessary and due to a childish lack of understanding of the situation. None of these lads seem to understand that opposite us here is a mad fanatical enemy whose one ambition is to kill as many of us as possible by any possible means before he gets killed himself.

Am much better today. The fever has gone and I'm left with a heavy cold. There's nothing I dislike more than riding in a tank. It's cold, cramped and uncomfortable. Every part of me that touches the tank is soiled or oiled. If there's no other means of progression and I have to travel on *Daring* then I get on at the last possible moment and get off directly when it stops. To Bobby's horror I'd rather face mortar fire in the open than sit in my tank!

Tuesday 12th September 1944

We have a very noisy ¾ hour just after 1am. A stream of mortars rain down on the leaguer and Arthur HB gets killed outright. He'll be a great loss. He's worked very hard and got a lot of tanks back on the road which might otherwise not have reappeared. We bury him up at the farm with a man from C Squadron who got creased at the same time.

Mellor and Atkins must be getting very fit. It's seldom they don't produce something for the pot: a running hen, a caged rabbit or sitting cabbage fall equally easily to their prowling. All the farms are full of livestock but the constant shelling keeps the inhabitants away.

The next big attack starts tonight and we are all packed ready to move at dawn. The artillery barrage starts at 10.30pm. It is a fearsome thing. Normally there's continual shelling which sounds like people kicking a football around on hard ground or a refractory horse kicking at a loose box or a few London omnibuses passing overhead but now it's one continuous roar.

Sleep is just about possible but fitful. It's a very cold night.

Wednesday 13th September 1944

Toward dawn, when our guns die down, the Hun starts replying. One would not have believed that anything could have survived this great barrage.

Now it's just daylight on a lovely fresh September morning with a little sickle moon in the sky and a wonderful view of countryside and seascape. Here we are throwing everything we can at the Hun and he at us. It's been going on for 5 years and, as far as the common man is concerned, all to no purpose. Pray God this will end soon and let us get back to peaceful days at home.

We get ordered to do more than we are capable of. John O pushes ahead to find out if a certain point is occupied. We are sure it is, at least, well covered. Division, including the general who comes to visit us, are sure it's ok. We lose five Shermans and one Honey in the attempt. One of the Shermans is completely blown up after being bazooka-ed with only one survivor, not Henry Hall. So that's the end of another of our nicer officers: fat, stolid, imperturbable and always cheery. He wasn't truly cut out to be a soldier but had adapted himself well and was of great value to B Squadron.

We get a panic order to move forward – very unnecessary and could have been avoided if my advice had been heeded earlier. To make the party complete the CO's wireless goes flat on him. We change tanks but meanwhile we lose sight of A Squadron which sets Bobby in a panic and he swans off, in full sight of the enemy, down the one road that he's always refused to let us use. As a result we get a packet. My tank gets a near miss knocking off a bogey and a roller. Buster gets a bit in the face.

I remain here for the night getting shit all night long. Spot some hens going up to roost so stalk out with my revolver and get four (in four shots). One is a runner and is retrieved by a Gurkha so I give it to him.

Thursday 14th September 1944
A Honey comes for me at dawn. I dash off after a quick brew up and change a bit of kit to the other tank. The track is blocked by an ambulance which turned over in the night so I continue to come out on the San Savivo ridge. I'm not at all popular in someone else's battle and get scowled at by friends and shot at by the enemy. It's an awful shambles with bodies sprawled everywhere, burnt out tanks and houses and a reek of carnage.

Turn back across shattered Passano to find the regiment in a valley where we are spasmodically shelled. We spend the day in this noisy dirty place and get very little done. Bobby insists on digging in for the night – most undignified!

Friday 15th September 1944
The day starts badly as Bobby does a recce and finds a place from which he can see right forward. He then does what I've striven to keep him off – that is directing the troops himself. He warns John V that there's a Tiger 100 foot ahead of him but it's an old MK IV abandoned several days ago! He is on the

verge of going all blue when the general sends for him. He gets very lost and I get sent to meet him halfway back to put him on the right road.

I like listening to the 25-pounder shells going over. They seem so cheerful and enthusiastic and make a noise like children going down a slide. I am writing this to the sound of them in the pitch dark.

Saturday 16th September 1944

We move at 8.30am to join up with A and C Squadrons. We reach the Marano River where we are halted and spend the rest of the day. It's a filthy place right down on the crossing and we get a lot of heavy stick.

I try to find a decent leaguer area and in doing so get sniped at. Creep round the farm where I think the shots came from only to find a nice wine glass and some fowls – bag a cockerel at 30 yards. The Germans killed a pig last night and our leaguer smells of roast pork.

Find two Tiger tanks that have gone over a twenty foot bank. I can't reason out the story at all. They are the most monstrous great things. A Sherman is to a Tiger what a Carrier is to a Sherman! The 88mm gun alone is as long as our Sherman tank!

Sunday 17th September 1944

We have an unpleasant night between two river crossings. They stonk [concentrated artillery bombardment] both hard during the night and we get some overthrows. I hear quite a few bits hit my tank but I'm secure under my mosquito net on the ground.

A few strong shells in the morning cause some alarm and despondency. One literally misses my ear by inches and gets my operator, Mellor, in the knee with a nasty wound.

I am left to hold the fort for most of the day as Bobby goes into division. Alex Williams comes in having found the remains of Peter Woods. He says it looks as if a tank had gone over him. A shell in B Squadron in the afternoon kills three and wounds one. Sergeant Lyon was one of the unlucky ones, a good chap.

They say there's only 3,000 Hun in front of us and that it's mostly artillery. The infantry have no casualties from bullets in an attack as there's no opposition but once in position they get shelled to hell.

An airborne division lands in Holland today[14] and the Siegfried Line seems to be well and truly pierced. The Hun talks of retiring to the Rhine where we will meet his 'real defences'.

---

14. Operation Market Garden was the unsuccessful airborne and ground assault on German forces in the Netherlands. The objective was to secure a series of nine bridges that would allow an invasion route into Germany, but the Allies were defeated when trying to capture the final bridge over the Rhine at Arnhem. With this defeat went the hope of being able to finish the war before the end of the year.

Monday 18th September 1944

Spend the day again in the same place – B Squadron suffer four more casualties. We move in the late afternoon to a very unhealthy ridge right in the foreground of the battle. Get some very unpleasant shelling and B Squadron lose another, a direct hit on the open co-driver's hatch. Very bad luck.

We sit in a sordid farm full of filth, dust and dead Huns. It's more like what one saw pictured in the last war. A few hens are picking around the corpses and an overturned Tiger adds to the scene of desolation.

I have to go into division after dark. I get stonked twice, choked up with dust and a sore throat from shouting at my driver who backs me over a drop fence once, onto a minefield once and into a Bren Carrier twice.

Tuesday 19th September 1944

Move early to another position where we again get stick – due chiefly to some of B Squadron walking around on the skyline and asking for it. We sit in our tanks for a bit. I give Atkins and Birkett my *Punches* to read to keep their minds off the noise. They enjoy them.

We stay in this spot all day and it's not so unhealthy after noon as the Hun has his attention turned elsewhere. I'm beginning to think our troops are getting very nervy. They duck and dodge at every shell noise. It's partly inactivity under shell fire and the disturbed nights.

If I were given an immediate wish now it would be a hot bath then a comfortable sofa or bed and no sound of any sort for 12 hours. The dirt and noise here is something we never had to compete with in the desert. The fresh figs and grapes are the saving grace of this country at the moment.

There's a wonderful new scheme just started called 'artificial moonlight'. When putting in an attack a row of searchlights are set back at 30° over the objective. The result is we can all see the ground as we advance and the enemy just strains his eyes into darkness.

Wednesday 20th September 1944

We don't move but I hadn't expected to. We sit 4 miles in front of the armoured brigade who had orders to move at first light and take three or four times as long to move as us so I can't see mathematically how we can. They start off after lunch.

We get tired of waiting and B Squadron go out on their own. They have a pretty good party against enemy infantry with no anti-tank guns so enjoy themselves madly. The general comes and sits near us in a six-wheel Greyhound. When the first shell of the day lands 100 foot off I've never seen people move so fast on to their faces or all-fours as those division staff! They leave in a hurry forgetting two telephones and the division HQ sign.

I, perhaps tactlessly, give them half an hour to reach their secure HQ before asking if he would like his division sign or whether we could keep it as a memento.

After dark the guns develop a most ominous sound, quite different to normal. Owing to searchlights one can't see the sky but it's evidently black and full of low rain clouds. This is confirmed at around 10pm when the heavens open and remain open all night long. The post holding the tarpaulin next to my tank breaks when it can no longer bear the strain of ½ ton of water and drenches the wretched A Squadron runner who is sheltering under my tank. David D and Irvine H, both a bit nervous, sleep in slit trenches and spend the night walking around. They salvage their bedding in the morning from a foot of yellow slime.

Thursday 21st September 1944
It continues to rain all day accompanied by a cold northerly wind. The ground is mostly underwater and is swept continuously by sheets of rain brought by violent gusts.

All day a string of refugees come past us returning to Coriano. I think they must have sheltered in San Marino, a strange little neutral state that we are on the borders of. They have nothing more than they can carry or sling onto a bicycle. Those with children usually have a goat on a rope.

B and C Squadrons did very well yesterday and get a special 'banana' from the general.

After lunch we decide to move up into one filthy room in a cottage. After sweeping out the rubble it becomes fairly habitable. A few shells have removed most of the walls but the roof is mostly intact. We pull the tanks up close and get headphones and telephones inside. Later we get a fire going and light a dim lamp. The scene really might be Flanders 1915. We thaw out a little but nothing can get dry.

My bedding is pretty wet but I have to sleep in it. I pile on dry, warm jerseys and put my feet in my fleece lined coat to push them to the bottom of my damp bed. No doubt I'll survive!

Friday 22nd September 1944
The congestion on the roads is terrible with two day's traffic crowded into one and blocks everywhere caused by vehicles ditched, overturned or locked.

My wish for quiet and a bed were very near to being fulfilled for all yesterday the guns were nearly silent and this evening I find a spring bed frame. I put my bed down on it outside (for Bobby has used our one room as a lavatory – dirty little man). About midnight I wake up being bitten by mosquitoes and an awful attack of indigestion.

Saturday 23rd September 1944

Feel bloody all day, can't be sick, can't shit and can't swallow anything. Oh hell, I hope it's not jaundice.

We hear that we were to be broken up with 4H going to an infantry division! Bobby develops a complex of being able to move at 10 minutes' notice. We've done 3 weeks of mild battling (from an HQ point of view) and he hasn't removed his underclothes, socks, jersey or trousers once. I am starting to get nervy with him and decide I am going to try to see less of him. I've been holding his hand too long.

Sunday 24th September 1944

I've definitely got jaundice. The question is how to stick it out as I live very close to the doc and he's pretty observant!

Have a good night but very early rise as we have to send a squadron forward. The Gurkhas are operating next to us and sleep till long after we've brewed up our breakfast.

Get two letters from Cara including some snaps of her and Christopher. He looks so fine that I have to keep a good hold on myself to prevent myself from becoming a bore going round showing him off! He looks so healthy and strong and intelligent and full of fun. There's a little devil lurking in his eye too!

Visit the Bays' 'cemetery'. They had an awful debacle yesterday – a gallant blunder – losing half their tanks and many officers and men. Their tanks are strewn all over an open forward face, turned at all angles, black and burnt, some complete, some mutilated. Two are completely over, balanced on their turrets.

I go on to visit A Squadron on the forward line and spend an hour examining the next features and plains beyond. Except for puffs of shells bursting or smoking farms and haystacks, the country looks so peaceful. It's sad to see this wonderful grape crop rotting on the vines but there is no one to gather it.

Monday 25th September 1944

Get the doc to give me a pill in the morning which makes him horribly suspicious. As I've eaten nothing for three days I'm feeling a little weak but manage a little porridge for breakfast.

We sit on a ridge being indolently shelled and watch A and C carry out a bloody job of making contact with the enemy north of the Marrechia River. They get a lot of shelling and mortaring but carry out their task well. They take a few prisoners, kill a few Hun and have some slight casualties.

At 3pm I depart back to RHQ where the doc orders for me to be evacuated – not even a bottle of sherry will make him relent. We leave after dark and take one wounded man and one prisoner to dump at a cage. It's a long roundabout route and it soon starts to pour. On arrival I am bedded down in an ambulance where I have a very comfortable night.

Tuesday 26th September 1944
Awake at 7am to a lovely sunny morning.

I head off to C Echelon, passing the scenes of our and other people's battles. By the smell there must still be a lot of corpses about. The locals are returning but they'll have to be quick to get their roofs built before the winter rains start, poor devils. The ground is a swamp and I only hope this rain hasn't given Jerry a second chance to escape. It's come at a very convenient time for him.

Arrive at Porto Recanati at 3pm. The hospital is right on the seafront, a nice building of white solid stone and blue shutters. The sisters are kind and don't seem as overworked as is usually the case. Kenneth Saville is in the next bed with jaundice and is bright yellow. I suppose I must be too.

It's announced that our troops have crossed the Rubicon.[15] That's our effort of yesterday.

Wednesday 27th September 1944
It's nice being next to Kenneth – we have so much shared past and mutual friends and when all else fails can swap big game hunting experiences. He has also shot in Kenya and was at Secunderabad for a year.

Thursday 28th September 1944
It rained heavily again in the night giving Kesselring a chance to recover himself. It means our tanks will be bogged down where they stand for several days I fear. I may even find them where I left them when I escape from here.

Jack White appears in the afternoon. He has worms and feels it is a good chance to be cured. It is gratifying to know I'm missing nothing but this vile weather.

Perhaps jaundice is getting me down but I truly believe we are unlikely to get the war finished this autumn and if that is so then it may well drag into next summer. What a dreary prospect. I must review my plans for the future.

Saturday 30th September 1944
The sister tells me that jaundice affects one's liver for 3 months and that ale is the worst possible thing. She advises keeping off it for at least a couple of

---

15. Julius Caesar's crossing of the Rubicon river in 49 BC was the final step leading to civil war.

months. Well, she may be right and I don't want permanent injury to my liver but 3 months takes one to 1945. I must try to find a doc with a more optimistic point of view.

Monday 2nd October 1944
The doc says Kenneth, though his water has been clear for 3 days, will yet be 10 days in hospital and at least another 10 convalescing. I therefore can't see myself out in under a fortnight and am seriously considering evacuation to where I can at least get a hot bath and better food.

Thursday 5th October 1944
The tonnage of stores being landed at Ancona and other places to the north must be terrific. Every day a convoy comes up; mostly three or four cargo ships, sometimes more, as well as hospital ships, warships, schooners and landing craft. One never sees a ship going south – one can only surmise they sail again after dark.

Have a 'water test'. It's clear of bile so from today onward I can get up and gradually find my legs to strengthen my muscles.

Friday 6th October 1944
Hawksworth arrives late in the evening. He's taken 8 hours getting down. The traffic apparently has been awful and many bridges have been swept away. He has a good mail for me and a parcel from Egypt.

There seems to be little news from the regiment. They are sitting as I left them and are changing to all-steel tracks. A few people are being allowed away for seven days leave.

Sunday 8th October 1944
Hawksworth goes in to Ancona to get 12 pints of blood. I'm all for helping these medical people who don't seem to get much aid from the army.

I think there's a real hanky-panky going on with our rations here. We live on short rations with no selection of any sort – it's spam or nothing for dinner. We should be getting generous rations as many are on a diet and hospitals are meant to get a good drawer. No doubt some soldier is making a pile and some Wops are growing fat at our expense.

Monday 9th October 1944
At dawn the sea is dead flat with the recently emerged sun swathed in low cloud. Close by, on the beach, a dozen fishermen are pulling in their net. The net lies in a great black loop on the surface of the sea. The men don't haul on the line but keep up a strange rhythm with their feet and swaying

bodies. When the sea gives them a little they hold it, never giving anything back and slowly drawing the net in ... It is a scene that might well have been the Apostles hauling in their net on the lake of Galilee.

Tuesday 10th October 1944

I am told I am due for discharge to the convalescent depot at Gigli's[16] house and get up directly after breakfast. I am a week ahead of schedule as this is my third day up. To my surprise I see my car arrive for me followed by another, from which the yellow faces of John O and Shagger Curwen emerge. I stay on an extra hour to put them in the picture of life here and to help them settle in.

Gigli's house is the strangest thing I've ever seen. The approach is painfully formal, one is diverted off and goes round a great sweep to the other end of the house. The house is like a wedding cake poised exactly on the highest spot of a hog's back ridge. It is so ugly it hurts but the view is quite magnificent.

Wednesday 11th October 1944

This place really is worth describing it's so incredible so I shall let my pen run on.

On each side of the main entrance are the kitchen, pantry and back stairs. The main hall runs the whole length of the house hung with chandeliers. On one side is the drawing room, heavily curtained and furnished in cheap imitation Louis XIV furniture. Mirrors adorn the walls, dolls in lovely silk and lace sit, stand and bedrape large glass-sided cabinets.

Opposite is the dining room with hand painted walls and great bowls of flowers. If one lets one's mind wander to the ceiling, great flashy thighs, bulging bellies and billowing bosoms meet the eye. I was warned I'd be able to count over 100 'tits' in these two rooms and now I understand!

The next floor up, reached by a great curving double stair, is another hall with a ten-foot statue of three ballerinas. Off the hall are seven bedrooms, four bathrooms and Gigli's dressing room. His dressing room has two wash basins and leads into an enormous bathroom with a sunken Roman bath in the centre of the floor. Alas this is now a sick bay and the bath is boarded over.

---

16. Beniamino Gigli (1890–1957), widely regarded as one of the greatest tenors of his generation, was the favourite singer of Mussolini and recorded the fascist anthem *Giovinezza* for him. He gave over a thousand benefit concerts and is said to have raised more money for charity than any other singer in history. His personal life was complicated, and he is understood to have fathered at least eight children by at least five women.

The next floor up contains more bedrooms and a billiard room. Above that is a roof garden, glassed in on three sides and a wall of imitation rock and moss. On a tree, unlike anything seen on this planet, a cock pheasant is perched while below it a buzzard hangs in an endless glide.

All the walls bear framed credentials of Gigli as a singer and various pictures and medals are displayed as testimonials to his popularity in every part of Italy. As he sang for the Germans, the now brave, loyal Italian people won't let him come on stage.

Saturday 14th October 1944
Amelio is the butler, majordomo and general factotum here. He twiddles the staff round on his little finger. He looks like a most terrible rogue but I don't believe he aspires to anything more than living happily. In the evening he gives a recital of Gigli's records. They sound quite good from afar but not quite so good close by. Deedes, who has less music in him than me, wonders loudly how the man could have made so much money.

Tuesday 17th October 1944
Deedes and I take a drive around. I regret very much that we call in to see my lovely Palazzino Antonelli. The Welsh are now there. All the care we took of the house and garden has been time wasted. The lawns are ploughed deep with wheel tracks, trees uprooted, the fountain filled with rubble, doors and windows pulled down and the lovely wallpaper ripped off the walls. It makes me wonder how Sotterley must be looking.

Saturday 21st October 1944
After saying my goodbyes, I leave at 9.30am to rejoin the regiment. Just at dark I find B Squadron. Ronnie Pitt has settled in a school with everything very comfortable – stoves, mats down and electric light! It's warm and far friendlier than anything the Con Depot could do.

If I'm quick I'll get back in time to go into battle again. I left the regiment the same evening it withdrew from the River Rubicon Line.

Sunday 22nd October 1944
Have a certain amount to do seeing various people and then inspect the billets. They've certainly got these shell-battered homes into a living condition with rubbish swept out and spare wood used for fires. The owners are pushed into one or two rooms and we take over the others. At first the civilians don't like it but soon find that not only are our troops kindly natured but that they get all sorts of pickings from the cookhouse and help in getting things straight. The children love it.

The new brigadier, John Combe,[17] and Peter PG, his 2i/c, arrive at the same time for a conference. We're just short of Cesena for which a battle royal is still in progress. We are waiting to go through when the crossing is made good.

Go round the squadrons in the afternoon and see most officers, including several new ones. I'm really rather pleased to be back to this life and hear the guns again (so long as not too close). After dark the low cloud is lit up by gun flashes and dozens of searchlights. The moon is quite outshone.

Monday 23rd October 1944

Walk up the hill with Irvine Harris after lunch. Take a stick and heavy boots as it's muddy under foot and stroll as if on a Sunday walk to see the battle for Cesena. We can't see much – just smoke, shelling, gun flashes and the constant vibration of machine gun fire. It's amazing if one climbs 300 foot one can see miles and miles over the plain which is absolutely flat, thickly orcharded and dotted with little red houses.

We hear an 'official' rumour that we are moving back tomorrow to form a brigade with the 3rd and 7th Hussars. We've all known this for a month yet we are only told 12 hours before we are expected to move. Everyone is standing to in readiness for the order and the wireless is kept open all night.

Thursday 24th October 1944

At 7.30am we get a telephone message to say 'no move today'. What a wonderful army this is where no one seems able to think ahead. If this sort of thing goes on in a perfectly straightforward move then it is easy to understand how perfectly chaotic our staff must be in battle with the continuous counter-orders.

At 11.30am we get an order to say we start to move tomorrow. Hold a hurried conference and decide that Senni and I are to head off to meet the advance parties.

---

17. Major General John Combe CB, DSO & Bar (1895–1967). After a distinguished Western Desert campaign, during which he was twice awarded the DSO, he was captured by the Germans on 6 April 1941 outside Msus. As a PoW in Italy he developed a reputation as an enthusiastic escaper, succeeding during September 1943 and joining a group of Italian partisans. In March 1944, guided by Italian resistance fighters, he undertook a 250-mile walk, partly across snow-covered mountains, to the coast, where he acquired a fishing boat. By May he was back in the UK and five months later returned to the Eighth Army in Italy.

Chapter 9

Barne's Taxi Service

Without consultation with the 4th Hussars, it had been decided to convert their light reconnaissance tanks into armoured personnel carriers. By removing the turret from their tanks and many of the internal fittings, notably the bulky ammunition storage racks, it became possible make room for ten fully equipped infantrymen. The RAF had recently switched from Browning machine guns to wing-mounted cannon, and these surplus Brownings were to be mounted above the driver's head. These modified tanks were known as 'Kangaroos'.

Kangaroos had originally been developed by the Canadians and first saw action in August 1944 during the later stages of Operation Overlord. It was soon found that 'debussing' (climbing out of the hull) was challenging under fire, and climbing rungs were added. They proved their worth in allowing foot soldiers to be delivered right to the point of attack, removing the need for an exhausting, exposed infantry march and helping significantly to reduce casualties. Given their success in France, the military authorities were keen to replicate this in Italy, where the well prepared German defences gave the enemy an advantage over attacking Allied troops.

* * *

Wednesday 25th October 1944
Rise terribly early having slept badly on a good bed. Eat our ration breakfast and then get a message from the Baroness [Francetti] to come down to her for breakfast. This consists of tea, bread and honey. All the servants are obviously family retainers and are well dressed even at 8am.

To brigade HQ where I set about allotting billets, trudging round the town drawing sketch maps for 4 solid hours. The 7H, who move tomorrow, give us lunch and couldn't be more friendly.

Back for a long talk with Cookie [Major General Ronald Cooke CB, CBE, DSO, 1899–1971]. He lays the plan for the 4H before me. It's been a well-kept secret and must remain so for several days. He asks my first impressions and I tell him frankly.

Thursday 26th October 1944

It's been pouring all night and continues to come down in a solid sheet accompanied by a bitterly cold wind.

Eventually B and C Squadrons arrive at 11am with one tank ditched when the road gives way. Do a recce of the area and find a thirteenth century castle with a farm nearby for the officer's mess. The owner is a delightful old squire, a late artillery colonel, wearing boots and breeches, a nineteenth century hat, a waistcoat and velveteen coat. He keeps a horse and is an amateur sculptor. The Germans, with a pistol literally in his coccyx, gave him 3 hours to clear out. We ask tentatively if we could have three rooms and he gives us more than he can spare, regretting he doesn't have sheets for all seven officers!

Get back to find Bobby has arrived and he goes off to brigade to receive the news. He comes back in the evening and we discuss the bombshell. The army have purposefully kept it from us until it's a *fait accompli* and then dropped the news on us. He is very upset and angry and is going to write to Winston tomorrow to tell him he's prepared to chuck his hand in. This means I may be left with the baby.

Friday 27th October 1944

Have to see Bobby before he goes to brigade to say if I'm prepared to take on the regiment in its new role. I've had a sleepless night to think it over and decide it's definitely in my interests, and probably that of the regiment, if I accept. It may not materialise but I'd be a fool to refuse after last year's fracas with HWLL.

Saturday 28th October 1944

We open up a fascist's store for furniture and Dick tries on one after another of the uniforms, hats etc. In one, like Musso loved being photographed in, he really did look very like Benito! We allow the locals to have their share and give all the clothing to the local poor and hospitals.

After lunch am summoned by Bobby to say he's going home and I'm getting command of the 4th Queens Own Hussars! He's been to no little trouble to impress on people that I am the most suitable, if not the only, person for the task. It is not an enviable job just now. I see little future for us in this new experimental role but it means promotion (long overdue) and, in all probability, that I'll take the regiment home in due course. I must now reapply my nose to the grindstone – I shall have 160-odd tanks under my command.

Monday 30th October 1944

In the afternoon I go over with Senni to the Baron Francetti's house where we play squash. The baron appears and I then have to play him. Beat them both. He is a very charming person, educated at Eton and with perfect manners.

Some of Arthur's kit is being disposed of today. People have little feeling about that sort of thing – clothes get bandied about and tried on and argued over. A pity but perhaps natural. I ask for a button hook and clothes brush but both seem to have disappeared. I should have liked some little memento of Arthur as I was fond of him.

Tuesday 31st October 1944

Day-by-day I take over more responsibility but the fact that Bobby is going is still kept secret. Nigel SS comes over with the brigadier and congratulates me.

Lieutenant Colonel Renshaw, aged 30 and with a DSO and MC, brings over a pilot to experiment with loading on to our carriers.

Wednesday 1st November 1944

A lovely crisp sunny morning. It's just the sort of day one might expect now in England with the trees turning to the lovely colours of autumn. Drink a glass of peach brandy to foxhunting in the evening – I wish it could have been a port in the Crown at Oakham.

Thursday 2nd November 1944

While getting ready for the gunners and infantry to come over for more loading tests we get told the army commander[1] is arriving at 11.30am. At 12.45pm he still hasn't arrived and we are told be will be here at 2.30pm. At 1.30pm Bobby and I are summoned to see him.

He seems awfully shy and not quite knowing what to say or do next – he hasn't the memory of other and great army commanders. I do know, however, that despite his unimpressive appearance he is absolutely genuine and a first

---

1. Sir Richard McCreery GCB, KBE, DSO, MC (1898–1967). McCreery won his MC for one of the last ever mounted cavalry attacks on a German machine gun post in 1918, capturing ten prisoners in the process. He was chief of staff to Alexander, and Montgomery's immediate superior during the Battle of El Alamein. He held various positions during the Italian campaign and ended up taking over command of the Eighth Army from Leese in December 1944. He maintained a high reputation throughout the war and was noted for detailed planning combined with strategic flair. His appointment was particularly fortunate for the 4th Hussars as he was an expert on the use of light armoured vehicles.

class soldier. He wanted to tell us the plans for our future but that it would be insecure to put it down on paper. Our object this winter must be to train for the final campaign and a spring attack.

Friday 3rd November 1944

Spend most of the afternoon with Archie, Corporal Howard and Sergeant Wallace separating out mess accounts. There's always a muddle with such things after a battle. In the heat of things one let's things go hang, saying it will be easily sorted out when we come in for a rest but by that time people are dead, items are lost or forgotten and receipts or signatures not taken.

Saturday 4th November 1944

Continue the problems of change over, both of role and command. I think people have been guessing that Bobby is departing – well, they'll know tomorrow.

We have a party in Bobby's room at 7pm with John V, John O, Paddy O'B, Jack W, Carlton P and John D. Bobby tells them the form and they listen in silence. I don't think Bobby is popular but he is trusted and respected. Anyone of any account appreciates the amount he has done to bring a rather scratch lot of officers and a second class unit up to a first class regiment with a very definite and strong spirit. He's ruled with a loose rein but nevertheless has guided it firmly – I think it's only his appearance which has prevented him going up much higher in the army. It's certainly given him an inferiority complex and has affected his manner towards his fellow man.

Sunday 5th November 1944

Bobby makes a farewell speech to the squadrons. He's not a little upset and I can well understand it. I'm sad to think we won't see his funny little angular figure with bowed legs, overlong trousers, peaked cap set back off his rodent-like face and permanently shrugged shoulders as though he were constantly freezing.

After lunch, Oliver Brooks of 1st Welch calls on me. To my surprise and pleasure he's bringing up his battalion to play with us in our training. The fates have certainly started kind.

Tuesday 7th November 1944

Bobby goes off at 8.30am. The whole of HQ and C Squadron turn out and line the road to cheer him off. I do hope all present 4H appreciate him.

I take the chair of office and it's remarkable how people's manner changes overnight. I only hope I don't alter for the worse. So many COs do once they get the feel of power as one's wish is taken as an order.

All our heavy baggage arrives up from Taranto including three large saddle bags of mine. My room suddenly feels very overcrowded but it's really quite exciting unearthing treasures one hasn't seen for years – photograph albums, books, Cara's ski boots (more a treasure of memory than anything else, bless her tiny feet), my best suit, more breeches, more boots, a dazzling red mess jacket and Uncle Seymour's guns.[2]

Saturday 11th November 1944

I go up to breakfast with the sky completely overcast and great black clouds covering the heavens. There are two large and definite waterspouts spiralling up from the black sea to the black clouds. It's an amazing and unusual sight. The bottom bit looks like an upheaval from an underwater explosion and then it becomes a black spiralling pillar which we watch rising.

Later the foul weather comes over with alternate sleet and snow storms. The locals look miserable. They are badly shod and seem to lack warm clothing. They say they've not known snow here since 1915.

Monday 13th November 1944

Run up to brigade for a five minute talk and am detained for over 2 hours. The first and best thing is that my posting as CO has gone through – I can now again hoist colonel's pips on my shoulders. The next big thing is arranging leave to UK for a few people and there's a chance of getting John D to staff college.

Lunch with B Squadron. It's a nice happy atmosphere but lacking in spit and polish. The men are fairly comfortable but as they were the last squadron for accommodation they've got bad billets. Three troops live in a church. It's been desecrated and is a cold, untidy looking place.

Wednesday 15th November 1944

I issue invites for a birthday party. Though it's at my expense it really is in aid of the regiment with reps from other units, town mayors etc. I shan't get £25 of fun out of it but I'm sure it isn't money wasted.

Saturday 18th November 1944

The advance party of 2/6 Queen's arrives and within an hour is ordered back to unit. Our training is now 'off'. No doubt this recent fine weather has

---

2. Captain Seymour Barne MC (1886–1917) won the Military Cross during the First Battle of Ypres as a captain in the 20th Hussars. He voluntarily transferred to the Royal Flying Corps as an artillery observer and was killed when his plane was shot down near Arras in April 1917. This was during the RFC's 'Bloody April', when the lives of aircrew were measured in weeks or days, as the British aircraft were no match for the latest German fighters.

made an opportunity to attack. If this continues I foresee our being needed at very short notice and very soon.

Alex has arrived on a special train to near our door and we have to guard him – the chief fear being a landing party coming in and carrying him off!

Monday 20th November 1944

There is masses of work on with more modifications on the tanks.

In the afternoon I turn my mind to the party. The tanks are all turned out of the square and a spotlight is rigged up on the doorway. John's room becomes the bar and the mess and ante room become the 'At Home'. We move out most of the furniture, leaving some tables with snacks and cigs on, and rig up our own lighting. Cup and 'snoopy-woo' are the drink – the latter being a real menace!

About sixty people turn up, including the brigadier and Baron Francetti, and we all work hard seeing everyone has a drink. Hawksworth, behind the scenes, tests each new cup and shaker that is made and so do several others. I don't begrudge them one bit – all the servants here are hardworking and charming. The party was meant to be 6 'til 8pm but doesn't end 'til well after 9pm.

Now I'm a year older I also have one less to live. I still think there's lots of life in me though. I wonder if I'll be commanding 4H this time next year?

Sunday 26th November 1944

Write all morning and afternoon. Have a clerk take up some official letters and write one to Winston.[3] Not a very good effort but should suffice. I find if I don't get what I want at the first attempt it's never any good.

The weather is fine at the moment but it looks as if next week is going to be very wet. It's our last week of training and, I suspect, about the time of staging that last big attack of winter. Would that it could have been arranged earlier. The ground will not again be so dry and later the cold will be a serious handicap.

Monday 27th November 1944

The scheme is postponed 'til 11am owing to weather conditions and then finally cancelled. I go out in the afternoon to the workshops to see my tank with the turret removed and to plan the interior seating and lighting. It should be very roomy and comfortable.

---

3. 'Will you reassure the Colonel of the pride of every man of the 4th Hussars in having him as their Colonel, and how much I personally appreciate the honour of being given active command of such a fine Regiment. It will be my constant endeavour always to uphold the good name of the Regiment and that of our illustrious Colonel.'

Tuesday 28th November 1944

C Squadron is off on the 3rd but I can't believe they'll do anything. Armour won't now operate 'til spring.

Walk around in the afternoon. The mess our tanks have made of the village street is terrible. It's a morass with manholes and cellars caved in and pavements crushed; I should not be surprised if the houses don't start cracking as the foundations have had such a severe shaking.

Wednesday 29th November 1944

When inspecting the tanks along a thoroughfare a stupid woman going hells bells on a bicycle runs slap into me. At least ten officers are standing in the road and why she chose me I can't think – no one saw her coming. I go for six and so does she but unfortunately failed to break her neck. I rise with as much dignity as I can muster and she's helped away. She seems to expect sympathy. It's lucky for her we are not the Hun – 'Lieutenant, take her behind this hedge before you shoot her!'

Thursday 30th November 1944

Plenty of work on hand. Have two men (Lowton and Andrew) up to read out the sentence of three years penal servitude for desertion when the regiment was ordered into battle. Also have an officer, John Paley, in to tell him he's been awarded the MC. He is absolutely overcome. The effect on him is more than I'd expected from the two prisoners. He stands and gulps and looks uncertain whether to laugh or cry. He saluted and rushed off in confusion. It means more to him than probably any other officer I know as soldiering is the whole world to him. His first comment was on how pleased his father would be with him.

Friday 1st December 1944

Well, this is the last lap of 1944 and may it be the last lap of the war too. It is just possible though one daren't think too much about it. The whole of the six armies on the Western Front are making an all-out effort and a big Russian drive has started in Hungary. Perhaps they'll get one going on the Warsaw Front.

I spend the morning with the brigadier going round the squadrons. 'A' is in first class trim. 'B' is only fair but one must take into account the lack of facilities and the poor accommodation.

Saturday 2nd December 1944

In the morning we clear a hillside and shoot our 5s on Honeys as the brigadier and others haven't seen them fire and have had good reports on them. The first few rounds, despite the wet ground, ricochet madly over towards the next village. No signal comes in during the day of any casualties in the neighbourhood so all is OK!

Sunday 3rd December 1944

At 8.30am the wheels of C Squadron and HQ start off. I go down to watch them. It's the first appearance of 'my' regiment since I've had command. Watching the tanks get loaded is a wonderful sight and it's perfectly organised. An officer stands in the square and by signal marries up the 34-wheeled transporters and tanks from different routes. Blocks are put down and fifty-three tanks climb onto the backs of fifty-three transporters. They look just like beetles performing the sex act.

One tank is ditched outside San Vito as the driver is blind drunk. I take immediate action and will see that he gets stick when tried.

Monday 4th December 1944

We leave at 9.50am with my car and jeep and my three servants, Chimery, Ashdown and Hawksworth. Strangely there is little traffic and we reach Cesena for lunch at 1pm.

My Tac HQ is a farm right on Route 9. It's a dangerous location and was strafed yesterday.

Tuesday 5th December 1944

Visit corps at 9am on a harried, raw, cold, foggy morning. The general is very affable and says he hopes to give us a show. Everyone does seem out to give us all the attention that they can.

I go on to see 10th Indian Infantry Brigade and then on to DLI. The CO is 'Crackers' May, an old friend. We have a good talk and laugh and get everything sorted for tomorrow over two glasses of gin. Move on to see my bogus Tac HQ, all part of some cover plan.

After numerous adventures get back for tea and then out to see C Squadron again before dinner. I have done over 150 miles today in two cars.

It's a very cold night and as I write the guns are going in a continual roar before an attack. My goodness, I'd hate to be 'going in' tonight. Poor old infantry, they do have an uncomfortable time.

Wednesday 6th December 1944

I don't think I've ever been so miserably cold. One's feet are permanently cold and wet. The house is only a cowshed, having no glass after shelling and frames and shutters taken as firewood. The cows are in the main part of the building and, darn the odour, it's the warmest place I know of.

Crackers brings over a company to try loading on to what are now known as Kangaroos. We stand in a bog in a steady drizzle. It seems scandalous to all concerned the way corps intend to use C Squadron as a livery stable and take as many or as few Kangaroos out whenever they want them for any purpose.

Sunday 10th December 1944

Sit in the office 'til 1230 when an urgent call from brigade sends me dashing in. It's quite incredible. The army have sat on the present line for a month and must have realised that certain formations would need a rest. We are told we are to take over the right of the line. I'd been assured there'd be a winter lull and so we've got men scattered everywhere; on leave, packing, on courses and out scavenging wine. We could not be taken more by surprise. Of course we can manage but it will be a strain.

7H are having to leave all their tanks and go up as infantry so the whole brigade is in turmoil. I'm told to take over 3H's tanks today. Just to get orders to A Squadron involves a 45-minute drive and 3H themselves don't get the order 'til after dark. I go down and they are very kind and helpful. Everyone feels sure it's one of those situations when it's right to disobey the brigadier and take over by morning's light. A takeover in the dark with sleepy, grousing, cold and potentially drunk men would be a failure.

The officer situation is becoming acute. Kenneth H writes to me to tell me he is going home to see an eye specialist. John Strawson looks like remaining in hospital for at least another 3 weeks and there is no news of Herbert and Elliot for whom I've applied.

Tuesday 12th December 1944

Have an early run up to Ravenna. A Wop driving an army lorry nearly puts me in the ditch. I give him two straight rights in the face but luckily I have my glove on. I take his identity card, write on it 'this man is a dangerous driver' and sign it across the page. Am I cruel? I don't think so – I am sure it is the only treatment they understand or respect.

We take up position in a sugar factory by the most lovely sixth century church, Sant'Apollinare. It's of brick with a round belfry tower. Alas every one of the windows is broken and much of the building is wrecked. The apse has been bricked up and covered with cotton wool but to no effect as a Hun threw a grenade in through a window. A dead horse by the altar rather spoils the air.

Ravenna has been knocked about a good deal. In places one can only get through where a bulldozer has cleared the street like a snowplough, leaving great banks of rubbish on each side. All the shops are shuttered and there's little sign of life.

Wednesday 13th December 1944

It's Mummy's birthday and I've clean forgotten to mention it in any letter. It's not easy sitting out here year after year to think of people having birthdays or that weddings and births and growing up are taking place. What a bloody old man I'm going to be when I return unless I'm very careful.

Go up for a recce with 7H. We are taking over from the Canadians. The front line is on a marsh and the dividing line with the enemy is a high marsh dyke wall. We have good, dry farms to live in. Upstairs one keeps a perpetual sentry to watch out for the Hun. By night we patrol and they patrol.

Thursday 14th December 1944

Paddy moves up with A Squadron. There's a box-up with brigade which causes them to sit all afternoon waiting. They are told to move at dusk in the bitter cold and take over new billets in the dark with restricted cooking possibilities as they are now in the line. It makes me very cross. I don't mind how much I, or my officers, are buggered about [but] I hate it happening to the troops.

Friday 15th December 1944

A fine sunny morning for a change, not that there's any heat in the sun but it makes everything look more cheerful and increases visibility. A good thing for me as I climb onto a roof to try and assess the German positions. There's not much to see and not much going on.

Aircraft have been buzzing about on their various missions. A cheerful sound when we have complete air supremacy.

Sunday 17th December 1944

I move Tac HQ after breakfast and then head out for the day.

I get back and find all settled. Irvine is sitting on a sofa in a centrally heated house and remarks it's like being on leave! It's pathetic that these chaps have been living rough all their service and 'leave' to them is as simple as warmth and comfortable furniture. Meanwhile there is a constant and distinct rattle of machine guns. What a strange war!

Wednesday 20th December 1944

There's a very big counter-attack going on in the Ardennes.[4] We are not giving away any information about it except to say it's serious and penetrated

---

4. The Battle of the Bulge, 16 December 1944–25 January 1945, the final German offensive on the Western Front. Focussed on the densely forested Ardennes region, it caught the Allies completely off guard. The German plan was to push west as far as Antwerp, split the Allied lines and encircle their armies. The advance was halted on 24 December 1944.

35 miles into Belgium – but even that news is 48 hours old. It's caught the First Army completely on the wrong leg, I fear. It may well prolong the war but, at any rate, will give a fillip to production and wake up those complacent, smug people at home and in America who think it's all over, bar the shouting.

Thursday 21st December 1944

Have an annoying case to deal with. A man of the LAD, with a Luger he has no business to have, shoots at a comrade when tight, strikes an NCO and then resists arrest. I have to make it a FGCM.

Bosworth returns with John D's jeep. He left on 8th as he was due in Taranto on 10th but went straight to Florence to see a South African nurse, then drops his bags in Taranto and returns to Florence via Rome and thence to Bari via Rome and Ravello. He's covered 2,955 miles in 14 days, run the bottom out of the jeep, purposefully missed his ship and arranged an air passage. This is additional coal to my fire of resentment to the way he's behaved with the belongings of deceased officers.

Saturday 23rd December 1944

After breakfast it starts to snow a bit. Dick H comes to lunch and says the snow is lying inland, further south it's lying deep on the coast road.

Some suicide parties have been dropped near here by parachute. They are out to disorganise HQ and assassinate senior staff officers and COs! One lot is reported in Ravenna today. I have put out security orders as one must take these things seriously.

Monday 25th December 1944

There is thick snow on the hills and all the roofs and fields are white. Attend Holy Communion at brigade HQ in the coldest schoolroom I've ever been in. The padre is late, the floor hasn't been swept and there's a lot of noise outside. I don't feel I've really benefitted spiritually or physically and no doubt this communion will be the direct cause of me getting a cold.

Drive on to A Squadron for breakfast where Corporal Ward has a fine feast ready and a large fire of 75mm ammo cartons to thaw us out. Spend the morning going around the patrols. There's an unofficial truce so things are very quiet. Make a speech to each patrol and shake a lot of hands!

Head back for an hour's work and wrap up some small parcels for my staff (servants, mess and *Dauntless* and *Daring* crews).

Have the most wonderful party in a big thatched barn. I get a terrific welcome and roars of applause when I take a hand in helping with the serving. All the sergeants and officers join in the spirit of the party. By now I'm nicely bottled and having made six previous speeches, my seventh seems to come out quite nicely.

Tuesday 26th December 1944

Just after dark a lone Hun plane drops an oversize bomb on the town. It fair shakes the place.

The PM has gone to Athens – gallant but foolish. Those Dago sods are more than capable of bumping him off. We hear ¾ ton of dynamite was found in a sewer by the Grande Bretagne hotel, now General Scobie's HQ. We're a mad nation to expect honesty or even decency from any of these continental types. I think only the Norwegians or Swedes are capable of honourable dealings.

Saturday 30th December 1944

There's a great sea running and the sky is full of snowflakes. I am summoned to brigade, rather in trepidation, but it's worse than I feared. A new SS division has entered the line and I have to get B Squadron up on Monday. They've not had a very fair deal but operations are operations and the SS are not to be trifled with.

Sunday 31st December 1944

Have an early breakfast and go off to see B Squadron to go round the troops. Go on with John O to see his troops. The Hun sits in houses 300 yards off and one can hear him talking. He doesn't shoot at us because he doesn't want us to shoot back! Live and let live.

Corps Commander Foulkes gives us a pep talk after lunch. He's a bright, strong sort of man and puts it across well. It looks as if we're static 'til April.

David Dawnay and Dick H-R come up to me after the conference. I wonder if I've aged like they have. They have such a careworn look about the eyes and I've been in battle far longer than them.

A grand mail in including a lovely picture of Linda. She sits opposite me now saying, 'When will you finish all this blasted writing and take me shooting?' Bless you, old girl, you'll retrieve a pheasant for me this very next October…

Monday 1st January 1945

10 Downing Street
Whitehall
1 January 1945.

My dear Colonel Barne,

Many congratulations on your appointment to command the Regiment and the gallant manner in which all ranks are facing their new task. I have talked this over several times with Field Marshal Alexander, and I can only tell you he considers the new rôle will be even more important than the former.

I hope to hear from you from time to time.
Yours sincerely
Winston S. Churchill

Wednesday 3rd January 1945

Decide to go to 'C' to oversee their battle tomorrow. It's the first time Kangaroos have been employed in Italy and Jack and I are probably the only real exponents. We arrive before dark and spend 'til 10pm driving around. The attack is extremely complicated and involves an enormous number of various types of carriers. The commander seems horribly optimistic and a large cage has been prepared for prisoners. Either we'll get nothing or receive a bloody nose. It's about time we realised the Hun is no fool as well as a very brave man. If he doesn't want to hold an area he'll quietly withdraw. But if he does, he'll hold it to the last man.

I go back to 2/6 Queen's for a late supper and a final run through of orders. It's a lovely clear night full of stars and searchlights and as we come home half a moon is rising.

Thursday 4th January 1945

'Home' consists of a boarded-off corner of a shell-battered house. A cobbler has set up shop in it and there's a wonderful smell of wax and leather. At 2am the Kangaroos with passengers in move off and I retire to bed. The Hun sounds very close but I think they are nervy and apprehensive, not offensive.

Get up at 6am and at 6.15am we move off to see the Kangaroos start in earnest. Get a bit lost in Frenza on the way. The area around the station really is a scene of frightful desolation. The bomb holes are now thickly iced and the white frosted tree stumps and rubble heaps make it look like a scene from a war film.

By lunchtime it is apparent that last night's criticisms of the plan were proving true. I leave just before dark to find a '*casa*' but can't find any reasonable house with a roof that is not already occupied by soldiery.

Friday 5th January 1945

Go back to the battle with the jeep. Swan forward through the battle area. It's heavily mined and prisoners are still coming in. Our guns have done a lot of damage and I've never seen so many wounded animals: cows, donkeys etc. Horrible.

Am forced right up much further than I'd like and make contact with Ralph Liney. He's good and steady under fire. That's the real test – I know he's efficient and the right type in barracks. Talk the operation over and later do the same with Minnow PP. All seem pleased.

Everyone is full of the A Squadron battle. I go to Paddy for details. Get the dope and there's no doubt they saved the situation. They fought this morning for 5 solid hours having had quite a battle yesterday too. Sergeant Beet and three others killed and one tank is bazooka-ed but not knocked out. See poor Louis, the hero, who has just returned from trying to extricate a driver from a tank but found him too stiff so took the rum ration in lieu.

The army commander sends me a personal message of congrats on the A and C Squadron show. It's all rather overwhelming as I've done so little towards it really.

Personal telegram Lt COL BARNE from ARMY COMMANDER (.) My very best congratulations to all ranks on important part taken by your regiment in very successful operation on ARMY FRONT yesterday (.) Your tank crews displayed a splendid fighting spirit and great gallantry in driving back with heavy losses to the enemy strong infantry attack against the left flank of 5 CDN ARMD DIV (.) In armour drive on 5 CORPS FRONT your regiment with their new equipment of KANGAROOS showed initiative skill and determination and played a vital part in a successful operation (.) Ends

On sober reflection I am wondering if it isn't a VC case for Louis [*see* Appendix B]. He really saved the day for the Canadians and many other troops have packed in under far less vicious or sustained fire.

Saturday 6th January 1945

It's a horrid dark morning, warmer but raining. Go to see B Squadron. All isn't going smoothly there but can't quite lay my finger on the trouble.

Return to Mezzano for Sergeant Beet's funeral. Such a sad, lonely figure laid in his grave wrapped in an army blanket. The squadron are very philosophical about it – I think everyone is these days. One can't win battles without losses.

Go up to Casa di Mezzo where the main battle was. The Hun is still only a few hundred yards away and proves it by putting down some mortar fire. There is a half turned-over tank lying there as well as the Huns who came too close. I can see at least six bodies, including one very young pale faced lad relaxed forever.

I am escorted by SSM Thomas, a really lovely man. He always looks after me as though I were his own boy. He insists on leading me through the mines as two men have lost a foot each on this track today. The thaw has brought old mines back to life. The mud is so thick as we walk in the fresh tank tracks that we sink up to the knees.

Write letters in the evening and a signal of congrats to 'A' and 'C' to go with the army commander's letter. I still have citations to do and to decide if Louis Jackson merits a VC or not. I've risked my feet today with that object in view!

Sunday 7th January 1945

Have a busy day gathering details of the Casa di Mezzo battle. The 12L have been very generous in their praise. There is no doubt that A Squadron in general, and 4th Troop in particular, have saved a very nasty situation. I write to the PM and take the opportunity of enclosing a copy of my letter to brigade to try and get the regiment home in May.

A very good mail comes in. I have a most difficult case in Wilson, an old friend of mine from the Royals. A friend of his writes to me to tell me that Mrs Wilson is pregnant but all due to one short night's dirty work she accepted more out of fear than anything else. He was a Canadian at that. Wilson is due home about the same the child is due. He's a terribly stubborn character with a strong moral code. I shall put the padre on to softening him.

I have many letters to write to the wives of Beet, Barlow, Cummington, Lowden and Spinks on their deaths. It's tragic they were all married men.

Tuesday 9th January 1945
Get the most wonderful cake from Nanny's sister, Mrs Parlor. It's a real 'brigade cake'. I open it and eat of it washing it down with a glass of port to keep it moist. I intend to make it last several days but from the look in other people's eyes I think I will find that hard.

Wednesday 10th January 1945
I give Tug Wilson an interview. He has as much moral as physical courage. He'd hate to think I saw it but I've never seen a man more broken. He's not hard on her and says, 'I know her, she's my best friend. I must send her a cable.' I shall always think of him as one of the finest characters I've known and more filled with Christian spirit than most professing Christians.

I follow this up with the exact opposite – Sergeant Brown. He was absent from his tank for 3 out of 5 hours of fighting on the 4th. I shall not court-martial him for the sake of the squadron but shall have him before brigade on a veiled charge of cowardice.

Friday 12th January 1945
Get the most charming letter from the PM. There is no doubt he takes a great interest in us.

I write a lot of letters. It's a good excuse for not going out as it's snowing hard and the roads are in a most dangerous condition. If ice covered with snow is not enough then superimpose an Italian division in British transportation and you reach the limit!

Saturday 13th January 1945
We move our HQ about 5 miles to Tagliata-Pangipani, north of Ravenna. It's a sordid little village not unlike Wrentham West End. I have an upstairs

room in a tobacconist's with two small windows that let in little light but lots of cold air, even when shut!

Tac HQ is a solid building with OR mess and clerks all under one roof. At one window where the rain has come in there is a large frozen puddle and a layer of ice up the wall. All this soon melts out when we get in occupation and the few fireplaces are effective. I intend to install diesel stoves. They can be made out of 25-pounder shell cases and give out a wonderful heat for nearly 12 hours.

I have to write two operation orders in the evening.

Sunday 14th January 1945

I do not look forward to this as a winter line. We are re-grouping which means a mass of orders and an equal number of counter-orders. The Canadians are leaving the line but on the whole they are a jittery, nervy, bomb-happy crowd.

Monday 15th January 1945

Civilians are being evacuated from north of the River Lamone. It's a pitiful sight in this bitterly cold weather; each family with all it possesses or can carry. The hire of a cart is 200 lira (£5) so they usually can't afford more than one and there is no going back. Each cart is piled high with furniture and bedding, usually with a baby stuck in somewhere wrapped in a shawl. A pair of poor bewildered cattle are in the shafts and the men pull and beat them. The women are in a state of hysterics and the men little better. They express themselves best with a stick on the cattle.

It's a wretched business, especially in this weather, but the men must have billets and to argue it out we must remember that these people backed Musso when he came into the war and they loved it when they thought they were beating us. One must think of our poor people at home who have been through much the same when bombed out and also the Wop prisoners ensconced in houses like Sotterley making love to our country girls (I'm told) while we live out in the open or sheds or bombed out houses.

Wednesday 17th January 1945

Wake in a leisurely manner and find on arrival at breakfast that 'B' have been fighting since 6am. That damn boy Irvine hasn't bothered to let me know! I give breakfast a miss and take the staff car as Hibbert has been wounded to send him back in comfort.

I arrive at 'B' HQ just as the second attack comes in. I stay for a couple of hours but only as a spectator – and an uncomfortable one at that. Take a first-hand report back to the Canadian division commander. He wants to send up flame-throwers but I reckon we can manage with our tanks.

Thursday 18th January 1945

I go up to B Squadron. John is out, likewise his officers. He has no idea of his responsibilities as a squadron leader and I find him within 300 yards of the enemy testing his Tommy gun prior to sallying forth to personally supervise the extraction of a Bren carrier and to plaster a house containing some Boche. Two jobs a corporal could carry out. However, sticking to my principle of riding my people on a light rein, I leave him to it.

Last night a wretched pointer was making such a noise in our yard that I had to go down and see what the matter was. As I suspected he was freezing so I took him in. He bounded round breaking everything, pulling coats off pegs and blankets off the bed. Seeing that I'd get no sleep with him in the room I put him in the passage where he soon settled down. He is the most delightful, if stupid, creature.

Saturday 20th January 1945

Go up with John to recce a farm held by the Hun with a view to 'creasing it'. We play Red Indian-Boy Scout tactics creeping round the vines and decide the place is already too battered to be worth shooting up more.

Closet myself in the secrecy of my room after lunch to write. There is a mass of paperwork to be done: honours, awards, Python scheme [repatriation of troops who had served for more than 4 years abroad] plus letters to next of kin.

Sunday 21st January 1945

Visit Casa Rasponi, a shell of a house 100 yards from the Boche. Dead Huns still lie about unburied. Grim-looking men living eternally in tin hats peer at one from dark doorways with an expression as if they constantly expecting to be attacked. Thank God I'm not an infantryman. We recce the house for the operation at hand and are very glad to get away from its morbid atmosphere. Go on to meet with Brigadier Cookie who approves of my plan.

Monday 22nd January 1945

Personal telegram for Field Marshal ALEXANDER from General MCCREERY (.) PRIME MINISTER may like to hear that his Regt 4 Hussars played a very important part in our successful operations on 4 Jan (.) Near ALFONSINE a sqn of 4 Hussars tanks moving at first light to assist infantry of 9 Armd Bde drove back enemy infantry inflicting very heavy losses on them (.) This enemy attack with three infantry battalions was directed against a vital sector on the left flank of 5 Cdn Armd Div (.) The enemy left 150 prisoners in our hands and some 100 dead in front of our positions (.) This result was largely due to the fine handling of 4 Hussars tanks under difficult conditions in the half-light at dawn (.) On the other flank 4 Hussars with their new KANGAROO equipment carrying 2/6 Queens played an equally important part in the armoured drive which has cleared the enemy out of a big salient he held East of R SENIO (.) In this new action the 4 Hussars showed great skill and enterprise in handling their new equipment (.) Ends

Personal telegram from PRIME MINISTER to Gen MCCREERY (.) I was very glad to see the signal which you sent informing me of the part played by the 4th Hussars in your operation on Jan 4th (.) Please tell them how proud their Colonel is of their exploits in their new capacity and assure them of my constant interest in all their activities (.) Ends

Tuesday 23rd January 1945

Start off very early for Operation Bolster. It is very simple and grossly over-insured.[5] We have air support, dive-bombing and strafing, artillery, tanks and the infantry all laid on to help. The whole show runs smoothly without incident and is finished by noon.

I do feel that at any time now, given a push, the Hun might pull right back. With the Russians marching on Berlin and their door back to their homeland being threatened they must be anxious to return to protect the Fatherland rather than defending the Italian mud.

A 109 Messerschmitt comes over just before dark. It's the first enemy plane I've seen for some time. He turns on one side and has a good look at us but is actually looking for the gun positions next door. If the Hun is not pulling out then we must expect some fireworks before dawn.

Wednesday 24th January 1945

I really believe the end is in sight. Every morning the news is terrific with Russians rolling on across the Prussian plains and in the west with us throwing a great weight of shells and bombs on the Hun, causing him maximum and ourselves minimum casualties. No one is keen to be killed at this stage of the war! What a relief it will be when it all ends but what an anti-climax. For many of us there won't be any physical relief – probably more work for senior officers. Crime will increase as there will be little to do and the men will become restive.

---

5. The Kangaroos were to carry Royal Engineer personnel and equipment to Casa Raspani, the forward position. The supporting air cover and artillery was to ensure the enemy was distracted during the operation as the Kangaroos would not have had sufficient firepower to defend themselves.

I receive the news that we are to be an entirely Kangaroo regiment. It will be a blow but we must get used to the idea.

Thursday 25th January 1945

There has been quite a heavy fall of snow in the night. I am up before daylight intending on going round Paddy's positions but he rings to say it's not advisable.

All the village girls and our troops are hard at it outside snowballing – an age-old sport, I suppose, in every country where there's snow. I used to hate it. I wonder whether Christopher will – somehow I don't think so as he's such a sturdy little chap.

Saturday 27th January 1945

There is still thick snow about and one feels very much a target when walking about. The trees and buildings show signs of the heat and there is one spot called Spandau Run where one has to be extremely quick.

Ronald W has the most wonderfully organised defences in his house. The Tommy guns and grenades are all at the upper windows and Brownings at apertures at ground level. They've turned the cows out to use their stalls.

Monday 29th January 1945

At 1100 hours I am rung up to be told a VIP is arriving at 1300. It can't be the PM so I guess Mark Clark.[6]

I'm right. Mark Clark, Fifteenth Army group commander, followed by McCreery, Cookie and Foulkes of the Canadian Corps, arrive amidst the snapping of cameras. Clark proceeds to address us. He's a fine looking man but spoilt by his untidy apparel of Yank waterproof jacket with no medals or insignia at all. McCreery seems very vague and vacuous and is too obvious in his efforts to make polite conversation all round. When talking to one he seems to be thinking more of who he is to speak to next and what he should be saying to him! A strange type to hold such a high rank.

They leave before lunch and 'Margot' Asquith calls in to arrange the takeover as we are to withdraw from the line and move to Pesaro.

Thursday 30th January 1945

My cold has come out and I feel miserable. The worthy Hawksworth looks after me so well that it's a pleasure to be ill. Alas he's due for a home posting in April and I shall be lost without him.

---

6. General Mark W Clark (1896–1984), the youngest four-star general in the US Army during the war. He was to command the United Nations forces during the Korean War and signed the Armistice in 1953.

Jack White returns in the evening with my car. He's had a slight smash in it. John V is 24 hours overdue. I only hope nothing awful has happened to him, like the two MPs who have now been missing a week.[7] They were only flying between Naples and Brindisi but I believe the snow is terrific on all those hills and it may be months before the wreck is found.

I intend on going to bed directly after dinner but hear that Hitler is to speak at 10.15pm. After all the news we've heard recently of Russian advances, to say nothing of pressure from the West, we feel this may be Hitler's 'swansong'.

At 10.10pm the radio plays *Lohengrin*. 'Ah', say the wise ones. This is followed by *The German Lament* and part of the *Valkyrie*. 'Yes', nod the wise ones again, 'this obviously denotes the fall of the Gods.' Every minute we get more optimistic and more worked up, sitting on lousy hard chairs with a dirty stone floor next to a filth-filled fireplace where a drip-fed petrol stove hisses and roars. Our glasses contain poisonous locally distilled alcohol they call whisky.

Presently Adolf H speaks, quietly at first but soon all the rage, fury, madness and passion are pouring into the room in an unintelligible babble [*see* Appendix A]. It's the voice of a raving lunatic. At times he is sobbing and at times yelling dire threats to his own people should they dare to lay down their arms. It seems the war will have to continue as we won't accept less than total surrender and Hitler will never offer that. He says surrender means death and a far worse death in the hands of the Allies than any death in the battlefield.

Thursday 1st February 1945
Go up to A and B Squadron for the last time before the takeover. Seldom can so many cavalry regiments have been in such close contact before: Bays, 4H, 7H, 9L, 10L, 12L, 27L, KDGs.

Just before dinner Ronnie rings me up to say the brigadier wants me to go home on a fortnight's leave. I get on to the brigadier but say 'no'. It's left me wholly stumped, leave to UK having been our main topic of conversation for so long and when it comes I refuse! I don't think I want to go unless Cara is also home. In any case I'd like to be here while all this change of organisation, personnel and tanks is taking place. It's extremely kind of Cookie and given me a new lease of life just to think such things are possible.

---

7. Two MPs, Robert Bernays and John Dermot Campbell, were visiting British forces in Italy as part of a parliamentary delegation. The wreckage of their plane was never found, but it is believed to have crashed in the Adriatic near Brindisi.

As I pee before going into my *casa* for the last time I can't help wondering if this is the last time the regiment will hear the sound of guns. I somehow think it is. I go to sleep to the popping of machine gun and Spandau fire.

Saturday 3rd February 1945
Go down to Pesaro after quite a good breakfast and a prayer of thanks that my car hadn't been looted. It is a frightful place but a block of summer villas has been put at our disposal. The 10th Royal Hussars have left things in a dirtier condition than the French would have dared! I am not pleased.

Sunday 4th February 1945
The mess is starting to take shape and the cold, damp dungeon atmosphere is clearing. We have three more new officers today, Cole, Curl and Baker. They don't look much and are very young but this can be remedied.

Colonel Nigel comes in for a drink. He's off home soon and won't go any further in the army. He wants to get back to his woman but I can't work out if she's not someone else's wife. He's been a very good light influence and has helped create this excellent spirit that is so noticeable in this brigade HQ.

Monday 5th February 1945
After lunch I see the troops on Python. It is an awful shock to see so many of our senior men on it. I reckon it must be 75% of the faces and names that I know. John M, QM and the doc have volunteered to stay on with the regiment. Highly pleasing. I want every 4H who will offer to stay behind as we're going through a bad time.

After tea I go on leave and feel like a schoolboy released. I could have worked myself into a serious, sombre mood but decide otherwise. Drive down to Jesi for a good old fashioned party. I go completely mad and enjoy myself immensely. As I handpicked the officers for the party myself it doesn't matter. In fact, I think they are rather impressed I could be so gay – I've kept myself in a dignified and serious manner for 18 months for their benefit! Eventually get to bed at 5am absolutely exhausted.

Tuesday 6th February 1945
Come to at 9am and leave by 10am, reaching Florence by 6.30pm. From Arezzo onwards the amount of wilful damage done by the Hun is appalling: masses of rolling stock burnt out, buildings and bridges blown up and great sections of hillside blown away to block roads.

Stay in Hotel the Savoia with the great joy of a bath with a plug that pulls. Find Alec Drew here who I last saw in Secunderabad in 1930. He's much the same as ever but becomes little pompous. That can soon be cured and I start the cure at dinner in front of his staff who have been addressing him as Sir!

Wednesday 7th February 1945

Shop gently after breakfast and stroll round the town. The shops have got the most lovely stuff in them but all at a fearful price. They must be making a packet as we soldiers, not having seen such nice things for so long, just can't resist.

The sun is shining when we come to the Arno and the Ponte Vecchio is more lovely than I could have imagined. The Hun has left the bridge intact but blown up all the period houses at each end. Many of the statues are still sandbagged or underground.

Thursday 8th February 1945

A regulation day. Breakfast at 9am, Hawksworth in to clean at 10am, out by 11am, drink 12–1, lunch, sleep, tea with locals, cocktails 6–9pm, dine on black market, dance, bed at 1am but sleep is difficult these days.

Today's lunch is with the old Baroness Francetti in a twelfth century villa looking down over the town. Poor old dear, the Hun put her in jail while they looted the house. In fact most of the women here have been in jail, some for speaking English, others for anti-fascist tendencies. They don't seem to mind and are certainly as chic and charming as any I've ever seen.

Drink at Donima's. All our 'own set' there and joined by Jack Profumo MP and a very good value blonde. She takes us on to the RAF night club. Dinner being on the black market was expensive and required plain clothes. I put on my own but Jack had to borrow a husband's blue jacket and was immediately named the Russian pianist. He doesn't look at all English!

Saturday 10th February 1945

Donima takes me to select a hat for Cara. I look at hundreds as she patiently tries them all on, redoing her hair every 5 minutes. A woman can be so intense when selecting apparel. She and the pansy hatmaker study Cara's photograph and decide what she'd want. Also get a lovely model jeep for Christopher and other odds and sods for Mummy and Cara.

Drink chez someone or other. A mother of about fifty, but chic as I've seen, is busy mixing cocktails. Can you imagine Mummy doing that!? Philip's wife Julianetta, Manetti and another girl join us at the Black Cat. Jack Profumo has Donima in a corner, there's not much doubt about his intentions tonight. [Profumo, when Defence Minister in the early 1960s, was to become notorious for his affair with Christine Keeler.]

Tuesday 13th February 1945

Leave at 10.30am and arrive back to my office. There is a mass of letters waiting for me but little news of the future. There seems no hope of leaving this spot soon. People are well settled in now and seem fairly comfortable.

Sunday 18th February 1945

We have our memorial parade at 10am. With so many on courses and leave, as well as the troop at Forli, we only muster 450. The turnout is excellent and the drill good. It's a horrible experience marching at the head of the regiment through crowded streets but with no band to keep step. At times one couldn't hear the footfalls of the squadron immediately to my rear and at other times the echo in the narrow streets put one half a beat out.

Colonel Nigel takes the salute and loves every minute of it. I read the roll of honour and the lesson. The singing is extremely poor even though we'd collected two fiddles, a piano, a trumpet and a saxophone!

Sunday 19th February 1945

Foote VC, a paunchy pleasant little colonel who has come to take over from Nigel SS, visits me. I fear I'm fast registering for the unemployment list. Foote looks at me with that amazed look of a staff officer who first sees an officer trying to help the war as opposed to himself. I have been foolish enough to try to keep the regiment operational at this period when the manpower question is acute and devised a scheme for keeping 600 men from sitting idle in a back area. I'm coldly told that it would be impossible to grant me the 'privileges' that I am asking for.

Well, 3 weeks remain for my colonelcy to become 'temp' as opposed to 'acting' and thereafter I don't think I really mind what happens. I'm due my pension in any case and the war will end within a few months. After than I'm not sure now I really want to go on soldiering and rocketing around.

Tuesday 20th February 1945

Maurice finds an old order stating that the medical officer must at intervals be 'at home'. He publishes a time in the regimental orders and sits waiting. His only visitors are a senior squadron leader and his 2i/c who come in shyly holding hands. 'We've discovered we're in love, doctor. Please tell us how we can have a baby!'

I suppose many people would condemn me for not discouraging this light spirit amongst the officers but, personally, I strongly approve. They have many years yet in which to grow old and serious. They are only in the army to win this war and in every case have done their share and shown up very well in battle.

Colonel Nigel SS comes in for a drink to say goodbye. He's already stinking but in great form. We are all very sorry indeed to see him go. Though he does a lot of clowning he also runs a very good show in Cookie's absence.

Friday 23rd February 1945

Every morning a mass of elderly women accompanied by a pretty daughter apiece visit the lines. I'm told they've come for washing. My nasty mind thinks not but after close study I've decided they do actually collect the washing but the pretty girl is used to charm the men out of scraps of breakfast.

One hears so much about the starving, ill-clothed people but where we are this is balls. They look well and are well clad with every doll in a fur coat. The thing that irritates one is the enormous number of unemployed men whilst roads, bridges etc are in such desperate need of repair.

Monday 26th February 1945
Rise at 6am. It's a lovely morning once it gets light. Spring really is in the air and a green haze has come all over the earth. The ordnance people can also feel spring and have issued us with a new shade of light green paint. It's quite pleasant.

The natives finally seem to be returning to the land. Everywhere they are busy pruning, ploughing and (a new labour) poking laboriously for mines left by the Germans.

Friday 2nd March 1945
Set off at 8.30am with Jack W, Coulter, Peter Q, John Gibb and James S to watch a tank demonstration. It's rather like a point-to-point with car parks, band playing, tote, spectators on the banks behind fences or walking the course. There are masses of people and lots of gossiping but little attention to the tanks. In fact, the tanks get well bogged and we are left to carry on our chatting in peace.

Tuesday 6th March 1945
Lunch at corps. It's a very intimate lunch in an enormous dining room painted to represent a great tent. BGS (Toby Lowe), GI and MS are in. It's a very good lunch with a glass of stout. I'm then taken into the holy of holies and hear things that have not yet been put before the War Cabinet! However, it is considered imperative that I should be in the know to train up the new 'toy' along the right lines.

Drive back to Forlimpopoli to tea with Brigadier Souperon, a tall, quiet, charming fellow commanding 11 Brigade. I may be doing the 'big thing' with him. I certainly hope so.

Return in time for a quick change and then out to the sergeants' mess to say farewell to the Python sergeants. Read and Spiers make first class speeches and I am put up to make one too. I leave at 11pm as things are getting very disorderly. I know there's nothing wrong with the spirit of the 4H sergeants' mess and they get together so seldom that they must be allowed a little licence.

Thursday 8th March 1945

I hold a conference and after telling all I know we go out to inspect the first of our new Priests [M7 Priest 105MM Howitzer Motor Carriage, built on the chassis of a Sherman tank and more durable and better armed than the first Kangaroos]. They are fine roomy vehicles and much more suitable than Kangaroos for the job we have in view.

At 5pm I say goodbye to thirty-one men leaving for good, including eight first class sergeants. Later I attend an HQ sergeants' mess farewell party. I'll be glad when they are all gone as this continuous saying goodbye and speech-making is rather wearing.

Friday 9th March 1945

Head up first thing to the mountains and by 9.15am we've climbed 5,000 foot into the snow of Termintillo. One doesn't realise how big the snowfields are until one gets up to the top, even with the snow line receding there's a run with a fall of 3,000 foot. Peter Lund and P Aitcheson (Olympic champs) are up here as instructors with Hamish Taylor as the commandant. It's hard to believe this is a military establishment. The instructors wear light khaki wind jackets with their badge of rank on their caps.

I get dressed, equipped and wax up my skis and head out onto the snow but the blazing sun makes me strip in no time. I flounder about and being to feel rather desperate as I seem to have lost any skill I ever had.

I'm too exhausted at lunch to eat so drink through and after half an hour with my feet up set out for the higher and steeper slopes. The ski hoist works from 2pm 'til 5pm and takes us 800 foot up. I recover my old form straight away and manage to prove I've not lost my nerve or grown too old!

By 5pm I'm flat out and stagger home. I take two aspirins with a stiff whisky and get under all the blankets I can find 'til the dinner gong goes. After dinner the pipers come in and we do an eightsome reel. It leaves the Yanks guessing!

Sunday 11th March 1945

At 10am we are assembled for the race. I run well 'til near the end when, trying to be too clever, I cut down through some trees, losing a ski and all my speed. I'm badly shaken and have another fall as consequence on the finishing line.

Spend the afternoon going down the standard runs, twelve times in all. By the last run I am exhausted with every muscle aching as well as a pulled shoulder and cut shins and forearms but I've enjoyed it.

John Adye is up here. I last saw him in Muttra 1933/34. It's fun talking pig and of the good old days and being called 'Tony' instead of 'Colonel'.

Even the girls call me 'Colonel' now and the hotel staff are most deferential with their '*Il Colonello*' even when I'm in plain clothes. Perhaps I am growing to look like one?

Monday 12th March 1945
The car comes for me at 10am. It's a lovely spring day. Almond and plum are out and look like white and pink puffs of cotton wool against the dark hillsides of olive and plough.

Arrive at 6pm to brigade HQ, set in a lovely great house overlooking a lake and up a 1½ mile drive. Eat a good and cheerful dinner and leave after seeing Cookie. Everything is shrouded in mystery, latrine screens and smoke. If the local spies weren't curious before they must be now!

Wednesday 14th March 1945
Watch the football against Pesaro town team. The Wop is very temperamental and there's nearly a scene. It was most amusing to watch but I kept wondering how I was going to handle the situation. I longed to wade in but I know it would have been regarded badly afterwards if there had been an incident.

Saturday 17th March 1945
A and B Squadrons moved off yesterday. At 6am I am waiting for C Squadron to come through. At 6.12am they arrive, trundling along in close formation. I'd appreciate the sight more if they were on time.

After breakfast all the furniture is packed to be sent to San Vito and at 10am the 'wheels' set off. The wretched Bakes has a dog and gets roundly cursed by me to leave the dog behind (you brute, Barne!).

Stop at Cesena for lunch and see lots of New Zealanders, who have probably never visited Ireland, celebrating St Patrick in no small way.

Arrive at our new area by 10pm. The guns are flashing and banging away not so far distant. One battery makes a sharp rap on my door like someone is knocking presumptuously.

Sunday 18th March 1945
Have a really full day. Have squadron leaders' conference then off to 8th Indian Division under Russell. Arrive back to hear we have an officer vacancy for home leave. John V takes it. I am a little surprised but he's mad keen. I don't think I'd have done the same in his place.

On to 56 Division under Whitfield, a very different division and commander. Then on to 24 Guards Brigade where I drink with Malcolm E.

It sounds like a social day but each visit involves a long talk with the commander and then planning with the gunnery instructors. The corps commander has said he's leaving the whole thing to me which may be complimentary but it's pretty amazing!

Tuesday 20th March 1945

I hear later of a terrible accident occurring in the afternoon's training. One of my Kangers drives on to a pile of lifted mines. Of the ten occupants, four are killed and, of the rest only one is not seriously injured. Two of the men fly over fifty feet and the shambles inside is quite ghastly.

Wednesday 21st March 1945

Spend the entire day at a 78 Division discussion on Kangers. I'm really rather an important person these days but, no doubt, will get the sack at some stage. I just hope it won't be 'til after the battle.

Arbuthnott, the division commander, is sweet. He is a scruffy little man, looking as though he'd just got out of bed but knows his stuff. I sit beside him and whisper in his ear and he responds nobly. As we shall be fighting under him I feel it important to be on the right side of him. Alexander appears with General Nye and I have a chat with him. He's friendly but though he's been on a Kangaroo won't commit himself.

Receive a letter from Cara on my return. She thinks the war is as good as over and wants to fly out here to join me. It's a lovely idea and wish it could materialise.

The doc and Ewan go off on leave today. They come in to see me before they go. They really are like a couple of schoolboys, with grins all over their faces but trying to be serious. A sterling pair.

Thursday 22nd March 1945

I go over to the 2nd Commando Brigade after lunch for a conference. I've never seen such a wild show and, pray God, I never have to work with them again in a big way. The brigadier is as scatty as a caged monkey. There is nothing quiet or orderly or regular about anything and the plan is equally scatty and complicated, breaking most of the principles of war.

Saturday 24th March 1945

My face is getting quite sunburnt again as I got very pasty-faced in the winter. I have a good all-over bath in the evening. Baths are scarcer here than in the desert and I'd rather not bathe at all than go to the military bath. The dust here really is worse than the average desert conditions. The tanks soon break up any surface of non-tarred road so that they're all three to four inches deep in fine powder.

Monday 26th March 1945

Hear on the wireless that the Royals were amongst the first to cross the Rhine.[8] The advance is going at a great pace with little opposition. There is great speculation about it all – some, including myself, think the end is very near but that an unpleasant guerrilla war may go on for months but not long enough to hold the large Allied forces.

Ride Jerry who goes along very nicely and we jump a few ditches. The peasants can't work me out at all as I am hatless and in plain clothes. However, they touch their caps to me and discuss me after I've passed. I notice that the various graves, whether German or British, are well cared for and even have flowers put on them.

Thursday 29th March 1945

I say farewell to about sixty of our best men as they have all completed 4½ years abroad. I make a little speech after inspecting them and then they file past and shake hands. Many have tears in their eyes and hold on to one's hand embarrassingly long and hard. Hawksworth will be my greatest personal loss but there are many key men from all trades. As they go off they give me three cheers and I feel the place definitely emptier for their departure.

Before noon a new lot turn up to take their place and in time we'll be equally sad to see them go. So does a regiment go on; fresh people writing new chapters in its history but in the background a strange sameness all the way through.

I get rather browned off when I hear that the Regiment and the Kangers are now being referred to as 'Barne's Taxi Service'.

Friday 30th March 1945

The lady who lives here with three charming children is nice looking but terribly grim. I discover her husband died of wounds in the retreat from Egypt so perhaps it's understandable. It could even be the Royals were responsible.

Ever since we've been up here I've been going to bed at 10pm or soon after and taking the minimum of alcohol. I don't believe that otherwise I'd be able to cope with all the work I need to get through.

---

8. On the night of 23 March, following a sustained 4-hour bombardment, the first Allied forces crossed the Rhine, the traditional German frontier that no foreign army had crossed since Napoleon's. On 25 March, Churchill, accompanied by Montgomery, also crossed the Rhine on an Allied landing craft, venturing as far as a bridge still under fire. This publicity stunt inevitably attracted plenty of criticism.

Sunday 1st April 1945

A real Easter morning and how one longs to be home on such mornings. Hawthorne takes the service at 11.15am and comes on to lunch. He brightens up a bit in the mess but I don't think he'd ever be really bright.

After lunch Guy, Jim S and I go up to see Buster and Louis who are doing an operation tonight. They are in a lovely pine wood right on the sea's edge and not 500 yards from the enemy. They are surrounded by secret weapons and are all very cheerful. It's nice to see how steady and businesslike they are in their preparations.

The Priests have to be waterproofed which is a big job. They got machine-gunned when moving into position so can't do any major jobs here. Occasional rockets are sent over too but none when I'm there. We wish them luck and leave just before dark.

Tuesday 3rd April 1945

The rush of battle arrangements is now full on. Everyone seems to drive a little faster and with a grimmer, more determined look on their faces. I go to see General Freyberg. The old boy is quite charming and remembers all sorts of details about the Royals and 4H. We chat for 10 minutes and then get down to work – he doesn't know much about Kangaroos and, like every other general, is keen to have us, just to add to his collection.

Go on to a flame-throwing demonstration. It's really quite awe-inspiring seeing great jets of flame hurtling into the black smoke of previous shots. The whole thing is completely silent.

Wednesday 4th April 1945

Dick McCreery gives his pre-battle talk today at Forli. It's good but doesn't really inspire one at all. He's more like a sloppy bishop drawling on with people coughing and coming in late. He inadvertently tells us D-Day which doesn't inspire one with any confidence in him as a leader. There must be something about him, though, that us in the stalls don't see.

Tuesday 5th April 1945

Brigadier Timmis comes in after lunch and wants the lowdown on everything. He leaves at 3.45pm and at 4.15pm Brigadier Cookie walks in and we talk for ¾ hour. When Timmis returns we waffle 'til after 6pm when I decide I must go as we are having a monster cocktail party. I find them still in my office when I return from changing and pack them off.

I am three-quarters of an hour late for my own party. We have taken the big government offices in Forli. The corps commander and 56 and 78 division commanders send reps but two CRAs and five brigade commanders all turn up plus some other red hats. Colonels are two a penny! We all enjoy ourselves greatly and the drink is so good that I keep it flowing 'til 9.45pm. There's no doubt it's of military value as well as giving the chaps a break after the very gruelling training they've been doing.

Thursday 7th April 1945
At 5.30pm I go with an empty head to address all the officers on the battle. As is usual, the less I can think beforehand the better I talk at the time. I think it goes pretty well despite the 8th division commander in person wishing to ask some point of me.

Am whacked by dinner time but have a bottle of beer thanks to the 6th Lancers. Write letters 'til midnight. A very strong north wind is blowing – is it blowing up for rain or blowing the clouds away?

Sunday 8th April 1945
A cold, windy morning. I talk to each squadron in turn during the course of the day regarding the forthcoming battle. Each talk takes over an hour and there's half an hour of driving between three of them. One talk is in a schoolroom, one behind a haystack and others in farmyards out of the wind.

We also have to move RHQ and have two conferences. My bus moves up while I am out so the moment I come in I can sit straight down and get the paperwork dealt with. With no increased staff I am directly working with three divisions and my own tank strength is about that of a brigade. Thank goodness the office staff are most capable, helpful and friendly.

Monday 9th April 1945 [First day of the Battle of Bologna]
There was a sharp frost in the night but it's a glorious clear fresh dawn. All is so peaceful and it's impossible to believe that in a few hours all hell is going to be let loose. I could not be more mentally content going into battle. I am sure I have the whole regiment behind me and we are as complete and well trained as I ever could wish. By the men's expression yesterday I feel certain they will go out and use their common sense and enthusiasm.

I dash down to Forli for a conference. There's nothing left behind, all the buildings vacated and the roads clear. After lunch the heavy bombers arrive. I've never seen them in such strength before, wave after wave at 20,000 foot, 700 planes in all. The smoke and dust the other side of the river is terrific. Then the barrage starts, followed at intervals by strafe attacks and then at 7.20pm the flame-throwers and infantry go in. The Hun must be going through hell.

My conference goes on so late that we drive back with the gunflashes and searchlights helping us keep on the road.

Tuesday 10th April 1945

Visit division HQ at daylight to listen to the units sorting themselves out. So far the battle has gone well and is up to the time programme. One 'wing' drops its load on us, including the divisional commander. About eighty Indians are wounded but I'm not sure how many killed. It is an inexcusable mistake.

I spend the day by my tank calling in at all hours for infantry. As we had predicted the bombing slowed things up as it causes a lack of ambition to get on. We seem to lose all drive and initiative. It's such a pity as we had started off so well. By dark our positions haven't noticeably changed and yet there seems to be little organised resistance. There is little chance of us moving tonight and the opportunity of a breakthrough is slight now. All most disappointing.

Wednesday 11th April 1945

I am called at 0001 hours and am on the go 'til 2300 hours. Nothing is done but one expends a lot of energy doing it. I eventually squeeze an order out of division but as soon as I move off they cancel it.

I have about 4 miles to move to the new division (78) HQ but foolishly obey an order and go 18 miles to get there. (The moral is not to obey orders). On arrival, and having collected my chaps, am then told to move back to the old place. We do an advance in the afternoon which should have been done last night and we lose seven Priests on mines. John O does very well in particular despite losing a tank and two good men.

Conference at division after dark. The Hun side of the Senio river is terribly knocked about by our shelling and bombing. There is not a house or tree that has not been damaged and the roads are in an awful state. There are quite a few locals about and give me a great welcome in the backstreets of Lugo where I seem to be the first tank through. By dark the stream of our traffic coming through is intense.

Thursday 12th April 1945

We sit outside Lugo all day having made a great effort to be ready to move off at first light and risked a lot to get the Priests on to the embussing point with only the scantest amount of maintenance. These people have no idea of how to put a move on. The Hun is now retiring and, as no one is pushing him, he is laying mines at leisure and destroying bridges etc. With the enormous preponderance of armour that we have, all the bridging and bulldozing equipment and armoured infantry carriers the roads can be ignored and we should be able to make a rapid and strong advance. There's a lot to be said for 'you never get bad troops, only bad officers' but one might really say 'bad staff'.

Sit in my command tank all afternoon playing backgammon with the doctor and drinking gin and vermouth. Get signal from high up to say we are all to move at 1735hours, i.e. 35 minutes. Get squadron leaders in who say no one else is taking any notice of it. Ring up division who say it's off and we are to move at 0400 hours tomorrow. I don't believe it and get ready to move at 0600 hours.

Friday 13th April 1945

We start off on the great dash at 0600 hours and cross the Santerno river, a formidable line if it had been held in strength. We sit and wait for 4 hours. There is little opposition in front of us and we have as many armoured vehicles in our column as the Hun has in all Italy!

At 1pm we start groping forward and by 5pm have covered 5,000 yards. We start settling down for the night – I am already settled as I shave off all the bolts on my driving sprocket.

We get a terrific reception at one farm where we stop for our brew up. The whole family turn out, rushing into the house to fetch vino, eggs, radishes, water and even more children. I take a group photo. It is a very pleasing scene of this happy, healthy peasant family amongst the flowering cherries. We can't help wondering quietly if they didn't treat the Hun in the same way when they arrived!

Saturday 14th April 1945

The houses are very English-looking here and countryside pretty with vines and fruit trees. We see an old man returning to find his little cottage demolished. He just sits down and cries and cries.

I sit in a road block with a dead Hun and horse beside me. He's a boy of not much more than 17 years lying as he lay in his mother's womb. He's clothed in a dirty green uniform and has a black trickle of blood dried on his face. Each successive vehicle gently lays another layer of dust on him. The horse looks ghastly with white of eye showing and stiff legs pointing skyward. Yet I think to myself 'poor horse' and 'well, that's another bastard accounted for'. The horse will work equally willingly pulling the crown jewels or a load of manure. The Hun has a brain and has chosen to fight for a man who has disturbed the whole world.

Sunday 15th April 1945

Go to see the troop leaders for a conference. They are all happy and growing fond of the New Zealanders they are serving alongside. Return along a lateral road very near the front. The heavy dew means there is no dust so I can drive fairly fast. Put my jeep into a shell hole and do some damage. That is how Jack was killed but going fast and in the dark.

Nothing doing when I get back. Everywhere one sees tanks, tanks and more tanks but men sitting doing nothing. It makes me very sad and ashamed. We should now be racing up towards the Po river. We are bound to win – not just by fighting but by weight of numbers and superiority of equipment and air power. The people to be proud are our factory workers at home.

Monday 16th April 1945
We sit until 5.30pm until moving. It is quite incredible and unforgivable. We are D+8 and are at the point where we could and should have been on D+2. They knew we had the Reno to cross but it seems to have come as a surprise and there are no preparations for the crossing.

We have a dusty drive and have to go a long way back to cross the Reno river. Arrive after dark in a very noisy place in front of some guns. I cannot understand why the Hun didn't fall back on the Reno. It appears to be the most magnificent natural line to hold. His bridging (mostly wooden) next to our Bailey Bridge [portable, prefabricated type of bridge] looks a very poor amateurish effort. They have no shortage of guts but we have the equipment.

It's so cold driving after sunset that I bring out my Bovril and we all have a strong cup of it. Very reviving.

Tuesday 17th April 1945
We are told to be ready at 7am and at 7pm are still sitting in our same ruts having had four or five alarms, orders and counter-orders.

Wednesday 18th April 1945
I take it we won't be told to move 'til late so got off to visit 9th Armoured Brigade in the morning. Thank God we aren't with them, partly because they aren't in the battle, but also the mosquitoes on the marshes are quite terrible.

Get back at noon after traversing some horrible roads and find the regiment is just moving. We move on sharply with 'A', 'B' and 9L pushing on far and fast, taking a lot of PoWs, guns, tanks etc. We have a scene in the late afternoon when a small counter-attack comes in on our flank. There are masses of vehicles around that don't seem to realise anything's on. I send out RSM who comes back having been shot at so send Arthur Smith who also gets brassed up. I order the local soldiery to stand to so as to hold the Argenta Gap![9] We get a few stonks and the Spandau fire gets very close but nothing comes of it. A good thing really as we were not very strong.

---

9. The town of Argenta, situated between the Adriatic coast to the east and a large wetland area to the west, was the key to securing the right flank of the Eighth Army.

John Ogier gets wounded and evacuated. I get Porgy [Archer] to take over B Squadron. I think the hunt has started. The Boche seem demoralised and on the run. It will be hard work keeping our forward troops supplied over the next few days.

Thursday 19th April 1945

We move before dawn. Have breakfast in an apple orchard and have a very good appetite for it. We've come quite far in the last 24 hours and are now held up by demolitions near Portomaggiore, 12 miles from Ferrara. Yesterday our brigade alone took over 500 prisoners and more are coming in now. They are a miserable looking crowd.

Peter Q collects a very nice bay gelding, he was being ridden by a Hun officer only this morning. Sergeant Brown, late Royals, hacks him back down the echelon for me in the evening. He's full of quality and has obviously been very well looked after.

Friday 20th April 1945

Start the morning in a temper and go in to brigade before breakfast to complain about being put under command of an infantry recce unit. At 9am I'm summoned and given orders to clear an area and form a bridgehead with 56 Recce, Northants and our B Squadron. I start off by showing I am in command and give my orders. All goes very well although the party is more sticky than I'd expected. We take 120 PoWs and knock out a gun. Unfortunately Porgy gets wounded early on and we have some more men and tank casualties. Things work out alright and I'm more firmly convinced of the good backing of all ranks in the regiment.

Toward the evening I go up to 11 Infantry Brigade during a lull. Waste a lot of time and return before dark and run up to B Squadron. I take my tin hat but it's not as fearsome as I'd expected. Get my first proper meal in a hardware shop at 9pm while holding a conference. Get to bed at 11.30pm in the same shop. At midnight a message comes from brigade with new plans and orders. After one of the busiest days I can remember it's turning out to be a busy night too.

Saturday 21st April 1945

The fresh orders mean that people will have to be buggered about so I decide I'd better do it in person. All are most amenable and fairly get cracking. I go up in the doc's Honey, complete with Red Cross flag, to give orders to B and Northants Squadrons. At 3.30am they set off. It's an eerie sight watching these great tanks in moonshine silhouette with their enormous gun barrels and infantry clinging to every point.

Get back at 5am and try to get an hour's cushy but get a heavy stonking by the big guns. The shells fall very close and the whine, bang then sound of falling masonry is very alarming. I begin to wish I'd chosen a bigger house. However, all is well.

I dash off at 6.30am and visit 11 Brigade. Breakfast and shave with 2 Armoured Brigade then back to my HQ where Guy joins me with *Dauntless*. Have an idle morning of bumf, lecturing new reinforcements and doing a little reorganisation. The new horse is tied to an apple tree and grazes peacefully next to us. The more I look at him, the more I like him.

At 2pm I move up and 12 hours later we stop moving just short of Ferrara. Our start is slow owing to traffic congestion and we are then held up while a bridge is stonked (without effect). The 9L with my two squadrons are leading the party. Sometimes they turn and we are left on a flank in which case we are the first into the farms etc. We pick up a few straggling Hun and they stonk us a bit. The locals come out flapping white towels or sheets and cry and cheer and seem genuinely hysterical. Everywhere one looks there are fires. In each farm the Hun has either set fire to the buildings or our tracer has set haystacks ablaze.

We push on with tanks of all sorts crowding for the defiles [steep-sided narrow gorges] like a hunting field for a gate with everyone pushing on, jealous of position. We get held up and lose a certain number of tanks. The guns are horribly close and on one occasion an 88 fires for some time down our road with great white tracer shells moving like comets and bursting with a crack beside us.

Casualties on both sides are light. At 1.30am we capture intact the bridge over the last river before the Po line. By 3am we are consolidated and withdraw non-essential vehicles as a stonk is bound to come down. It does but not heavily and the only casualty is poor Louis. He gets a piece through the back. It's the last place you'd expect him to take one as there's no braver fighter in the regiment.

Sunday 22nd April 1945

Manage nearly 2 hours on my back and then we stand to as we are many miles behind the enemy and he may object to us. He contents himself though with spasmodic shelling. I am forced to loan two troops of B Squadron to the 56 Recce Regiment. They've been at it two days and two nights continuously and if they are as tired as I am they may not be at their best.

Since the beginning of this campaign I've lost four of my five majors one way or another. I now intend to get Dick Hidden up as my 2i/c as I have no responsible person with me when I go off. I tell Peter to put up major's crowns and retain command of B Squadron with Aubrey as his 2i/c. It's a youthful combination but I have no doubt it will be efficient.

Monday 23rd April 1945

Jim S and I leave early to visit C Squadron as the rest of the regiment is doing nothing up here. I travel 135 miles in my search for crossings over the Reno and looking for 'C'. Everywhere bridges are blown and no one seems to have a clue.

Meet up after lunch with C Squadron's echelon but fail to meet Jim F. They've gone on too far and the traffic is frightful. I doubt I'd get back even if I'd struggled against it all night. Get home at 6pm very weary and dusty. The mess has come up and we are very comfortable and cheerful.

At 9pm we are ordered to be at 2 hours' notice. Send for Paddy who comes in rather drunk. I keep my temper but am a little annoyed. There will be time to drink later on. This is not the moment.

Tuesday 24th April 1945

We move forward in the night and mop up the area between Ferrara and the Po. We collect 160 PoWs and knock out twelve Mark IV tanks.

We spend the night in the gloomy portals of a parsonage. It has the most depressing effect. I try to get up to our leading troops but there's so much traffic on the road that I am forced off. Get out on to a lane hoping to get around but find myself in hostile territory and get a stonk all to myself – luckily without effect!

The Brigadier comes up and I have a chat with him. He is very complimentary on the way our tanks have been kept on the road.

Wednesday 25th April 1945

I swan out before anyone else about. Find all the country that last night was thick with vehicles is now empty. Advance very cautiously using my field glasses with Tommy gun at the alert. Pick up three Huns with a portable wireless who I hand over to partisans, keeping the wireless of course.

Move up towards the Po and have a hectic morning collecting people up and settling down in a concentrated regimental area. Go 26 miles west of Ferrara to visit C Squadron. They are in very good shape but James F is out visiting me! We make contact on the road home.

Call in on Freddie G. He has his mess at the local nightclub and has got a lot of girls in to give his officers a dance. Unfortunately don't see Freddie but leave a message to say I'll be writing to his wife!

Get back to a late dinner and 'A' and 'B' come in. It's what I've wanted and I feel that we are, at last, as much of a happy family as ever the Royals were in the desert days. The chatter makes one think of people who haven't met for 10 years instead of a group who see each other almost daily. The regiment really is a team now. There is no one who isn't pulling in accord and the cheerful spirit that prevails is partly respite from our hard labours and partly from a feeling that this really is the end of the war. I could not be happier, unless perhaps I commanded the Royals, and I think if I were offered promotion now I'd refuse it.

Thursday 26th April 1945

I am woken at dawn to hear my first cuckoo calling. I've had my ear cocked for it for several weeks now. Maybe the gunfire has put it off but this is a normal date for England (24th I always used to reckon).

There's a telephone message after I'm in bed to say another twenty-five Shermans are on their way to us. I don't take particular interest and go back to sleep.

Friday 27th April 1945

Wake violently at 5am, my subconscious self having examined the message in the night. Of course it's obvious now that B Squadron is to be disbanded. It's pouring with rain but I paddle out in galoshes and duffle coat holding up my pyjama bottoms to wake Guy. He comes over and we work solidly on figures and establishments 'til 8.30am.

Head to corps. The roads are in an awful state with masses of lorries on the road. GI takes me on to BGS after studying how I'm taking the bombshell. BGS wants to take me to GOC but GOC has tactfully gone out!

Dash on to Army HQ at Imola. It's a long way back and go through the fine city of Bologna. Demand to see the army commander and am taken to chief of staff (Floyd). He starts by blustering but I stand up to him and tell him I'm being serious. He becomes more affable but I feel my chances of winning are slight. I put up all sort of suggestions but all are shot down. Everywhere I receive the most embarrassing amount of compliments on how we've done but I'm not in the mood to listen to those. Blast them all!

Return at 6.30pm to the news that Mussolini has been caught.[10] As I sit here amongst friends, the world seems a better place.

---

10. With Allied troops advancing into northern Italy, Mussolini and his mistress set off for Switzerland, intending to escape to Spain. They were captured on 27 April by communist partisans near Lake Como and summarily shot the following day. On 29 April the bodies of Mussolini and other executed fascists were taken to Milan where they were hung upside down from the roof of a petrol station. Mussolini's body was later buried in an unmarked grave. On Easter Sunday 1946 it was dug up by neo-fascists and only relocated five months later.

Sunday 29th April 1945

It's clearer today and I can distinctly see sunshine on the alpine snow. Our move today has been postponed, probably on account of the recent weather. So far as we're concerned the war is over. Rumour and counter-rumour are rife, not only with the troops but also on the wireless.

I lose an enormous gold crown to a molar while eating an excellent piece of Parmesan cheese captured by 'B' off a German cook's lorry.

I have a ride on the big bay. He's a lovely ride with a beautiful action and well-schooled. I can only give him a slow hack as he has a badly fitting shoe.

Monday 30th April 1945

Following from Prime Minister to Lt Col BARNE. 'I was glad to receive your excellent report 14 dated April 9th and I congratulate you and all ranks on the progress made in training for your new work. I am confident that the proud bearing of the regiment will be enhanced in this last victorious phase of the campaign in Italy. Consideration will certainly be given to your proposal for representation of the regiment in any parade which may be held to celebrate our victory.'

We are going to become very bored here. There's nothing to do and nowhere for the men to go. I now rise late and bed late and don't mind a few drinks after dinner or a kip in the afternoon. All very different to my life over the last 6 months!

Archie comes over in the evening and stays to dinner. He loses over £15 to pontoon, half of that being to me! He's in a rather difficult pompous mood. They have done nothing in this campaign and are very touchy on the subject. Stupidly he keeps trying to show us what an active part they've taken. I discover the next day that after leaving me at 12.30am he calls on the HQ2 mess where he stays 'til 3.30am. He then wanders down a road on the bank of the Po on his way home and falls in a shit trench!

Tuesday 1st May 1945

Dick Hidden and I drive up to find C Squadron. We pass through the abandoned Adige Line [the Germans' third, and final, defensive line behind the Po, an intricate system of trenches, dugouts and machine-gun emplacements reminiscent of the Great War]. What fools the Hun were to hang on with twenty-seven divisions on the Winter Line with little reserve or rest when they could have held this far stronger line with seven or eight divisions and released the rest for Austria or Germany itself. The country is perfectly lovely between Padua and Venice with glorious old houses facing on to the canals and fine trees and gardens.

Return at 8.30pm wet and weary. Sit talking and playing backgammon 'til midnight when we hear the pleasant news that the second dictator is now dead.[11] I think he was the incarnation of all the world's evil and cruelty.

Wednesday 2nd May 1945
A lovely day. Doze in the sun in the afternoon and at 4pm we hear that Vietinghoff with all German troops amounting to over 900,000 men had unconditionally surrendered on Sunday.[12] The ceasefire sounded at noon today.

Churchill pays us the tribute of 'one of the most gallant armies that ever marched'. Well, it's all over now and I'm glad I've seen it through to the end of active service. If I hadn't I should have always been a little ashamed of myself. I know I've done nothing particularly brilliant but I've neither done anything cowardly nor been altogether a failure on movement control or in G-plans or as a squadron leader or as a regimental commander. I've certainly had as much fun out of these 5 ½ years as anyone could have in wartime and my only real regret is that it's been such a waste of the good years that might have been spent with Cara and Christopher.

Thursday 3rd May 1945
Over the Po again to settle in my holding parties. We have a mass of humble cottages spread along both banks of a canal. It will be ideal for the men as they love getting into these *casas* and making themselves part of the family. They are delightful peasants and very friendly. When we tell them the war is over they look at us like saviours. Some ask about certain German towns where their husbands are being held in concentration camps.

---

11. Hitler had retreated to his Berlin Führerbunker in January in preparation for the battle for the German capital. The Red Army's advanced stalled during March, but April saw a fresh and sustained attack on Berlin. By 19 April the Russians were attacking the city's final defensive line to the east, with the Americans less than 50 miles to the west but advancing rapidly. At a situation conference on 22 April Hitler suffered a nervous collapse, followed by his first stated acknowledgement that the war was lost. By the 27th he was in paranoid turmoil, having sacked Göring from all his posts and had Himmler's SS representative shot on account of Himmler's offer to surrender to the Allies. After midnight on 29 April he married Eva Braun, hosted a modest wedding breakfast, dictated his will and instructions for his succession and then went to bed. On the afternoon of 30 April, having heard the news of Mussolini's undignified ending and with the Red Army less than 500m from the bunker, Eva Braun took poison and Hitler shot himself.
12. On 29 April, Generaloberst Heinrich Von Vietinghoff, supreme German commander in Italy, ordered his representatives to sign a surrender to become effective from noon on 2 May.

Tim Rogers tells me the Hun tried to destroy their horses when they couldn't get them back. They poured petrol over them and set light to them – he actually saw some of the less badly burned horses. Such people can't be human and should not be treated as humans when we come to settle with our enemies.

Saturday 5th May 1945

Get orders to move. I hope we are to become part of the force to occupy Austria under the name of 'Freeborn'.

I ride with Tim after breakfast on the two bay geldings. The stables really are a sight now and we have eight stalls occupied. The horses look very well and the five big bays would not disgrace a hunt stable in the shires.

Monday 7th May 1945

The regiment arrives in the Padua area. Write all morning in the C Squadron house. It's a lovely great house at the top of an acacia-covered hill. Looking down the cypress avenue from the chapel I feel more in the Italy of my imagination than at any other time or place.

Everyone on tiptoes all day in the expectation of Peace in Europe. I believe it was signed at 0241 hours at Rheims. The official announcement doesn't come out, however, though the ceasefire sounded at noon. The gradual leakage of news has somewhat spoilt the effect.

Have a hot bath at the Albano Therme hot sulphur baths. It is spoilt by there being Germans about. They even go into the cafés. One offered my chaps a drink and they got up and walked out.

Tuesday 8th May 1945 [VE (Victory in Europe) Day]

At 9.30am I address the regiment. I meant to speak for 15 minutes but actually go on for 45 minutes standing on *Daring*. Afterward the padre holds a short service of thanksgiving. A goose attended the whole ceremony and when the regiment marched past the goose in a solemn and dignified manner marched past too!

After dinner we sit up listening to the wireless with scenes from London, HM's speech, the PM's appearance at Whitehall [*see* Appendix A] etc. I wish Cara and I could have been home for all this. At 0002 hours on Wednesday morning, as I write this, they are sounding the ceasefire for all arms and nations in Europe after 5 years, 8 months of total war.

Wednesday 9th May 1945

Take Philip and the two cars to visit Venice and then on to Trieste on duty. We look into St Mark's and meet several old friends including strangely a colonel I put onto a ship in Tobruk in 1940. Lunch at an entirely Italian restaurant with no meat but beautifully cooked. It costs 15 lira for three courses and in a week's time will cost 1,000 lira.

At 2pm we push on to Trieste along the coast. It is lovely fresh green country, large unspoilt by the war. Stop at corps to find the form as we've seen Chetnik[13] prisoners returning and long columns of weary, scruffy, long-haired, leather-faced, dark men of the mountains straggling along the road. They are laden with Bren guns, Sten guns, German revolvers and knives. A few wild-looking women travel with them and old wagons pulled by tired thin shaggy ponies. It's a scene straight from the last war but these are Tito's[14] men marching into Italy filling Trieste and the hinterland.

Tension is high in Trieste and the troops are walking about armed. There are Yanks, New Zealanders and Scots Guards. Tito's girls are very much in evidence in red skirts and white bodices with a blue sash. They are on a sort of propaganda march, carry no kit and seem to have no organisation. They look carefree and irresponsible and will sleep wherever they are offered a bed.

Reach Miano at dusk. B Squadron have just got in after 24 hours on the road. We sit drinking while all around us partisans and Jugs send up Very lights and bursts of tracer.

Thursday 10th May 1945
Wake to see lovely fresh green fields with great mountains on three sides. Guy and I head north and explore most of south Austria. It's absolutely beautiful beyond all description: neat houses and Swiss-style chalets, clean villages, mountains topped with snow, pine and beech woods, green rivers and happy peasants in traditional dress.

See the division commander who seems vague so I decide what I'll do and then go to tell corps with my plan purporting to come from division! On the way find the most perfect house in a little village called Paternion. Decide at once that it should be my HQ. We drive about 220 miles.

---

13. Serbian nationalists who led resistance against the Axis occupation of Yugoslavia. They also employed terror tactics against Muslims, Croats and Communists with a view to creating an ethnically pure state of Greater Serbia. Many Chetnik groups collaborated with their occupiers to enable ethnic massacres and to position themselves to take control of Yugoslavia after the war.

14. Josip Broz, known as Tito (1892–1980), the successful leader of the Yugoslav Partisans, the Communist-led resistance to Axis occupation. He was recognised by King Peter II of Yugoslavia and the Allies as Prime Minister from 2 November 1944. After signing an agreement allowing Soviet troops into Yugoslavia, he succeeded in breaking the German lines and forcing them out of the country. With the occupiers gone, the various factions and ethnicities began fighting each other, and many atrocities and massacres were reported. Tito remained in power until his death in 1980.

All the Austrian roads are packed with German soldiers; tired, hot, hungry, they plod with all they can carry with no officers and no future. It doesn't bear thinking of should we have lost the war what our plight might have been. It's hard to tell who is who. There are Germans, Chetniks, Jugoslavs, Caucasian Russians and Cossacks (both madly anti-Bolshevistic) and Serbs all trekking about the roads. We also pass the complete Hungarian Army at the end of our nearest lake. The Hun is still being chased by the Russians through our territory and is threatening to take up arms again unless we protect them. There are several years ahead of clearing up this mess.

Friday 11th May 1945
Settle in to my new home at the baronial *schloss*! It is a most lovely house and wonderfully appointed. There are two separate houses forming a courtyard with great horse chestnuts against the hillside. John and I have the bridal suite, and the six best bedrooms and two drawing rooms form the mess. The spring water tastes so good one really doesn't want ale.

Everyone here is terrified of the Russians. I have a Hungarian general and his staff hiding here and all the German troops beg us not to let the Russians or Tito get hold of them.

Saturday 12th May 1945
We are given the Viking SS Division[15] to put in a cage. They are 2,000 arrogant Huns who claim not to be PoWs – the last guards let the officers keep their arms to save trouble! I wouldn't mind the trouble if only I had a few more men. The camp is an ex-British one and very comfortable. C Squadron come up and I put them up in a very luxurious Hitler Youth camp.

We have a bit of trouble with the Vikings over their women. They bring 100, a sordid lot and mostly in pod. There are three Polish girls who say they don't want to sleep any more with the Huns. I certainly don't want to assist any Hun to get his greens.

Visit division in a heavenly spot down on a lake. See my old friend General Arbuthnott who is overworked and harried and, to my mind, not definite enough in policy or action. There are now over six million prisoners to be fed and a whole divided country to be cleared up but everyone seems to be swanning about having a good time.

---

15. The 5th SS Panzer *'Wiking'* Division was made up of foreign troops from Denmark, Norway, Sweden, Finland, Estonia, Belgium and the Netherlands under German officers. They were driven back from Czechoslovakia by Soviet forces before surrendering to the Americans in Austria on 9 May. Despite being comprised of foreign troops, the division was cited for war crimes, including the burning down of a Ukrainian church with 200– 300 Jews inside. Early in the war, it was the division of Dr Josef Mengele, notorious for his experiments on prisoners at Auschwitz.

Sunday 13th May 1945
The Viking Division move off complete at dawn but the campsite soon fills up again with stragglers of all types. It's lucky for all that the surrender came in summer and there are a lot of Hun still up in the hills who will have to be rounded up.

Monday 14th May 1945
Another day spent heading around the camps and recce-ing the area. The turmoil is getting worse instead of better. C Squadron now have over 2,000 in their camp and we are in the midst of some very heavy storms.

Wednesday 16th May 1945
A very early start but this time for fun. Leave at 1.30am in a thunderstorm and drive for an hour. Leave the car and do over 2 hours of the most strenuous climbing imaginable in the dark. As we scramble up by the light of a hurricane lamp my mind wanders off to those we have lost over the last years, leaving me with a heavy heart.

My stalker smells, as all keepers do, of dogs, gunpowder and tweed. Near daylight we stop and listen and soon pick up a cock caper [capercaillie, the largest of the grouse family] calling. Our lights go out and coats etc are deposited and then follows the strangest stalk I have ever known. When the bird is silent or calling we remain frozen but if unalarmed every 30 seconds it makes a strange noise like water coming out of a bottle. During these couple of seconds one can make all the noise and movement one wants, only to freeze again like a game of grandmother's footsteps. One has to be as agile and alert as a boxer. It's a great thrill when first I see him. It's exactly as in every picture. There he is perched on a high bough of a larch, right on the edge of a precipice against the dawn sky. His great fantail is erect exulting in his sexual strength. It's a grand scene; the wild snow-capped mountains, windswept trees and this mysterious great bird dominating it all.

Stupidly I have accepted the stalker's 16-bore and have spurned his telescopic sight. Having regained my breath I take careful aim. There is a spurt of flame in the dark and I see the head droop and fan tail close. '*Kaput*', says the stalker excitedly. I reload the single-barrelled gun and take a second shot. That also hits home but the bird doesn't fall. As I reload for a third time he spreads his great wings and sails down into the valley. A little after we hear the crash of his fall.

We wait 'til it's properly light and descend the mountain to look for the body. It's like looking for the proverbial needle and we return to the stalker's house. He puts up a bit of paper and makes me take a shot at 50 yards to satisfy himself. I produce a good pattern but in my opinion a 16-bore with five shot at 100 feet is not strong enough for such a big bird.

I return at 7.15am for a hot bath and a normal day's work. In the evening the stalker comes in with my caper. He found it after a long search. It is a magnificent bird and causes much excitement.

Sunday 20th May 1945
Tension with Tito is high and there are all sorts of rumours floating about. We are now ready to use force and my Kangaroos are on their way up.

I go down to see Paddy. His camp is an amazing sight: hundreds of horses roam lush water meadows dotted with gypsy-like encampments of every conceivable form of primitive shelter populated by scruffy German soldiery, nervous prostitutes and women with children or expecting more. It is a sordid picture.

On my way home I see a most magnificent Maybach [German car manufacturer, now part of Mercedes-Benz] broken down with four German officers. I rush back to LAD and they go out instantly to put the car back on the road. It all works like a charm and I end up with the car.

Tuesday 22nd May 1945
McGowan returns from Venice with fishing tackle. We go out after tea and catch a lot of small fish on the fly.

For dinner we eat my caper. It's extremely good with very dark, gamey meat. It looks rather like overdone beef.

Wednesday 23rd May 1945
Two young chaps come to stay. They are searching for a *Gauleiter* [local Nazi party leader] Dr Rainer,[16] who is hiding up in the hills. It was his family that Kenneth and I chatted with the first time we visited. He has seven children, the youngest of which is 3 weeks old, but is quite prepared to lose them all to save his own skin. He is a high-grade war criminal. His propaganda is that England and Russia will be fighting within 6 months and that all good Germans who are now lying low can rise again and hold world mastery by 1950!

Thursday 24th May 1945
Drive down to Villach to see Frankie Reed. He has three regiments to run two camps with approximately 640 Hungarians in. The amount of bellyaching

---

16. Friedrich Rainer (1903–47). After the war he appeared at the Nuremberg Trials as a defence witness and was then extradited to Yugoslavia in 1947. He was found guilty of crimes against the people and sentenced to death by hanging. Despite his widow receiving a death certificate in 1947, there has been speculation that Tito's secret police used him as an informant as late as 1950.

over this job has to be seen to be believed. James F with one squadron holds up to 8,000 prisoners, Paddy holds nearly 1,000 prisoners and 840 horses plus women and children, B Squadron hold a large number of vehicles and run patrols all day while HQ hold a road block and all vehicle recovery.

In the afternoon we hear a rumour about Rainer and we persuade corps to let us take a risk and search the area of the mines. We do it with four troops (one from the Surreys) and I go with them as I know the country. We round up some suspects and grill a horrid deformed little farmer. We then go down the mines – an eerie job with drawn pistols but sadly it's a wild goose chase.

Friday 25th May 1945
Spend the morning getting ready for McCreery, the army commander. He turns up punctually at 4.15pm and is supposed to spend 15 minutes here but after I've introduced him to all the officers he settles down for three cups of tea. We move on to C Squadron and I drive with him and General Arbuthnott and General Keighly. He seems very interested, talking all the time. He leaves half an hour after schedule and gives up the rest of his tour – 11 Brigade must be cursing us!

We return to the *schloss* to be met by Arthur to say he has got the regimental band together for Sunday's parade. It's a miracle. We also start plotting for a monstrous party for officers on Wednesday, sergeants on Tuesday and men on Monday. There are plenty of 'ifs' but I am certain if anyone can do it it is the 4H.

Sunday 27th May 1945
It dawns fine, thank God. It's hot and sunny but not too hot for the parade. The band have arrived in the night and everything is set. The general arrives to Grey sounding a salute and I go to meet him. The service is very nice, the altar being on a platform against an unhewn stone wall. I then lead the march past while the general stands on a rostrum guarded by two tanks with great 17-pound guns reaching out into the street. The local population turns out in force and seem suitably impressed.

I feel on top of a wave at the moment. Cara is writing happily, the regiment is in very good order and good odour with the powers-that-be. The weather has improved, I'm winning packets at backgammon and we've got all the wine for our party and all the beer for the men's. The pressure of work has now died down sufficiently for us to enjoy ourselves.

Tuesday 29th May 1945
It looks as if we'll be here another month. The Tito trouble doesn't seem to have fully subsided yet and I suppose we still have to eject him from Trieste. [The city was claimed by both Yugoslavia and Italy.]

Work 'til 6pm then take my rod, reel and pockets stuffed with worms, flies, knife etc and trek downstream from Kreutzen. I find by wading upstream and fishing back to myself at the tail end of a pool I get a lot of fish (twenty in all). On my way home as it's getting dark the trout are making the water boil, turning somersaults clean out of the water in a sort of high jump competition. I put on a fly and catch a very nice fish on my second cast. I try again and again but by common consent the trout have agreed to leave the fly alone.

Wednesday 30th May 1945
The party is a great success. The food is excellent although perhaps not quite enough and the wine goes down well. There is an enormous and varied collection of guests including some Yanks. It rains about midnight but no one seems to notice.

Late in the evening Kenneth gets some 'hot' information and goes off into the mountains, taking Guy and Peter Q.

Thursday 31st May 1945
Kenneth comes in shortly after breakfast with Rainer himself and most of the others of his gang [Kenneth Hedley was made a MBE (Mil Div) for his efforts leading to the capture of these wanted men]. He also captured twenty gold sovereigns and two women. A very good show indeed!

I go to inspect the arrested men. One is kept apart as there is nothing but his face to incriminate him. He says he hopes to get away but I say he's suspect and must be put inside. He walks off accompanied by Sergeant Sowler and falls down. We put the doc on him but he's taken the easiest way out like Himmler. He must have had a phial of prussic acid [cyanide] behind his gums all morning. The women are then brought down and put in the cooler having been shown the body of Globočnik.[17] They and the rest of the thugs are very upset at the sight but it helps make them talk.

The police come to take the prisoners and leave us to bury the body in the nearest unconsecrated piece of ground we can find. It's all very dramatic.

---

17. Gruppenführer Odilo Globočnik (1904–45) was responsible for the 'liquidation' of the Warsaw Ghetto, containing 500,000 Jews. It is thought he was the originator of the idea of using extermination camps for industrialized murder and proposed this to Himmler in 1941. He was directly responsible for the setting up of camps at Belzec, Sobibor and Treblinka. Following his suicide, his body was taken to a local church, but the priest refused to bury him in consecrated ground and he was interred without ceremony outside the churchyard. He was captured along with seven other wanted Nazis, including his second-in-command, Sturmbannführer Höfle. Despite reliable reports of Globočnik's suicide and photographs of his body, he became the subject of conspiracy theories suggesting he was secretly handed over to US Intelligence.

Tuesday 5th June 1945
Put on my best gabardine and belt to meet Alexander, the supreme commander. He arrives 15 minutes late in a superb supercharged grey Mercedes. He wears an Indian blue flannel shirt as a bush shirt and his high rimmed peak cap makes him look very German-looking! He has an enormous entourage but only corps commander and div commander, Buffy, come round with us. Alex recalls our meeting at Recanati and asks a lot of shrewd questions of me. He speaks to the Hun in their own language and seems interested and pleased to hear what they say. One cannot suppress the feeling that one is talking to a VERY GREAT MAN.

Tony Lascelles from AFHQ is in the mess on my return and fixes many of my problems. He also promises to get me to England next week for regimental business. Our officer situation is looking very bleak indeed and I can see another thirteen leaving before the end of the year.

Wednesday 6th June 1945
Out at 4.30am when it's not quite light. Pick up Schnell, the forester, and go up towards Farchter See. He brings his sweet little dachshund, Sensi. She has a wonderful nose and is chock full of intelligence. See a good buck just as it's getting light but regret to say I miss it. See nothing else any good, stalk a chamois but it has a poor head. He looks grand in the sights with forefeet on a tree stump and head held proudly and motionless. He barks in a most disconcerting way when disturbed that deafens the whole mountain side.

Perhaps I'm getting old for I'm now just as happy watching game as I was shooting it. Years ago I felt I must produce proof of the size of the beast I'd seen and how clever I'd been. Now I know that no one cares what AM Barne has seen or done so I enjoy things for themselves and the pleasure they give me.

Return to a heavy day's work writing bumf, signing bumf and reading bumf.

Monday 11th June 1945
Was due to start my trip back to UK at 4.30am but yesterday's heavy rain means a delay. Leave eventually at 10.30am and fly half an hour to Udine. It's cold over the bare granite-topped Alps but hot again on landing. It's then 40 minutes to Trevino where we have a long hot wait for the next flight to Florence.

At Florence the US officialdom becomes more noticeable. Their idea of control is to make a simple thing more complicated so we get hustled round from our plane to a waiting room and then back for a long wait in the same plane without food. We get a snack at Rome after another flight and then a final flight gets us to Naples at 5pm. See thousands upon thousands of large planes sitting idle. God knows what will happen to them or the big car dumps we flew over.

At 6pm after various ceremonial signing in I go to see Major General Horace Birks. I'm told he's busy and can't give me long. In any case my trip to the UK has been vetoed by him. He's sitting in a large bare room of the Caserta Palace idly flipping the page of a file while he patiently waits for a fly to come within range of his swatter. I blame myself for coming, keep off the subject of the PM and only mention casually that the army commander in person had approved me going. I evidently strike the right note for in half an hour he melts, pours his soul out to me and starts working out how to get me home in comfort.

Tuesday 12th June 1945

Dine with Charles in the evening. He is looking very much older, despite his tan, and the first exuberance of meeting me soon dies off. They seem very much in the dark at AFHQ about the future of regular officers. He seemed totally unprepared for anyone to displace me and would fight against it. I shall not resent an ex-prisoner 4H but will fight like hell against anyone else.

Wednesday 13th June 1945

Awake at 5am. Tonight I shall be in England. It's so wonderful that I can't take it in to the full yet and don't dare let my mind dwell on it too much as I get terribly nostalgic (I think that's the word to describe one's feelings when one's eyes get embarrassingly moist?).

At 8am we move off in a Warwick. It has comfortable seats and is converted to a passenger plane. It's a 6½ hour flight and as I write this we are 8,000 feet up passing over Montecristo set like a model on a blue carpet. My pen is misbehaving as it is not used to such heights.

We arrive at 2.40pm but our fast timing is spoilt by being kept for 3 hours before a bus takes us to Victoria. England hasn't changed much. There is less traffic, the gardens are less tidy and, of course, there are a lot more people in uniform.

Elizabeth has a delightful little flat at 162 Sloane Street. She is looking awfully well and the goddaughter is a sweet little thing. She's been much maligned as undernourished but she seems very well shaped. Mummy looks a good deal older I'm afraid but is very gay and full of energy. She puts on a little make-up for dinner at a very dilapidated pub in Basil Street and we have a very happy evening.

I walk round to the club. A lot of windows are boarded up and it's very understaffed but all the old fogies are there looking just the same, talking just the same and living in the past. Soon I shall be joining them.

Meet old Tom Pragnell and we talk 'til nearly 1am. Wintle comes in. He is as mad as ever and is standing as a Liberal against Duncan Sandys [Churchill's son-in-law and a minister in Conservative governments of the 1950s and 1960s].

Thursday 14th June 1945

Breakfast is a rude shock at the hotel: one lump of sugar, one pat of butter and one tiny sausage. Now I know what I've long suspected – that England has had a very thin time of it but never by letter has there been any hint of it. I've had the best of this war and now feel ashamed.

Spend the morning at the War Office. As ever, one talks and walks miles but gets nowhere. The whole atmosphere is one of obstruction though well concealed and done with charm.

Lunch with Jack W's father then tea with Mummy and Elizabeth. Back to meet some 4H: Bobby as dapper as ever, Peter W who is now working with Winston and Eric North who has been rung by Thompson to bid me to lunch at Chequers on Saturday.

Head back to the club and talk talk talk 'til the small hours. I find there's a 'back to the cavalry' movement but don't know where it will end. I think the 4H have adopted me and want me to stay on as commanding officer. I believe it would be the wisest course to remain – I'll never command the Royals now.

Saturday 16th June 1945

Call at Trumpers for a haircut. They are very pleased to see me. Old Trumper is now dead but otherwise there is no change at all. Gloriously refreshing.

Lunch with PM at Number Ten annex (1 and 2 Storey Gate Buildings). Only Mrs Churchill and WSC present. It's extremely pleasant and interesting.[18] At 4pm rather worse for wear with brandy I stagger out and call on Ma where I stay 'til 7pm.

---

18. From AMB's notes: 'During the lunch he paced up and down, trying different poses in a large mirror in preparation for a forthcoming cabinet speech. He said that few know how near we were to utter extinction – it was a hair's breadth. He was very interested in the amount of casualties the regiment had suffered in the whole war and also since he had last visited. He was much less interested in the fate of the vanquished Nazis in Austria: "Are we in future to put every Foreign Secretary of a beaten nation to death because he went to war? No, let them kill themselves. Given them a banquet and give them a cup filled to the brim. Say 'This is poison, you are welcome to it'." At the end of the lunch Jock Colville [Churchill's private secretary] came in and said, "Your cabinet awaits, sir", to which he replied, "But my time is my own." On Colville's second prompting, we said our farewells.'

Sunday 17th June 1945

Go to church at St Michael's in Eaton Square with Mummy. Then on to the club where Michael is awaiting me. We lunch well and then take a bus to visit the city. We walk around St Paul's and a perfectly heavenly Norman church, St Bart's. The bombed area is very much greater than ever I'd believed possible but all very tidily cleaned up.

Dine at the club and see Nigel C. I feel so awful not knowing he'd been a PoW for four years and has lost a leg. I am ashamed at having come through with a whole skin.

Monday 18th June 1945

Twice meet Monty face-to-face in the War Office. He's grown very thick at the waist and wears normal battle dress. He knows who he is alright and intends everyone else to know too!

Wednesday 20th June 1945

Visit Mr Spink in his beautiful showrooms to discuss the Old Comrades badges. The PM has taken a dislike to the one we've had made. Purchase tax on silver is now 100% which rather handicaps our selection.

After tea with Ma I call into the club but am determined to remain sober. One whisky leads to another, sherry to beer and am then reminded I'm entitled to a bottle of pop followed by vintage port and a couple of brandies. I stagger home laden with parcels and pack ready for an early start.

I must have met 40 or 50 people in the last week. They all seem very pleased to see me. I've done a good deal of regimental and a little self-propaganda. I must have spent close to £5 – prices are quite terrible. A whisky and soda in the club is 2/7 [two shillings and sevenpence]. I've not eaten an egg, although they don't seem scarce, and I've hardly touched any meat.

Thursday 21st June 1945

Leave at 7am. It comes on to rain heavily and at Blackbushe the officials tell us it is too bad for flying. Michael [Barne] sends a car for me and I spend the day with him at Pirbright. After lunch it clears so we go over to Woking. It's a lovely little house and it makes me rather jealous that they've had the whole war, bar a few months, living in such peace and luxury. No doubt there have been bad moments but to have been able to escape, discard uniform and fall straight into a perfect well-ordered home life with wife, children, dogs … Well, it can't have been bad.

The spacious regimental office and orderly peacetime soldiering with mess life of pipers playing the retreat and bowls with a cigar after dinner are just as I remember it. It certainly is a contrast to the noise and squalor, the continuous uncertainty of the future, the gypsy nomadic life and all the changes of scenery and companions of my last 7 years.

After tea we take out a gun. Linda recognises that and it evidently strikes a chord in her memory. She had naturally been friendly when I arrived but connected me with Michael as I was wearing his old trousers. Later she lay near me, studied my face and came over several times to sniff me. Six years is a long time to a dog and I was not expecting any recognition.

Friday 22nd June 1945
After an excellent breakfast one of Michael's men takes me to the 'drome. I embark on a Warwick and after 5 hours 40 minutes, most of which spent asleep, we land in Pomigliano. Roberts, who is with me, fixes us a car and we are put up comfortably.

Saturday 23rd June 1945
Have a chat with Peter Wrightson. It's gone all round AFHQ that I'd spent the weekend at Chequers. That won't do any harm!

Charles C is out all day but rings me in the evening. The general tells me a bit about the future. It won't please Cara very much! We are due to take over from the 'Loathsome and Bawdy' [the Lothians and Border Horse, a Yeomanry regiment] right on the Jugoslav border. A wild bit of country and it may prove interesting. We will therefore remain in Austria but as we will then be the Imperial Reserve it is quite possible that we'll then go to Palestine.

Sunday 24th June 1945
Get away at 10.15am and eventually arrive at 4.45pm. Ashdown meets me with the Humber as the Maybach is still off the road. The regiment is just as I left it with John O, Porgy and the RSM all back. Everyone seems very fish-minded and keen on their flies.

Maurice Leigh goes into hospital and the same day we hear has been posted home on Python. We shall miss him very much. A nicer doctor it would be hard to find; he's good with the troops and has a wonderful dry sense of humour.

Tuesday 3rd July 1945
There seems to be a lot of work on hand. Our move is still very indefinite. Strange considering that we only have the difficulties and indefiniteness of our own administration to cope with. I hear the Russians are being a bit difficult about their withdrawal.

Fish after tea. Don't do much good. Move on a big fish but he's not really interested.

Wednesday 4th July 1945

John V is not feeling well. He complains that he finds it hard to get up in the morning, I recommend less kümmel!

Do my office work in the morning and then drive down to Ebensdorf to the 26th Armoured Brigade Horse Show. It's so cold I wear a duffle coat. There are lots of good horses from all over the country but a poor standard of riding and jumping. Eat a good lunch and see a lot of old friends.

Later we all go on to a party. It's in the most perfect setting on a small lake with our band and local glee singers. I drink too much and talk too much. Am taken out in a speedboat by Freddie W and we do figures-of-eight in and out of the searchlight beams.

Sunday 8th July 1945

Reach the Russian frontier [the border of the Russian-occupied zone of Austria] at 10.30am. There are three or four Russian officers on our side and even ask to see over a Staghound [American armoured car] and yet we'd be shot if we put a foot over the line! We move off at 11am. Everything seems normal and there are a few Russian troops about but not a single vehicle on the road. The locals rush out to cheer us and wave as if we're a liberating army but they also seem on very friendly terms with the Russkis.

We have a nasty accident at Trieben when a car overturns and two 17/21st troops have their legs badly mangled. We get them into a Russian hospital but the column is held up on a mountain road. I proceed alone and bluff my way through the various roadblocks. I recce the area we are moving to as best I can – it should be alright but it is the back of beyond.

Drive 'til after dark into the high mountains where it's very cold but invigorating. Doss down in a chalet where an English-speaking girl makes me up a bed and undertakes to cook our breakfast.

Monday 9th July 1945

Leave our chalet at 7am. Mary, who looked after us, and her three sisters are looking after forty little boys, all refugees from the Russkis in Vienna. How they live God only knows.

It's bitterly cold and the road climbs up steeply as any road I've ever been on. We get up to great heights and the wild scenery is magnificent.

Head back to the new mess at Grafenstein for lunch. My room is in house of an ex-commandant of a German SS regiment.

Friday 13th July 1945

Drive a Staghound for the first time. They are dead easy; change gear themselves, pull themselves up to a halt and have semi-automatic steering. I wish we'd had these cars in the desert or on the chase up to Tripoli.

Receive a letter from Ma to say that Cara arrived home on the 8th and all is well.

Thursday 19th July 1945
I can scarcely believe it but am told I'm off tomorrow. I refuse to think about it too much in case something goes wrong.

Friday 20th July 1945
Ride first thing but it comes on to pour with rain. Many crops are still out and I fear the harvest will be a poor one unless this is normal weather for these parts.

Spend a final morning in the office and then go off after lunch to Alamein Camp, the starting point of the overland leaving route. Am sent to a rest house at Velden where we laze about, bathe in the lake, drink and play backgammon.

Saturday 21st July 1945
Get away at 7.30am. It's a lovely road and there is little traffic. Stretch our legs at 10.30am then on to Linz, back into Italy and then up the Brenner Pass. The damage done by the air force is an incredible sight. In one place we see a hospital train that hit a crater and left the rails. It spilled over a 50 foot drop like a waterfall. The heap is most awe-inspiring.

Lunch with 56 Division Rest Camp. It's very well run and they are very obliging. The French have taken over the Tyrol. There are a lot of dark Moroccans about and by the look of it the next generation here won't be blondes by any means.

Get into Germany at Mitterwald where I lost my passport in 1937. Recollect several places Cara and I had noticed then. There's an *autobahn* from Augsburg, a wonderful but boring method of motoring. The Hun used it as a runway for jet-propelled aircraft. The machines lay hidden in the woods bordering the road.

Reach Ulm at 7.15pm having done 350 miles. We intended to go on but hear eight Yanks were caught last night by Werewolves[19] and were shot. That will smarten anyone up.

---

19. *Werwolf* was the Nazi plan for a resistance force to operate behind enemy lines as the Allies advanced through Germany. The plan was secretly initiated by Himmler as early as summer/autumn 1944 but was not made public for fear of appearing defeatist. As the German defeat became inevitable, Radio Werwolf broadcasts reminded Allied soldiers that 'every friendly German is a disguised soldier of hate ... their hatred and their anger ... are buried in their blood. A smile is their weapon by which to disarm you ... in heart, body and spirit, every German is Hitler.' In practice, the effectiveness of the movement was limited, and the war-weary German population was not prepared for further sacrifice in the name of a lost cause.

Sunday 22nd July 1945

Get away at 5.45am. The *autobahns* are good to Mainz with no traffic but then turn bloody awful. From Ulm to Luxembourg one hardly sees a town or village. It's full of wonderful crops or forestry – yet the Hun cries out for *Lebensraum*!

As it's Sunday everyone one sees are in their best clothes. Everyone looks surprisingly healthy and well turned out. The big towns are absolutely flattened by bombing but there's no sign at all of any war just having taken place over the countryside.

Have a puncture but otherwise the car goes very well. We cover over 400 miles today. Dine at Sedan where we have a bottle of Veuve Cliquot 1934 for dinner.

Monday 23rd July 1945

Reach Calais at 1310 hours – we've done just over a thousand miles. The road today has been dull on good roads through nice cornfields. It's amazing how little is to be seen of the war.

The transit camp is most helpful. There is a mass of documentation to be done to ensure the wrong people don't get across but it seems very well organised. We can't get a boat today so stay put.

The old Humber still bears the 9th Armoured Brigade white horse sign. It is probably the only white horse to have come as far as Calais and within sight of England. I feel it is end of an era and of this diary, kept daily often with great difficulty, sometimes written when dog-tired, sometimes when under fire, sometimes when things looked black and desperate but more often in sunshine and optimism and surrounded by good fellows who kept one cheerful and helped one through the sad and difficult times. I shall continue to be a soldier but not to keep this diary going.

Tuesday 24th July 1945

Am up very bright and early to organise my baggage and car. The boat is very crowded with three trainloads. Am made commanding officer thereby getting a carriage to myself and avoiding customs.

We get a lot of cheering at Folkestone – they evidently look out for the leave train to give the lads a welcome home.

Lunch at the club. It's funny to be back so soon. Have a haircut and then get the 4.05pm to Diss. To my delight I find that Cara has come to meet me. She's looking so radiant and well. Nigel is also on the station. Alas he's off to the Far East tomorrow but it's nice to see him. The son is asleep when we get in.

Epilogue

At the end of August, when his leave finished, my grandfather rejoined the 4th Hussars in Austria. Free from the pressures of war, they were able to enjoy themselves in the stunning countryside and within touching distance of the temptations of Trieste. John Strawson, later to command the regiment en route to becoming a major general, was a junior officer at the time and described my grandfather thus:

> We could not have had a finer commanding officer to set us on the right lines for peacetime. He led by example, was always immaculately turned out, excelled at horsemanship, shooting and yachting, and understood that after nearly six years of war, provided proper standards of excellence in all military matters were maintained, all ranks of the regiment should be allowed to enjoy themselves.

In December my grandfather was mentioned in dispatches and awarded an OBE 'in recognition of gallant and distinguished services in Italy'. During his two periods of command, the Royals Dragoons had won two battle honours and the 4th Hussars had won eight.

In May 1946 he returned to the UK to attend Staff College, the course required to be promoted to a substantive, not temporary, lieutenant colonel. As bad luck would have it, the commandant at Staff College was the same general he had goaded in September 1944 for scampering at the first sign of bombing and then sarcastically asked what he should do with his abandoned ensign. It appears the general had not forgotten this impertinence, and Barne's card was marked. The general, later to become chief of staff, wrote a damning report, and despite two approaches about brigadier jobs, my grandfather was not to progress any further.

He remained in the army until 1953, stationed at various bases around England. His final posting was as commandant of the Royal Armoured

Corps Training Regiment in Bovington, Dorset. My grandparents loved the area and on retirement they bought a farm nearby called Culeaze.

Culeaze was to be their beloved home for the next four decades and where they raised my father. They spent their time developing a beautiful garden, riding, travelling and sailing in the nearby Solent (he had won the Round the Island Race in 1949). My grandmother became a magistrate and my grandfather kept in touch with the RAC camp in Bovington, developing a programme to teach soldiers to sail. The strong desire expressed in the war diaries to put down roots and settle into a quieter life had been fulfilled.

Christopher, my father, followed his father into the army and joined the Blues and Royals (the Royals had merged with the Royal Horse Guards in 1969). He had two eventful tours of Northern Ireland and spent time in Germany, Cyprus and British Malaya prior to its independence.

I was born in 1978 and spent the first few years of my life in an army barracks in Germany. In due course we also settled at Culeaze, living a few hundred yards from my grandparents. They were a huge influence on me, unfailingly supportive and interested, and as their only grandchild I was fortunate to have a close relationship with them. Like many of that generation they rarely spoke of the war, but it was always present in the background. I was fascinated by the unusual memorabilia dotted around their home: the piece of Italian fighter fuselage painted with *fasces* and riddled with bullet holes, the military hats, swords, drums and, a particular favourite, the enormous red Nazi flag that was used to decorate beneath the Christmas tree (swastika not actually visible).

They died in quick succession when I was eighteen and living in New Zealand for the year. It was devastating. As always when a generation passes on, we lose the wealth of their experiences, and a link to a bygone era is lost forever. Having often wished I had paid more attention to the old tales, I could not believe my luck when I stumbled upon the war diaries some years later when clearing out Culeaze following the death of my father.

It has been a genuine privilege to edit the diaries and gain an unvarnished snapshot into my grandfather's life and character at a similar age to my own. There is no doubt that compared to many others he was fortunate during the war; he saw his family often, had stretches without much danger and found time for plenty of late night antics in Cairo. More importantly, he survived unscathed while many of those around him were killed or maimed, and finished the war with no long term mental or physical injuries. In the parlance of the day, he 'had a good war'.

Whilst his story is not the most exceptional or filled with any particular moments of great personal valour, it is testament to years of fortitude, often in the face of unfavourable and arbitrary odds. It is worth remembering that his generation were brought up soon after the Victorian era, when it was not seemly to boast of one's exploits or achievements. This is seen all through the diaries, from the downplaying of numerous skirmishes to the infuriatingly brief account of lunch alone with the Churchills. Set against today's culture of continual self-aggrandisement, the tone of the diaries is refreshingly of a simpler, more honest time.

In this spirit of honesty, my grandfather does seem aware of his own failings. The intensity of life in a war zone must lead to heightened emotion and strained relationships. To be sacked from his own regiment, an institution he obviously held extremely dear, must have been a huge blow and carried some stigma amongst his contemporaries. Whatever the failings (if any) of Humphrey Lloyd who replaced him, my grandfather must carry some of the responsibility of not trying to finding a way to work with him.

Central to the diaries is the relationship of my grandparents. Unlike many of their friends they were extremely lucky to be together for the first couple of years of the war and produce a healthy son in the middle of it. This does not detract from the risks my grandmother took in crossing Europe alone in 1940, sailing down the African coast in 1942 or bearing the burden of raising a son without knowing if/when the fateful telegram might arrive. Reading the diaries it is obvious what a strong and devoted team they were. My grandfather seemed to capture this perfectly when writing his memoirs in his later years. He started them with this dedication:

> This is a brief résumé of the main highlights of my life. The first and the most important of which was my marriage to Cara and all affection, faithfulness and inspiration that came with her. The rest to follow are my own personal minor achievements.

Appendix A:
Speeches Mentioned in the Diaries

3 September 1939, Chamberlain
This morning the British Ambassador in Berlin handed the German Government a final note stating that, unless we heard from them by 11 o'clock that they were prepared at once to withdraw their troops from Poland, a state of war would exist between us. I have to tell you now that no such undertaking has been received, and that consequently this country is at war with Germany.

2 October 1939, Churchill
I cannot forecast to you the action of Russia. It is a riddle wrapped in mystery inside an enigma; but perhaps there is a key. That key is Russian national interest ... Through the fog of confusion and uncertainty we may discern quite plainly the community of interests which exist between England, France and Russia to prevent Germany carrying the flames of war into the Balkans or Turkey ... Directions have been given by the Government to prepare for a war of at least years.

That does not mean that victory may not be gained in a short time. How soon it will gained depends upon how long Herr Hitler and his group of wicked men, whose hands are stained with blood and soiled with corruption, can keep their grip upon the docile unhappy German people. It was for Hitler to say when the war would begin, but it is not for him or his successor to say when it will end. It began when he wanted it, and it will end only when we are convinced that he has had enough.

7 October 1939, Hitler
Neither force of arms nor lapse of time will conquer Germany. There never will be another November 1918 in German history. It is infantile to hope for the disintegration of our people. Mr Churchill may be convinced that Great Britain will win. I do not doubt for a single moment that Germany will be victorious. Destiny will decide who is right. One thing only is certain. In the course of world history, there have never been two victors, but very often only losers. This seems to me to have been the case in the last war.

As Führer of the German people and Chancellor of the Reich, I can thank God at this moment that He has so wonderfully blessed us in our hard struggle for what is our right, and beg Him that we and all other nations may find the right way, so that not only the German people but all Europe may once more be granted the blessing of peace.

27 October 1939, von Ribbentrop
Fully conscious that right is on her side, and that up to the end she did everything in her power to avoid this utterly senseless war which was forced upon her, Germany will fight this war to the finish, backed by the tremendous impetus of the whole nation. That this decisive struggle for the future of the German nation can only end in a great German victory is assured for us by our own strength and by our faith in the man who is the embodiment of our highest ideals in the world – Our Führer!

25 December 1939, HM King George VI
The festival which we all know as Christmas is, above all, the festival of peace and of the home. Among all free peoples the love of peace is profound, for this alone gives security to the home. But true peace is in the hearts of men, and it is the tragedy of this time that there are powerful countries whose whole direction and policy are based on aggression and the suppression of all that we hold dear for mankind.

It is this that has stirred our peoples and given them a unity unknown in any previous way. We feel in our hearts that we are fighting against wickedness, and this conviction will give us strength from day to day to persevere until victory is assured.

At home we are, as it were, taking the strain for what may lie ahead of us, resolved and confident.

25 December 1940, HM King George VI
But how many more children are there here who have been moved from their homes to safer quarters? To all of them, at home and abroad, who are separated from their fathers and mothers, to their kind friends and hosts, and to all who love them, and to parents who will be lonely without them, from all in our dear island I wish every happiness that Christmas can bring. May the New Year carry us towards victory and to happier Christmas days, when everyone will be at home together in the years to come.

18 March 1941, President Roosevelt
In this historic crisis, Britain is blessed with a brilliant and great leader in Winston Churchill. But, knowing him, no one knows better than Mr

Churchill himself that it is not alone his stirring words and valiant deeds that give the British their superb morale ... The British people and their Grecian allies need ships. From America, they will get ships. They need planes. From America, they will get planes. From America they need food. From America, they will get food. They need tanks and guns and ammunition and supplies of all kinds. From America, they will get tanks and guns and ammunition and supplies of all kinds ... And so our country is going to be what our people have proclaimed it must be – the arsenal of democracy.

27 April 1941, Churchill
No prudent and far-seeing man can doubt that the eventual and total defeat of Hitler and Mussolini is certain ... There are less than seventy million malignant Huns – some of whom are curable and others killable ... The peoples of the British Empire and of the United States number nearly two hundred millions in their homelands and in the British Dominions alone.

They possess the unchallengeable command of the oceans, and will soon obtain decisive superiority in the air. They have more wealth, more technical resources, and they make more steel, than the whole of the rest of the world put together. They are determined that the cause of freedom shall not be trampled down, nor the tide of world progress turned backwards, by the criminal dictators.

10 November 1942, Churchill
Rommel's army has been defeated. It has been routed. It has been very largely destroyed as a fighting force. This battle was not fought for the sake of gaining positions or so many square miles of desert territory. General Alexander and General Montgomery fought it with one single idea. They meant to destroy the armed force of the enemy and to destroy it at the place where the disaster would be most far-reaching and irrecoverable ... Now this is not the end. It is not even the beginning of the end, but it is, perhaps, the end of the beginning.

25 December 1942, HM King George VI
So let us brace and prepare ourselves for the days which lie ahead. Victory will bring us even greater world responsibilities, and we must not be found unequal to a task in the discharge of which we shall draw on the storehouse of our experience and tradition.

Our European Allies, their Sovereigns, heads, and Governments, whom we are glad to welcome here in their distress, count on our aid to help them return to their native lands and to rebuild the structure of a free and glorious Europe.

On the sea, on land, and in the air, and in civil life at home, a pattern of effort and mutual service is being traced which may guide those who design the picture of our future society.

A former President of the United States of America used to tell the story of a boy who was carrying an even smaller child up a hill. Asked whether the heavy burden was not too much for him, the boy answered, 'It's not a burden, it's my brother!'

So let us welcome the future in a spirit of brotherhood, and thus make a world in which, please God, all may dwell together in justice and peace.

22 March 1943, Churchill

Therefore I tell you around your firesides tonight that I am resolved not to give or to make all kinds of promises and tell all kinds of fairy tales to you who have trusted me and gone with me so far, and marched through the valley of the shadow, till we have reached the upland regions on which we now stand with firmly planted feet.

However, it is our duty to peer through the mists of the future to the end of the war, and to try our utmost to be prepared by ceaseless effort and forethought for the kind of situations which are likely to occur. Speaking under every reserve and not attempting to prophesy, I can imagine that sometime next year – but it may well be the year after – we might beat Hitler, by which I mean beat him and his powers of evil into death, dust, and ashes. Then we shall immediately proceed to transport all the necessary additional forces and apparatus to the other side of the world to punish the greedy, cruel Empire of Japan, to rescue China from her long torment, to free our territory and that of our Dutch allies, and to drive the Japanese menace forever from Australian, New Zealand, and Indian shores.

26 March 1944, Churchill

The hour of our greatest effort and action is approaching. We march with valiant Allies who count on us as we count on them. The flashing eyes of all our soldiers, sailors and airmen must be fixed upon the enemy on their front. The only homeward road for all of us lies through the arch of victory.

The magnificent armies of the United States are here, or are pouring in. Our own troops, the best trained and best equipped we have ever had, stand at their side in equal numbers and in true comradeship. Leaders are appointed in whom we all have faith. We shall require from our own people here, from Parliament, from the press, from all classes, the same cool, strong nerves, the same toughness of fibre which stood us in good stead in those days when we were all alone under the German blitz.

Britain can take it. She has never flinched or failed, and when the signal is given, the whole circle of avenging nations will hurl themselves upon the foe and batter out the life of the crudest tyranny which has ever sought to bar the progress of mankind.

30 January 1945, Hitler

Therefore I expect every German to do his duty to the last and that he be willing to take upon himself every sacrifice he will be asked to make; I expect every able-bodied German to fight with the complete disregard for his personal safety; I expect the sick and the weak or those otherwise unavailable for military duty to work with their last strength; I expect city dwellers to forge the weapons for this struggle and I expect the farmer to supply the bread for the soldiers and workers of this struggle by imposing restrictions upon himself; I expect all women and girls to continue supporting this struggle with utmost fanaticism.

However grave the crisis may be at the moment, it will, despite everything, finally be mastered by our unalterable will, by our readiness for sacrifice and by our abilities. We shall overcome this calamity, too, and this fight, too, will not be won by central Asia but by Europe; and at its head will be the nation that has represented Europe against the East for 1,500 years and shall represent it for all times: our Greater German Reich, the German nation.

8 May 1945, Churchill

My dear friends, this is your hour. This is not victory of a party or of any class. It's a victory of the great British nation as a whole. We were the first, in this ancient island, to draw the sword against tyranny. After a while we were left all alone against the most tremendous military power that has been seen. We were all alone for a whole year.

There we stood, alone. Did anyone want to give in? Were we down-hearted? The lights went out and the bombs came down. But every man, woman and child in the country had no thought of quitting the struggle. London can take it. So we came back after long months from the jaws of death, out of the mouth of hell, while all the world wondered. When shall the reputation and faith of this generation of English men and women fail? I say that in the long years to come not only will the people of this island but of the world, wherever the bird of freedom chirps in human hearts, look back to what we've done and they will say, 'Do not despair, do not yield to violence and tyranny, march straightforward and die if need be – unconquered.'

Appendix B

The obituary of Lieutenant Louis Jackson MC (1922–2009) from the *Daily Telegraph*:

On January 4 1945, Jackson was commanding a troop of tanks in the 4th Queen's Own Hussars. At about 5am he was ordered to assist an infantry post at a farm north-west of Ravenna which was being heavily attacked by three German companies.

Although under fire, he dismounted and directed his tanks into position. One of his tanks was then hit by a bazooka at close range. Jackson was standing in front of the tank, which had got bogged down in a gateway on the farm. While the force of the charge left the crew killed or badly wounded, Jackson merely had his hat blown off. Having given orders to his remaining tanks, he went into the ruined farm complex. He steadied the hard-pressed infantry and organised their defences, but the Germans, using smoke and the cover afforded by the vineyards, surrounded the buildings. At 7am the ammunition ran out. Jackson called for more and then scrambled out of his tank, wrestled an automatic rifle from a German, jumped back into the tank and went on firing at the enemy.

During a lull in the fighting he extricated two wounded men from the tank which had been knocked out. He later recalled the nightmare of injecting one of them in the arm with a painkiller – only to find that it had no effect because the limb was not properly attached to the body. One man died and the other was evacuated.

The attack was renewed an hour later, and after the Germans infiltrated the farmyard – where they were safe from small arms – high explosive was fired from as little as 50 yards. During the fierce fighting, which lasted for nearly 5 hours, Jackson quietly walked from one position to the next giving fire orders and directing operations. His determination and gallantry frustrated the enemy and inflicted on them a costly defeat; 150 prisoners were taken and more than 200 killed or wounded.

Acknowledgements

I have loved typing up, editing and annotating these diaries over the last two and a half years. It would not have been possible, however, without the support of many people. I would like to thank my mother, Liza Barne, Miles Barne, Tish Lombe Taylor, Judy Russell, Gavin Black, Harry Boyt, Rowley Gregg and many contributors on www.ww2talk.com (including the 95-year-old Ron Goldstein, who served under my grandfather in Italy); Mills Leask for the idea of having the diaries published; Randall Nicol for his encouragement having edited my great-grandfather's diaries from the First World War; Richard Laird and Archie for producing the brilliant maps; Philip Young and George Chamier for their incredible patience in proofreading the diaries; and Robert Smith, who has proved a great ally as an agent.

I am particularly pleased to be able to support Ed Parker and the fantastic charity, 'Walking With The Wounded'. Their efforts to support vulnerable veterans to integrate back into society and maintain independent lives are incredibly important and just as relevant now as for my grandfather's generation.

Finally, a huge thank you to my gorgeous girls, Cara and Posie, for all the joy they bring and to my amazing wife, Tory, and for all the affection, faithfulness and inspiration that come with her.